What Lies Ahead

What Lies Ahead

A Biblical Overview of the End Times

J. B. HIXSON AND MARK FONTECCHIO

"looking for the blessed hope
and glorious appearing of our
great God and Savior
Jesus Christ"

(Titus 2:13)

Table of Contents

Index of Charts, Diagrams, and Illustrations

Acknowledgments

J. B. Hixson wishes to thank:

WENDY, BETHANY, BROOKE, Morgan, Landry, Faith, and Abby, whose patience with me as a husband and father is worthy of great reward in the Kingdom.

Mark Fontecchio for his partnership in this project. His contribution was invaluable and made this book a much better product.

Rev. L. O. Hixson, my grandfather, who is "present with the Lord." He taught me to love and long for the blessed hope—the soon coming of our Lord and Savior, Jesus Christ.

Morgan Hixson for his tireless and diligent work in creating the Scripture index.

Drs. Walvoord, Pentecost, Lightner, and Stallard, my professors, each of whom helped to mold my eschatology in significant ways.

Mark Fontecchio wishes to thank:

D R. J.B. HIXSON for affording me the opportunity to work with him on this project. His scholarship and friendship have been, and continue to be, a great joy in my life.

Barbara and Caroline for their diligence, time, and expertise in proofreading this work.

Micah, Hannah, and Anika for their loving support and sacrifice. Their teamwork makes it possible for me to dedicate my time to serving Christ.

Angie for being the unsung hero of my life. Her patience and commitment to being my helpmate is an inspiration. Thank you for the countless hours you spent assisting, proofreading, and editing this book. I pray the Lord will give us many more years together. Of all men, I am truly blessed.

J. B. Hixson's Preface

IN A WAY, this book has been in the making for over thirty years. As a teenager, I would sit and listen to my grandfather, Rev. L. O. Hixson, talk about topics like the Rapture, the Second Coming, and the Millennium during visits to his home in Austin, Texas. He was passionate about the end times. I was fascinated. Having piqued my interest, those conversations would continue with my father during our family's drive back to our home in Houston, and any other time I could bait him into a theological discussion. Between my father and my grandfather, I suppose I come by my fascination with eschatology honestly.

As I progressed through college and seminary, my knowledge of and interest in this topic grew. It quickly became one of my favorite subjects to preach and teach. After more than twenty years of teaching eschatology, including fifteen years at the college and seminary levels, I decided it was time to collate all of my research, course notes, charts, and handouts into a book. I was delighted when the Lord allowed my friend and colleague Mark Fontecchio to join me in this endeavor. Mark shares my passion for this subject, and it has been a true joy to collaborate with him on this project.

Why another book on eschatology? There is no shortage of material already in print on the subject. And surely there are writers more qualified and gifted than I to communicate these biblical truths. Truthfully, my reasons are selfish. The older I get the more burdened I have become with the desire to leave behind a legacy for my own six children. I have been blessed to study under some of the greatest theological minds the world has known. My mind is filled with knowledge about God's incredible plan of the ages. I want my children to know what is in my heart and, someday, to pass it on to their own children. This was my primary motivation.

Secondarily, I wanted to create a comprehensive presentation of my views for use in future classes. Up to this point, each semester I have provided students with hundreds of pages of notes. With the publication of *What Lies Ahead*, students have access to my teaching on this subject in one source.

Finally, while there may be an abundance of eschatology books already in print, none that I have found covers the material in precisely the same manner as Mark and I cover it here. Our goal was to strike a balance between scholarship and readability. We were not driven to produce another academic textbook. Rather, we wanted to provide the Body of Christ at large with a resource that can be used in the home, in the church, or in the classroom.

Years ago, one of my professors, Dr. J. Dwight Pentecost, said, "There is no higher activity in which the mind can be engaged than the pursuit of the knowledge of God." This is certainly true. And I would add that *specifically* the pursuit of knowledge about the coming Messianic Kingdom on earth and the culmination of God's plan of the ages is paramount if we are to truly "fear God and give glory to Him" (Rev. 14:7).

J. B. Hixson, www.NotByWorks.org

Mark Fontecchio's Preface

I VIVIDLY REMEMBER the first time I heard the word *eschatology*. It was almost twenty years ago when, somehow, as a new believer I ended up on a pastor search committee. Even then, deep within me, I think I knew I had no business being in such a position at that time. The denominational authorities had provided us with a list of questions for potential candidates. There, hidden in those questions, was a foreign term. The word was *eschatology*. Gradually, I began to fully comprehend the significance of the doctrines relating to the end times. Eschatology is a foundational teaching within the Word of God.

It would not be until a few years later, while in Bible college, that I heard another word that was unfamiliar to me. This time the word shrouded in mystery was *dispensationalism*. Very few books favorably mentioned the teachings of dispensationalism. Even fewer churches were proclaiming them.

Over the years, I have come to learn and believe that correctly understanding these doctrines is essential to rightly dividing the Word of God. Presented in *What Lies Ahead* is a sincere and humble effort to provide clarity where it is lacking. It is my desire to help explain these foundational truths of Scripture, and to help eliminate the confusion that surrounds the end times. My prayer is that this study will help you grow in the grace and knowledge of the Lord Jesus Christ (2 Pet. 3:18).

"Now to the King eternal, immortal, invisible, to God who alone is wise, be honor and glory forever and ever. Amen" (1 Tim. 1:17).

Mark Fontecchio, www.LiteralTruth.org

CHAPTER 1

Getting Our Feet Wet -
Why We Study Bible Prophecy

But the boat was now in the middle of the sea, tossed by the waves, for the wind was contrary.

- Matthew 14:24

JIM WAS IN serious trouble. He loved to take his father's old fishing boat out on those warm summer days. It helped him to relax, thinking of all the good memories he had shared with his father. Now it was only Jim and his faithful black lab, Shadow. Growing up on the shores of Lake Superior meant that Jim knew all the risks of the big lake. This was something his dad had made sure of. Jim was certain that high pressure had settled in, which meant no clouds in the sky, and the waves were expected to be less than two feet. It looked like a perfect day to head out far past the Apostle Islands. This was when the trouble began.

Jim and Shadow had barely arrived, when Jim first noticed that the waves seemed to be much rougher than originally forecasted. Shadow probably noticed it first. The clear skies were giving way to clouds. Turning on the weather radio was the first order of business. The National Weather Service was warning of a quick moving cold front that was coming from the northwest. This ferocious storm was about to turn the calm water into a violent nightmare.

Jim began to think he had another problem. Not only were the waves getting higher, but the boat was starting to sit lower in the water. This could only mean one thing; they were taking on water. Jim headed below deck to see how bad it was. The water filling the cabin confirmed his worst fears. There was simply no way to see where the water was coming from.

Jim started to think through his options. Eventually, the water would kill the engines and the power. "Could he make it all the way back to shore?" It seemed impossible. "Could he make it to one of the islands?" "Perhaps a freighter in the shipping lanes would spot him in time?" Jim knew there was only one thing to do. He put in a desperate call for help, hoping that he could be rescued.

Having grown up in the region, Jim knew there was a Coast Guard rescue station in Duluth, Minnesota. He also knew there was a smaller post on the southern shore, in Wisconsin. Jim put in the call on the marine radio. The jagged voice on the other end instilled comfort. He relayed his situation and location, and then the radio went dead.

It turned out that Jim had even less time than he had first thought. Enough water had come on board to kill the power and both engines. Those small two foot waves had grown significantly higher. At some point, Jim and Shadow were going to be in the water. The water temperature at this time of year would not be much more than forty degrees Fahrenheit. Jim knew that once they went into the water, they had less than an hour before hypothermia would set in. With the waves crashing upon them, hope of lasting that long was unthinkable. "Had the Coast Guard heard him?" "Would the Coast Guard even be able to find him in the storm?" As these questions raced through his mind, he recognized that it was time to abandon ship. His feet were already wet, and his boat would soon be underwater. Strapping his lifejacket on, Jim and Shadow plunged in.

Are you wondering what happened to Jim and Shadow? We don't like it when we don't know the end of a story. We would never accept it with a good novel, or in a movie, so why do Christians accept not knowing about the end times and God's eternal plan for mankind? Our future with Christ is much more important than just a good story in a book! Our Savior spoke of this when He proclaimed in Revelation 22:7, "Behold, I am coming quickly! Blessed is he who keeps the words of the prophecy of this book." This is precisely why we set out to study Bible prophecy.

The Importance of Studying Bible Prophecy

Unfortunately, many Christians shun Bible prophecy because of the assumed controversy that surrounds it. Prophecy is relegated to a secondary doctrine, which is seen as not essential to wrestle with. The assumption of perpetual disagreements on this issue has led many to a defeatist attitude. Why bother studying something that nobody seems to agree on? Others speculate, incorrectly, that the book of Revelation is the first place in Scripture we should turn to for the study of God's plan for the ages. Then when they try reading the book of Revelation, without any prior understanding of prophecy, they come to the decision that it is exceptionally tough to comprehend. Based on this limited experience, a conviction is made that studying prophecy in Scripture will be hard and simply not worth the effort.

Prophecy is a substantial portion of Scripture, and when Christians neglect it they are cheating themselves of some of God's Word. In reality, prophecy is an absolutely critical part of theology. If you cut out the prophetical portions of Scripture that deal with the end times, you would be left with a much shorter Bible than we have now. Prophecy is a major teaching of Scripture. We remind ourselves that the Apostle Paul wrote, "*All Scripture* is given by inspiration of God, and is profitable for doctrine, for reproof, for correction, for instruction in righteousness, that the man of God may be complete, thoroughly equipped for every good work" (2 Tim. 3:16-17, emphasis added). In other words, God wants us to study His prophecy found in His Word. It is a part of His will for every believer in Jesus Christ.

There is overwhelming confusion today about what the afterlife will bring for the believer in Christ. Bible prophecy cuts through this confusion, and teaches us that the afterlife is nothing like what is being portrayed in most movies and books today. As we come to understand prophecy, we see that our future involves serving, ruling, reigning, and working.

It is a common misconception that our work is merely a product of the fall of man into sin. The assumption is made that if sin were not present in this world we would not have to work. Genesis 2:15 reveals a notable contrast to this idea, by teaching, "Then the LORD God took the man and put him in the garden of Eden to tend and keep it." Adam tended the garden *before* he sinned. One prominent effect of sin is that our work is now much more difficult. Adam was told, "Because you have heeded the voice of your wife, and have eaten from the tree of which I commanded you, saying, 'You shall not eat of it': Cursed is the ground for your sake; in toil you shall eat of it all the days of your life" (Gen. 3:17).

For believers in Christ, we can know that our work will continue on in eternity, but without the negative effects of the Fall. Luke 19:11-27 informs us that our work will be considerably different than it is now, but it will continue. Thinking about Bible prophecy, and the end times, gives us a better perspective on life. It helps us to understand that this life is not all there is; there is a much higher calling.

Prophecy also provides us with hope for the future. When we lose a loved one we would like to know what the future holds. This is why Paul pointed out, "If in this life only we have hope in Christ, we are of all men the most pitiable" (1 Cor. 15:19). Scripture instructs us that when believers die, there is no reason to mourn them as the world does. Prophecy teaches that we will be reunited with them (1 Thess. 4:13-17). This hope carries over to our longing to be with the Lord. We look forward to receiving our glorified bodies (Rom. 8:23-25). We crave to know more about our future. Bible prophecy is God's answer for our hunger to know more. The Apostle Paul teaches us, "For our citizenship is in heaven, from which we also eagerly wait for the Savior, the Lord Jesus Christ, who will transform our lowly body that it may be conformed to His glorious body" (Phil. 3:20-21).

This same hope permeates our attitude. We should always be, "looking for the blessed hope and glorious appearing of our great God and Savior Jesus Christ" (Titus 2:13). Far too many Christians obsess themselves with the here and now, instead of the life to come. The study of prophecy gives people a reason for the hope that is within them.

Knowing of our future with Christ gives us cause to consider another reason for studying prophecy. When Christ returns for His Church, every believer will stand before Him at the Judgment Seat of Christ. Our good works will be rewarded as we give an account for the things done while in the body (1 Cor. 3:10-15; 2 Cor. 5:10). 1 Corinthians 4:5 reveals to us that the counsels of the heart will be the determining factor at the Judgment Seat of Christ. What will happen if we spend most of our time living for the world? The Bible has the answer, "And now, little children, abide in Him, that when He appears, we may have confidence and not be ashamed before Him at His coming" (1 John 2:28). No believer in Christ should want to be ashamed when we stand before the Lord. What a disgrace it would be if a believer is living in sin (out of fellowship with the Lord) at the moment the trumpet sounds and we are called up together to meet our Lord in the air! Knowing our future should be a persistent motivation for us to live to please our Savior, Jesus Christ. Jesus Himself testified, "lay up for yourselves treasures in heaven" (Matt. 6:20).

We see this identical teaching in other passages from the New Testament. Luke 19:11-27 helps us to recognize that while Jesus is gone we should be actively carrying out the work He has asked us to do, because one day we will each give an account when we stand before Him at the Judgment Seat of Christ. Realizing the day of accounting is approaching should be a motivation for godly living. This day of accounting is certainly a part of Bible prophecy. The reason many Christians today do not know much about the Judgment Seat of Christ is because they neglect the prophecies that teach about it in the Word of God. The reality of the imminent return of the Lord to rescue His Church from this present evil age gives us motivation to get out of bed each day and to live for Him. Jesus promised, "And behold, I am coming quickly, and My reward is with Me, to give to every one according to his work" (Rev. 22:12).

Colossians 3 confronts us with more reasons to study prophecy. There are two commands in the first two verses. We are to, "seek those things which are above, where Christ is, sitting at the right hand of God" and "set your mind on things above, not on things on the earth" (Col. 3:1-2). Studying prophecy helps us to obey these commands. Both of these directives help us to put our lives in perspective. They remind us that no matter what happens in this life on earth, God is at work setting in motion His plan for the ages. Paul reminds us, "When Christ who is our life appears, then you also will appear with Him in glory" (Col. 3:4).

We dare not forget that a great deal of prophecy has already been fulfilled. This should build our confidence in God's Word because the fulfilled prophecies validate the truthfulness of Scripture. When we begin to look at the prophecies of the Messiah, and see how many of these were fulfilled at the First Advent of Christ, it reminds us that we serve a God who is faithful to His promises. Many prophecies of the Messiah await future fulfillment in the context of the Second Advent, and we can count on these prophecies being fulfilled. As our faith in the Word of God deepens, we are led to worship our sovereign Creator. What great peace we can have knowing that He is in complete control of human history! The more we understand God's plan for the end of the age, the deeper our appreciation is for His sovereignty.

Rescue is Available

Jim and Shadow spent about fifteen minutes floating in the waves of the icy cold waters of Lake Superior. Jim's faith in the Coast Guard had paid off. Just as his legs were beginning to go numb, he heard the welcome sound of the rescue helicopter. Safely aboard the Coast Guard helicopter, Jim had time to reflect on how fortunate he was. Had he taken any other course of action, he would have perished. Jim was rescued because his faith was placed in the right object.

As we chart this course to study eschatology together, let us never forget that the focus of all Bible prophecy is *Jesus Christ*. He is the only one who can rescue us from an eternity in hell. As the Apostle Peter boldly testified so long ago, "Nor is there salvation in any other, for there is no other name under heaven given among men by which we must be saved" (Acts 4:12). *Saving faith is the belief in Jesus Christ as the Son of God who died and rose again to pay one's personal penalty for sin, and the one who gives eternal life to all who trust Him and Him alone for it.* The study of eschatology tells us the end of the story regarding the eternal salvation of those who trust in Jesus Christ to rescue them from the penalty of sin.

Discussion Questions

1. Why do Christians tend to shun Bible prophecy?
2. How would you rate your understanding of Bible prophecy?
3. What are some of the reasons that we should study prophecy in the Bible?
4. What benefit does fulfilled prophecy play in the life of the believer?
5. What is your eternal future? Have you trusted in Jesus Christ to rescue you from the penalty of your sins?

CHAPTER 2

Holding on to the Truth - Postmodernism vs. a Biblical Worldview

Take firm hold of instruction, do not let go; keep her, for she is your life.

- Proverbs 4:13

SOMETIMES THE TRUTH can be much stranger than fiction. Pilot Henry Dempsey never could have anticipated the horrifying experience that was awaiting him on September 2, 1987. It was a routine flight to Boston on a fifteen passenger airplane; on this particular trip, no passengers were on board.

Copilot Paul Boucher had noticed an unusual noise toward the rear of the airplane. Dempsey turned control of the aircraft over to the copilot, and went to investigate. At the back of the plane Dempsey saw something terrifying. He could see daylight poking through one of the corners of the rear door to the plane. Dempsey went to get a closer look, and at that exact moment the aircraft hit some turbulence, triggering him to bump against the door.

It took time for Dempsey's mind to catch up with what had happened to him. On this particular airplane, when the door opens it swings down to form stairs that end within inches of the ground (except when you are flying several thousands of feet in the air at over 180 miles an hour). Dempsey grabbed on to whatever he could, which in this case was the railing to the stairs. Upside down, he was now lying on the steps outside the plane; only his feet were touching the fuselage. The wind tore at him, but Dempsey held on. He could see the waves of the ocean crashing thousands of feet below.

In the cockpit, the copilot knew they had a problem. A red light had begun to flash, warning him that the door was open. The plane began to pitch to one side. The rushing air out of the cabin made the situation obvious. He looked back and could not see the pilot, but he knew the door was open. With all of the noise, he never heard Dempsey's desperate cries for help. It seemed inescapable to Boucher that his good friend had fallen to his death.

Copilot Paul Boucher urgently radioed the control tower. It was time to declare an emergency, and for the Coast Guard to search for the remains of his close friend. Diverting from Boston, Boucher knew he needed to land immediately at Portland International Jetport. Little did he know, that turning the plane almost cost him his friend's life. The increase in centrifugal force nearly ripped Dempsey from the stairs.

Flying a plane with a door hanging open is a bit of a challenge. Boucher made his focus on landing the plane before anything else could go wrong.

Meanwhile, Dempsey started to face the reality of another problem, "Even if he could hold on that long, would he survive the landing of the plane?" Thoughts of hitting the ground headfirst entered into his mind. At most, he knew that his head would clear the ground by about ten inches. If the plane bounced during the landing, Dempsey and the door erny anwould be torn right off. He pushed himself up as much as he could, and watched as the wheels unfolded and came into place.

As the plane landed safely, officials raced to evaluate the situation, "Was the Coast Guard still needed? Did the pilot really get blown out of the plane?" An air traffic controller spotted Dempsey lying on the stairs. There was no need for the Coast Guard because Henry Dempsey had held on. In fact, a firefighter had to pry his bloody fingers from the door![1]

The degree to which we hold on to the truth of Scripture depends, in part, on how much we recognize our problem. Without an absolute standard of truth there would be nothing to base our future hope on. There are many forces at work that are trying to loosen our grip on the Word of God. Without the anchor of God's Word we would be, "tossed to and fro and carried about with every wind of doctrine" (Eph. 4:14). At the forefront is the issue of postmodernism.

In order to understand how we interact with the Word of God, we need to first exegete the current culture. In other words, we have to know about the age in which we live. You simply cannot avoid the fact that for roughly 2,000 years Christians have been reading the Bible through the lens of their own culture.

A textbook example can be found in the pages of Church history, in regard to the nation of Israel. A survey of history reveals that we do not find many books written before 1948 that refer to a future for the nation of Israel. The reason is amazingly simple; there was no Israel. Israel was not on the map in modern times until it declared statehood in 1948. Not many Christians were thinking much about Israel's future. From the time Israel became a nation in 1948, there has been a steady and constant increase in the number of books written about its future.

It is hard to avoid the truth that we are a product of our culture. We do not want to make the devastating mistake of interpreting end time events in Scripture through the lens of our culture. This is becoming a considerable problem in the Western church. It is essential for a proper interpretation of the Word of God, especially prophecy, to transcend culture and look at the timeless truth of the text. In order to help us do this more effectively, we need to be aware that our current culture is postmodern. Postmodernism is a term that describes the mindset of our current culture—a collective mindset that is markedly different from the mindset of the previous era (the modern era). We are living in the postmodern era. One writer put it this way, "Postmodernism is the intellectual mood and cultural expressions that are becoming increasingly dominant in our contemporary society." These expressions call into question the ideals, principles, and absolutes that lay at the heart of biblical Christianity. Postmodernism is not a conspiracy; it is not a group of people who consciously decided to attack the Christian faith. Postmodernism is simply a natural development in cultural thinking over time. Some aspects of postmodernism are quite positive. Yet, at its very core are philosophical beliefs that attack and challenge the values and principles of biblical Christianity.

If we think of human history in three separate categories, there are the pre-modern, modern, and postmodern eras. Putting it into historical perspective, the pre-modern era essentially took us up to the Age of Enlightenment (the Scientific Revolution, the Age of Reason, the Industrial Revolution, those general historical benchmarks). Most people point to 1789 (the storming of the Bastille in France) as marking the end of the pre-modern age and the shift into the modern age. The modern era was comparatively short (1789-1989); the postmodern era is from roughly 1989 to the present. Thus, we have just recently witnessed a major cultural shift in thinking.

What Does This Mean?

Recognizing these historical changes is of little value if there is no knowledge of the resulting influence on our approach to faith, the Scriptures, and the absolute truth of God's Word. Consider the different approaches to faith.

In the pre-modern era the key word was *faith*. People had a deep devotion (believers and unbelievers alike) to a creator god. People understood that there was something beyond themselves that existed, and they had a general trust in their creator. Even if they had not trusted in Christ for salvation, they undoubtedly had a reverence for a creator. Amongst the lost, faith was generally not considered something to be mocked. Faith in a god was an acceptable part of culture.

In the modern era *reason* eclipsed *faith* as the new standard. If you could not prove it using the scientific method, it did not exist. This had a lasting and dramatic impact on the Christian faith. Science now eclipsed theology as queen of the sciences. Men had become too smart for their own good. When the imperfect science of men contradicted the Bible, science was to be believed. Compulsory schooling laws and public education further added to the corrosion of faith. Churches began to propagate an erroneous theory, which proclaimed that the science of men was perfect and without error. Much of what was taught as science, were in reality the theories of unredeemed men. This was particularly true in regard to the Darwinian evolutionary theory of the origin of man. Men and women began to accept these theories as factual, and the end result was tragic. Believing that science cannot be rejected, they approached the Bible thinking it needed to change to conform to science.

This led to a torrent of liberalization of the Scriptures. People began to reject the biblical accounts of Adam and Eve, Jonah and the whale, the parting of the Red Sea, and the sun standing still for a day. Eventually, this led them to reject the virgin birth, the deity of Christ, and the Resurrection of Christ. The reasoning was straightforward; none of these events could be scientifically proven.

Following this dangerous approach, many churches and seminaries quickly became liberal. A downward spiral ensued that changed the early seminaries and churches in the United States. Institutions that were once rock solid, built on the foundation of the Word of God as their only authority for life and practice, became leading outposts of mockery and ridicule of the Bible.

The minute someone begins to say that the Bible contains errors, it is only a matter of time before none of it is of any value to them. Do not ever buy into the argument that the principles of the Bible are to be respected, but the Scriptures themselves have scientific errors. This will lead to the rejection of the central truths of Jesus Christ. The Word of God stands as a unit.

Today, in the postmodern era, the key word is now *bias*. Everyone has his own viewpoint and perspective on life. Some people may still hold to reason; others may hold to faith. Or, it may even be a combination of both reason and faith. The bottom line is that everybody approaches life through his own individual bias.

In the pre-modern era people were quite comfortable with supernatural explanations. In the modern era everything had to have a natural explanation. Today, in the postmodern era, there are no explanations because it just does not matter. This can be witnessed in mass media and marketing. Some of the most successful marketing campaigns are those that make absolutely no sense at all, but they are so bizarre that they are memorable. It seems there is no need to connect the advertisement to the actual product; it just needs to be bizarre and memorable. In the postmodern age no explanation is needed.

In the pre-modern era the five senses were considered to be incomplete. People understood that there was something beyond what you could touch, feel, smell, hear, or see. In the modern era everything had to have a natural explanation. If you could not experience it with the five senses, it did not exist. It is quite remarkable that today, in the postmodern age, we have returned back to the concept of the five senses being incomplete. People recognize that there is something more to life. They recognize that the optimism of the modern age, that everything could be solved by science, was overstated. It is well known that you cannot prove everything scientifically. The problem now is that so often people are searching for answers in all the wrong places. Instead of turning to Jesus Christ and the Word of God, they are looking into Eastern Mysticism, pagan religions, and the New Age Movement. Their souls are famished, but they are willing to feast on any spiritual food that they stumble upon.

During the pre-modern era revelation from God (the Bible) was accepted. In the modern era the scientific method was the standard for truth. Today, in the postmodern era, there is no absolute truth. Truth is now a construction of each individual. There are multiple truths, but there is no all-encompassing, single, grand metanarrative, or universal truth that is true of all people of all times.

Remember, in the pre-modern era people generally had a high view of the Bible. This changed substantially in the modern era because then people generally had a low view of the Bible. They denigrated it and ridiculed it. The Bible was under constant attack, while science and reason were elevated. Those with the postmodern view really have no view of the Bible. Any text is just as functional or valuable as any other text. To the postmodern mindset there is no stake in the ground that creates an absolute standard.

This type of thinking can be seen today in our justice system. The United States Constitution is no longer seen as the governing document for our country. As a result, justices in our courts are making their own laws because the Constitution is no longer seen as a regulating document to which they must be beholden. These justices see themselves as a truth unto themselves.

With this same postmodern mindset, men and women (both Christians and unbelievers), who have disregarded the Bible as their only authority, are acting like gods unto themselves. They consider themselves to be the only standard that they need to follow. People with this approach will use the Bible if there is a benefit to them, but not because *it is the absolute standard*.

The Shift

There can be no denying that we have lived through a major cultural shift. The recent move from the modern era to the postmodern era has resulted in countless significant changes in our culture. Quite often these attitudes and beliefs are showing up within the Church. This directly impacts our ability to communicate with each other and interact with the Word of God. Before continuing our study of the end times, it is helpful to examine briefly this substantial cultural transformation.

Our ability to communicate is foundational. The goal of communication in the modern era was the transfer of knowledge. Under postmodernism the goal of communication is about participation and acceptance. It is thought that you have not really communicated unless *you have felt where the other person is coming from; you need to respect everything the other person is saying*. It is no longer about the transfer of information. According to the postmodern mindset, you share the blame if someone does not understand your words when you communicate with them. It is now just as much your fault, as it is theirs, because you did not know where they were coming from. This creates a whole new category of political correctness. The attitude or motive of the speaker is no longer taken into consideration. If the person receiving the communication wants to be offended by the words spoken, then the speaker is at fault. The speaker should have been striving for acceptance.

In the modern era there was a definite emphasis on truth. Today this has shifted to a focus on image and perception; truth is no longer valued as it once was. Again, the witness of this can be seen in the media. There used to be a clear distinction between truth and fiction. News broadcasts are no longer just about the events of the day; they have shifted to become all about entertainment. There is now a focus on re-creating history, theme songs, and slogans. The emphasis is now on image and entertainment. The distinct lines between the truth of news and fiction have become blurred.

Before the postmodern era there was a general respect for the societal institutions of authority. Today each person is now the ultimate authority; self is the authority. This emphasis on self has manifested another change. Under the modern age the worldview of most people was anthropocentric. People were looking out for the greater good of mankind. Today that focus has become egocentric; it is all about self.

Postmodernism: Good and Bad

The move to postmodernism creates fresh challenges and new opportunities for the Church of Jesus Christ. Should we embrace postmodernism? Should we reject it all together? The Church needs to reflect on how we are going to deal with some of the issues that have arisen because of postmodernism.

Many believers in Christ are still trying to evangelize the way it was done in the modern era. Then, the focus was on evidential apologetics. Evangelism was concentrated on proving the Resurrection and the biblical accounts of Christ. Systematically explaining the rational truth of the gospel message was the emphasis. This approach does not work with people who have a postmodern mindset. They are completely at peace with letting *you* believe in the Gospel of Christ. If you ask them if Christ rose again, they will typically answer, "Yes, He probably did." They have no objections to the idea that Christ rose again. They may even believe it, but for a different reason. Now what are you going to do?

This underscores the importance of recognizing that evidential apologetics has not prepared us to deal with individuals, like an Eastern mystic, who agree with everything we say. If we do not think through some of these issues, it can make for a thorny playing field when dealing with people.

Certainly there is still a place for looking at the evidence and rationalizing through the truth of Scripture as a method of apologetics. Yet, we need to be aware that things have definitely shifted in our culture. We could find ourselves armed with twenty-seven reasons which prove the Resurrection is a historical fact, but before we even get through the first point the Eastern mystic responds by saying, "Yes, I believe in the Resurrection." Now what do we do? This development of individuals each having their own personal truth can make witnessing much more challenging. The great obstacle in witnessing to people with the postmodern mindset is getting them to recognize that the Word of God is the authoritative and absolute standard on which to base their beliefs.

Another major setback of the postmodern era is the pervasive movement toward complexity and not clarity. This is often a very subtle distinction that we see today; the greater the complexity the greater the value. Whether it is an article, a book, a lecture, or a piece of art, the more complex it is the better. Simplicity has lost its value in the current culture. Even television shows have become more complex. They bounce back and forth in time because the old simple chronological approach is no longer accepted.

There is a definite departure from clarity today. Much of what people say is overanalyzed. Quite often we observe the words spoken, "He said this, but I wonder what he really means." It is hard for those with the postmodern mindset to recognize that at times people simply say what they mean. We witness this same phenomenon when metaphors or exaggerations are overanalyzed. Obvious figures of speech are meant to convey a point. The tendency to overanalyze them offers no value.

The death of absolute truth is a frightening development in the present age. In the modern age we were all on the same playing field; most people agreed that there was absolute truth. The skeptics and unbelievers thought absolute truth was found through science. Believers in Christ understood absolute truth to be the Word of God, but at least we all acknowledged that there was some unqualified standard. Today, most people do not have any standard. This makes it difficult to communicate if the truth is always shifting. It makes teaching others about God's eternal plan for mankind much more challenging.

Closely related to the death of absolute truth in the culture is the abandonment of certainty. People go out of their way to avoid saying anything that might sound dogmatic. Most people are not certain about anything. They are afraid to speak in absolutes and will seldom give definitive answers. A person with the postmodern mindset would typically say, "I *think* my way is better. I *think* you are wrong." However, they would never say, "I am right and you are *absolutely morally wrong.*" The abandonment of certainty is a central aspect of our current culture. It is not often that people will speak in unqualified and absolute terms.

In the postmodern era there is the epistemological dance between Scripture, culture, and tradition. Epistemology refers to the reasons why we believe something. Today the reason people (in the Christian faith) have certain beliefs is because of this interconnected concept of Scripture, culture, and tradition. Scripture is usually a part of the mix somewhere, but culture and tradition are typically placed on equal footing. In many books written today, we see this faulty idea that the basis of our beliefs cannot be Scripture alone; it has to be the Scripture, our culture, our tradition, and our own interaction with them.

With the postmodern shift came the intensification of experience-based religion in evangelical churches. The teaching of doctrinal truth has been replaced with entertaining people and helping them to have a good experience. The quality of a church service is now based on subjective feelings more than on the accuracy of what is taught.

Consider the advertising campaign of a massive church in Houston, Texas. The satellite campus model of Second Baptist Church makes them one of the largest churches in the country. The model they adopted was to contract with AMC Theaters. Sunday morning services from the main campus are simulcast onto movie screens in high definition-digital format. In marketing the grand opening of one of these area movie theater satellites, an e-newsletter was mass distributed by e-mail with the headline, "Same Experience. Comfier Seats."[2] This was the marketing slogan; no reference was made to Scripture, or the content of their message. The focus was on having the same experience as the main campus, but with comfier seats. The posters, billboards, and other marketing media around Houston contained the same slogan. Second Baptist Church has launched similar movie theater satellite campuses throughout the United States. Such an approach to marketing, while creative and perhaps effective in attracting crowds, runs the risk of undermining the biblical authority on which this particular church's message is supposedly built.

Today, in the postmodern church, the focus is often on the quality of the nursery, the parking, the availability of free doughnuts and coffee, the playground for the kids, and whether or not the pews are comfortable. There is little focus on what is being taught by the church. The specific goal of many churches is to make sure people are comfortable to the exclusion of content, substance, and doctrinal teaching. Postmodernism has led to this intensification of experienced based religion; what matters most is how you feel, not the accuracy of the content. What matters most is how you perceive it. The church is seen as having succeeded when the message comes across well, regardless of the substance being taught.

It would be one-sided to only mention the negative aspects of the culture. There are some positive components that have been ushered in by postmodernism. It is certain that the Church now holds the rational high ground in our culture. The viewpoint of the modern era, that everything had to be provable by the scientific method, has been replaced. People might not accept your faith, but they are comfortable with faith being an option. Now we must convince men and women that the Christian faith is the *one true faith* amongst all the systems of belief in our world. No longer is it a philosophical battle between religion and science; religion has won. Science was proven to be bankrupt because we cannot scientifically prove everything. Science does not solve all of the world's problems. The exaggerated claims of modern science have been dethroned. This will inevitably lead to a realignment of churches and theological schools. It is forcing churches to take sides, and this is part of what is known as the *remnant principle*.

The Remnant Principle

The *remnant principle*, as seen in Scripture, is that historically God moves in the minority. This can be seen all the way back with Noah, in Genesis 6-7. Noah and his family survived, but everyone else perished. Genesis 18-19 once again reveals the *remnant principle* to us with Abraham and Lot. Or, consider the nation of Israel; it was the minority of the people who came back from exile because most of the Jewish people had turned away from God.

Think of the words of Jesus in the Sermon on the Mount where He said, "Enter by the narrow gate; for wide is the gate and broad is the way that leads to destruction, and there are many who go in by it. Because narrow is the gate and difficult is the way which leads to life, and there are few who find it" (Matt. 7:13-14). Surely in our day we can witness the principles of these words, as most people during the Church Age reject salvation found in Christ. As we look forward in time, we recognize that even in the Tribulation the vast majority of people are going to take the mark of the Beast.

To be sure, there are exceptions to the *remnant principle*, where pockets of revival breakout. The pages of history indeed account for great revivals taking place, in certain geographic locations, where the majority of people have come to faith in Christ. However, this is still the exception. A quick survey of the people groups of the world demonstrates that most individuals on earth are not believers in Jesus Christ. The *remnant principle* is a truth of Scripture that will not be reversed until the Second Coming of Christ. Until that time, Satan is the prince of this world and his army is going to have the appearance of the majority.

Postmodernism is forcing churches to take sides. Churches are splitting over issues like open theism, the emergent church, the seeker sensitive movement, and the purpose driven movement. This is a part of the *remnant principle* that is healthy for the Body of Christ. How much better it is for the Bride of Christ to take a stand for the Savior, rather than just trying to get along with the world and concede to the doctrines of men.

Final Thoughts on Postmodernism

Another helpful aspect of postmodernism is that it provides an opportunity for interaction with people about their worldview. People with the postmodern mindset are dialoging on this issue, and there is no shortage of books about worldviews. Kids today often go to worldview camps or retreats to learn about other religions. The propagation of other religions is not helpful, but at the very least this creates apologetic opportunities. Postmodernism has opened the door to discussions with people who hold to other worldviews.

Postmodernism also forces us to examine our own historical context. It calls us to realize that we are living in a shift of historical thinking.

Before the onset of postmodernism in our culture we really did not think about what things were like before 1789, or 1989, and how things have been affected in recent times. Postmodernism has compelled us to examine our worldview.

A Biblical Worldview

Given the current culture that surrounds us, how can we develop and implement a consistent biblical worldview? We need to begin by thinking through the worldview process.

"Theology is the discovery, systematizing, and presentation of the truths about God."[3] How we think about God determines how we view the world. Ultimately, our source for truth is the written revelation of God (John 17:17).

How do we arrive at an accurate understanding of the Word of God? It starts with pre-theology (figure 2.1). Hermeneutics deals with how we approach the Scriptures. How are you going to study the Bible? What method of interpretation will you use? Will you allegorize the text, or will you take it in its literal meaning?

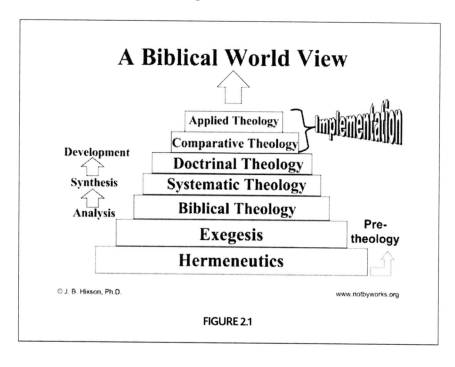

FIGURE 2.1

18

Exegesis deals with the original text. This is where we look to the original languages of the Bible. This includes word studies and understanding what the text means in its original context. Biblical theology, systematic theology, and doctrinal theology are the development phase of arriving at a biblical worldview. Comparative theology and applied theology are the implementation.

Another way of stating our approach to Scripture can be seen in figure 2.2. There are five steps in the Bible study process: study, link, summarize, compare, and apply. Step one corresponds to biblical theology. This is using the literal-grammatical-historical method of interpretation to look at the specific passage and the immediate context that surrounds it. Step two corresponds to systematic theology. The focus is expanded by cross-referencing Scripture with Scripture. At this step we integrate, or synthesize, truths from various passages in the Word of God. This is also called theological cross-referencing. Step three corresponds to doctrinal theology, which is where we analyze, synthesize, and develop the truths we have studied. This is where we categorize our conclusions into a logical, systematic summary. Step four brings us to comparative theology.

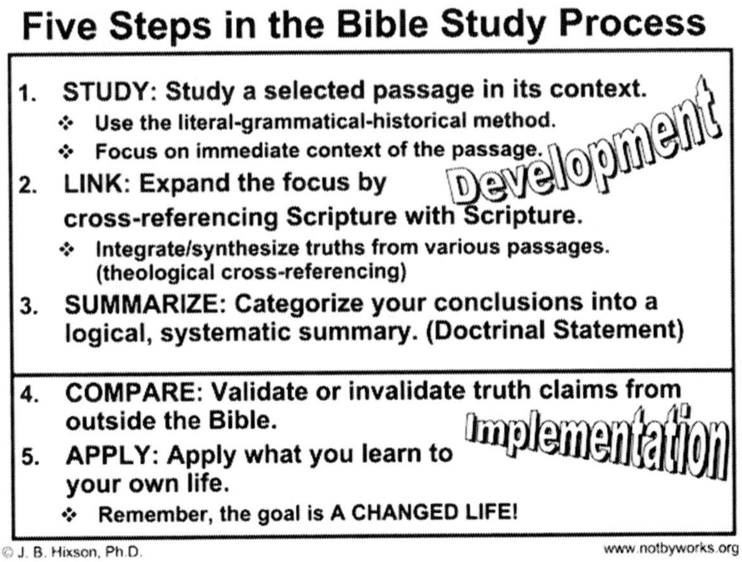

Five Steps in the Bible Study Process

1. **STUDY: Study a selected passage in its context.**
   ❖ Use the literal-grammatical-historical method.
   ❖ Focus on immediate context of the passage.
2. **LINK: Expand the focus by cross-referencing Scripture with Scripture.**
   ❖ Integrate/synthesize truths from various passages. (theological cross-referencing)
3. **SUMMARIZE: Categorize your conclusions into a logical, systematic summary. (Doctrinal Statement)**

Development

4. **COMPARE: Validate or invalidate truth claims from outside the Bible.**
5. **APPLY: Apply what you learn to your own life.**
   ❖ Remember, the goal is A CHANGED LIFE!

Implementation

© J. B. Hixson, Ph.D.   www.notbyworks.org

FIGURE 2.2

Now that we have summarized the truths from the Word of God, we can compare what we are hearing or reading from outside the Bible and validate or invalidate those truth claims. Our final step, step five, is applied theology. This is the final part of the implementation phase where we apply what we have learned to our own lives. The goal is always a changed life! The result is a biblical worldview.

What is the relationship between worldview and theology? Theology is the process of developing and using (or implementing) a worldview. The objective is to take all of the claims to truth that we are confronted with (from Bible study books, commentaries, experience, tradition, philosophy, science, nature, reason, television, radio, etc.) and filter them through the Bible. We are able to make sense out of all the claims to truth in our day because we can know that whatever does not line up with the truth of Scripture is in error. Theology is simply the process of connecting the dots of Scripture and developing a grid of interrelated beliefs or doctrines that are constructed as a model of reality. This is your worldview, or how you see life.

Dispensationalism and a Biblical Worldview

At the forefront of many theological discussions is a central truth of Scripture known as dispensationalism. This particular word carries great importance. What is it, and how does it fit into our biblical worldview?

Dispensationalism is an understanding of Scripture that relates to our theological process and our worldview. It is the understanding that God communicated to us a plan for the ages in His Word, from Genesis to Revelation, which makes sense out of everything that we see in Scripture. In other words, this is the grand story, or plotline, of human history. It begins with creation and ends with re-creation, with a great amount of truth recorded in between. Dispensationalism is the biblical system that most accurately portrays what God is trying to reveal to us in His Word. A consistent literal interpretation of the Word of God will inevitably lead to a dispensational perspective.

Where does the term *dispensation* come from? It may surprise you to learn that it actually comes from the Bible. It comes from the Greek word *oikonomia*. We see that both the King James translation and the New King James translation, in Ephesians 1:10 and Ephesians 3:2, actually use the word *dispensation*.[4] The New American Standard translation uses the term *administration* in Ephesians 1:10 and uses the word *stewardship* in

Ephesians 3:10.[5] The general idea is that of accountability, stewardship, or management. The understanding is that God, at various times in human history, interacted with man according to different sets of rules.

Let us be particularly cautious at this point. *This does not mean that dispensationalism teaches that God has different methods of salvation for men during different periods in human history.* One of the recurring criticisms against dispensationalism is the myth that dispensationalists teach different approaches to salvation in the Old and New Testaments. There is absolutely no truth to this claim. This is an assumption critics make out of ignorance and theological bias. Dispensationalists passionately affirm that salvation in all ages is by grace through faith alone.

Dispensationalism is a clear truth from Scripture. It is self-evident that God interacted differently with mankind over time. It is indisputable that God interacted differently with Adam and Eve than He does with us today in the Church Age. It is obvious that God interacted with Noah differently than He does with us today. It is also clear from Scripture that God has dealt with Israel differently than the Church. These changes have nothing to do with how we receive eternal life. Mankind has always received individual salvation by faith, although it is evident that the content of that faith changes over time. Abraham did not believe the full content of the Gospel of Christ that we preach today. Abraham did not believe in Jesus Christ of Nazareth who died on the Cross to pay our penalty for sin. Yet, he certainly believed in God. He believed in Yahweh to provide a Redeemer in substitutionary atonement for him. Abraham may not have known the Redeemer's name, but the Bible clearly teaches us that his salvation was by faith. The Apostle Paul wrote to the churches of Galatia, "Just as Abraham *'believed God, and it was accounted to him for righteousness.'* Therefore know that only those who are of faith are sons of Abraham" (Gal. 3:6-7). Salvation has always been by grace through faith in every age; this has not changed. However, the precise content of that faith has changed as more of God's revelation has been made known to mankind.

Consider the following: "Corporate Jewish hope for the advent of the Messiah developed dynamically from the period of David's reign when it was prophesied that his kingdom would endure to the end of time (2 Sm 7:16). Israel was told that, through David's descendants, his throne would exert a never-ending dominion over all the earth (22:48–51; Jer 33)."[6] This is a significant point to be understood because this is what the Jewish people were looking for in the first century concerning the Messiah. Yet, when people receive the Gospel of Christ today they seldom have any understanding of the Messianic promises to Israel. As men and women respond to the Gospel of Christ, very few understand that Jesus is the Son of David who will one day take the Davidic Throne to rule with a rod of iron. This is not a problem. In the Church Age you can receive eternal life without knowing that Jesus will one day establish a never-ending Kingdom. There is no need today to understand all of the Jewish implications of the Messiah in order to be saved.

The Gospel of Christ that must be preached during the age of the Church includes the understanding that Jesus is the sacrificial Lamb who died for our sins and rose again. Paul states this very truth in 1 Corinthians 15. This is the content of the gospel, "For I delivered to you first of all that which I also received: that Christ died for our sins according to the Scriptures, and that He was buried, and that He rose again the third day according to the Scriptures" (1 Cor. 15:3-4). Christ took our place on the Cross; He bore our penalty for our sins. Anyone who recognizes these truths, while placing their faith in Christ alone, is saved. There is no requirement in the present age to understand the Kingdom and the Jewish Messianic implications of the Savior for eternal salvation. The great majority of people today, when they come to faith in Christ, have little understanding of the Davidic Covenant, the Messianic Kingdom, or that Jesus is the Messiah of Israel.

The content of the message of salvation was also different during the ministry of Jesus. He came testifying, "Repent, for the kingdom of heaven is at hand" (Matt. 4:17). Matthew also records, "In those days John the Baptist came preaching in the wilderness of Judea, and saying, 'Repent, for the kingdom of heaven is at hand!'" (Matt. 3:1-2). The King was amongst them; He was offering the Jewish people the Kingdom. You could not (whether you were a Jew or Gentile) reject Jesus as the Messiah, who will rule on the throne of David, while accepting Him as Savior because those two aspects were connected. To believe in Jesus for eternal life was to trust that He is exactly who He said He is, the Messianic King of Israel. This is what the entire Gospel of John is all about. Jesus claimed to be the Son of God, which has clear Messianic implications.

When Scripture speaks of the time of the Tribulation, we once again see a shift in the terminology of the gospel. The wording changes, and the good news is now referred to as the Gospel of the Kingdom. This can be seen in Matthew 24 where we read, "And this gospel of the kingdom will be preached in all the world as a witness to all the nations, and then the end will come" (Matt. 24:14). Why is different wording used? This is where we need to put the pieces together. Revelation 7 teaches us there will be 144,000 Jewish missionaries. In other words, there will be 12,000 servants of God from each of the 12 tribes of Israel pronouncing the same message that both Jesus and John the Baptist were proclaiming at the First Advent of Christ. Both John the Baptist and Jesus were proclaiming to the people that they should get ready because the King and His Kingdom were coming. During the Tribulation this will once again be the message that is proclaimed before the Second Coming of Jesus Christ.

Jesus promised, while speaking to the Jewish leaders, that Israel as a nation would not see Him again until the people corporately cry out, *"Blessed is He who comes in the name of the LORD!"* (Matt. 23:39). Jesus was quoting Psalm 118, which is a Messianic Psalm. During the Tribulation the content of saving faith will have Messianic implications as the witnesses proclaim the coming of the Messianic King and His Kingdom. People will be told to believe in Jesus the Messiah, the One who is coming to take the throne to rule and reign. In the Tribulation the Gospel of the Kingdom will have a very Messianic tone; in order to be saved, people will have to believe more about Him than we do in the present age.

Dispensationalism recognizes the teaching of Scripture which proclaims we are in a different dispensation today. Ephesians 3 makes this quite clear. Notice what Paul wrote to the church at Ephesus, "For this reason I, Paul, the prisoner of Christ Jesus for you Gentiles— if indeed you have heard of the dispensation of the grace of God which was given to me for you, how that by revelation He made known to me the mystery (as I have briefly written already, by which, when you read, you may understand my knowledge in the mystery of Christ)" (Eph. 3:1-4). These words have significant implications. The word *revelation* means the unveiling of something by God to man. In other words, Paul was testifying that God revealed something to him. The word *mystery* means something previously undisclosed. This was something new; it was new information. Paul was proclaiming that by revelation God gave him new details about His plan of the ages.

Take another look at verse 4 along with verse 5, "By which, when you read, you may understand my knowledge in the mystery of Christ, which in other ages was not made known to the sons of men, as it has now been revealed by the Spirit to His holy apostles and prophets" (Eph. 3:4-5). Again, this was something totally new. When non-dispensationalists talk about the continuity between the Old Testament and the New Testament they ignore this important phrase in verse 5 that says, *"which in other ages was not made known to the sons of men"* (Eph. 3:5, emphasis added). Paul was announcing that the Church was not revealed in the Old Testament. Israel is not the Church. Israel is not the Bride of Christ. Israel was not baptized by the Holy Spirit into the Body of Christ. Israel was not positionally in Christ. This was new information.

Notice what Paul proclaims:

> Which in other ages was not made known to the sons of men, as it has now been revealed by the Spirit to His holy apostles and prophets: that the Gentiles should be fellow heirs, of the same body, and partakers of His promise in Christ through the gospel, of which I became a minister according to the gift of the grace of God given to me by the effective working of His power. To me, who am less than the least of all the saints, this grace was given, that I should preach among the Gentiles the unsearchable riches of Christ, and to make all see what is the fellowship of the mystery, which from the beginning of the ages has been hidden in God who created all things through Jesus Christ (Eph. 3:5-9).

The word translated *fellowship,* in verse 9 of the New King James translation, is once again the Greek word *oikonomia*. There is usually a note in most Bibles which indicates the meaning of *stewardship* or *dispensation*. It is the same exact word that was translated in Ephesians 3:2 as *dispensation*. This is precisely the point of what we are talking about. Replace the word *fellowship* with some of the other accepted definitions of *oikonomia,* and then we would have: to make all see what is the *plan* of this mystery, to make all see what is the *stewardship* of this mystery, or to make all see what is the *dispensation* of this mystery. Paul explicitly proclaimed the dispensation of this mystery, "which from the beginning of the ages has been hidden in God who created all things through Jesus Christ" (Eph. 3:9).

Again, another word of caution is in order. This was not new to God, but it was newly revealed by God. In other words, God did not have a *Plan A* and a *Plan B*. God was not taken by surprise when Israel rejected the Messiah. He was not wondering what to do next. The Church was not created by God just because He had a problem now that the people of Israel had rejected their King. This was a part of God's plan all along; it actually goes back to the Abrahamic Covenant. Daniel 9 specifically tells us that there is going to be a gap of time in God's plan with Israel. Even though the Church is not predicted in the Old Testament, the Old Testament plan allows for it. The New Testament is simply God giving the rest of the story. He was filling in the missing pieces, which is why the two testaments fit together perfectly. They are not the same, but there is progressive revelation. God was unfolding and revealing His plan that involves, in the present age, a mystery called the Church.

A natural question arises at this point: how many dispensations are in the Bible? Most dispensationalists recognize seven ages, as seen in figure 2.3. These would include:

- Innocence (the Garden of Eden) in Genesis 1:28-3:6
- Conscience (Adam and Eve's Family) in Genesis 3:7-6:7
- Human Government (Noah) in Genesis 9-11
- Promise (Abraham) in Genesis 12-Exodus 19
- Law (Moses) in Exodus 20-Acts 2
- Church (Christians) in Acts 2-Revelation 3
- Kingdom (Christ) in Revelation 19-22

There is no right or wrong answer for how many dispensations there are because God does not directly tell us that there is a specific number. It is a matter of interpreting Scripture and observing when there is a major shift in the way that God deals with mankind.

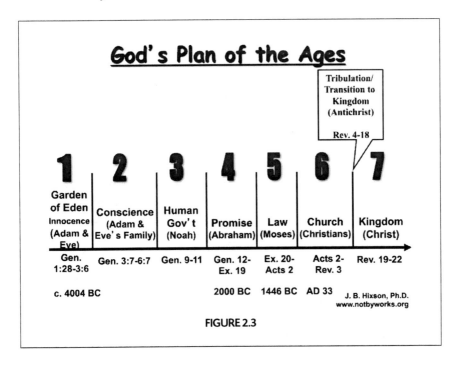

FIGURE 2.3

In the pages to come, we will be examining the dispensation of the Kingdom in much more detail. But it is worth mentioning at this point that some scholars suggest that, in addition to the Kingdom Age, there are other dispensations yet to come. One of these is the Tribulation. While this is not a point worth contending over, let us remember that the Tribulation is really just an extension of the fourth dispensation—God dealing with the nation of Israel. God promised in Daniel 9 that His program for Israel would last 490 years before the Kingdom would come. Specifically, it would be 490 years from the decree of Artaxerxes (to restore and rebuild Jerusalem) until the time when the Kingdom would arrive. Daniel 9 is quite clear that 483 years would pass and then there would be a gap in time in which the Messiah would be cut off (crucified). Then, after the Messiah would be cut off, the city of Jerusalem would be destroyed. After this, there would still be seven more years.

This final seven years (referred to as Daniel's Seventieth Week or the Tribulation) is really just the end of this 490 year period. We happen to be living in an inter-advent age, the time between the cutting off of the Messiah and His return to take the throne. In regard to the Tribulation, God's way of dealing with mankind will not be new. It certainly will change from the way He is dealing with us right now, but it will not be new. It will just be reverting back to the way He dealt with Israel before. God will once again deal with Israel, this time through the 144,000 witnesses. God will be confronting Israel once more with the truth about the Messiah.

Another future dispensation that is sometimes suggested in addition to the Kingdom is the Eternal State. Those who see the Eternal State as a distinct dispensation usually refer to the Kingdom age as the Millennial Kingdom. However, it is best to see the Millennium and the Eternal State as two aspects of the future earthly kingdom. According to Scripture, the Kingdom actually encompasses both of these. When Christ comes back to take the throne, the Kingdom begins. Scripture is clear (as we will see in chapter 3) that it is a Kingdom without end. The distinction between the Millennium and the Eternal State is the location. The first 1,000 years (known as the Millennium) will be on the old heavens and old earth, and the rest of it (for all eternity) will be on the new heavens and new earth. There will be some obvious changes between the two, but not from a dispensational perspective.

In contrast to the dispensational understanding of God's plan of the ages is *covenant theology*. Unlike the term *dispensation*, *covenant theology* is not actually a biblical phrase. Covenant theology is based upon two hypothetical covenants that are not mentioned anywhere in Scripture; these were supposedly made in eternity past between God the Father, God the Son, and God the Holy Spirit. It is all theological construction. There is no Scripture verse that specifically mentions covenant theology, but as we have seen, Scripture explicitly says there is a mystery, a new dispensation, one that God had just instituted. Recognizing these dispensations in Scripture is only a part of dispensational theology.

Consider the following definition from Paul Enns:

> Dispensationalism is a system of interpretation that seeks to establish a unity in the Scriptures through its central focus on the grace of God. Although dispensationalists recognize differing stewardships or dispensations whereby man was put under a trust by the Lord, they teach that response to God's revelation in each dispensation is by faith (salvation is always by grace through faith). Dispensationalists arrive at their system of interpretation through two primary principles: (1) maintaining a consistently literal method of interpretation, and (2) maintaining a distinction between Israel and the church.[7]

A much more concise definition is, "Dispensational Theology can be defined very simply as a system of theology which attempts to develop the Bible's philosophy of history on the basis of the sovereign rule of God. It represents the whole of Scripture and history as being covered by several dispensations of God's rule."[8]

Charles Ryrie gives a well-known and well thought out definition of dispensationalism. Ryrie suggests three distinctions that make up the *sine qua non* of dispensationalism. This Latin term, *sine qua non*, simply means *that without which it would not exist*. Another way of stating this, is that these are the core essentials of dispensationalism; without them dispensationalism would not exist. One of these three core essentials is the important distinction of a consistent literal interpretation.[9]

The dispensational method of interpretation is referred to as the literal-grammatical-historical approach. The words on the page mean something in their context. When the words were first written down, God was intending to communicate something. Dispensationalists do not search for the deeper, hidden, mystical meaning of the text. Instead, a literal interpretation means taking the words and sentences of Scripture as they would be understood in their plain meaning, the way that words are normally used to communicate. The literal meaning of words is the very basis of communication. It is impossible to communicate with words, if the words themselves do not have a normal meaning. A literal interpretation is the normal, plain, customary usage of language. Literal interpretation does not preclude the use of figurative language because we use figures of speech all the time. In fact, *all the time* is a figure of speech. People do not stumble over this phrase, *all the time*. We understand what people mean when they say, "I am so hungry I could eat a horse" or "the kids are driving me up a wall." Literal interpretation does not preclude the use of figures of speech. Literal interpretation takes into account the grammatical-historical context of a passage. It precludes spiritualized or allegorical interpretation.

According to Ryrie, a second core essential of dispensationalism is the distinction between God's program for Israel and His program for the Church.[10] God clearly has a program for Israel that has not been completed. If you believe the Bible is true, you cannot deny this fact from Scripture. This will be part of our focus in chapter 3.

Finally, the third aspect of Ryrie's definition of dispensationalism involves the doxological purpose of God in human history.[11] Part of God's plan involves the redemption of individual human beings, but that is not the ultimate goal of the plan. Human history, biblical history, and the metanarrative of Scripture are all about bringing God glory.

How we approach the Bible greatly impacts our ability to grow in Christ Jesus. These beginning foundational principles will demonstrate themselves to be essential in understanding the beautiful truth of God's Word. They will prove to be the keys that unlock the glorious future hope we have in Christ Jesus!

Discussion Questions

1. What is postmodernism?
2. How does postmodernism impact a person's approach to Scripture?
3. What are the good aspects of postmodernism? What are the bad?
4. What is the remnant principle?
5. What are the steps to arriving at a biblical worldview? Why is a biblical worldview important?
6. What is dispensationalism?

7. Why is it critical to understand postmodernism, biblical worldview, and dispensationalism before studying the end times?
8. How consistent are you in your biblical worldview?

Endnotes

1. John Lovell, "Death's Door," http://new.yankeemagazine.com/article/deaths-door (accessed April 8, 2012).
2. From an e-mail sent October 19, 2006 from news@second.org to subscribers of Second Baptist's online newsletter. The subject line was "Cypress Campus Grand Opening."
3. Charles Caldwell Ryrie, Basic Theology: A Popular Systemic Guide to Understanding Biblical Truth (Chicago, IL: Moody Press, 1999), 15.
4. *The Holy Bible: King James Version.*
5. *New American Standard Bible*, 1995 Update (LaHabra, CA: The Lockman Foundation, 1995).
6. Walter A. Elwell and Barry J. Beitzel, *Baker Encyclopedia of the Bible* (Grand Rapids, MI: Baker Book House, 1988), 1446.
7. Paul P. Enns, *The Moody Handbook of Theology* (Chicago, IL: Moody Press, 1997), 513.
8. Renald E. Showers, *There Really Is a Difference! A Comparison of Covenant and Dispensational Theology* (Bellmawr, NJ: The Friends of Israel Gospel Ministry, 1990).
9. Charles Caldwell Ryrie, *Dispensationalism*, Rev. and expanded. (Chicago, IL: Moody Publishers, 1995), 46-48.
10. Ibid.
11. Ibid.

CHAPTER 3

Is There Any Hope? - Dispensational Theology vs. Covenant Theology

If in this life only we have hope in Christ, we are of all men the most pitiable.

- 1 Corinthians 15:19

IT WAS DECEMBER of 1927, and night was about to fall off of the coast of Massachusetts. A Navy S-4 submarine was conducting submerged trials, and as it surfaced it collided with a United States Coast Guard destroyer. The submarine quickly sank in 110 feet of water. Lifeboats were lowered from the Coast Guard vessel, but all that was found was a small amount of oil and some air bubbles. Rescue operations were started, but there was little that could be done. A nor'easter was upon them, and the underwater currents blocked any attempts to rescue the six known survivors who were trapped in the forward torpedo room. The men had been able to exchange a series of signals with rescue divers by tapping on the hull. Using Morse code, the six men tapped out a question, "Is... there... any... hope?"[1]

Hope is a central part of life. Hope for a better future tugs at our hearts. The cry of the heart of the redeemed is to be with our Savior for all of eternity. The Apostle Paul reminds us that we are citizens and, "members of the household of God" (Eph. 2:19). We should be looking forward to the day when we will live in the eternal Kingdom of God. Unfortunately, the resurgence of covenant theology has left many Christians wondering, "Is there any hope for a future literal Kingdom of Christ?"

A Literal Kingdom

Eschatology means the study of the last things (the end times). Eschatology starts with the Old Testament promises of God to Israel. The Davidic Covenant, established in 2 Samuel 7, is one of these important promises. David was told, "And your house and your kingdom shall be established *forever* before you. Your throne shall be established *forever*" (2 Sam. 7:16).[2] "The descendant of David through whom God will fulfill His promises completely is Jesus Christ."[3] The message of Scripture is clear; the nature of the Kingdom is eternal.

This same teaching is observed throughout the New Testament. In the Gospel of Luke the promise was made to Mary, "And behold, you will conceive in your womb and bring forth a Son, and shall call His name Jesus. He will be great, and will be called the Son of the Highest; and the Lord God will give Him the throne of His father David. And He will reign over the house of Jacob forever, and of His kingdom there will be no end" (Luke 1:31-33). It is essential to recognize, at the outset, that the Kingdom of Jesus Christ will be eternal.[4]

The Sermon on the Mount

The Lord Jesus Christ made the teaching of His Kingdom a part of His public ministry. The Sermon on the Mount, in Matthew 5-7, is the first major recorded discourse that Jesus preached in His public ministry. The Gospel of Matthew was written to a Jewish audience with the intention of proving Jesus is the Messiah. The central message during this discourse was the Kingdom of Heaven. In Matthew the term *kingdom* always refers to the promised Kingdom of Israel. It should be noted that there is no distinction between the *Kingdom of Heaven* and the *Kingdom of God*. In the Gospel of Matthew these two terms are used interchangeably.[5] The Kingdom of Heaven simply means the Kingdom that comes from heaven. The Kingdom of God refers to the Kingdom that belongs to God. The point of both of these expressions is to convey the idea of God's Kingdom on earth. Neither phrase is intended to teach that this Kingdom will be located in heaven.

The historical situation of the Sermon on the Mount is riveting. The Jewish people were deeply concerned about getting into the Kingdom of God. Rumors were beginning to swirl that perhaps this man, Jesus, was the long awaited Prophet of Israel. "Could it be that He was going to usher in the Kingdom of Israel?" Matthew 4:17 records that Jesus had been proclaiming the Kingdom of Heaven was at hand. This led to a very natural question, "Who would make it into the Kingdom?" The only group who appeared to have a standard of righteousness was the religious leaders of Israel. Who would dare to question their ability to get into the Kingdom?

Jesus was that person. Even a quick reading of the Gospels reveals that Jesus had many run-ins with the Pharisees. The miracles Jesus performed had already stirred up a lot of trouble. Against this backdrop, Jesus began discussing the Kingdom in Matthew 5.

Matthew 5:20 is a key verse within the Sermon on the Mount. Jesus said, "For I say to you, that unless your righteousness exceeds the righteousness of the scribes and Pharisees, you will by no means enter the kingdom of heaven" (Matt. 5:20). These were powerful words. What a rebuke to the religious leaders of Israel! In effect, Jesus was teaching, "If you really want to get into the Kingdom, let me tell you how. You have to be righteous, but not just any kind of righteousness. You have to be more righteous than even the Pharisees and the scribes." What a shocking statement this was! It was common knowledge to the people of Israel that their leaders were arrogant, but there was still a respect for their service to God. No one could argue that their leaders did not have a deep reverence for the laws of God. It was assumed by many Jewish people that the Pharisees and the scribes were on the correct path to getting into the Kingdom.

As you look at the Sermon on the Mount, try to think about the intent of Jesus. The people certainly knew the teaching of the Old Testament (in Exodus 20:13) forbidding murder, but Jesus told them, "But I say to you that whoever is angry with his brother without a cause shall be in danger of the judgment" (Matt. 5:22). The people also knew that Exodus 20:14 instructed them not to commit adultery, but again Jesus told them, "But I say to you that whoever looks at a woman to lust for her has already committed adultery with her in his heart" (Matt. 5:28). Jesus was breaking down their misconceptions in the Sermon on the Mount. He was trying to get the people to understand that the focus should be on the status of their hearts rather than their outward behavior. Jesus wanted them to identify that what was taking place within their hearts was more significant than the external actions that men could see.

The highpoint of the teaching, in this section of Scripture, is when Jesus proclaimed, "Not everyone who says to Me, 'Lord, Lord,' shall enter the kingdom of heaven, but he who does the will of My Father in heaven" (Matt. 7:21). This raises an important question, what is the will of His Father? The answer is found in John 6:40, "And this is the will of Him who sent Me, that everyone who sees the Son and believes in Him may have everlasting life; and I will raise him up at the last day." By believing in Jesus Christ we become righteous. Paul expounded on this later, in the Church Age, by saying that, "Christ is the end of the law for righteousness to everyone who believes" (Rom. 10:4).

Set aside our study in Matthew for a moment. In Romans 9 the Apostle Paul, under the inspiration of the Holy Spirit, gave us the doctrinal foundation that Jesus alluded to in the Gospels.[6] Paul put together the pieces doctrinally for us, and it synthesizes perfectly with everything Jesus had said in the Sermon on the Mount (as well as the teaching of our Lord throughout the Gospels). The Gentiles were considered by the Jews to be dirty, rotten, filthy people who had no respect for the sacred Law. Yet, Paul teaches:

> What shall we say then? That Gentiles, who did not pursue righteousness, have attained to righteousness, even the righteousness of faith; but Israel, pursuing the law of righteousness, has not attained to the law of righteousness. Why? Because they did not seek it by faith, but as it were, by the works of the law. For they stumbled at that stumbling stone (Rom. 9:30-32).

Building off of this, Paul continued to teach about Israel, "I bear them witness that they have a zeal for God, but not according to knowledge. For they being ignorant of God's righteousness, and seeking to establish their own righteousness, have not submitted to the righteousness of God. For Christ is the end of the law for righteousness to everyone who believes" (Rom. 10:2-4). *Christ being the end of the Law* means that *Christ is the goal of the Law.*

When Jesus presented Himself to the nation of Israel, He offered the Jews the Kingdom. The bottom line is that Israel had drifted. It had been roughly 400 years since Malachi, the last writing prophet. Over the generations the people of Israel had wandered, and had gotten off track with their understanding of the Kingdom promises. Traditions had been added, the Scriptures reinterpreted, and the Law had been recast into man's image. This all had a devastating effect; the Jews had turned the Law into a legalistic standard for entrance into the Kingdom. The Jewish leaders then turned around and proclaimed their own righteousness because they lived by the same rules they had created. How convenient this was for them!

This is what Jesus was up against. Jesus stepped onto the scene, and completely opposed this line of thinking. Jesus taught that if a person wanted to be righteous, *it must be faith righteousness, not self-righteousness.* If the people of Israel would have turned from the misconceptions they had created about the Kingdom, they would have received their King and His Kingdom.

The Centurion

Immediately after the Sermon on the Mount in Matthew, we see the Lord's interaction with the centurion. Pay close attention to the interaction in these verses:

> Now when Jesus had entered Capernaum, a centurion came to Him, pleading with Him, saying, "Lord, my servant is lying at home paralyzed, dreadfully tormented." And Jesus said to him, "I will come and heal him." The centurion answered and said, "Lord, I am not worthy that You should come under my roof. But only speak a word, and my servant will be healed" (Matt. 8:5-8).

This was an incredible response by the centurion in verse 8. He understood that he was not even worthy to have Jesus come under his roof. At the very heart of this was the recognition that when Jesus spoke, it was God speaking. The centurion acknowledged who Jesus was, and how unworthy he was before God. What a contrast this was with the Pharisees, who were counting on their own righteousness to justify themselves before God. The definitive teaching of the Word of God, regarding our eternal salvation, is that we are completely unworthy before a Holy God. There is absolutely nothing that we can muster up, in our own self-righteousness, to make us worthy before God.

The dialogue continues, "For I also am a man under authority, having soldiers under me. And I say to this one, 'Go,' and he goes; and to another, 'Come,' and he comes; and to my servant, 'Do this,' and he does it. When Jesus heard it, He marveled, and said to those who followed, 'Assuredly, I say to you, I have not found such great faith, not even in Israel!'" (Matt. 8:9-10). This is the key, faith righteousness.

Verse 11 is a significant verse, "And I say to you that many will come from east and west, and sit down with Abraham, Isaac, and Jacob in the kingdom of heaven" (Matt. 8:11). Do not miss the teaching of our Lord. These people will sit in the Kingdom of Heaven.

This same verse also contains another key teaching on the Kingdom. This will be a global kingdom; it will be much more than a Jewish kingdom. Jesus was teaching that when He comes back a second time, many people will come from both the east and the west (many will be Gentiles, like the centurion who had great faith). They will sit down in the Kingdom with Abraham, Isaac, and Jacob. Right now these great leaders of Israel (Abraham, Isaac, and Jacob) are in the presence of God, but their bodies will be resurrected. They will most certainly be in the Kingdom of God.[7]

Matthew 8:11 forces us to recognize the global nature of the Kingdom; this is the point Jesus was making. It was for the benefit of everyone who could hear Him. He wanted them to know that the Gentile centurion understood this critical truth: it is faith righteousness that is essential for getting into the Kingdom. Jesus was trying to tell the people that there will be many Gentiles in the Kingdom of God.

In the very next verse Jesus mentions the *sons of the kingdom*, which is a reference to Jews, and in this context it obviously refers to unbelieving Jews. They will be, "cast out into outer darkness" (Matt. 8:12). This was sure to rattle the people of Israel! Jewish people without faith would not make it into the Kingdom. Jesus was testifying that if the Jewish people had faith, like the centurion, they will be there with Abraham, Isaac, and Jacob. Without this faith, they would become like the Pharisees and Sadducees who will be cast into outer darkness. The idea in Matthew 8 is that Jesus was declaring that He had not seen such great faith, even in Israel (Matt. 8:10).

What is so truly remarkable about this passage is the nature of the Kingdom. The Jewish people had been trained by their leaders to have self-righteous piety, and as a nation they had little concern for the Gentiles. Jesus confronted their pretentious attitude.

It is certainly true that salvation is of the Jews. The Messiah came through Israel, but the Kingdom was always intended to be global. The people of Israel were supposed to usher the Kingdom in, which is what they will do when Jesus comes back the second time. Jews who do not receive the mark of the Beast (because of their faith in Christ) will usher in the Kingdom of Christ.

If you were listening to Jesus as He first spoke these words, what would you have understood the Kingdom to be? Or, if you were reading about these events after the Gospel of Matthew started circulating in the churches, what would you have recognized the Kingdom to be? There was only one answer for the Jewish people living at that time. It was the Kingdom that was promised to David, the Kingdom that was reiterated through the prophets, the Kingdom that was proclaimed when Gabriel announced the birth of Christ, and the Kingdom that Jesus had referred to in the Sermon on the Mount. No one would have had any reason to think that the Kingdom was spiritual, and not a literal kingdom.

When God promised David, in 2 Samuel 7:16, that his descendant will reign forever upon the throne, what did David envision? David himself was a king who sat upon a literal throne. David did not picture some mystical, spiritual, hypothetical throne. He understood the throne the only way it was ever understood at that time, as a literal throne. Likewise, when the Messianic King had come, He was also talking about a literal kingdom. This is exactly what the people were expecting.

Parables of the Kingdom

By the time we reach Matthew 13, it is evident that the nation of Israel was not going to receive Jesus as their King. The only crown the people would give Jesus was a crown of thorns before they crucified Him. It is precisely for this reason that there is a dramatic shift in Matthew 13. At this point, Jesus began to speak the parables of the Kingdom.

Great confusion has crept into the Church surrounding this chapter. Even amongst those who hold to the premillennial return of our Lord, it is often thought that the parables of the Kingdom are about the Church Age. The idea proposed is that Jesus introduced a *mystery form* of the Kingdom. An examination of the text reveals that Matthew 13 never uses the word *form*. In context, this chapter does not say anything about the Church at all.[8] The purpose of this section of Scripture is entirely different. Israel had clearly rejected the Kingdom of Christ. In light of this, Jesus was explaining that the Messianic Kingdom would be postponed.

In Matthew 13 Jesus was also explaining, through parables, that when the Kingdom did arrive, it would be slightly different from what many of the Jews were expecting. There will be unbelievers living in the Kingdom (because eventually there will be some unbelievers in the Millennium). The Kingdom will start small like a mustard seed, and then explode. This points us to the understanding (just as we see elsewhere in Scripture) that at the end of the Tribulation the earth will be sparsely populated because a majority of the people will have died. It will be a small remnant of people that enter the Kingdom.

The Kingdom of Christ starting small should not be a surprise to us because this is in keeping with God's remnant program throughout all of human history.[9] It is a remnant (only believers living at the time of the Rapture) who will be raptured during the Church Age; it is a remnant on earth who will be ushered into the Kingdom. This latter point is best seen in Matthew 25, where we learn that Jesus will separate the sheep and the goats, and say to the believers, "Come, you blessed of My Father, inherit the kingdom prepared for you from the foundation of the world" (Matt. 25:34). To those without faith in Jesus He will say, "Depart from Me, you cursed, into the everlasting fire prepared for the devil and his angels" (Matt. 25:41).

All of these parables, in Matthew 13, are related to the future Kingdom of Christ. They are certainly not about the Church Age. The original audience would have understood these parables as references to a literal kingdom.

Obsessed with the Kingdom

As we make our way through the Gospel of Matthew, we see repeatedly that the disciples were obsessed with the Kingdom. In Matthew 18:1 the disciples asked Jesus, "Who then is greatest in the kingdom of heaven?" In chapter 19 Peter asked a bold question, "See, we have left all and followed You. Therefore what shall we have?" (Matt. 19:27). The Lord's response was astounding, "Assuredly I say to you, that in the regeneration, when the Son of Man sits on the throne of His glory, you who have followed Me will also sit on twelve thrones, judging the twelve tribes of Israel" (Matt. 19:28). Or, consider the words of the mother of two of the disciples, "Then the mother of Zebedee's sons came to Him with her sons, kneeling down and asking something from Him. And He said to her, 'What do you wish?' She said to Him, 'Grant that these two sons of mine may sit, one on Your right hand and the other on the left, in Your kingdom'" (Matt. 20:20-21). None of these passages sounds like a spiritual kingdom. The reason is remarkably simple; all of these people were expecting a literal kingdom.

The Olivet Discourse

As we approach the Olivet Discourse, we observe that the Cross was drawing near. It would only be a matter of hours before Jesus would be betrayed, arrested, and crucified. Within Matthew 23, Jesus had given some scathing rebukes to the religious leaders (this is seen with the eight *woes* listed in verses 13-36). In verse 37, we have a powerful and passionate lament by Jesus. This is a key display of emotion by our Savior for His people of the nation of Israel when He cried out, "O Jerusalem, Jerusalem, the one who kills the prophets and stones those who are sent to her! How often I wanted to gather your children together, as a hen gathers her chicks under her wings, but you were not willing!" (Matt. 23:37). The repetition of a noun (Jerusalem mentioned twice) is a demonstration of great emotion. Our Lord was agonizing over the reality that His people had rejected Him and His Kingdom.

Our focus moves to the next two verses. "See! Your house is left to you desolate; for I say to you, you shall see Me no more till you say, *'Blessed is He who comes in the name of the Lord!'"* (Matt. 23:38-39). The *house* of Israel was the Temple (1 Kings 9:7-8). The words of Jesus came true within forty years when the nation was ransacked and the Temple was destroyed by the Roman general, Titus. Let us not miss the important words of the Lord to Israel. Jesus specifically told them that they would not see Him until they say, *"Blessed is He who comes in the name of the Lord!"* (Matt. 23:39). This quote is from Psalm 118, which is a Messianic Psalm. Most Christians recognize the words of part of this Psalm, "This is the day the Lord has made; we will rejoice and be glad in it" (Ps. 118:24). The *day* referred to is the Second Coming of Christ. This is the day when the Messiah will come and usher in the Kingdom.

Just a few days before Jesus taught the Olivet Discourse, the people had cried out as Jesus entered Jerusalem, *"Hosanna to the Son of David! Blessed is He who comes in the name of the Lord! Hosanna in the highest!"* (Matt. 21:9). Before long those calls of, "Hosanna! Hosanna!" turned into, "Crucify Him!" The outcome of the Lord not taking the throne at that time is a delay of when His Kingdom will be ushered in. Jesus predicted this delay of His Kingdom in the parables of the minas recorded in Luke 19. In Matthew 23:39, Jesus was now making this delay in His Kingdom apparent. Jesus was revealing that Israel will not see Him again until the people as a nation come together and receive Him as their King crying out, "Hosanna! Hosanna!"

The disciples were quite troubled by this. They still did not comprehend everything that the Lord was teaching them. Despite the Old Testament prophecies of the suffering Messiah, and the Lord's teaching about His death, the disciples were still confused. In Matthew 24:1 it appears the disciples were alarmed over the Lord's statement about the Temple being left desolate. Their response was curious; they approached Jesus and pointed out how beautiful the Temple was. Jesus responded with absolute clarity regarding the Temple, "Do you not see all these things? Assuredly, I say to you, not one stone shall be left here upon another, that shall not be thrown down" (Matt. 24:2).

The Temple being destroyed in the future raised another question. Mark 13:2 informs us that it was Peter, James, John, and Andrew questioning the Lord. There was one basic question, "When will this happen?" They wanted to know when the Kingdom will be ushered in, but they asked it three different ways, "Tell us, when will these things be? And what will be the sign of Your coming, and of the end of the age?" (Matt. 24:3). The disciples were asking for some signs so that they could be ready. This is truly a significant principle of the Olivet Discourse. The entire Olivet Discourse is in response to verse 3. It contains the signs which precede His coming (and it explains His second coming) so they would know what to look for.

This raises an intriguing question, why did Jesus give all these signs to the disciples, if He knew that He was not going to come back in their generation? Certainly Jesus knew they would die well before His return. The answer is straightforward if we look at the broader context of prophetic Scripture. The prophets often spoke to the existing generation as representatives of the whole nation. A great number of prophecies made in the Old Testament were spoken to the current generation even though the prophecies were not fulfilled until later. A helpful example is demonstrated in Micah 5:2, which predicted the Messiah would be born in Bethlehem. The Messiah most definitely was not born in Bethlehem when Micah 5:2 was first written. Jesus was following this pattern by speaking to the disciples as representatives of the Jewish nation.

It is necessary to remember that the Olivet Discourse, in Matthew 24-25, relates to the Tribulation. It is a mistake to try to fit the Church and the Rapture into the Olivet Discourse. Jesus was talking about the signs of His second coming to usher in His Kingdom.

Take a look at Matthew 25:31, "When the Son of Man comes in His glory, and all the holy angels with Him, then He will sit on the throne of His glory." What kind of throne is this? This is a reference to a literal throne. Is there any reason to believe, from anything Jesus said in three and a half years of ministry, that He was talking about a spiritual, nonliteral kingdom? There is nothing to suggest this at all! The only way you can arrive at this conclusion is by bringing into the text the idea that the Kingdom is spiritual and not literal.

The Disciples' Continued Obsession

Fast forward in time; Jesus was betrayed, arrested, crucified, and had risen again. Afterwards, in Acts 1, Jesus was talking with His disciples on the day of ascension. It is amazing, but they were still obsessed with the Kingdom. Notice what they said in Acts 1:6, "Lord, will You at this time restore the kingdom to Israel?" If the Kingdom is not literal, then this would have been the perfect opportunity for Christ to set the record straight. Christ should then have broken the news to them that the Kingdom will be different from what they expected. He should have communicated that He was going to reign figuratively in their hearts from the clouds of heaven. Jesus did not do this! Instead He responded, "It is not for you to know times or seasons which the Father has put in His own authority" (Acts 1:7). The Father has determined the timing, but Jesus confirmed that the Kingdom is still going to come.

Jesus had already instructed the disciples to wait in Jerusalem for the baptism of the Holy Spirit (Acts 1:4-5). The wording of the ascension of Jesus is fascinating. "Now when He had spoken these things, while they watched, He was taken up, and a cloud received Him out of their sight. And while they looked steadfastly toward heaven as He went up, behold, two men stood by them in white apparel" (Acts 1:9-10). The disciples were standing there gazing up into heaven. It leaves us wondering if the disciples even understood at this point that there would be a long delay (the Church Age) before Christ ushers in His Kingdom. Did they think Jesus would ascend to heaven, grab the keys to the Kingdom, and head right back down to earth to usher in His Kingdom? This is when the men in white apparel said to the disciples, "Men of Galilee, why do you stand gazing up into heaven? This same Jesus, who was taken up from you into heaven, will so come in like manner as you saw Him go into heaven" (Acts 1:11). Jesus left in bodily form and will return in bodily form (not spiritually or figuratively).

The disciples made their way back to Jerusalem and met in the upper room. One of the first acts of business was to choose a new disciple. Judas had proven himself to be an unbeliever (and had killed himself) so they needed a replacement. This was an urgent matter of business for them. Remember, Jesus had promised them that in the Kingdom the disciples would reign with Him upon twelve thrones (Matt. 19:28). We are left wondering if the reason for the disciples urgency in replacing Judas was because they did not want that twelfth throne to be left empty.

Later on, Peter was preaching in Solomon's Porch. We read in Acts:

> But those things which God foretold by the mouth of all His prophets, that the Christ would suffer, He has thus fulfilled. Repent therefore and be converted, that your sins may be blotted out, so that times of refreshing may come from the presence of the Lord, and that He may send Jesus Christ, who was preached to you before, whom heaven must receive until the times of restoration of all things, which God has spoken by the mouth of all His holy prophets since the world began (Acts 3:18-21).

The disciples were still looking for Christ to come back. We see this continued focus on the promised return of Christ in the New Testament epistles.

The Testimony of Scripture

It is necessary to recognize that there is never a single hint, in all of Scripture, that the Kingdom of Christ is a spiritualized kingdom. The Kingdom in the Bible has one meaning, an eternal Kingdom that was first promised in the Old Testament. It is self-evident that the Word of God always refers to a literal earthly Kingdom for Jesus Christ, the eternal Son of God, to rule and reign with a rod of iron in perfect peace and justice. This Kingdom, according to Bible prophecy, will be inaugurated when Christ returns at the Second Advent. This eternal Kingdom will be on the old earth for 1,000 years (the Millennium). After the old heaven and old earth are destroyed, this Kingdom will continue on for all eternity in the new heaven and new earth. Scripture indeed teaches that Jesus is the King of Kings, but He is not reigning on earth as the King today. His reign on earth awaits His second coming.

The Word of God gives no indication that the Kingdom of Christ is a spiritualized kingdom, with Christ figuratively reigning in the hearts of His believers. Unfortunately this has become the predominant view in the Church. To believe in a *literal* return of Christ to establish a *literal* kingdom on earth with a *literal* throne from a *literal* rebuilt temple in Jerusalem, places you in the vast minority of Christians today.

Three Approaches to Understanding Bible Prophecy

There have been three general approaches to Bible prophecy throughout Church history. Let it be noted that these approaches are not specific views about the timing (or lack thereof) of the millennial aspect of the Kingdom of Christ (which is the discussion at hand when we examine premillennialism, amillennialism, and postmillennialism). These three approaches focus on the broader fulfillment of prophecy. Looking at figure 3.1 we recognize that historically A.D. 33 was the birth of the Church and A.D. 70 was the destruction of Jerusalem. The Preterist view teaches that the prophecies of Christ, the prophecies written by the Old Testament prophets, and the prophecies of the book of Revelation were all fulfilled by A.D. 70. How is this conclusion reached? The Preterist view allegorizes the text; any unfulfilled prophetic passages in the Word of God are not subjected to a literal interpretation. This popular view teaches that the Second Coming of Jesus Christ was a spiritualized second coming.

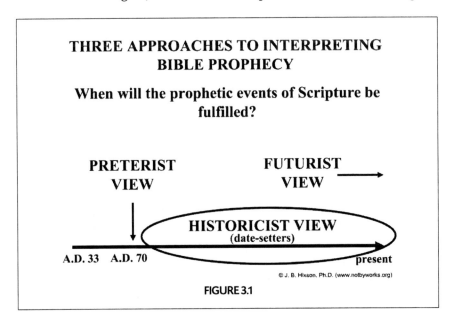

THREE APPROACHES TO INTERPRETING BIBLE PROPHECY

When will the prophetic events of Scripture be fulfilled?

PRETERIST VIEW

FUTURIST VIEW

HISTORICIST VIEW
(date-setters)

A.D. 33 A.D. 70   present

© J. B. Hixson, Ph.D. (www.notbyworks.org)

FIGURE 3.1

How Matthew 24 is handled is illustrative of this approach. Consider the text:

> For as the lightning comes from the east and flashes to the west, so also will the coming of the Son of Man be. For wherever the carcass is, there the eagles will be gathered together. Immediately after the tribulation of those days the sun will be darkened, and the moon will not give its light; the stars will fall from heaven, and the powers of the heavens will be shaken. Then the sign of the Son of Man will appear in heaven, and then all the tribes of the earth will mourn, and they will see the Son of Man coming on the clouds of heaven with power and great glory (Matt. 24:27-30).

The Preterist approach is to allegorize this section of Scripture. Therefore, it is suggested that this passage refers to the smoke billowing up over the ruins of Jerusalem in A.D. 70, after the Roman general, Titus, burned the Temple. This is thought to be the fulfillment of the lightning stretching from the east to the west; the flames and smoke of the Temple being destroyed is believed to be a fulfillment of Matthew 24. Christ's second coming was supposedly symbolized by the fire and smoke billowing over Jerusalem when the city was destroyed. The belief is that Christ never intended to return all of the way to earth to rule and reign. Instead, Christ is thought to be ruling and reigning spiritually in our hearts. However, if we examine Matthew 24, there is nothing in this passage that suggests such an implausible interpretation. The text speaks of the coming of Christ *as* lighting from the east to the west. The intended teaching is that Christ's second coming will be a global event. There is no justification for allegorizing this prophecy.

The Preterist position sees no future significance, prophetically, for the nation of Israel. We should recognize that Israel is seen as having the same political and human rights as any other nation of the world. Yet, Israel is not believed to have any special favor before God. Again, the reason is tied back to the spiritualized view of the Kingdom of God. The Church is believed to be the new Israel.

This brings us to the Historicist view (figure 3.1). Those who hold to the Historicist view tend to be date-setters. The typical approach is to have a corresponding reality in current events to the unfilled prophecies of the future found in the Bible. The Historicist view believes that we are living inside the bubble of fulfillment. In other words, things are happening each day (current events) that are the fulfillment of Bible prophecy. Most of us have run into people who hold to this approach. Every time an earthquake rattles part of the globe, it is claimed to be a fulfillment of Matthew 24:7.

Perhaps the most obvious example of the Historicist view can be found by looking at the re-establishment of the nation of Israel in 1948. When Israel became a nation again, many Christians were certain this had prophetic significance. This was even true of Christians who typically held to a literal interpretation of the Bible. Some believers took it so far as to say that the generation living in 1948 was the terminal generation. Their belief was that a generation is forty years; therefore, adding forty years to the year 1948 led them to think that 1988 would be the year of the Rapture.

This presents an important question, was the re-establishment of Israel as a nation in 1948 the fulfillment of prophecy? It *seems likely* that 1948 was noteworthy in regard to events that will lead up to the Tribulation. Yet, can we say with one hundred percent certainty that Israel becoming a nation again in 1948 *is* the fulfillment of end time prophecies? Would it shake your theology if Israel is destroyed as a nation during your lifetime? What if Israel no longer existed for another 1,500 years? God *appears* to have re-established Israel as a political and national entity in preparation for what will happen in the Tribulation with the Antichrist. However, it is conceivable that God's timing is much different. Israel could cease to exist and then become a nation again in the distant future (even after the Rapture). We can only be certain if 1948 (the re-establishment of Israel) was prophetically significant after the Rapture of the Church when the Antichrist takes charge and protects Israel from a Northern invasion. Then it will be safe to conclude that the re-establishment of Israel in 1948 is directly tied to the events of the Tribulation.

It is imperative to exercise caution when we look at current or historical events. We should not assume that they have prophetic significance. On the stage of God's end time events, the rising of the curtain is the Rapture. Right now the stage is being set, but we cannot say when the curtain is going to rise. The Director may yet have other things to bring in, or props on the stage that still need to be moved. Eventually, the curtain is going to rise. Only then will we be able to see how things came together prophetically.

A consistent literal interpretation of the Bible can only lead to the Futurist view. This understanding recognizes the great number of prophecies in the Word of God that have not yet been fulfilled because they await a future literal fulfillment. Recognizing the promises of our future should give the believer in Christ tremendous hope. With great expectation we can look forward to the Rapture, and serving our Savior for all of eternity in His Kingdom when the prophetic promises of Scripture have been fulfilled.

Dispensational Theology vs. Covenant Theology

Is this glorious hope in the coming Kingdom of Christ the standard belief amongst Christians today? The surprising answer is, no. The root of the problem is covenant theology. We must recognize that most scholars today, within evangelical Christianity, are covenant theologians. Yet being in the majority should not be confused with being correct.

Dispensational theology has been greatly misunderstood. It is often equated with either a specific view of the end times or a belief in different dispensations (time periods) within Scripture. The distinctions between dispensational theology and covenant theology extend much further than just these two aspects; the differences are vast. Regrettably, there is not a lot of recognition within the Church of these critical distinctions. The contrast extends as far as our entire approach to Scripture (studying the Bible) and our salvation. Getting these issues right is central to our faith.

In chapter 2, we examined some brief definitions of dispensational theology. We observed that Charles Ryrie's *sine qua non* of dispensational theology has three aspects. It includes a consistent literal interpretation of the Word of God, the distinction between God's program for Israel and His program for the Church, and the doxological purpose of God in human history.

Covenant theology has its own core essentials. The *sine qua non* of covenant theology involves four aspects. These are the four essentials that truly define the perspective of covenant theology. First, under covenant theology, the Bible is viewed through the lens of two theological covenants: works and grace. Notice that these are *theological covenants* and not *biblical covenants*. Dispensationalism is based on four *biblical covenants* that are actually mentioned in Scripture. Covenant theology is based on *theological covenants* which are a creation of man. Second, the basic Bible study method of covenant theology is to read the New Testament back into the Old Testament. Third, covenant theology teaches that the Church has replaced Israel in God's plan. Fourth, under covenant theology, God has only one program or purpose in human history, and it relates to the redemption of man.

Constructed Theological Covenants

Practicing a literal hermeneutic (method of interpretation) leads to the discovery of several covenants that God has already made with mankind through certain individuals in the Word of God. These four covenants (five if you count the Mosaic Covenant) stand out, and together they are the key that unlocks our understanding of God's program for the ages. God's program is described in detail by these covenants, and a proper understanding of them is critical to arriving at a sound understanding of eschatology.

Covenant theology takes a much different approach. Covenant theologians do not look at the biblical covenants in Scripture quite the same way. Instead, they look through the lens of their theology, and have created two (sometimes three) theological covenants that are never mentioned in Scripture. The major tenet of covenant theology is that the Bible is viewed in terms of these two theological covenants: works and grace (see figure 3.2). All covenant theologians understand and believe in a covenant of works and a covenant of grace. Some also add a third covenant, the covenant of redemption.

The covenant of redemption is said to have been made in eternity past between the Father, Son, and Holy Spirit. It is believed that the Triune God made a covenant amongst themselves to redeem the world. The redemption of mankind becomes the key focus. According to this view, God decided in eternity past to redeem a people whom He had never created, who had never fallen, and who had no need yet of redemption; this was His plan. Then God made a covenant of works with Adam in the Garden of Eden. If Adam had obeyed God he would have lived forever. Adam sinned, and the covenant of works was eliminated. For this reason, God immediately instituted a covenant of grace which supersedes all of the rest of human history. This is what we are considered to be living under now.

47

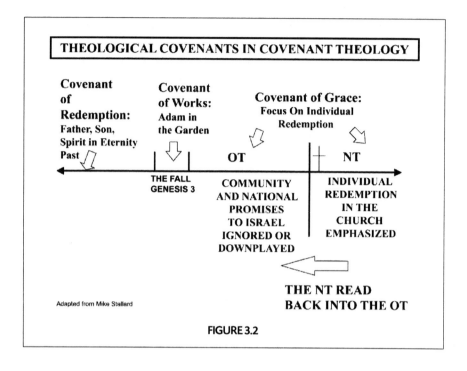

FIGURE 3.2

The Priority of the New Testament in Bible Study

The basic Bible study method of covenant theology is to read the New Testament back into the Old Testament. The approach is to start with the New Testament, and focus everything on the Church as the climax of God's purpose in human history. The teaching of the New Testament is then superimposed onto the Old Testament.

Dispensational theology believes that we should practice the priority of earlier revelation. Later revelation can never change the meaning of earlier revelation. Dispensational theology starts with the Old Testament and reads forward, but covenant theology starts with the New Testament and reads back into the Old Testament.

We should recognize the priority of the Old Testament in biblical interpretation. This corresponds with the concept of the progress of revelation. God, over a period of approximately 1,500 years, unveiled Himself to mankind through His written Word. This started in 1446 B.C. and ended in A.D. 96. Over that period of time, using three different languages and some forty different authors, God revealed Himself to mankind. In trying to understand His written revelation, it is completely illogical to begin with later revelation (the New Testament) and read it back into earlier revelation (the Old Testament).

When we read an Old Testament prophecy like the Davidic Covenant (when David heard the promise of a kingdom), literal hermeneutics requires that we understand it in its literal-grammatical-historical context. In other words, how would David have understood it? David did not have all of the completed teachings of the Old Testament, and he had none of the New Testament. To interpret 2 Samuel 7:16 using the New Testament is to do something that David could not have done. This approach requires the conclusion that David could not have possibly understood what God was saying to him.

It is often suggested, at this point, that an Old Testament text like this has two meanings; one for David and one for us. Let us think this through. If an Old Testament passage can have two meanings, why not three? Why not four meanings? The next thing you know you have a multiplicity of meanings, and there is no stake in the ground for understanding the author's intent of the passage.

We all have a tendency, to some degree, to read the New Testament back into the Old Testament. The reason is simple; we are much more familiar with the New Testament than the Old Testament. We need to be careful to avoid this. It is for this reason that we practice the priority of the Old Testament in hermeneutics. Why? It is because the Old Testament came first. Consider how our schools have historically taught kids math. First, they are taught pre-algebra, then algebra, geometry, and trigonometry. They would not start with calculus, and then try to understand basic algebra. There is a natural progression. The same is true with the revelation of the Word of God.

When we say that dispensational theology practices the priority of the Old Testament in hermeneutics, we are not suggesting that the Old Testament is a rule of life today. The New Testament, as the latest revelation, gives us the instructions for life in the present Church Age. The Epistles of the New Testament were written directly for the benefit of the Church. We recognize that because we are living in the present Church Age, we find in the New Testament principles for the function of the Church, offices in the Church, leadership in the Church, and Church government. All of these teachings come to us directly from the New Testament. Dispensational theology practices the priority of the New Testament in life and practice, not the Old Testament. However, it practices the priority of the Old

Testament in hermeneutics. Later revelation can never reinterpret or change the meaning of prior revelation. This is a very important rule of hermeneutics.

The problem is that covenant theology reads the teaching of the New Testament back into the Old Testament. The result is that the national promises to Israel are either downplayed or ignored. Consider Jeremiah 29:11, "For I know the thoughts that I think toward you, says the LORD, thoughts of peace and not of evil, to give you a future and a hope." Even though the context clearly demands that this is referring to Israel, covenant theologians individualize this promise by applying it to Church Age believers. Likewise, 2 Chronicles 7:14 teaches, "If My people who are called by My name will humble themselves, and pray and seek My face, and turn from their wicked ways, then I will hear from heaven, and will forgive their sin and heal their land." Under covenant theology this is not taken in context as a promise to Israel; instead, this is said to be a promise to Church Age believers.

This is a key point to understand; regarding hermeneutics, covenant theology practices the priority of the New Testament and dispensational theology practices the priority of the Old Testament. It is a fundamental rule of interpretation that later revelation can never alter the meaning of earlier revelation. We should first read the earliest written revelation from God as our foundation.

What God revealed to Abraham in Genesis 12, or to David in 2 Samuel 7, had meaning in its original context. We do not need the New Testament to understand the meaning of the Old Testament. With only the Old Testament Scriptures in hand, we could definitely understand its meaning. This is necessary to recognize. Otherwise, if you believe that you need to have the New Testament in order to understand the Old Testament, it leads to theological chaos. This is the path covenant theology takes you down. The end result of this line of thinking is that the original recipients of the Old Testament would have been helpless to comprehend God's Word. The original recipients could have never understood what God was communicating to them because the New Testament did not exist until hundreds of years later. Even Malachi was written 400 years before the New Testament.

If covenant theology is correct, this means God revealed Himself to these people, in a historical context and setting, through written documents which they could do absolutely nothing with. It would have been gibberish to them because they did not have the New Testament.

This is why dispensational theology is careful to point out that we do not need the New Testament to understand the Old Testament.

The New Testament helps us to put all the pieces together; it gives us additional information. But it does not contravene the original information. The Old and New Testaments do not contradict each other; they complement each other. Covenant theology does not see a distinction (dispensational theology does) between the Old Testament and the New Testament because it does not see a distinction between Israel and the Church. The belief is that God has one people. Covenant theology sees more continuity between the two testaments, while dispensational theology recognizes the distinctions and the discontinuity. The New Testament was written primarily for the benefit of the Church, and the Old Testament was originally written to the nation of Israel.

An Inconsistent Approach to Bible Study

Looking at this second essential belief of covenant theology brings us to the following question, how does each system of theology handle the interpretation of the Word of God? Traditional dispensational theology holds to a literal interpretation of the Bible. It has often been described as the literal-grammatical-historical interpretation of Scriptures; this is the approach dispensationalists take in studying the Bible. Covenant theologians practice a more allegorical approach to studying the Bible, particularly with the prophetic portions of Scripture.

It is important to recognize that many covenant theologians are now claiming to believe in a literal interpretation, but it is inconsistent at best. These theologians hold to a literal interpretation of some passages (historical passages including the First Advent of Christ), but when it comes to prophetic passages that have yet to be fulfilled, they suddenly switch to an allegorical method of interpretation.

In the 1950's it was an accepted truth that covenant theologians practiced allegorical hermeneutics, and that dispensationalists practiced literal hermeneutics. Now everybody in contemporary theology *claims* to practice a literal method of interpretation. It would be hard to find a covenant theologian today who says, "I don't think you should take the Bible literally." This is not what leads them to incorrect interpretations of Scripture. What leads them down the path of error is simultaneously professing that we should practice a literal-grammatical-historical hermeneutic while continuing to spiritualize vast portions of Scripture.

To be fair, it is also worth mentioning that not all dispensationalists are consistent in their literal interpretation. It could be suggested that when we go astray in our interpretation of Scripture, it is not because we have abandoned our belief in a literal hermeneutic, but because we are simply not employing it effectively. All of us need to strive to be consistent. We all at times waver in the consistency of our methodology of studying Scripture.

So what exactly is a literal interpretation? Paul Enns provides a solid answer, "Literal interpretation means the words and sentences of Scripture are understood in their *normal* meaning—the ways that words are understood in normal communication. It is a literal or normal meaning of words that is the basis of communication. Biblically, there is precedence for interpreting the New Testament literally. Old Testament prophecies like Psalm 22, Isaiah 7:14; 53:1–12; Micah 5:2 have all been fulfilled literally."[10] We do not read something and try to seek the meaning mystically by meditating on it and wondering, "What does the author really mean?" When we read anything that is written we can understand it because words have meaning in their grammatical construct; there is a subject, a noun, a verb, and a clause.

The same is true of the spoken word. Try to think back to the last time you walked into a McDonald's. If you ordered a Big Mac you got a Big Mac (well...usually anyway), and not a chocolate shake because they understood what you meant. They did not say, "Well, he ordered a Big Mac, but I think the hidden meaning of what he really wanted was a chocolate shake." We understand language because it has inherent meaning.

Let it be rightly noted that a literal interpretation does not preclude the use of figurative language, but it does preclude spiritualized or allegorical interpretations. The allegorical approach to Bible study is to search for the hidden deeper meaning of the text. This involves reading the text, and then trying to look beneath the words on the page to figure out *what it really means*. This approach connects imaginary dots based on a meaning that has been concocted in the reader's mind, rather than based on the words of the text.

Covenant theology has some regulating principles that are theological constructions. One of these is called *sensus plenior*. This Latin phrase means *the fuller sense or the deeper sense*. This is a regulating principle for how covenant theologians approach the Bible. Their approach, as they study the Bible, is to dig deeper beyond the actual words on the page to find *the real spiritual meaning*. They are looking for *the fuller deeper sense of the verse.* Covenant theologians are quite comfortable spiritualizing the Word of God, and arriving at meanings that are formulated somewhere other than the text, even though the words on the page do not support their interpretations.

It is helpful to take a moment to clarify these terms. *Sensus plenior* is the technical phrase for the meaning of a text that a covenant theologian is trying to arrive at. They are looking for the deeper sense of a passage. *Allegorical* is their overall approach; it is the system of allegorizing the Scripture. A person allegorizes the Scripture when they seek the sensus plenior, or the fuller deeper sense. Covenant theologians do not like their system of interpretation being labeled as *allegorical.* They prefer the fancier, Latin phrase *sensus plenior.* They will often proclaim, "We interpret the Bible literally. We are just looking for the deeper sense." Somehow this is thought to make it sound better.

This should help us to understand how covenant theologians get off track. When studying a prophetic portion of Scripture, they have a different understanding of how to handle the words *throne* and *kingdom.* Even though these words have a literal meaning within the text, their approach is to spiritualize them and proclaim that the Kingdom of Christ is metaphorical. This is why they will teach that the *throne* is a *symbolic throne.* The Kingdom of Christ is said to be Jesus reigning in our hearts today. The throne is thought to be a spiritual reign in the heart of each believer in Christ; this is the belief of covenant theology. Where does the Bible say these things? Nowhere! Yet, covenant theologians come to these conclusions by building an entire theological framework that spiritualizes the text.

Sometimes the *sensus plenior* makes for creative preaching. This imaginative approach can be very insightful, and make you think about some connections in Scripture that you have never thought of before. The problem is that the text does not support it. At best, it is just speculation. When people hear this type of preaching they often think, "Wow, this man is spiritual. Look at what he saw in the text. I never saw any of this when I read it!" Christians would be much better off if they recognized that the reason they do not see these things in the Word of God is because they are not there. Rather than letting the words on the page dictate the meaning, the search is made for the deeper hidden meaning. Under this line of thinking, the more spiritual you are the greater the sense you will have of what God is really trying to communicate. It is the *goose bump approach* to studying the Bible.

Is this the way God really intended to communicate? Dispensational theology suggests that the meaning of the Bible is simple to understand in its normal and natural reading. This is how language works, and this is the way that God has chosen to communicate. God has communicated to mankind by using the words on the page. There is no need to search for the hidden meaning. We do not conceive a deeper meaning of the Bible in our minds. Instead, we find it through the words on the page in their normal grammar and context.

The allegorical approach to Scripture leads to numerous inconsistencies. The greatest of these is the difference in how the two advents of Christ are handled in the Word of God. Covenant theology approaches all of the Old Testament prophecies concerning Christ's first advent literally, but does not take this same approach regarding the Second Advent of Christ. This theological system recognizes that Jesus was *literally* born of a virgin (Isa. 7:14); it also identifies that Jesus was *literally* born in Bethlehem (Mic. 5:2). Covenant theologians understand that Jesus *literally* had a forerunner (John the Baptist) as predicted in the Old Testament (Mal. 3:1). These Old Testament predictions are all understood *literally*.

Yet, when they come to passages on the Second Coming of Christ and the inauguration of His Kingdom they change their approach and take those passages *spiritually*. They fail to accept the promises of the Kingdom of Christ and His second coming as Scripture that will be fulfilled literally. This is an enormous inconsistency in their approach. There are far more passages in the Word of God that deal with the promises of a kingdom than there are about Christ coming the first time as a suffering servant. There is no Scriptural justification for taking all of these passages allegorically. Indeed, many passages related to the Second Advent are very explicit. They give precise dimensions and boundaries of the Kingdom (Gen. 15); they give incredible, architectural details about the future temple (Ezek. 40-48); they describe life in the coming Messianic Kingdom in breathtaking detail (Isa. 65).

This leads directly to a significant distinction between covenant theology and dispensational theology. Dispensational theology holds to a literal earthly kingdom. Covenant theology believes in no earthly kingdom, as the Bible describes it. Covenant theologians would say that it is an earthly kingdom, but in spiritual form. To them the Kingdom is now, but the reign is not a geographic reign; it is not in a physical temple with an actual throne and physical dimensions. Instead, Jesus is reigning in each believer's heart. Under covenant theology, we are in the Kingdom *right now*.

Charting out the view of the end times according to covenant theology would show nothing but a line with a dot at the end of it. The *a* of *amillennial* means *no*; the exact meaning is *no millennium*. Covenant theology denies a literal fulfillment of much of what the Bible predicts, including the Rapture, the Antichrist, the signing of the peace treaty, the rebuilt Temple, the Abomination of Desolation, the seven-year Tribulation, the Battle of Armageddon, the Second Coming of Christ, and the Millennium. Under this system of theology, the entire book of Revelation is seen as the Church Age. It is called the Recapitulation view of Revelation because each section is said to be about the Church (see figure 3.3). The seals, the bowls, the trumpets, and the Millennium are all thought to be symbolic of this present age. This view understands the book of Revelation as retelling the story of the present age repeatedly; Revelation is not seen as sequential.

Covenant theology does teach that Christ will come back (once) at some point in the future (known only to God); at that time, those redeemed in Christ will go to heaven and those who are not will go to hell. This is why the end times chart of covenant theology can be thought of as a line with a dot at the end of it. It teaches that right now (during this age which could be represented as a line) the only thing left to happen in the future (represented by a dot) is for Christ to come back one final time.

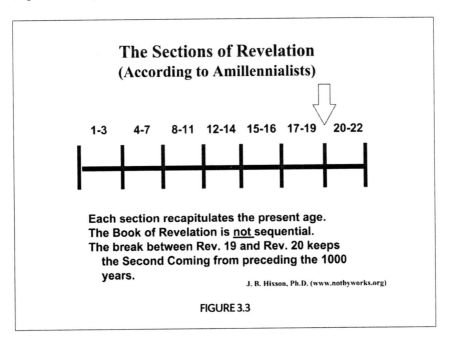

**The Sections of Revelation
(According to Amillennialists)**

1-3   4-7   8-11   12-14   15-16   17-19   20-22

**Each section recapitulates the present age.
The Book of Revelation is not sequential.
The break between Rev. 19 and Rev. 20 keeps
the Second Coming from preceding the 1000
years.**

J. B. Hixson, Ph.D. (www.notbyworks.org)

FIGURE 3.3

What a remarkable contrast this is with the teaching of the Bible! The Word of God reveals that we (Church Age believers) will rule and reign with Christ for 1,000 years over an unprecedented time of peace and justice! Take comfort from knowing (according to the Word of God) that even though we face constant inequities in this life, it is not always going to be this way. In this present age bad things do happen to good people. Dirty, rotten, filthy scoundrels get away with crime; juries are made up of imperfect men and women. We have great miscarriages of justice that take place. As Christians, we should look forward to the time when this will no longer be a reality of life. In the Millennium, when someone commits a crime there will not have to be a trial by jury. Jesus Christ Himself will be sitting upon the throne and will be handing out perfect justice. This is the teaching of Revelation 19:15, where we learn that Christ will rule with a rod of iron.

The reason for taking the time to set the stage, with the biblical understanding of the Kingdom of Christ, is to make sure that we are not intimidated by the fact that dispensational theology is the minority view. There is a ground swell resurgence of popular teachers proclaiming that we are living in the Kingdom right now. This is the viewpoint that many Christians are seeing, hearing, and reading about. Believing in a literal interpretation of the Bible, a future for the nation of Israel, and a literal kingdom places you in the minority of believers today. Take comfort from knowing that all throughout Church history God has had a remnant of believers who have held to His truth.

The Replacement of Israel

Another key distinction in theology relates to Israel and the Church. Dispensational theology teaches there is a distinct program for both Israel and the Church. Covenant theology sees them as one and the same; the Church has replaced Israel. This is often referred to as replacement theology. Supercessionism is another term for it; the Church has superseded Israel. Under this belief-system the Church is now spiritual Israel, which means there is no prophetic future for national Israel. It is thought that the nation of Israel played an important role historically in the past, but will not play a significant role in God's plan in the future. Covenant theologians believe the Church has replaced Israel in God's plan.

Think of the entire world and God's program as a stage. Right now, and at any given time throughout human history, God has a certain group of people on center stage who are His envoys to mankind. The early act of God's program was Adam and Eve, and then it was Noah and his family. At different times it was Abraham, Jacob, and then Moses and the children of Israel. The story of Israel was center stage in the program of God for many centuries. Dispensationalists recognize that right now Israel has exited stage right, as it were. Ever since A.D. 33 (the day of Pentecost) God's ambassadors have been members of His Church. The Church is center stage (in the spotlight), and Israel has exited stage right. According to the Bible, the Church is now His envoy to represent Him and to spread the gospel.

The resurgence of covenant theology means that many Christians now conclude that when Israel exited stage right, it left center stage for good. Under covenant theology, Israel will never play a role on center stage in God's program again. The idea is that there is no future prophetic significance for the nation of Israel.

Dispensationalists correctly understand that, according to the Bible, one day the Church is going to exit stage right (at the Rapture), and Israel will once again take center stage. God is not through with the people of Israel; they are just in the dressing room waiting for the right time to come back on stage. God has a future for national Israel on earth. As we will see in the pages to come, His covenants with Israel were unconditional. He has not abandoned His promises to Israel.

Even in the Kingdom, God has a distinct and different plan for Israel. Ultimately, all of God's people will be in the Kingdom. The Bride of Christ (the Church) will be serving, ruling, reigning, and a part of the fellowship of God's people in the Kingdom. We will all be together as the people of God, but the Church will have a different function and identity that is distinct from the nation of Israel. The Church and Israel are not the same; God has a separate plan for both. A consistent literal interpretation of the Word of God naturally leads to an understanding of a future for Israel.

Under covenant theology God has one people. They were called Israel in the Old Testament, and the Church in the New Testament. Covenant theologians arrive at this conclusion because they prioritize the New Testament in their reading of Scripture. As they read the New Testament back into the Old Testament, they come to the belief that the Church is spiritual Israel.

God's Purpose in Human History

The differences in theology even have a dramatic effect on what is seen in Scripture as the purpose of God in human history. Dispensational theology teaches that the purpose of God in human history is to bring glory to God; this is the ultimate purpose. Covenant theologians certainly agree that the chief end of man is to glorify God, but they focus on the redemption of mankind as the ultimate purpose of God's plan. Everything from Genesis to Revelation is understood to be about redeeming mankind. They believe that from eternity past (before He spoke the world into existence at creation) He decided to redeem mankind whom He had not yet created, who had not yet fallen, and who did not yet need a Savior. God chose in eternity past to create this covenant decree (it is referred to as eternal decrees) to save mankind. Everything else God has done is about saving mankind; this is said to be God's purpose.

Dispensational theologians surely believe that the redemption of mankind is a part of the plan, but it is not the end-all, be-all of the plan. Let us understand that God redeemed mankind because He is the Creator of mankind. Why did God create mankind? God created mankind to bring Himself glory. The redemption of mankind is *a part of the larger plan* to bring God glory. The tendency to overemphasize the individual redemption of mankind, by covenant theologians, has led to skewed thinking in a number of theological areas. This is why they downplay the national or historical aspect of Israel; Israel is not thought of as a nation or corporate entity. Israel is seen as a gathering of individual people who need to be saved. The Church and Israel are considered to be less significant; the focus is primarily on how we come to Christ.

This exaggerated focus on individual redemption is a key mistake of covenant theologians. They often refer to the *scarlet thread of redemption.* As they read the Old Testament they allegorize it, making passages refer to Christ and redemption. This is not sound exegesis. It may lead to the compliments of men, but it is not rightly dividing the Word of God. The greater the creativity in interpretation the more profound it is thought to be. This leads to some bizarre interpretations of Scripture; even the most obscure reference to *red* in the Old Testament is said to be a reference to the blood of Christ at Calvary. Once again, the reason they commit this mistake is because they try to force the teaching of the New Testament into the Old Testament, and they feel free to assign symbolic meaning to a word or phrase that is not justified in the context.

The concentration in covenant theology on individual redemption ties back directly to the belief in theological covenants that are not spoken of in Scripture. Remember that the covenant of grace is said to cover people living during the times of the Old Testament and the Church Age; therefore, there is nothing unique about Israel or the Church. The national promises to Israel are downplayed. The focus on individual redemption, under covenant theology, is emphasized in the Old and New Testaments. This is the primary lens through which covenant theologians view Scripture.

What does the Bible say? In the Old Testament if someone came to faith in Yahweh it meant he was following the God of the Hebrew people. To be saved was to believe in the one true God, Yahweh (understanding that Yahweh was the only one who could redeem him from his sins). This person became a proselyte to the Jewish faith. When God led the people of Israel across the Jordan River into the Promised Land, their task was to use the land as an outpost to evangelize the pagan countries around them. Instead of evangelizing their neighbors, the people of Israel married them! The nations surrounding Israel swayed the Hebrew people to leave their God. Despite some times of success (Nineveh is a notable example) Israel failed to reach the nations with the message of Yahweh. In the New Testament there is a definite shift. There is now no need to identify with one nation, or even one particular local church. Salvation is found by identifying with Christ by faith alone in Him.

The point is to recognize that individual redemption is definitely emphasized in the New Testament. The New Testament is saturated with passages that call for men and women to come to faith in Christ! The New Testament persistently proclaims the individual sinfulness of mankind, the need for a Savior, and a personal response of faith alone in Christ alone! In the Old Testament salvation was by faith alone, but the emphasis on individual salvation was dramatically less. Instead, the focus was much more on the national promises to God's chosen nation, Israel.

Truthfully, there is not even all that much said about heaven or hell in the Old Testament. The Old Testament concept of *Sheol* is the grave, but it is not very often that we get a hint in Scripture that the Old Testament Saints had a *firm* understanding of the afterlife. Certainly, the teaching of the afterlife is taught in the Old Testament, but it is not as prominent. You have to really search for it. In great contrast, it is very much emphasized in the New Testament. This is all a part of the unfolding of God's plan of progressive revelation.

Covenant theology seeks to change the emphasis of the Old Testament by forcing the New Testament focus on individual redemption back into prior revelation. The belief that the ultimate purpose of God's plan is the redemption of mankind has a direct and disastrous effect on how covenant theologians approach the Old Testament.

There is a much better outline for the purposes of God in human history (see figure 3.4). Dispensational theology sees God's work over time in human history as having two aspects, creation and redemption. The Bible tells a grand story that begins with creation and works toward redemption. It begins in Genesis 1 with the creation of the world.

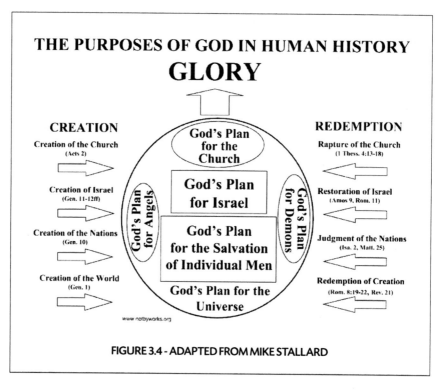

FIGURE 3.4 - ADAPTED FROM MIKE STALLARD

Taking a closer look at figure 3.4, we recognize that everything inside the circle represents some of the things God is doing on earth. Working our way through the Bible from creation to redemption, from Genesis to Revelation, we get a glimpse of the plan of God. If we start in the bottom left of the chart, the first thing that we see is the creation of the world in Genesis 1. Then we observe the creation of the nations after the flood in Genesis 10. The creation of Israel is seen with the Abrahamic Covenant in Genesis 11-12. As we make our way to the New Testament, we take note of the creation of the Church in Acts 2; this is the creation of the Body of Christ, with Jews and Gentiles united into one body.

As we head down the second column, on the top right, we have the redemption phase. This involves: the rescue, or the Rapture, of the Church in 1 Thessalonians 4:13-18; the redemption and restoration of Israel to the Promised Land (on earth in the Kingdom), which is promised in Amos 9 and Romans 11; the judgment of the nations who rejected Christ, seen in Isaiah 2 and Matthew 25; then the ultimate redemption of all creation, recorded in Romans 8:19-22 and Revelation 21. The redemption phase comes full circle back to the new heaven and new earth. It begins with creation and ends with re-creation; along the way God is busy at work doing a number of things.

This certainly is not an exhaustive list of all that God is doing. We recognize that God (as the sovereign Creator) has a plan for the whole universe. God has a plan for the salvation of individual men, Israel, the Church, the angels, the demons, and Satan. This is referred to as the *doxological purpose of God* in human history. In all that God is doing in creation, He is seeking to bring Himself glory.

Covenant theology has pulled out the *part of God's plan* dealing with the salvation of individual human beings and elevated it to the *entire plan of God*. The Bible is not as simplistic as covenant theology makes it out to be. The Gospel of Jesus Christ is a central *part* of the message of the Word of God, but it is *not the totality* of God's plan. The individual redemption of men is only a part of God's overall goal for His creation. God's ultimate plan is to bring Himself glory. Recognizing God's program keeps us from making the mistake of reading the New Testament back into the Old Testament. This is the error of covenant theology.

Covenant theologians would not deny that God's purpose is to bring Himself glory. In fact, the Shorter Catechism of the Westminster Confession states, "What is the chief end of man? To glorify God, and to enjoy Him forever." However, while covenant theologians recognize *the chief end of man is to glorify God* they fail to recognize the totality of God's plan, which involves God bringing Himself glory through creation and redemption.

Why does this matter? What happens when an overemphasis is made on the individual redemption of men? The result is to view all of Scripture through the lens of individual redemption. In turn, this leads to a theological system that makes its entire focus on man. This leads to the misinterpretation of many passages, including those dealing with the end times.

A Word about Salvation

Most dispensationalists believe in Free Grace salvation. This was certainly the classic view of C. I. Scofield, Lewis Sperry Chafer, and John Nelson Darby. Free Grace teaches that saving faith is the belief in Jesus Christ as the Son of God who died and rose again to pay one's personal penalty for sin and the one who gives eternal life to all who trust Him and Him alone for it.

Covenant theologians typically espouse a different gospel. Most covenant theologians hold to reformed theology concerning soteriology (the doctrine of salvation). The belief is that in order to be redeemed by Christ you must repent of all your sins, and fully commit yourself in obedience to God. Saving faith is said to involve a decision to make Jesus Christ the Lord of your life, or fully surrendering to the lordship of Christ. This is why this position is referred to as Lordship Salvation. In reality, it confuses the biblical distinction between salvation and discipleship. Lordship Salvation is about what you do for God; if you make enough of a commitment to Jesus Christ, He will save you.

Lordship Salvation is not seen (by those who hold to it) as two steps to salvation. The idea is not step one *believe in Christ* and step two *make a firm commitment to Christ*. Rather, those who hold to Lordship Salvation equate the two. It is said that *real faith* (to really believe in Christ) is to pledge full allegiance and obedience to Him. *Real faith* is thought to include repentance of sins, a pledge to stop sinning, and becoming a person that does good works. If a person has done all of these things, then they have *really believed*. Therefore, it is taught that if a believer in Christ falls into consistent sin, it proves that they were never truly saved to begin with. Each believer is supposed to be guaranteed to persevere in consistent good works. Of course, covenant theologians disagree on precisely how consistent we must be in our good works in order to prove that we are really saved. Lordship Salvation is a very heavily performance based, works based approach. It is not explicitly works based like Roman Catholicism, which teaches directly that you must do good works to get saved. Instead, Lordship Salvation teaches if you want to go to heaven, have faith. What does faith supposedly mean? It means to promise to be good and to actually fulfill that promise. No good works; no faith. No faith; no salvation.

Lordship Salvation has started to infiltrate the ranks of dispensationalists. The historic position of dispensational theology (based on a consistent literal interpretation) has been Free Grace. Nevertheless, a trend has emerged in recent years where dispensationalists are becoming confused about the Gospel of Christ, as they wade into the waters of Lordship Salvation. A return to a consistent literal hermeneutic would lead to a return to the Free Grace position.

Take Caution

One of the easiest mistakes we can make is to be inconsistent in our literal approach to the Word of God. This is especially true when synthesizing one part of Scripture with another. The excitement of finding *what appears to be connections* to other sections of the Word of God, can in reality lead us to taking the Bible out of context. The only remedy is to study each individual passage to ensure that we have not dislodged it from its original meaning.

We also must be careful that we do not blur the distinction between Israel and the Church, particularly when interpreting the Gospels. All of the New Testament was written for the benefit of the Church. Circulated after the Church was formed, the New Testament Scriptures were written for the instruction of the Body of Christ. Even so, we need to recognize that the events which occurred historically within the Gospels happened before the Church was in existence. The Gospels do not record Jesus interacting with members of the Church; He was predominantly interacting with the people of the nation of Israel.

A correct approach to prophecy guides our way to the glorious hope we have in Jesus Christ. Therefore, as we examine the Scriptures it is imperative that we do not look for multiple meanings for any given text within the Word of God. Every passage in Scripture has only one correct interpretation. The more consistent we are in our literal hermeneutic, the more accurate we will be.

The Need for Hope

Our world today is crying out for hope. Wars, crime, injustice, and the frailty of life all make us hunger for something more. Our loving Creator has intervened in the affairs of men and has promised an eternal hope. Part of this great expectation includes His coming Kingdom. Should there not be a shared confidence in Christ's return to set up His Kingdom? What led us to the point where covenant theology has become the dominant teaching of the Church? The answer can be found by skimming through the pages of Church history; we turn our attention there next.

Discussion Questions

1. Define eschatology.
2. What is the literal-grammatical-historical method of interpreting Scripture? How do covenant theologians differ in their method of interpretation?
3. What does the Bible teach about a literal kingdom?
4. Describe the three approaches to understanding Bible prophecy. Which one is the correct approach we should use?
5. State the four essential beliefs that define covenant theology. How does dispensational theology differ?
6. What does it mean to practice the priority of earlier revelation in interpreting Scripture?
7. How would you describe replacement theology?
8. What is the purpose of God in human history?
9. What is Free Grace salvation?
10. Do you have hope for the future? Are you eagerly awaiting the Kingdom of God?

Endnotes

1. Department of the Navy – Naval Historical Center, "USS S-4 (Submarine # 109, later SS-109), 1919-1936," http://www.history.navy.mil/photos/sh-usn/usnsh-s/ss109.htm (accessed May 31, 2012).
2. 2 Sam. 7:16, emphasis added.
3. Tom Constable, *Tom Constable's Expository Notes on the Bible* (2003), 2 Sam. 7:4.
4. The Kingdom of Jesus Christ is not restricted to the 1,000 years of the Millennium; His Kingdom is eternal. For this reason, we want to avoid

referring to His Kingdom as the *Millennial Kingdom*. This conveys the false impression that Christ's Kingdom is only for 1,000 years. Christ will reign for 1,000 years on the old earth and He will continue to reign in the new heaven and the new earth. It is more accurate to refer to the time of Christ's reign on the old earth as the *Millennium*.

5. This can be plainly seen in Matthew 19:23-24, "Then Jesus said to His disciples, 'Assuredly, I say to you that it is hard for a rich man to enter the kingdom of heaven. And again I say to you, it is easier for a camel to go through the eye of a needle than for a rich man to enter the kingdom of God.'"

6. It is important to remember that we build our doctrines based on the Epistles, and not on narrative literature.

7. The soul of each believer, of every age, goes immediately into the presence of the Creator when they die. Their bodies will be resurrected at different times to receive their glorified bodies. According to Daniel 12 and Isaiah 26, for Old Testament believers this will take place at the Second Coming of Christ. These precious Old Testament Saints will be resurrected, and will enjoy the Kingdom of Christ. It is after all, a Jewish kingdom.

8. The Church is not mentioned in any of the Gospels, except in Matthew 16, when Jesus used the future tense, and said to Peter, *I am going to (in the future) build My Church*. Even in Matthew 18, the famous discipline passage, the Greek word for *church* is best translated *assembly*. The Church did not exist yet.

9. See the remnant principle in chapter 2.

10. Paul P. Enns, *The Moody Handbook of Theology* (Chicago, IL: Moody Press, 1997), 176.

CHAPTER 4

The Road to the Future - Eschatology in Church History

There is no remembrance of former things, nor will there be any remembrance of things that are to come by those who will come after.

- Ecclesiastes 1:11

A MYSTERIOUS ILLNESS has started to infect your neighbors. Purplish black spots have begun to appear on them, and after a few days they suffer a painful death. This was the horrifying experience for the citizens of Europe, which began in the year 1347. The Black Death, also known as the plague, swept through the land killing significant portions of the population. It was caused by bacteria that were spread through fleas, which were feeding on the blood of infected rats.

The people of Europe were struck with fear. The plague was spreading slowly over the trade routes that were used by the merchants. Everyone knew the plague was coming, but they stood powerless to stop it. As the plague progressed, people could see their future. What was happening in villages and towns down the road was certain to hit them next. Not knowing the cause of the plague meant the cure escaped them. Death overshadowed Europe. Despair set in, and people were looking for answers.

The Jewish people became an easy target to blame. Public wells were the standard source for drinking water, but the Jewish people were getting their water from the natural springs. The struggle for survival made suspicion a necessity. This seemingly odd behavior of the Jews led to the accusations leveled against them; the Jews must have been poisoning the wells. Why else would the Jewish people refuse to drink the water? The result was tragic. A great number of Jews were rounded up and burned at the stake.

The most common approach to cure the plague by doctors was bloodletting. This came from the idea that the plague could be drained out of people. The doctors would cut into a vein and then let it bleed. Sometimes the doctors would cut directly into the sores. The blood that would come out of the sores on the skin was black, thick, and smelt horrible. This attempt at a solution never saved anyone.

The religious community had their own understanding of what had brought this terrifying situation to Europe. Their claim was that the Black Death was God directly punishing people for their sins, and another drastic solution was proposed. A group, known as flagellants, came onto the scene. At times, thousands of people joined their ranks. Marching through the villages and towns, these people would flog each other. This was intended to release them of their sins, thereby sparing them from getting the plague.

The people of Europe agreed on their problem. Death was the enemy, but a lack of identifying the true source of their problem led to social chaos. A basic comprehension of the problem (fleas and rats) would have brought about immediate clarity, and millions of lives could have been saved. This demonstrates an important principle; ignorance of the root problem can send men and women down a path that leads to utter confusion.

Admittedly there is widespread confusion within the church at large surrounding the doctrine of the end times. This lack of clarity can be directly attributed to an inadequate understanding of the source of the problem. In order to recognize the root cause of the confusion surrounding the end times we need to take a look back in Church history. Understanding the historical road that has brought us here helps us to see more clearly the path to our future in Christ Jesus!

The Historical Road

The early Church was put into a remarkable situation. The nation of Israel had put its hope in a *political* Messiah who would come and break the shackles of the Roman Empire. The Jewish people believed this would free them to live in the Kingdom of the Messiah. Now that the Church was born, when would the Messiah return? This question burned in the hearts and minds of the early believers in Christ. As days turned into months, and months turned into years, hope began to fade for Christ's quick return and establishment of His Kingdom.

The testimony of Scripture tells us that the early Church certainly believed that Jesus Christ would return for His Church at the Rapture. This is clear enough from the words of the Apostle Paul, "But I do not want you to be ignorant, brethren, concerning those who have fallen asleep, lest you sorrow as others who have no hope. For if we believe that Jesus died and rose again, even so God will bring with Him those who sleep in Jesus" (1 Thess. 4:13-14). The Church was to take comfort from knowing that when Christ returns for His Bride, He will bring with Him those who have already died in Christ. This will take place at the Rapture.

Furthermore, the early Church expected a literal return of Christ at the Second Coming to establish His Kingdom. Consider the evidence we have already examined. The consistent testimony of Scripture is that the Kingdom of Christ is a literal kingdom.

Fast forward one generation to the early second century Church. This was the generation who had ties to relatives and friends who actually walked with Jesus Christ. Their hope for the return of Christ was still strong. This generation held tightly to the words spoken to the disciples, "This same Jesus, who was taken up from you into heaven, will so come in like manner as you saw Him go into heaven" (Acts 1:11). This generation of believers expected the return of Christ any day. There was excitement, and they were filled with hope.

History is filled with evidence that many from this generation believed in the return of Christ to establish His literal Kingdom. Consider the following statement from Justin Martyr (A.D. 100-165), "But I and others, who are right-minded Christians on all points, are assured that there will be a resurrection of the dead, and a thousand years in Jerusalem, which will then be built, adorned, and enlarged, [as] the prophets Ezekiel and Isaiah and others declare."[1] Another fascinating statement from Justin Martyr points to this same belief, "And further, there was a certain man with us, whose name was John, one of the apostles of Christ, who prophesied, by a revelation that was made to him, that those who believed in our Christ would dwell a thousand years in Jerusalem; and that thereafter the general, and, in short, the eternal resurrection and judgment of all men would likewise take place."[2] This is the clear witness from this stage of Church history.

Another couple of generations went by and a normal human reaction took place; the hope of the return of Christ began to wane within the Church. Many Christians still believed Jesus would *one day* return, but as time passed the everyday hope and excitement that it could be today began to fade.

Around A.D. 185, Origen was born. He went on to become the father of the allegorical interpretation of Scripture. Origen began to suggest that maybe the Church was misunderstanding the writings of the Apostles and the unfulfilled prophecies of Scripture. It was alleged that perhaps Jesus was not talking about a literal kingdom. Origen suggested an allegorical approach to the Word of God, and because of this many Christians began to spiritualize (or allegorize) the text of Scripture.

In the early fifth century, Augustine wrote his famous work *The City of God*. Augustine recast Scripture into a cosmic battle of good versus evil; the Church was presented as the Kingdom. This monumental work helped to crystallize the allegorical approach to the Scriptures. Let us not forget that during this time the early foundations of the Roman Catholic Church began to dominate the face of Christianity.

In the Dark Ages, it was a desperate scene for the Church of Jesus Christ. This is not to say that there were no Christians during this time who believed in a literal return of Christ to establish His Kingdom. However, the dominance of the Roman Catholic Church and the limited access to the Word of God naturally reduced the number of people with a scriptural understanding of the end times. The Roman Catholic Church grabbed hold of the views that Augustine put forth in *The City of God*. The Catholic Church was considered to be the Kingdom, and therefore there was no widespread study of eschatology.

This strikes at the heart of the problem that we are confronted with today. One of the underlying reasons widespread disagreement exists about eschatology is because of the historical reality that for approximately 1,400 years these doctrines were not studied or taught. There is more unilateral agreement on Christology, theology proper, and other major doctrines of the faith because they have been studied longer. When Augustine wrote his book *The City of God* (which, essentially, in the fifth century propagated this whole concept that we are the Kingdom), it virtually shelved the study of eschatology for 1,400 years.

The Protestant Reformation forever altered the landscape of the Christian faith. For the first time, the Scriptures were much more accessible to the common people. As men and women read the Bible, they began to realize for the first time that salvation is by faith alone, not by keeping the sacraments and buying indulgences.

The Protestant Reformation did not immediately clear up the confusion surrounding the doctrines of the end times. We note that most of the reformers themselves were amillennial. It is also imperative to remember that at this stage of history, Israel was not a nation. This meant that even after the Reformation, as men and women began to read the Scriptures more, their current historical situation directly impacted the way they viewed the Word of God. As they read about Israel, the tendency was to think of an ancient nation from the historical days of the Bible. This made it much more difficult for people to come to the conclusion that God was talking about a future for the nation of Israel.

As individuals began to reintroduce themselves to the Scriptures, they began to read it in its normal plain sense. Truthfully, they were just going back to how the Church read and understood the Scriptures in the first century. Reading the Scriptures this way, they began to recognize that there is going to be a literal Kingdom of Christ that is coming. Men and women began to see that these promises from God have yet to be fulfilled. A Davidic Kingdom will come; Jesus will return to rule and reign!

This gave rise to the birth of dispensationalism. John Nelson Darby (A.D. 1800-1882) is considered the father of dispensationalism as a system. This does not mean that Darby created or fabricated these doctrines. It simply indicates that Darby recognized the same truths from Scripture that had been recognized by men of the early Church, and he put them into an organized system of belief. The name *dispensationalism* was given to the historic doctrines that had been taught throughout Church history, particularly in the early Church. The doctrine was not new; only the systematizing (putting the pieces together in Scripture) and the specific label of this theology as dispensationalism were new.

The vast majority of Christians today are completely unaware of the early Church's firm belief that there is a definite future for the nation of Israel. Christians have let the traditional teachings of Origen and Augustine, which have been handed down over the centuries, blind them to the truth of God's promised future for Israel. This is another one of the underlying reasons many Christians today insist there is no future for Israel.

A Closer Look at the Road

Examining the path of Christians who have walked before us helps us for at least two basic reasons. First, it forces us to examine why certain doctrinal positions have been handed down to us in the faith. Secondly, looking at the dangers of those who have strayed from the way of truth keeps us from making the same mistakes.

Precisely for these reasons, let us go back to the beginning and look a little more closely at the detailed pages of Church history. The Patristic era was from A.D. 100-400. During this time, the early Christians looked for three things: the return of Jesus Christ, a cataclysmic end to the present age, and a bodily resurrection. We do not find the term *premillennial* used during this time in history because it was referred to as *chiliasm*. Even though this teaching went by another name during this stage of history, let us understand clearly that they looked for a literal return of Christ to establish His Kingdom. Notable premillennialists in the early Church included: Papias (A.D. 60-130), Irenaeus (A.D. 130-200), Justin Martyr (A.D. 100-165), and Tertullian (A.D. 160-225). Every one of these men espoused in their writings the teaching that is now referred to as premillennialism.

This is not a minor point that can be easily overlooked. Covenant theologians love to argue their view of the end times from Church history, rather than from Scripture. The erroneous statement is often made that all of the Church fathers were amillennial. This is simply not true. The pages of history do not support these claims.

Furthermore, let it be noted that while many covenant theologians try to focus the attention primarily on history, there is a looming fundamental question that they cannot answer. All of the promises in the Old Testament regarding the First Advent of Christ were fulfilled literally. Jesus was born of a virgin in Bethlehem, with a forerunner who we know as John the Baptist. Yet, when it comes to the prediction of the Second Advent of Christ in the Old Testament, covenant theologians spiritualize those promises. What is the justification for this? Truthfully, there is none. It is an arbitrary decision to bring their theology into the text.

Augustine (A.D. 354-430) is often referred to as the *father of amillennialism*. He abandoned premillennialism because of what he considered to be the excesses and carnalities of this view. Augustine considered Mark 3:27 to be a reference to the present binding of Satan. The text in Mark records, "No one can enter a strong man's house and plunder his goods, unless he first binds the strong man. And then he will plunder his house." This is a clear example of reading into the text more than what is actually written. Nevertheless, Augustine's book *The City of God* was significant in the promotion and acceptance of amillennial thinking in the Church.

The Medieval era could be defined as the years from A.D. 430-1500. Unfortunately, the Augustinian amillennial view was the accepted and predominant teaching of the Church during this period. Before we jump to the conclusion that this means amillenialism, therefore, must be the correct view, let us think this through. During this same period of time in history, salvation by works through the sacraments and the sale of indulgences was the undisputed teaching of the Church. This was the incorrect view of eternal salvation propagated by the Roman Catholic Church. Should we also start teaching this false gospel of works because it was taught during Church history? May it never be!

We would also do well to remember that during this time underground churches were facing the constant persecution of the Roman Catholic dominance. When the teaching materials of these groups were found by the Roman Catholic authorities they were quickly destroyed, leaving very little historical record of their actual beliefs.

The Reformation era lasted from A.D. 1500-1650. The primary reformers, including Martin Luther (A.D. 1483-1546) and John Calvin (A.D. 1509-1564), accepted the commonly held view of amillennialism. Most of us are a product of our culture and to some degree the reformers were no different. Luther was a historicist, meaning that he held the position that the end time prophecies of the Bible were being fulfilled in his day. Luther believed that the Roman Catholic Pope was the Antichrist, which was a view that was passed down all the way to C.I. Scofield.

The Modern era of Church history is considered to be A.D. 1650 to the present. During the eighteenth century postmillennialism became a popular teaching. The beginnings of modern postmillennialism are usually associated with the works of Daniel Whitby (A.D. 1638-1726). Jonathan Edwards (A.D. 1703-1758) was also a postmillennialist who viewed the First Great Awakening as the beginning of the Millennium. Other men that were associated with this line of theology included B.B. Warfield and Charles Hodge.

After the Reformation, it was an exciting time in the eighteenth and nineteenth centuries. The Scientific Revolution, the Age of Enlightenment, and the Industrial Revolution meant that optimism ruled the day in Western thinking. This optimism carried over to how many people viewed the Scriptures. It led to the idea that if the message of Christ could be preached to the entire world, this would usher in the golden age of the Kingdom. This view embraced the belief in a kingdom on earth. Yet, it was referred to as postmillennial for a specific reason. Counting back 1,000 years from the Second Coming of Christ was said to be the experience of the Kingdom. The experience of the Kingdom was defined as taking the gospel out to the world to bring everybody on board, which would usher in the Second Coming of Christ. This view began to die out as a leading view in theology with the ushering in of World War I. Wars and the major loss of life defeated the optimism.

Not many Christians today would claim to be postmillennial. Unfortunately, however, this same teaching has once again arisen under other names. Reconstructionism, Dominion Theology, and Theonomic Ethics are essentially the reintroduction of postmillennialism. This type of Christian activism teaches that if we can elect enough Christians to political office, we then can impose Christian laws on the world and usher in the Kingdom. This repackaging of postmillennialism fails to understand the unmistakable teaching of Scripture. When Jesus Christ the Prince of Peace returns, then the entire world will be evangelized; it is not the other way around.

Dispensationalism, as an organized system of theology, arose in the middle of the nineteenth century. John Nelson Darby (A.D. 1800-1882) is known as the father of dispensationalism. Darby documented the different dispensations found within the record of biblical history. A consistent literal hermeneutic led him to the understanding, from Scripture, of the Rapture of the Church and the Second Coming of Christ to establish His Kingdom. Darby also believed in a future literal fulfillment of the Old Testament promises to Israel.

As time marched forward, C.I. Scofield (A.D. 1843-1921) spread and popularized the teachings of dispensationalism. Dispensational theology continued to be advanced from 1883-1897 through the Niagara Bible conferences. This had a significant impact on helping to advance Bible institutes and Bible colleges in the years that followed. The groundwork was started for Moody Bible Institute in 1886. Philadelphia School of the Bible was started by C.I. Scofield and Dr. William Pettingill. Lewis Sperry Chafer, a disciple of Scofield, passed on the baton by starting Dallas Seminary (then called Evangelical Theological College) in 1924. The combination of conferences, Bible institutes, and Bible colleges helped to spread the historic biblical teachings known today as dispensationalism.

These are the pages of Church history that have brought us to the present day. Mistakes have been made and battles for the truth have been both won and lost. Now the challenge lies before us, how do we make sure that we are understanding prophecy correctly? What road should we embark on to help us understand the future as outlined in the Word of God? It would be remiss to move forward on our journey of studying eschatology without first charting out our course. This brings us to the issue of interpreting prophecy in the Word of God.

Eight Principles for Interpreting Prophecy

Our road to the future starts with eight basic principles for interpreting prophecy. First, let us remember that we should, *follow the customary usage of language.*[3] In other words, there is nothing mystical or spiritual about prophetic passages. They use verbs, nouns, and subjects just like every other part of Scripture. There is no need to turn off our normal rules of hermeneutics when we study Bible prophecy.

Second, let us make certain that we, *commit no historical-cultural blunders.* This means we need to make sure that we always read the text of Scripture in the context of its culture. An illustrative example of this is the phrase *outer darkness* and how it is used in the Gospel of Matthew. This expression is used three times in Matthew and simply means *out in the dark.* Consider Matthew 8:12, "But the sons of the kingdom will be cast out into outer darkness. There will be weeping and gnashing of teeth." This is the first occasion of this expression being used in Matthew. In the Jewish culture the wedding feast was held at night, and torches and lamps were used to light up the festivities. This can be clearly seen in Matthew 22:13 with the parable of the marriage feast and in Matthew 25 with the parable of the virgins and their lamps.

Jesus was speaking about the Jewish people missing the Kingdom. The first event in the Messianic Kingdom, at the beginning of the Millennium, is the Marriage Supper. The marriage will take place in heaven but the wedding feast (the supper) will take place on earth. Jesus was teaching in Matthew 8:12 that some of the Jews will not be able to participate in the Marriage Supper of the Lamb because of their lack of faith in Christ. These Jews will be out in the dark, and not in the light taking part in the celebrations of the Marriage Supper. In every case in Matthew, with the use of this phrase *outer darkness*, this is precisely what Jesus was talking about. Some of the Jews will not be enjoying the wedding feast because of their lack of faith in Him.

Taking these passages out of the cultural context in which they were written has caused confusion. This had led to the bizarre idea that the phrase *outer darkness* refers to some sort of Christian purgatory, where really bad Christians go for 1,000 years to be punished before ultimately ending up in heaven. Such an absurd view is clearly not the point of these passages. The outer darkness passages have nothing to do with either the Church Age or Christians. Outer darkness in Matthew is always in reference to the Jews missing the Kingdom. To miss the Kingdom means the person will ultimately be in hell. At the end of the tribulation, when Christ returns to take the throne, those who refused to trust Him for eternal life will be excluded from the Kingdom. To them He will say, "Depart from Me, you cursed, into the everlasting fire prepared for the devil and his angels" (Matt. 25:41). On the other hand, those on earth at that time who believed in Him will ultimately be in heaven. The Lord will say to them, "Come, you blessed of My Father, inherit the kingdom prepared for you from the foundation of the world" (Matt. 25:34). If we are not careful to put these passages into their proper historical and cultural context, we will miss the plain meaning of the text.

Third, we must, *make Jesus Christ central in all of our interpretations.* This is certainly not meant in an allegorical sense. Rather, let us recognize that God's entire Kingdom program points to the eternal Son of God who became the Son of Man to rule, reign, and manifest God's glory to all. We should never lose sight of the truth that the Son of Man is going to come back to rule and to reign.

Fourth, let us be, *conscious of context.* Ignoring the surrounding context of any given prophetical passage is a sure way of coming to an incorrect interpretation. Look at the verses before and after the passage you are studying to make sure you have the original context of the given passage.

Fifth, *interpret by the analogy of faith.* This simply means that every interpretation must be in harmony with the uniform teaching of Scripture. Again, note that this means something different from how covenant theologians use this phrase the *analogy of faith.* Covenant theologians think that the analogy of faith gives them the right to reinterpret Old Testament passages allegorically. This takes us back to what they call in Latin *sensus plenior,* or a fuller, deeper, hidden sense. As covenant theologians read passages that describe a Kingdom for Israel, they look beneath the words of the page and look for the hidden sense of the passage. This is not what is meant, according to dispensationalists, to interpret by the analogy of faith. Instead, the belief is that every interpretation must be in harmony with the uniform teaching of Scripture. Our interpretation of prophetic Scripture must not contradict the full counsel of the Word of God.

Sixth, let us be aware of and, *recognize the progress of revelation.* An excellent example of this can be found in regard to the teaching of the Kingdom. With the completion of the New Testament we have more information about the Kingdom of Christ than the Jews living when Christ was first beginning His ministry. In the Gospels, Jesus began to explain that the Kingdom will look a little different from what many of the Jews were expecting. The Lord also revealed that there will be a delay before the Kingdom will be ushered in.

A fitting illustration of this revelation can be found in Luke 19. This is a central passage for premillennial dispensationalism. In Luke 19:11-28 Jesus made it clear that the King (Jesus Himself) would go away to receive the Kingdom. While the King is away we need to be doing the business of the Father. Someday Jesus is going to come back, and when He does He is going to ask us to give an account for what we have done while He was gone. We will give account to the Lord Jesus at the Judgment Seat of Christ. Before Luke 19 was written, this teaching was not as clear. This illustrates the importance of the progress of revelation.

Seventh, make sure to only, *grant one interpretation to each passage.* There is no such thing as a multiplicity of meanings. Christians often teach that a prophecy can have several fulfillments. This is often asserted in regard to Isaiah 7:14. Isaiah records, "the virgin shall conceive and bear a Son" (Isa. 7:14). It is stated that this passage has both a near fulfillment and a far fulfillment. The idea put forth is that the Hebrew term for *virgin* can mean *young maiden.* In this line of thinking it is assumed that all Isaiah was actually prophesying was that a young maiden would have a child. The child born in Isaiah 8:1 would be seen as the corresponding near fulfillment and the ultimate fulfillment is found in Jesus Christ.

There is simply no reason for this approach to Scripture. Matthew saw the birth of Christ as a complete fulfillment of Isaiah 7:14. This is why Matthew quoted Isaiah and said, "So all this was done that it might be fulfilled which was spoken by the Lord through the prophet, saying: *'Behold, the virgin shall be with child, and bear a Son, and they shall call His name Immanuel,'* which is translated, 'God with us'" (Matt. 1:22-23). We need to recognize that there cannot be two different meanings of the same prophecy. If there can be more than one meaning, then there could be an infinite number of meanings. We would never know when to stop applying different meanings to a prophetic passage. This is why this is such a critical point to recognize.

Eighth, as we study prophecy and seek to interpret it we should, *choose the simplest interpretation*. In other words, do not overcomplicate it. Quite often Christians make prophecy harder to understand than it should be. The book of Revelation is actually one of the easiest books of the Bible to outline and understand. Certainly it contains apocalyptic literature. However, if you recognize the apocalyptic genre, the rich symbolism, and do not try to stretch the metaphors, it is not as complicated as some people make it out to be.

Three Categories of Prophetic Fulfillment

As you study Bible prophecy you will inevitably come across some unexpected twists and turns in the road. This is why we must recognize that every prophecy in the Bible falls into one of three categories. The first of which is *complete fulfillment*. This type of prophecy is fulfilled in one event. Examples of this would include Isaiah 7:14 and Micah 5:2. Micah 5:2 was fulfilled in one event when Jesus was born in Bethlehem. This is revealed to us in Matthew 2:6. We will be dealing with the complete fulfillment of prophetic passages often in our study of the end times.

Partial fulfillment of a prophetic passage is when a prophecy is fulfilled in stages. Daniel's Seventy Weeks in Daniel 9 is one clear example of this type of prophecy. The first sixty-nine weeks, or sixty-nine periods of seven years (483 years), were fulfilled from the time of the decree of Artaxerxes in 444 B.C. to the time of Christ. There are still seven more years that await future fulfillment. This is the Tribulation, which is also referred to as Daniel's Seventieth Week. Let us recognize that this is still only one prophecy in Daniel 9, but not all of it has been fulfilled yet.

Another example of partial fulfillment can be found in Luke 4. The context is that Jesus was just beginning His Galilean ministry. Take a look at the passage:

> So He came to Nazareth, where He had been brought up. And as His custom was, He went into the synagogue on the Sabbath day, and stood up to read. And He was handed the book of the prophet Isaiah. And when He had opened the book, He found the place where it was written: *"The Spirit of the Lord is upon Me, because He has anointed Me to preach the gospel to the poor; He has sent Me to heal the brokenhearted, to proclaim liberty to the captives and recovery of sight to the blind, to set at liberty those who are oppressed; to proclaim the acceptable year of the Lord."* Then He closed the book, and gave it back to the attendant and sat down. And the eyes of all

who were in the synagogue were fixed on Him. And He began to say to them, "Today this Scripture is fulfilled in your hearing" (Luke 4:16-21).

Jesus intentionally chose this specific prophecy from Isaiah 61 to read. The prophecy is a Messianic Kingdom promise. The Jewish people were openly looking for a Deliverer to come, to usher them into the Kingdom. Do not miss the truth that Jesus intentionally picked this passage. Jesus already had a reputation for reading from the Scripture in the synagogue on the Sabbath (Luke refers to it as His custom). Notice the reaction of the people in verse 20. Luke reveals that the, "eyes of all who were in the synagogue were fixed on Him" (Luke 4:20). As Jesus told them the Scripture was fulfilled that day Luke records their reactions. The people, "bore witness to Him" and they, "marveled at the gracious words which proceeded out of His mouth" (Luke 4:22). The people were amazed at the words of Jesus. They were wondering, "Does this man think this prophecy refers to Him?"

Why is this passage in Luke so significant? The answer is found by comparing Isaiah 61 with the portion of Scripture that Jesus actually quoted in Luke. Isaiah teaches us, "The Spirit of the Lord GOD is upon Me, because the LORD has anointed Me to preach good tidings to the poor; He has sent Me to heal the brokenhearted, to proclaim liberty to the captives, and the opening of the prison to those who are bound; to proclaim the acceptable year of the LORD" (Isa. 61:1-2). Jesus quoted this part of the prophecy but stopped midway through the sentence and said, "Today this Scripture is fulfilled in your hearing" (Luke 4:21).

The rest of the prophecy that Jesus *did not quote* from Isaiah 61 is referring to the Kingdom. The portion of Scripture that Jesus *did quote* was fulfilled at the First Advent of Christ. This is why Jesus stopped midsentence at this point in the text and told the people it was being fulfilled right before their eyes! The rest of the prophecy from Isaiah 61 will not be fulfilled until the Second Advent of Christ when Jesus comes to inaugurate His Kingdom. This is a textbook example of one prophecy being fulfilled in two stages. Part one was fulfilled at the First Advent, and part two will be fulfilled at the Second Advent of Christ.

Luke 4 and Isaiah 61 are unique in one sense. We do not have any other passages in the New Testament that are so clearly delineated, where Jesus literally stopped in the middle of reading an Old Testament passage. However, this does not mean we do not have other prophecies that have been partially fulfilled. Certainly there are other Old Testament prophecies of the coming of Christ where the First and Second Advents are merged into one.

The Old Testament prophets did not understand that they were looking at a telescopic view of prophetic events. It has often been pointed out that partial fulfillment of prophecy is like looking through a telescope at one mountain, with another mountain situated right behind it. From a distance it is impossible to tell that there is a huge valley between the mountains. For the prophets it looked as if there was only one event ahead, when in reality there were two.

It is imperative to remember that the Apostle Paul referred to the Church as a *mystery* in Ephesians 3. This simply means that something previously undisclosed had now been made known by divine revelation. The Church Age was not revealed in the Old Testament. It is understandable that the prophets of the Old Testament would speak of the events surrounding the First Advent of Christ (His suffering and crucifixion) and the events surrounding His second advent (Christ the victorious warrior and the establishment of His Kingdom) as one event. Partial fulfillment means that part of a given prophecy has already been fulfilled and the rest will be fulfilled at a later time.

The third type of fulfillment of prophecy has been accurately described as *analogical fulfillment*. In this type of fulfillment all or part of a prophecy is referenced twice. This is when a New Testament writer will take an Old Testament prophecy and use it as an analogy. In this type of fulfillment the New Testament writer is clearly not intending to suggest that it is being fulfilled in that moment. Rather, he is using it as an analogy. Prophecy looks forward and predicts what will happen in the future, but an analogy looks back to provide a comparison.

Matthew is certainly one Gospel writer who made use of analogical fulfillment. The reason for this is fascinating. The Jewish people were well versed in the Hebrew Scriptures. Matthew was trying to prove to a Jewish audience that Jesus was the Messiah, and he used the Old Testament Scriptures to support his teaching. Reading through Matthew, it is hard not to notice that Matthew pulled some Old Testament prophecies wildly out of context and applied them to the life of Jesus. How is this justified? Are these mistakes in Scripture? This is where analogical fulfillment comes in.

Take a look at some specific examples.[4] In Hosea 11:1 we read, "And out of Egypt I called My son." In the context of Hosea, it is obvious that this is a reference to the Exodus of the people of Israel out of Egypt. Israel had been held in bondage to Egypt, but was called out and rescued.

Matthew took Hosea 11:1 completely out of context and suggested that this prophecy applied to Joseph and Mary who fled to Egypt for safety. The biblical record is quite clear that Joseph and Mary were not in bondage to Egypt like Israel had been. Rather, they were being protected during Herod's reign of terror, when he was killing all the male children two years of age and younger. Matthew 2:15 teaches that Joseph took Mary and Jesus to Egypt, "and was there until the death of Herod, that it might be fulfilled which was spoken by the Lord through the prophet, saying, 'Out of Egypt I called My Son.'" Notice that Matthew used the word *fulfilled*; it is the Greek word *plēroō*. It is a mistake to assume that this word always means a one for one equivalent. Plēroō can also be used to refer to an analogy, which is how it is used in Matthew 2:15.

As we make our way through the Gospel of Matthew we see this same type of usage of plēroō in several other places. Why did Matthew do this? Charles Dyer, in *Issues in Dispensationalism*, makes an interesting observation. If you follow the argument of Matthew throughout his Gospel record, he was trying to establish that Jesus Christ is the true Israel. Jesus is the true and ultimate seed of Israel, the seed of David, who will usher in Israel's future. Matthew, in his Gospel, was contrasting Israel's failures with the victories of Christ. Matthew was demonstrating every step of the way that where Israel failed as a nation, Christ succeeded.

With this in mind we look again to Matthew 2:15. Matthew argues that just as, Israel was called from Egypt as a child (Hosea 11:1) in its early stages as a nation, Christ was also called from Egypt as a child (Matt. 2:15). As the nation of Israel was called out of Egypt, the people fell into disobedience. Shortly after they arrived in the wilderness they started bickering, fighting, and that generation failed to make it into the Promised Land. By way of contrast, Christ came out of Egypt and was obedient in all things to His Father in heaven.

It is helpful to remember, as we look at Matthew, that the Gospels were not always written chronologically. They were not intended to record every single event in the life and ministry of Jesus Christ. They were written for a theological purpose. A Gospel is a compilation of selected events that were put together in a specific order, by the particular author, to make a point. Matthew followed the history of Israel to show that where it failed as a nation, Jesus Christ succeeded. Matthew constructed his Gospel to make this point.

If you follow the history of Israel, as soon as the people had departed from Egypt the very next thing that happened to them was that they were, baptized as a nation in the Red Sea (Exod. 14; 1 Cor. 10:1-2). The next thing that Matthew records about Christ is that Jesus was baptized by John the Baptist (Matt. 3). It was only a matter of three days after Israel was baptized in the Red Sea that the people were disobedient to the Lord (Exod. 15:22). When Christ was baptized He received the great commendation from the Father, "This is My beloved Son, in whom I am well pleased" (Matt. 3:17).

Working our way into Matthew 4 we remember that Israel went into the wilderness where she was tempted for a period of forty years. Matthew 4:1-2 reveals that, "Christ went into the wilderness where He was tempted for forty days." What is the great contrast that we see? Israel failed the temptations at every turn, but Christ passed each temptation.

In the Sermon on the Mount we see this comparison between Jesus and the nation of Israel once again. Exodus 19 records that, "Israel went to Mount Sinai to receive God's law." This was the next significant event in the history of the nation of Israel. In Matthew 5-7, Christ went up on a mountainside and expounded upon the law. Israel broke the Law (Moses even literally broke the tablets), but Christ fulfilled the Law. Jesus told the people, "Do not think that I came to destroy the Law or the Prophets. I did not come to destroy but to fulfill" (Matt. 5:17).

The Gospel of Matthew does not specifically record that Matthew laid out the text this way. For this reason, we should be careful that we do not press this line of thinking too far. Yet, the pattern of following the history of the nation of Israel and comparing it to the life and ministry of Christ seems obvious. At the very least, it helps us to understand why Matthew used these analogies of Old Testament prophecies out of context; Matthew was building a case.

Let us recognize that not all of the prophecies within the Gospel of Matthew are analogical, but some of them definitely are. Just because Matthew used the word *fulfill,* we should not assume that a prophecy is a direct fulfillment. The problem is that we use the word *fulfill* both literally and figuratively (as an analogy). We must always look at the context to determine the intended meaning. Is the author making an analogy or is he telling us this is the actual fulfillment of the prophecy?

The Roadmap

As we set out together on this path to better understand our future with Christ, let us remember that the principles for understanding prophecy are the signposts on the side of the road which will guide our way. Recognizing the types of fulfillment of prophecy in Scripture will help us navigate through the bends and curves in the road. There will be times when we study Scripture where we will need to slow down and examine what type of prophetic fulfillment is before us. Keeping our map in hand will guide us safely through this journey of understanding the end times. Our next stop is the Abrahamic Covenant.

Discussion Questions

1. How has ignorance of Church history impacted the Church?
2. What was the early Church expecting from the Messiah? What specifically did the Apostle Paul not want the Church to be ignorant of?
3. What happened over time to the hope of believers toward the return of Christ?
4. Who is Origen and what impact did he have on the Church? What was the impact of Augustine?
5. What role did the Protestant Reformation play in Church history?
6. What are the origins of dispensationalism?
7. Why is it important to follow the eight principles for interpreting prophecy?
8. What are the three categories of prophetic fulfillment?
9. Can there ever be two different meanings for the same prophecy? Why or why not?
10. Why did Matthew make good use of analogical fulfillment?

Endnotes

1. Alexander Roberts, James Donaldson, and A. Cleveland Coxe, *The Ante-Nicene Fathers Vol. I: Translations of the Writings of the Fathers Down to A.D. 325* (1997), 239.
2. Ibid., 240.
3. These eight rules for interpreting prophecy are adapted from Paul Lee Tan, *The Interpretation of Prophecy* (Rockville, MD: Assurance Publishers, 1974), 97-123.
4. Much of the material used in these examples was adapted from Charles Dyer in *Issues in Dispensationalism*. Wesley R. Willis and John R. Master, eds., *Issues in Dispensationalism* (Chicago, IL: Moody Press, 1994), 53-55.

CHAPTER 5

A Promise to be Kept -
The Abrahamic Covenant

Now the Lord had said to Abram: "Get out of your country, from your family and from your father's house, to a land that I will show you. I will make you a great nation; I will bless you and make your name great; and you shall be a blessing. I will bless those who bless you, and I will curse him who curses you; and in you all the families of the earth shall be blessed."

- Genesis 12:1-3

CATHY HAD TEARS bubbling up in her eyes as she looked at the wedding photo and remembered when Steven had first proposed. It seemed so long ago; those were the happiest days of her life. The smile on the photo exposed her happiness. Steven had promised her the world. Three kids and eleven years later it all seemed like a distant dream. Her marriage, her wonderful life, it had all fallen apart.

No one really plans to have a bad marriage. The pressures of life begin to creep in. You find yourself without enough money to pay the bills, so you take a second job. The car falls apart, the plumbing needs repairs, and then kids come along swallowing up both your time and money. The passionate love between couples fades as they become nothing more than roommates.

This was a perfect description of life for Cathy and Steven. Keeping up with their expanding lifestyle meant they had to work harder to pay for it. Long gone were those little moments of life when they could share a smile, or a touch. Cathy often found herself wondering if Steven was truly working late, or had he found someone else? As she sat at the kitchen table with the divorce papers in hand, Cathy realized she had lost all faith in her marriage. Those wonderful promises from the beginning days of their relationship had never come true.

It is a desperate situation when men and women view the promises of God like the broken promises of men. In the beginning pages of the Bible, God made some foundational promises to Abraham that have yet to be completely fulfilled. Should we give up on the promises of God? The Word of God answers, "O seed of Abraham His servant, you children of Jacob, His chosen ones! He is the Lord our God; His judgments are in all the earth. *He remembers His covenant forever*, the word which He commanded, for a thousand generations, *the covenant which He made with Abraham*" (Ps. 105:6-9, emphasis added).

The Covenants

Studying Bible prophecy is a part of examining God's plan of the ages, with a particular focus on the end of the plan. In order to understand the end of God's plan you must first recognize His entire plan. Any study of eschatology should start with the beginning, which goes back to Genesis and the Abrahamic Covenant.

The covenants in Scripture are the key to understanding God's program for the ages. God's eschatological program is described in detail by these covenants, and a proper recognition of them is critical to arriving at a sound interpretation of eschatology. As we think of God's program for human history, we see five major biblical covenants in Scripture. These are the Abrahamic (Gen. 12:1-3), Mosaic (Exod. 19-20), Land (Deut. 30), Davidic (2 Sam. 7:16), and the New Covenant (Jer. 31). Four of these covenants are unconditional; only one is a conditional covenant.

What is the difference between a conditional and an unconditional covenant? The conditional covenants are *if/then statements* in the Word of God. With a conditional covenant God is testifying, "If you will obey, then I will respond in a certain way." In this case the fulfillment of the covenant depends on the recipient's response. Unconditional covenants are *I will* statements in the Bible. God is proclaiming, "I will do this." With an unconditional covenant there are no *if* statements attached. The fulfillment depends solely on the one making the covenant.

The Mosaic Covenant

The Mosaic Covenant is a conditional covenant. It was intended to be a rule of life. If you obeyed you would be blessed, and if you disobeyed you would be cursed (Deut. 28). The four unconditional covenants include the Abrahamic Covenant, Land Covenant, Davidic Covenant, and New Covenant. These four covenants contain God's covenant plan of the ages. Through these covenants God set in motion a plan that will come to fulfillment at the end of the age.

The Mosaic Covenant stood alone; it was not of the same nature and type as the other biblical covenants. The Mosaic Covenant was a rule of law. The Apostle Paul teaches us in Galatians 3:19, "What purpose then does the law serve? It was added because of transgressions, till the Seed should come to whom the promise was made; and it was appointed through angels by the hand of a mediator." The Seed is an obvious reference to Christ. Paul continued, "Now a mediator does not mediate for one only, but God is one" (Gal. 3:20). The Abrahamic Covenant was a unilateral covenant with no mediator necessary. God gave Abraham the covenant by promise. The Mosaic Law was different, "it was appointed through angels by the hand of a mediator" (Gal. 3:19).

Galatians 3:21-22 informs us, "Is the law then against the promises of God? Certainly not! For if there had been a law given which could have given life, truly righteousness would have been by the law. But the Scripture has confined all under sin, that the promise by faith in Jesus Christ might be given to those who believe." This is the same teaching that is found in Romans 10. There we read, "For Christ is the end of the law for righteousness to everyone who believes" (Rom. 10:4). It is faith in Christ that makes us righteous and reconciles us to God.

Verse 23 in Galatians records, "But before faith came, we were kept under guard by the law, kept for the faith which would afterward be revealed" (Gal. 3:23). The idea of being kept under guard by the Law carries the idea of being a steward.

This brings us to the important words found in Galatians 3:24, "Therefore the law was our tutor *to bring us* to Christ, that we might be justified by faith." The words *to bring us* are not in the original text. This is why they are italicized. They were inserted in the English translations to smooth out the reading. Without those words, in the English, it reads, "Therefore the law was our tutor to Christ." Our focus is on the word *to*. It is a preposition in Greek, and prepositions can be translated a number of ways. The best way to translate the preposition in this instance is not the word *to*. A better translation would be the word *until*. This is the same as verse 19 where we read, "Till the Seed should come" (Gal. 3:19). If we read verse 24 with this wording it teaches, "Therefore the law was our tutor until

Christ" (Gal. 3:24). It is a mistranslation to write that the Law was put into place *to bring us* to Christ.

The Law was put in charge of God's people (Israel) to help be a steward to them. It was there to give them guidelines for living, but it had no hope of bringing people into righteousness. Instead, the Law actually served to highlight the unrighteousness of men. The Law was put into place until Christ came.

Now that Christ has come, the Church is living under a different steward. Our steward is the Holy Spirit. We are to live by faith and not by sight (2 Cor. 5:7). We are to walk after the Spirit and not after the flesh (Gal. 5:16). The clear teaching of the New Testament is that it is not the circumcision of the flesh that matters, but rather the circumcision of the heart through the Spirit.

The Mosaic Covenant was a rule of law, a stewardship, and not an unconditional promise. The other four major biblical covenants are unconditional. Figure 5.1 helps us to visualize these covenants. *Before the Law* refers to the time in human history before the Law was given at Mount Sinai. As we work our way to the right, across the bottom of the chart, *Israel and the Law* refers to the time when Israel was center stage in human history and was living under the Law. Making our way further to the right we see the *Church* and the *Kingdom*.

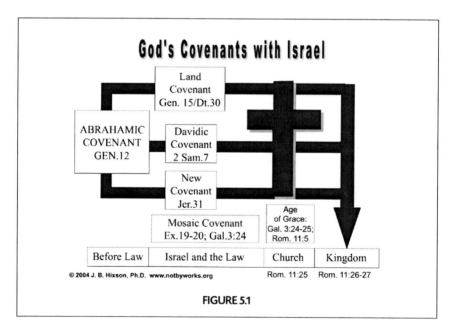

FIGURE 5.1

The Foundational Promise

It is essential to recognize that before the Law was given, God gave the Abrahamic Covenant. This is the foundational covenant for all of human history. The Abrahamic Covenant is the basis for God's entire covenant program. In the days of Abraham, when this covenant was first given, most of the people on earth did not have faith in God. People did not understand what it meant to have a relationship with the Creator by faith. As a part of His plan for the ages, God envisioned a time that would involve global recognition of who He is, global acceptance of Him as the Creator, and a time of perfect righteousness. God promised a Seed who would one day bring blessing to the whole earth. The Abrahamic Covenant was made unconditionally to Abraham, and it had three elements to it.

The first component of the Abrahamic Covenant is the land, "Now the LORD had said to Abram: 'Get out of your country, from your family and from your father's house, to a land that I will show you'" (Gen. 12:1). Do not underestimate how important the physical land of Israel is to God. This teaching is pervasive in the Old Testament. God's promise to Abraham involved a physical land.

The Abrahamic Covenant also has a seed component, "I will make you a great nation; I will bless you and make your name great; and you shall be a blessing" (Gen. 12:2). The phrase *great nation* obviously implies the seed of Abraham; from him would come a great nation. What an incredible promise to a seventy-five year old man with no children!

The third component of the Abrahamic Covenant is the general spiritual blessings that were promised. We read, "I will bless those who bless you, and I will curse him who curses you; and in you all the families of the earth shall be blessed" (Gen. 12:3).

The land, seed, and spiritual blessings were the three components of the foundational Abrahamic Covenant. Then, in the unveiling of God's revelation, God amplified these three aspects with three subsequent unconditional covenants.

The first of these is referred to as the Land Covenant (referred to as the Palestinian Covenant in older literature). The Land Covenant can be seen in Scripture in Genesis 15 and Deuteronomy 30. Genesis 15:18 reveals, "On the same day the LORD made a covenant with Abram, saying: 'To your descendants I have given this land, from the river of Egypt to the great river, the River Euphrates.'" God told Abraham He would give his people this land.

The seed component of the Abrahamic Covenant involved the promise to make a great nation out of the descendants of Abraham. Consider the teaching of 2 Samuel 7. We read in verse 12, "When your days are fulfilled and you rest with your fathers, I will set up your seed after you, who will come from your body, and I will establish his kingdom" (2 Sam. 7:12). This verse refers to Solomon. What about verse 13? "He shall build a house for My name, and I will establish the throne of his kingdom forever" (2 Sam. 7:13). Solomon did not reign forever; this points us forward to Christ.

God elaborated on the seed aspect of the Abrahamic Covenant in the Davidic Covenant. David was told, "And your house and your kingdom shall be established forever before you. Your throne shall be established forever" (2 Sam. 7:16). This ties back to the promise to Abraham that God would make him a great nation. Christ is the ultimate seed of Abraham.

The New Covenant explains the blessings of Genesis 12. Jeremiah 31 reveals a future period of time of unprecedented blessings that will come. God will write His law on the hearts of the people of Israel. This is the covenant that God promised to make. Do not miss the important words found in Jeremiah 31:33, "But this is the covenant that I will make with the house of Israel after those days, says the LORD: I will put My law in their minds, and write it on their hearts; and I will be their God, and they shall be My people." The Lord said that in the future He would make this covenant with Israel. The Abrahamic Covenant was made in Genesis 12, the Land Covenant was established in Genesis 15 and Deuteronomy 30, and the Davidic Covenant was put into place in 2 Samuel 7. Jeremiah 31 does not teach that God, at that time, was making a covenant with Israel. Instead, God proclaimed He would make a covenant with Israel in the future.

The first three of the unconditional covenants were put into place in the Old Testament. The New Covenant was different; it was predicted and promised in the Old Testament, but was not actually made with the people of God until the New Testament. In the Upper Room, on the night Jesus was betrayed, the Lord instituted the New Covenant when He proclaimed, "For this is My blood of the new covenant, which is shed for many for the remission of sins" (Matt. 26:28). When Jesus was crucified a day later, this was the ratification of the New Covenant; the shed blood of Jesus was the blood of the New Covenant.

Figure 5.1 demonstrates that all of these covenants were given under Israel and the Law. The New Covenant, even though it was not given until Calvary, was still ratified under the Old Testament Law. The Church did not come into existence until forty days later, on the day of Pentecost, in Acts 2.

Are We There Yet?

All four unconditional covenants have been put into place. The question that remains is have they been fulfilled? Have they been inaugurated? There is a substantial difference between ratifying a covenant and inaugurating a covenant. The Bible does not teach that any of the unconditional covenants are in force today. The blessings, as outlined in each of these covenants, are not being realized in the present age. The only way that theologians can claim these covenants are in effect is to spiritualize the text of Scripture. This way, the normal plain reading of these passages is overlooked.

For the point of illustration, consider the New Covenant. Like all four of the unconditional covenants, the New Covenant is part of a program that will be fulfilled in the Kingdom. Of the four unconditional covenants this is the one where we find the most disagreement. The Scriptures teach us that when the New Covenant is in effect, it will be a time when there will be perfect righteousness. Jeremiah teaches:

> Behold, the days are coming, says the LORD, when I will make a new covenant with the house of Israel and with the house of Judah. … But this is the covenant that I will make with the house of Israel after those days, says the LORD: I will put My law in their minds, and write it on their hearts; and I will be their God, and they shall be My people. No more shall every man teach his neighbor, and every man his brother, saying, "Know the LORD," for they all shall know Me, from the least of them to the greatest of them, says the LORD. For I will forgive their iniquity, and their sin I will remember no more (Jer. 31:31, 33-34).

Believers in Christ will universally obey the commands of the Lord. Furthermore, during this time there will be no need to teach anyone about the Lord Jesus Christ because they will all know of Him, from the least to the greatest.

It is quite obvious that this is not a description of the existing reality. In the present age, believers continue to sin. The need to teach others about Jesus Christ is enormous. The command given to the disciples for believers during this time is to, "Go therefore and make disciples of all the nations, baptizing them in the name of the Father and of the Son and of the Holy Spirit, teaching them to observe all things that I have commanded you; and lo, I am with you always, even to the end of the age" (Matt. 28:19-20). The exhortation in this present age, that we go out and teach others, contradicts the future actuality under the New Covenant when teaching will be unnecessary. Clearly, the New Covenant cannot be in effect today.

Notice again that Jeremiah 31:31-33 teaches us that the Lord would make this covenant with the house of Israel and the house of Judah, which is not the Church. This is a big point of contention. Even most dispensationalists tend to capitulate to the view of covenant theology, which teaches that the Church is fulfilling the New Covenant today. It is a direct result of the tendency to read the New Testament back into the Old Testament.

A better illustration is found in Ezekiel 36. Here again we see a description of the New Covenant. Ezekiel 36:25-27 teaches, "Then I will sprinkle clean water on you, and you shall be clean; I will cleanse you from all your filthiness and from all your idols. I will give you a new heart and put a new spirit within you; I will take the heart of stone out of your flesh and give you a heart of flesh. I will put My Spirit within you and cause you to walk in My statutes, and you will keep My judgments and do them."

A superficial reading may lead us to the impression that Ezekiel 36 is referring to the Church. Verse 26 speaks of a new heart, which could be taken to be a description of someone during the Church Age. Before we jump to conclusions, we need to focus on the rest of the text. Again, notice verse 27, "I will put My Spirit within you and cause you to walk in My statutes, and you will keep My judgments and do them" (Ezek. 36:27). As Church Age believers, even with the Spirit of God living in us we still sin. If this text is said to be about the Church, this creates tension with the actual words of verse 27. Instead, Ezekiel is teaching us that when the New Covenant is in force believers will not sin; this will take place in the Kingdom.

What we are experiencing now in the Church Age is very similar to what will be universally true of believers in the Kingdom. However, this does not mean this is a fulfillment of the New Covenant. Similarity does not mean identity. The Church today serves as a microcosm, a hint, at what life will be like universally when the long-awaited Kingdom is inaugurated.

The Church was never mentioned in the Old Testament. The mystery of the Church is described by Paul in Ephesians 3. This new work was revealed by God through the Apostle Paul. The new entity called the Church, the Bride of Christ, in many ways represents or pictures what God will be doing when the King takes the throne someday. It is imperative to remember that the Church is not a fulfillment of the Kingdom.

In Romans 11, Paul directly addressed this issue and revealed that one of the purposes of God for the Church is to provoke Israel to jealousy. Romans 11:11 teaches, "I say then, have they stumbled that they should fall? Certainly not! But through their fall, to provoke them to jealousy, salvation has come to the Gentiles." This is a reference to Israel being provoked to jealousy by the Church. Part of the plan of God for the Church is to provoke Israel to desire the type of relationship that we have with God through Jesus Christ.

The Church, the Bride of Christ, is most certainly important to the Lord (Eph. 5:29). God even has a specific plan for the Church in His Kingdom. Yet, it is a mistake to equate this love for the Church with the fulfillment of God's covenant program. God's covenant plan centers on the people of the nation of Israel. Jesus Himself proclaimed a similar reminder when He said, "salvation is of the Jews" (John 4:22).

The Great Commission instructs believers to, "go therefore and make disciples of all the nations" (Matt. 28:19). The Church is striving to reach the people of the world. Unfortunately, the Church will not succeed much more than Israel did in the Old Testament. The people of the world will not be completely evangelized until Jesus Christ returns to establish His Kingdom. When Christ takes the Davidic Throne to rule and reign, Jerusalem and Israel will be the center of the global worship of Jesus Christ.

The New Testament teaches that the Spirit of God indwells believers today. The Spirit of God indwelling believers in the Church Age is similar to what is predicted under the New Covenant. Again, similarity does not mean that they are equated. Within the Church Age believers can grieve the Holy Spirit (Eph. 4:30). Believers in Christ can quench the Spirit (1 Thess. 5:19). It is our responsibility to yield ourselves to the Spirit of God. If this was not true, all believers would be perfect because we all have the Holy Spirit living in us, and He is perfect. The very fact that there are different levels of maturity within the Body of Christ makes it self-evident that our sanctification process is dependent on believers yielding themselves to the Spirit. In the Kingdom this will be notably different.

The covenant program of God has been ratified, but it has not been inaugurated. It will be fulfilled in the future at the Second Coming of Christ. When the New Testament mentions the Church participating in the blessings of Abraham, it does not mean that the Church is fulfilling the Covenant of Abraham. This is an important distinction. To participate in the blessings does not equate with fulfilling the covenant.

The death and resurrection of Jesus Christ is the ultimate event of human history. The death of Christ ratified the New Covenant. By necessity, it had to precede the establishment of the Kingdom. Undoubtedly, the death of Christ was also essential to redeem mankind and usher in the Church Age. Church Age believers are connected to Abraham's promise through the Seed of Abraham, Jesus Christ. Our identification with Jesus Christ (the Seed of Abraham) results in many blessings. These are not to be mistaken for the fulfillment of the Abrahamic Covenant. The Church is now experiencing some of the blessings that will be manifest globally when Christ comes back and takes the throne, but it is a mistake to assume that the Church is the *fulfillment* of the Abrahamic Covenant.

The people of Israel and the Church share the Mediator of the New Covenant. This is referred to in Hebrews 8:6, 9:15, and 12:24. It is incorrect to look at these references and assume that the New Covenant is in force today. This is not the teaching of Hebrews. Rather, the instruction is that we serve the Mediator of the New Covenant. We serve the Christ who mediated the New Covenant with Israel.

Galatians 3:14 is one passage in the New Testament that speaks of the blessings of the Abrahamic Covenant affecting the Church. Paul teaches, "that the blessing of Abraham might come upon the Gentiles in Christ Jesus, that we might receive the promise of the Spirit through faith" (Gal. 3:14). A covenant theologian's approach to this verse is considerably different from a dispensationalist's approach. Believing that the Church is Israel, they assume that passages like Galatians 3:14 are teaching that the Church is the fulfillment of the Abrahamic Covenant. Notice, however, that the text does not use the word *fulfilled*. The New Testament teaches that the Church is participating in the blessings. Consider it a sneak preview of what is to come!

The promises of the New Covenant are much better than what can be witnessed within the Church today. It will be a time of universal knowledge of Christ, with believers living in perfect obedience and righteousness. The Church is a microcosm of what life will be like in the

Kingdom. This was also true of Israel in the Old Testament; Israel was to be a microcosm of what life will be like in the Kingdom. God is unfolding His plan, but the Church is no more fulfilling completely this covenant program than Israel did in days gone by. Therefore, it is incorrect to state that the Church is experiencing a partial fulfillment of the covenant promises. None of the covenant promises have officially begun. God's covenants await a future literal fulfillment.

Are You the Seed of Abraham?

As we have already noted, the Abrahamic Covenant contains a seed component. The question of who is the seed of Abraham leads us to an important discovery in Scripture. The Word of God identifies four different seeds of Abraham. The *natural seed* of Abraham refers to all of the physical descendants of Abraham (ethnic Jews).

The *natural-spiritual seed* is the physical descendants of Abraham (Jewish people) who have believed the gospel. The Apostle Paul mentioned the distinction between the natural seed and the natural-spiritual seed in his letter to the church at Rome. Paul proclaimed, "For they are not all Israel who are of Israel" (Rom. 9:6). He was making it known that being a physical descendant of Abraham is not the same as being a physical descendant of Abraham with faith in Jesus Christ. There will be many unbelieving Jews in hell because of their lack of faith in Christ.

The *spiritual seed* of Abraham consists of believing Gentiles. These are people who have no ethnic claims to Judaism but have trusted in Christ for their eternal salvation. The New Testament often refers to Church Age believers as being the spiritual descendants of Abraham. This does not mean that the Church has taken the place of Israel. It simply means that by faith we have entered into a relationship with the Creator. Because of this, we are experiencing some of the blessings of the Abrahamic Covenant.

The *ultimate seed* is Jesus Christ. We read in Galatians, "'And to your Seed,' who is Christ" (Gal. 3:16).

Broken Promises?

God's covenant program (all three components of it: land, seed, and blessing) has been ratified but not inaugurated. Does this mean God has broken His promises? Remember, the Abrahamic Covenant specifically teaches, "I will make you a great nation; I will bless you and make your name great; and you shall be a blessing. I will bless those who bless you, and I will curse him who curses you; and in you all the families of the earth shall be blessed" (Gen. 12:2-3). How will the Abrahamic Covenant be fulfilled?

Through the fulfillment of the Land Covenant Israel will one day receive the land they have been promised by God (Gen. 15:18-21). By the fulfillment of the Davidic Covenant, a King will reign upon the Davidic Throne. The inauguration of the New Covenant will bring about the ministry of the Holy Spirit whereby believers are enabled to live in perfect righteousness. In the Kingdom, believers will not be able to grieve or quench the Spirit of God. The priority of the Abrahamic Covenant can be witnessed repeatedly in the New Testament (Gal. 3:14, 29; 4:22-31; Rom. 4:1-25; Matt. 22:23-32; Acts 26:6-8).

The dawn of the Church Age was a significant event in God's eternal plan. The Messiah had come to Israel, born of a virgin. Jesus lived a perfect, holy, and sinless life. After Jesus was betrayed, arrested, crucified, buried, and resurrected, the Church was born on the day of Pentecost in Acts 2. This ushered in a new program. Did this mean the end of the promises of God to the people of Israel?

The Apostle Paul addressed this issue in his letter to the church at Rome. Regarding the Jewish people Paul instructed, "Even so then, at this present time there is a remnant according to the election of grace" (Rom. 11:5). Not all of the Jewish people have rejected Jesus Christ. Some have placed their faith in Jesus as their Savior and have become a part of the Body of Christ. In Romans 11:1, Paul even used himself as an example!

In Romans 11:25 the Apostle Paul continued to instruct, "For I do not desire, brethren, that you should be ignorant of this mystery, lest you should be wise in your own opinion, that blindness in part has happened to Israel until the fullness of the Gentiles has come in" (Rom. 11:25). *Blindness in part* means that not every Jewish person in the Church Age is an unbeliever. A remnant of the Jews has recognized that the Messiah has come, and they have trusted in Christ for their salvation. These Jewish believers are a part of the Church. At some point in the future the people of Israel are going to receive their King and usher in the Kingdom.

The covenant program that God has with the world through Israel has not been abrogated. It has been delayed, but not nullified. Yet, covenant theology proclaims the exact opposite. The belief is that these promises of God were conditional and when Israel crowned Jesus with thorns, God decided to send the Kingdom through the Church.

The Kingdom of Christ will still have a future fulfillment, which is exactly what Paul stated in Romans 11:26-27. The specific teaching we find in verse 26 is that, "all Israel will be saved" (Rom. 11:26). This means that the whole nation will be delivered. Corporately, as represented by the leadership, the people of Israel will come back together and recognize Him as the Messiah. Paul was not teaching that every individual Jew will be saved. Instead, he was demonstrating the remarkable contrast with the Church Age. Right now, it is only a remnant of Jews who are eternally redeemed.

The nation of Israel has already rejected the Messiah once. This is the reason we see the scathing woes to the Pharisees, Sadducees, and Scribes in Matthew 23. When Jesus returns at the Second Coming, Matthew 24 teaches us that Christ is going to send out His angels to the four corners of the earth to gather the elect, which is a reference to Israel. Jews who believe the Gospel of the Kingdom will be regathered, and the people of Israel will receive their Kingdom.

Notice what the Apostle Paul wrote, "And so all Israel will be saved, as it is written: *'The Deliverer will come out of Zion, and He will turn away ungodliness from Jacob; for this is My covenant with them, when I take away their sins'*" (Rom. 11:26-27). The covenant mentioned in verse 27 is a reference to the New Covenant. The penalty of the sins of believers has already been taken away, but in the Kingdom believers will live in unbroken fellowship with God.

The Promises of the Abrahamic Covenant

The Abrahamic Covenant contains specific individual promises to Abraham. These include the promise to Abraham that his name will be great, to make Abraham the father of a great nation, and the land which will be given to him personally (as well as to his seed) as an everlasting possession (Gen. 12:2; Gen.15; Gen. 17:8).

The nation of Israel can also look forward to the national promises of the Abrahamic Covenant. The Lord promised that a great nation would come from Abraham (which is Israel) (Gen.12:2). From out of this nation a King would be born (2 Sam. 7:16). The land will be given to Abraham and his seed (Gen. 15; Gen. 17:8). When Jesus Christ comes back there will be no question of who owns the land.

The universal promises (or global promises) of the Abrahamic Covenant have a striking impact on the future of the world. Through Abraham all of the families of the earth will be blessed (Gen. 12:3). Abraham's descendants will be as numerous, "as the stars of the heaven and as the sand which is on the seashore" (Gen. 22:17). Abraham would become the father of many nations (Gen. 17:4). We are also reminded that Abraham was promised, "I will bless those who bless you, and I will curse him who curses you" (Gen. 12:3).

The Blessing of the United States

Is the United States being blessed today because of our support for Israel? The promise in Genesis 12:3 that God will bless those who bless Abraham and curse those who curse Abraham often gives rise to this claim. It is a very common belief among Western Christians to say that this is the reason the United States has not yet fallen. Is this a biblical reality?

We need to be careful not to stretch the application of Genesis 12 beyond what God intended. The blessing and curse of Genesis 12:3 is a promise that pertains to the nation of Israel related to the millennial aspect of the Kingdom. The nation of Israel is not dwelling in the land corporately with belief in Jesus, the Messiah. The land, seed, and spiritual blessings of the Abrahamic Covenant have not yet been fulfilled. Genesis 12:3 points to the Millennium. During that time the King of kings (the ultimate Seed of Israel) will be upon the Davidic Throne reigning from Jerusalem, and those who bless Israel will be blessed and those who curse Israel will be cursed.

Certainly, we should be sensitive to how we deal with Israel. It would be an obvious mistake to mistreat the people of Israel. Unbelieving Jews are enemies of the Gospel of Christ, but because God has established His covenant plan through Abraham, Israel is beloved (Rom. 11:28). The people of the nation of Israel today continue in unbelief. The Israel of Genesis 12, where this promise is recorded, will be living with belief in the Messiah within the Kingdom.

The Promise Will be Kept

The prophetic implications of the Abrahamic Covenant demand a literal future for Israel (Gen. 17:19). This certain truth should help us to rest in the promises of God regarding the future. It should cause to us to marvel at the unconditional love and immeasurable grace that He has shown to both Israel and the Church. We can rest with confidence that the Lord will return to bring to fruition all of the promises rooted in the Abrahamic Covenant!

Discussion Questions

1. Why is it important to understand the entire plan of God when studying eschatology?
2. How many biblical covenants are mentioned in chapter 5?
3. What is the difference between conditional and unconditional covenants?
4. What was the role of the Mosaic Covenant?
5. Explain the components of the Abrahamic Covenant.
6. How do we know that the unconditional covenants have not been fulfilled today in the Church Age?
7. Should we show support to Israel? Why or why not?
8. How can we be sure that the promise of the Abrahamic Covenant will be fulfilled?

CHAPTER 6

Title Deed to the Land - The Land Covenant

He is the LORD our God; His judgments are in all the earth. He remembers His covenant forever, the word which He commanded, for a thousand generations, the covenant which He made with Abraham, and His oath to Isaac, and confirmed it to Jacob for a statute, to Israel as an everlasting covenant, saying, "To you I will give the land of Canaan as the allotment of your inheritance."

- Psalm 105:7-11

A MAN WITH a dream is someone who has found a reason to live. Dr. Eric Price stumbled upon his dream in central Idaho, shortly after medical school. Decades of methodical planning were finally pushing his plan into action.

Dr. Price's first passion was always medicine. As one of the best surgical oncologists in his region, his skills were in constant demand. Saving lives meant forfeiting the time to establish a family of his own, but the financial realities of his career made his dream possible. Price would soon be escaping California to head for the mountains of Idaho. He had purchased forty acres of land outside of Hailey, Idaho and construction would now begin on his retirement home.

The arrival of a court order from the sheriff's department alarmed him. A married couple from Ohio had surfaced and was taking legal action to prove their claim to the same land that he had just paid for. A court order had been issued forcing construction on the property to be stopped before it could even begin. The court would determine who rightfully had the authentic title deed to the land.

Dr. Price had purchased the land through a local real estate company. He even had a notarized deed from the seller. It seemed to be inconceivable that someone else could have a valid claim to his land.

Price was the victim of an imposter who had thoroughly done his homework. The fraudulent seller had spent time at the local courthouse, searching the public records to find a piece of property that was owned by a family living outside of Idaho. The next step in his elaborate plan was to forge and record a deed to a fake identity. Assuming this identity, the man had then listed the property for sale. This imposter was long gone, with Dr. Price's money.

Dr. Price had taken the proper legal steps to secure the land, but it legally belonged to another family. Their legitimate deed went back decades before Price's recent claim to the land, and the fact is *the rightful owner of the land is the one who holds the original title deed.*

Who Owns the Legitimate Title Deed?

On a much larger scale, the battle over land continues to play itself out in the headlines of our time. The struggle for the land surrounding Jerusalem continues to rage, and the varied claims to it go back thousands of years. Through the fog of confusion that surrounds this pivotal issue, one essential question stands above the rest, "Who owns the original and legitimate title deed to the land?"

In the very first sentence of the Bible we read, "In the beginning God created the heavens and the earth" (Gen.1:1). On the third day of creation we read, "Then God said, 'Let the waters under the heavens be gathered together into one place, and let the dry land appear;' and it was so. And God called the dry land Earth, and the gathering together of the waters He called Seas. And God saw that it was good" (Gen. 1:9-10). It should not be missed in this discussion that God is the Creator of the dirt, the rock of the earth, and the things of creation that we take for granted. Christians often fail to recognize that this earth, and all of creation, belongs to God. It is often overlooked that God indeed has a specific plan for all of creation, which includes a future global kingdom. This coming kingdom includes specific physical boundaries for the nation of Israel. The capital city of the Kingdom will be Jerusalem.

As we have seen, the Land Covenant is part of the foundational covenant program of God. Within the Abrahamic Covenant God promised land, seed, and blessing. The covenant program of God serves as a title deed to the land. God's covenant program is what entitles the Jewish people to the land.

This takes us back to Genesis 12. Notice the emphasis on the land. "Now the LORD had said to Abram: 'Get out of your country, from your family and from your father's house, to a land that I will show you'" (Gen. 12:1). In our study of the Old Testament, we need to pay attention to the number of times the Scripture emphasizes the land. Genesis 12 is early in the progress of revelation, but yet we see the first indication that God has something special in mind related to the land. The Lord told Abram to go to the land.

Next we turn our attention to Genesis 15, where God amplified the details about this land. In verse 18 we read, "On the same day the LORD made a covenant with Abram, saying: 'To your descendants I have given this land, from the river of Egypt to the great river, the River Euphrates'" (Gen. 15:18). The land that God has promised to the nation of Israel has specific boundaries. It is inconceivable to spiritualize the promise of land given that God explicitly mentioned the future boundaries of Israel.

Genesis 15:18 also reveals two other points that need to be examined. First, and foremost, only the nation of Israel can legitimately lay claim to the land. The unconditional promise of God to the people of Israel, given long ago, serves as their title deed to the land. The more recent creation of the Islamic faith and the fraudulent claims to the land do not negate this original title deed. It is a misguided notion to assume that because the nation of Israel was displaced from the land for many centuries that this means the land does not belong to her. Whether or not the nations of the world currently recognize Israel's right to the land is irrelevant. The Creator has assured that Israel will one day take possession of *all the land that rightfully belongs to the descendants of Abraham.* What a glorious day that will be!

The second matter for discussion, from Genesis 15:18, involves the future boundaries of the nation of Israel. Notice again the boundaries of the land described by God, "To your descendants I have given this land, from the river of Egypt to the great river, the River Euphrates" (Gen. 15:18). Among dispensationalists, the discussion surrounding the boundaries of Israel's covenant land centers on the river of Egypt. The varying possible locations of this river result in estimates of land that will encompass 10,000 - 300,000 square miles. It depends on where the river of Egypt is located. Charles Feinberg suggested boundaries that would include 300,000 square miles.[1] This is the view held by a majority of dispensationalists.

Ultimately, a greater point must be made. Any boundary within that range is much larger than the current boundaries of Israel. Even at its peak, the people of Israel never controlled all of the land that has been promised to them. It is not even close. If God's Word is to be trusted, there is a future for national Israel.

Again, this begs the question, "What did God mean in Genesis 15:18 when He said, 'To your descendants I have given this land, from the river of Egypt to the great river, the River Euphrates'?" There has to be a plain normal sense of how Abraham would have understood this. Israel is one day going to take possession of its rightful claim to a very large piece of real estate. This still awaits a future fulfillment.

An interpretive mistake is sometimes made in regard to the Land Covenant. The issue surrounds a passage found in Joshua. Consider the text:

> So the LORD gave to Israel all the land of which He had sworn to give to their fathers, and they took possession of it and dwelt in it. The LORD gave them rest all around, according to all that He had sworn to their fathers. And not a man of all their enemies stood against them; the LORD delivered all their enemies into their hand. Not a word failed of any good thing which the LORD had spoken to the house of Israel. All came to pass (Josh. 21:43-45).

At the very heart of the matter, is whether or not this text teaches that God fulfilled the Land Covenant at that time. *Simply stated, Joshua 21:43 cannot be the fulfillment of the Land Covenant. We know this to be true because in later revelation the Word of God continued to predict that one day Israel will possess the land.* Amos 9:14-15 instructs, "'I will bring back the captives of My people Israel; they shall build the waste cities and inhabit them; they shall plant vineyards and drink wine from them; they shall also make gardens and eat fruit from them. I will plant them in their land, and no longer shall they be pulled up from the land I have given them,' says the LORD your God." These types of passages demonstrate that the later revelation of God continued to predict a complete fulfillment of the Land Covenant. Therefore, Joshua 21:43 must refer to something else.

If we carefully study the biblical record, we learn that God had a specific plan for the nation of Israel at this stage in its history. Numbers 34:1-18 outlines the land that Israel would possess when it entered the land of Canaan. However, it was not part of God's plan for the people of Israel to take it all at once. God told them, "I will not drive them out from before you in one year, lest the land become desolate and the beasts of the field become too numerous for you. Little by little I will drive them out from before you, until you have increased, and you inherit the land" (Exod. 23:28-30).[2] This is why Joshua 23:5 records that the people still had more land to possess. God's plan for Israel was for the people to take possession of the land a little at a time. Without a population base sufficient to cultivate and inhabit the land, taking possession of it all at once would turn much of it into wasteland. As the years unfolded, Israel failed to drive out the remaining nations and take full possession of her land.

The summary statement witnessed in Joshua 21:43-45 immediately follows the military campaigns of Joshua. It was intended to show that God gave the people rest after Israel took the initial step of taking possession of the land. They had all of the land that God intended them to have *at this point in time in history*. The context demonstrates that this was not intended to mean a fulfillment of the Land Covenant found in Genesis 15. Only after the return of Christ, at the Second Coming, will the Land Covenant be fulfilled.

The Significance of the Land

The significance of the Promised Land in the Word of God can easily be overlooked. This directly ties into God's eschatological plan of the ages. Our attention turns to Deuteronomy 30:

> Now it shall come to pass, when all these things come upon you, the blessing and the curse which I have set before you, and you call them to mind among all the nations where the LORD your God drives you, and you return to the LORD your God and obey His voice, according to all that I command you today, you and your children, with all your heart and with all your soul, that the LORD your God will bring you back from captivity (Deut. 30:1-3).

A common mistake is to read this passage as a conditional statement. Notice carefully that we do not read an *if/then* statement. Instead, it is a statement of *when it will happen*. These things will come to pass when the people of Israel, "return to the LORD your God and obey His voice" (Deut. 30:2). At that time, the Word of God teaches:

> That the LORD your God will bring you back from captivity, and have compassion on you, and gather you again from all the nations where

the LORD your God has scattered you. If any of you are driven out to the farthest parts under heaven, from there the LORD your God will gather you, and from there He will bring you. Then the LORD your God will bring you to the land which your fathers possessed, and you shall possess it. He will prosper you and multiply you more than your fathers. And the LORD your God will circumcise your heart and the heart of your descendants, to love the LORD your God with all your heart and with all your soul, that you may live. Also the LORD your God will put all these curses on your enemies and on those who hate you, who persecuted you. And you will again obey the voice of the LORD and do all His commandments which I command you today. The LORD your God will make you abound in all the work of your hand, in the fruit of your body, in the increase of your livestock, and in the produce of your land for good. For the LORD will again rejoice over you for good as He rejoiced over your fathers, if you obey the voice of the LORD your God, to keep His commandments and His statutes which are written in this Book of the Law, and if you turn to the LORD your God with all your heart and with all your soul (Deut. 30:3-10).

There are some statements in this passage that deserve our attention. Notice in verse 5 that the text directly states, "Then the LORD your God will bring you to the land which your fathers possessed, and you shall possess it" (Deut. 30:5). It is a matter of fact that Israel will one day possess the land that has been promised to the nation.

Verse 6 also contains an important statement, "And the LORD your God will circumcise your heart and the heart of your descendants, to love the LORD your God with all your heart and with all your soul, that you may live" (Deut. 30:6). God will be the one doing the work in the hearts of the people of Israel. The instruction given does not teach that the Jewish people should work to clean up their outward behavior in order for God to give them this land. Instead, the Lord is going to do a work in their hearts. The promise of God to circumcise the hearts of the people of Israel is a reference to the New Covenant.

The New Covenant is the linchpin for the entire covenant program. All three aspects of the Abrahamic Covenant are unconditional, but the timing requires Israel's obedience. The only way the people of the nation of Israel will be obedient is if God does a work in them through the New Covenant.

Again, we read in verse 7, "Also the LORD your God will put all these curses on your enemies and on those who hate you, who persecuted you"

(Deut. 30:7). This ties back directly to the Lord's promise to Abraham, "I will bless those who bless you, and I will curse him who curses you" (Gen. 12:3).

Deuteronomy 30:10 brings us to another statement that we need to examine carefully. There we read, "if you obey the voice of the LORD your God, to keep His commandments and His statutes which are written in this Book of the Law, and if you turn to the LORD your God with all your heart and with all your soul" (Deut. 30:10). A common error is to assume that because the word *if* is used, that this automatically means this should be taken as a conditional statement. It actually refers to the timing of the events referenced.

The key that unlocks verse 10 is to keep it within the context of the entire passage. In verse 9 God had promised the people of Israel that He would bless them. Verse 10 reveals that this would happen if they obeyed, "the voice of the LORD your God" (Deut. 30:10). Clarity is brought to this passage when we remember that in verse 6 God had already promised, "And the LORD your God will circumcise your heart and the heart of your descendants, to love the LORD your God with all your heart and with all your soul, that you may live" (Deut. 30:6). This is why verse 8 testifies, "And you will again obey the voice of the LORD and do all His commandments which I command you today" (Deut. 30:8). *God was telling the people of the great things He will do for them when they obey Him, but they will obey because of the powerful work He will do within them.* It is an exegetical error to ignore the context before verse 10, which describes how this condition is going to be met; verse 10 is not a conditional covenant. God was proclaiming that He will do the work within the people of Israel, causing them to obey Him. When they do, they will receive the blessings of the land.

Our attention shifts once again to Deuteronomy 30:3, "The LORD your God will bring you back from captivity, and have compassion on you, and gather you again from all the nations where the LORD your God has scattered you." The New Testament gives us the added details of when this will happen.

The specifics are found within the Olivet Discourse (Matt. 24-25). Matthew 24:29 begins by testifying, "immediately after the tribulation of those days." This is a reference to Daniel's Seventieth Week (Dan. 9:27). In Matthew 24:15 we even see that Jesus had already mentioned Daniel by name. Jesus also taught:

Immediately after the tribulation of those days the sun will be darkened, and the moon will not give its light; the stars will fall from heaven, and the powers of the heavens will be shaken. Then the sign of the Son of Man will appear in heaven, and then all the tribes of the earth will mourn, and they will see the Son of Man coming on the clouds of heaven with power and great glory. And He will send His angels with a great sound of a trumpet, and they will gather together His elect from the four winds, from one end of heaven to the other (Matt. 24:29-31).

This will be the fulfillment of Deuteronomy 30:3. The return of the Lord Jesus Christ at the Second Coming is when this great end times regathering into the land will take place. We remember that Jesus had specifically said, "For I say to you, you shall see Me no more till you say, 'Blessed is He who comes in the name of the LORD!'" (Matt. 23:39). This statement was directed toward national Israel because as a nation the people had rejected the Christ. After the Tribulation, the nation of Israel will embrace the Messiah (Zech. 13:8-9). Christ will usher in His Kingdom, and at that time He will regather the Jewish people into the land.

The Prominence of the Land

A quick survey through the Old Testament prophets reveals the prominence of the land in God's program. The phrase *My land*, is pervasive throughout the Old Testament.

In the book of Joel we read, "For a nation has come up against My land" (Joel 1:6). Once more, referring to the Second Coming of Christ and His judgment Joel records, "I will also gather all nations, and bring them down to the Valley of Jehoshaphat; and I will enter into judgment with them there on account of My people, My heritage Israel, whom they have scattered among the nations; they have also divided up My land" (Joel 3:2). Here we specifically witness that God associated the people of Israel with the land that He has given to them. God is jealous for His people and the land that belongs to them. Imagine someone stealing your son's brand new bike. Immediately you are filled with jealousy because you simply want your son to have what rightfully belongs to him. This is the type of jealousy that the Lord has about the land because He has given it to the nation of Israel. It is for this reason we see the expressions, "on account of My people, My heritage Israel" and "My land" (Joel 3:2).

Consider some more examples from the Old Testament prophets. In Isaiah 14:25 God promised, "I will break the Assyrian in My land." In Jeremiah 2:7, the weeping prophet described Israel as having, "defiled My land." God's jealousy for His land extends to whoever defiles the land, even if it is His own people. Once the Jewish people crossed the Jordan River they had a habit of defiling the land. They sacrificed to pagan gods and intermingled with the people of pagan nations, which provoked the jealousy of God because it is His holy land. What does holy mean? It means separated unto God, which is what the land should be.

Our brief survey of the Old Testament takes us to Ezekiel. The context of Ezekiel 36 is the New Covenant. The promise is given of a new covenant for Israel and judgment for her enemies. Verse 5 proclaims, "Therefore thus says the Lord GOD: 'Surely I have spoken in My burning jealousy against the rest of the nations and against all Edom, who gave My land to themselves as a possession, with wholehearted joy and spiteful minds, in order to plunder its open country'" (Ezek. 36:5).

A few chapters later we see another reference to the land belonging to God. This time the context is the end time Battle of Gog and Magog in Ezekiel 38-39. This takes place after the Rapture, but right before the Tribulation and the signing of the peace treaty (Dan. 9:27).[3] The Scriptures record, "You will come up against My people Israel like a cloud, to cover the land. It will be in the latter days that I will bring you against My land, so that the nations may know Me, when I am hallowed in you, O Gog, before their eyes" (Ezek. 38:16). Any battle that involves Israel is a battle that involves His land.

2 Chronicles 7:14 is another passage that is often taken out of context. The Word of God records, "If My people who are called by My name will humble themselves, and pray and seek My face, and turn from their wicked ways, then I will hear from heaven, and will forgive their sin and heal their land" (2 Chron. 7:14). God spoke these words to Solomon after the completion of the Temple. Once again, the land refers to the land of Israel. If the people of Israel turned to the worship of false gods, the Lord warned, "Then I will uproot them from My land which I have given them" (2 Chron. 7:20).

The Priority of the Land Promise

The priority of the land promise can be witnessed by its prominence in the covenant program of God. The significance of the land is emphasized within the Abrahamic Covenant, the Davidic Covenant, and the New Covenant. Each of these unconditional covenants underscores the importance of the land. This is why the Land Covenant should be thought of as the title deed to the land.

The priority of the land promise is easily demonstrated in the Abrahamic Covenant. We remember that Genesis 12:1 records, "Now the LORD had said to Abram: 'Get out of your country, from your family and from your father's house, to a land that I will show you.'"

Again, we witness the specific focus on the Land Covenant in Genesis 15, "On the same day the LORD made a covenant with Abram, saying: 'To your descendants I have given this land, from the river of Egypt to the great river, the River Euphrates'" (Gen. 15:18). Deuteronomy also teaches us, "Then the LORD your God will bring you to the land which your fathers possessed, and you shall possess it" (Deut. 30:5). The priority of the land promise is expressly demonstrated within the actual Land Covenant.

The Land Covenant was reaffirmed with Isaac in Genesis 17:19, "Then God said: 'No, Sarah your wife shall bear you a son, and you shall call his name Isaac; I will establish My covenant with him for an everlasting covenant, and with his descendants after him.'" In Genesis 26, we see the Land Covenant reaffirmed again:

> Then the LORD appeared to him and said: "Do not go down to Egypt; live in the land of which I shall tell you. Dwell in this land, and I will be with you and bless you; for to you and your descendants I give all these lands, and I will perform the oath which I swore to Abraham your father. And I will make your descendants multiply as the stars of heaven; I will give to your descendants all these lands; and in your seed all the nations of the earth shall be blessed; because Abraham obeyed My voice and kept My charge, My commandments, My statutes, and My laws" (Gen. 26:2-5).

The Land Covenant was even reaffirmed with Jacob in Genesis 28:

> And behold, the LORD stood above it and said: "I am the LORD God of Abraham your father and the God of Isaac; the land on which you lie I will give to you and your descendants. Also your descendants shall be as the dust of the earth; you shall spread abroad to the west and the east, to the north and the south; and in you and in your seed all the families of the earth shall be blessed. Behold, I am with you and will keep you wherever you go, and will bring you back to this land; for I will not leave you until I have done what I have spoken to you" (Gen. 28:13-15).

The Davidic Covenant stands with the other unconditional covenants in demonstrating a priority of the promise of land. We read in 2 Samuel 7:10, "Moreover I will appoint a place for My people Israel, and will plant them, that they may dwell in a place of their own and move no more; nor shall the sons of wickedness oppress them anymore, as previously." It would require hermeneutical gymnastics to claim that this verse has already been fulfilled. The borders of Israel are in constant dispute and the oppression is fierce.

Ezekiel 37 speaks of the future reign of Christ:

> Then say to them, "Thus says the Lord GOD: 'Surely I will take the children of Israel from among the nations, wherever they have gone, and will gather them from every side and bring them into their own land; and I will make them one nation in the land, on the mountains of Israel; and one king shall be king over them all; they shall no longer be two nations, nor shall they ever be divided into two kingdoms again. They shall not defile themselves anymore with their idols, nor with their detestable things, nor with any of their transgressions; but I will deliver them from all their dwelling places in which they have sinned, and will cleanse them. Then they shall be My people, and I will be their God. David My servant shall be king over them, and they shall all have one shepherd; they shall also walk in My judgments and observe My statutes, and do them. Then they shall dwell in the land that I have given to Jacob My servant, where your fathers dwelt; and they shall dwell there, they, their children, and their children's children, forever; and My servant David shall be their prince forever'" (Ezek. 37:21-25).

The King of verse 22, who shall reign over all the people, is a reference to Jesus Christ. Another important statement is made at the end of the next verse, "Then they shall be My people, and I will be their God" (Ezek. 37:23). This is a distinctly prophetic and Messianic phrase which refers to the time when the Kingdom is inaugurated. This type of terminology was used often by the prophets to speak of the final and ultimate intimacy with God. At that time, "Then they shall dwell in the land" (Ezek. 37:25). Notice again that verse 25 specifically uses the word *forever*. The consistent testimony of Scripture is of the eternal nature of the Kingdom. When Christ takes the throne after the Second Coming, the Kingdom begins and it never ends. Within these promises of the Kingdom of God we see the continued emphasis on the land.

The New Covenant also proclaims the priority of the land promise. Jeremiah 31:8 demonstrates this in two different parts of the verse. First we are told, "Behold, I will bring them from the north country, and gather them from the ends of the earth" (Jer. 31:8a). Further, "a great throng shall return there" (Jer. 31:8b). The context dictates that this is a reference to the land.

Jeremiah 31:17 offers great hope to the people of Israel, "There is hope in your future, says the LORD, that your children shall come back to their own border." Verse 21 of Jeremiah continues this same line of thinking, "Set up signposts, make landmarks; set your heart toward the highway, the way in which you went. Turn back, O virgin of Israel, turn back to these your cities" (Jer. 31:21). The Word of God clearly reveals that God is passionate about His land. This is once again witnessed in verse 23, "Thus says the LORD of hosts, the God of Israel: 'They shall again use this speech in the land of Judah and in its cities, when I bring back their captivity'" (Jer. 31:23).

The passion and priority of God for His land is again established by looking to the words of the prophet Joel, "Then the LORD will be zealous for His land, and pity His people" (Joel 2:18). Further, we are told, "Fear not, O land; be glad and rejoice, for the LORD has done marvelous things!" (Joel 2:21). Joel 2:28-32, which was quoted by Peter in Acts 2, refers to the New Covenant. Yet again, we read, "For in Mount Zion and in Jerusalem there shall be deliverance" (Joel 2:32).

Ezekiel records stimulating words regarding the New Covenant. The prophet referred to the significance of the land by proclaiming the words of the Lord, "For I will take you from among the nations, gather you out of all countries, and bring you into your own land" (Ezek. 36:24). Regarding the New Covenant Israel was told, "I will give you a new heart and put a new spirit within you; I will take the heart of stone out of your flesh and give you a heart of flesh. I will put My Spirit within you and cause you to walk in My statutes, and you will keep My judgments and do them" (Ezek. 36:26-27). Notice in verse 28 another emphasis on the land, "Then you shall dwell in the land that I gave to your fathers; you shall be My people, and I will be your God" (Ezek. 36:28).

Chapter 37 of Ezekiel opens with the valley of dry bones. Contrary to popular belief, the valley of dry bones is not referring to individual believers today. Instead, it refers to a time when Israel is reinvigorated and repositioned into the land after the Tribulation. The people of Israel will be deposited into the land supernaturally by the angels. At that time, they will thrive again like a person that has been reborn. It will be the direct result of the New Covenant.

Ezekiel 40-48 contains the millennial vision. In addition to the strong emphasis on the future Temple, there is also a definite focus on the land. The boundaries of the land of Israel will be expanded to fulfill the promise of God. The New Covenant and the final chapters of Ezekiel have a repeated testimony of the importance of the Promised Land.

The importance of the Land Covenant must not be underestimated because it is the absolute death knell of covenant theology. The physical land promises of God are an insurmountable obstacle which blocks the attempts of men to spiritualize the Word of God. The repeated testimony of Scripture is that God promises the nation of Israel physical real estate.

The Perpetuity of the Land Promise

The land promise has not been abrogated, nor has it been abandoned. This is evident from the reiteration of it within the New Testament.

The first chapter of the Gospel of Luke records the angel, Gabriel, announcing to Mary the future virgin birth of the Messiah, Jesus. Within this announcement Gabriel proclaimed about the Christ, "He will be great, and will be called the Son of the Highest; and the Lord God will give Him the throne of His father David. And He will reign over the house of Jacob forever, and of His kingdom there will be no end" (Luke 1:32-33). In order for there to be a kingdom there must be land. Gabriel reiterated the covenant promises of God.

Our focus once again moves to the Gospel of Matthew. The record teaches that John the Baptist came proclaiming, "Repent, for the kingdom of heaven is at hand!" (Matt. 3:2). This is the same message that was proclaimed by our Lord, "Repent, for the kingdom of heaven is at hand" (Matt. 4:17). The intended meaning, of both John the Baptist and the Lord Jesus, to the people of Israel was to repent because their long awaited Kingdom had arrived. It is self-evident that God's sovereign plan involved the Kingdom being offered and rejected. This means the Kingdom would be delayed and finally ushered in at the Second Coming of Christ. But chronologically speaking, from man's perspective, had Israel received the Messiah and believed in Him as the Son of God who alone can provide individual salvation, then there would have been no Church Age. Christ would have then just ushered in His Kingdom. Jesus would have been crowned with David's crown instead of a crown of thorns. This is what both Jesus and John the Baptist meant in the context of these passages. The people were being called to repentance because the Kingdom was legitimately being offered to them.

This same teaching was present in Jesus' Sermon on the Mount in Matthew 5-7. The Sermon on the Mount is about the Kingdom. Consider some of the key teachings:

- Blessed are the poor in spirit, for theirs is the kingdom of heaven (Matt. 5:3).
- Blessed are those who are persecuted for righteousness' sake, for theirs is the kingdom of heaven (Matt. 5:10).
- Whoever therefore breaks one of the least of these commandments, and teaches men so, shall be called least in the kingdom of heaven; but whoever does and teaches them, he shall be called great in the kingdom of heaven (Matt. 5:19).
- For I say to you, that unless your righteousness exceeds the righteousness of the scribes and Pharisees, you will by no means enter the kingdom of heaven (Matt. 5:20).
- Enter by the narrow gate; for wide is the gate and broad is the way that leads to destruction, and there are many who go in by it. Because narrow is the gate and difficult is the way which leads to life, and there are few who find it (Matt. 7:13-14).
- Not everyone who says to Me, "Lord, Lord," shall enter the kingdom of heaven, but he who does the will of My Father in heaven (Matt. 7:21).

The Sermon on the Mount is all about Kingdom truth. Throughout His ministry, the Lord Jesus continued to teach about the Kingdom. This is illustrated for us in the parable of the wedding feast in Matthew 22. Jesus directly stated that the intention of the parable was to convey truth about, "the kingdom of heaven" (Matt. 22:2). The people of Israel had become ethnocentric. They had come to believe that when the Kingdom arrived it would only involve the Jewish people. After years of oppression, and under the rule of Rome at the time, the people had developed a complex. What they never seemed to understand was that the Kingdom was always intended to be global in nature. When Israel crossed the Jordan River the people were to expand and glorify God over His earth, in His land. The people of Israel never accomplished this. Pockets of revival and periods of obedience did occur, but it never universally happened. Jesus sought to address this particular problem with the parable of the wedding feast.

Within the parable, the people originally invited to the wedding did not accept the invitation. As a result, the servants were eventually instructed to go out into the highways to invite people to this great feast. Regarding Matthew 22, Arno Gaebelein taught:

> The third verse speaks of the offer of the Kingdom as made to Israel by the King and His disciples. It was refused. In verses 4-6 there is a repeated offer and how this second offer was treated. This took place after the cross ("all things are ready"; the cross of Christ has done that). The beginning of the Book of Acts reveals that offer made exclusively to Jerusalem. Those who had rejected Christ and crucified Him had a chance to repent. They did exactly with the message and the messengers what our Lord predicts in this parable. Verse 7 is a prediction of what should befall Jerusalem. This was fulfilled in the year 70. The city, which had become a city of murderers (Isa. 1:21) was burned. Then the King predicts the world-wide offer made to the Gentiles (verses 8-10).[4]

A physical kingdom was offered to the nation of Israel.

The Lord Jesus made an interesting statement regarding this in the latter part of His ministry. Speaking to the chief priests and the Pharisees Jesus proclaimed, "Therefore I say to you, the kingdom of God will be taken from you and given to a nation bearing the fruits of it" (Matt. 21:43). A misunderstanding of this statement has led many to incorrectly believe that God has taken away the Kingdom of God from the Jews and given it to the Gentiles. This is not at all what Jesus meant.

The key to understanding the original intent of this verse is found by first looking at the broader context and the audience to whom Jesus was addressing these words. Verse 23 reveals that Jesus was in the Temple and was speaking to, "chief priests and the elders of the people" (Matt. 21:23). Verse 45 confirms that the chief priests and the Pharisees heard the words of Jesus. His message was clearly directed toward these religious leaders, but what message was the Lord giving to them? Jesus was not proclaiming that the Kingdom would be given to a Gentile nation. *The rulers of Israel had rejected their King and consequently the Kingdom of God would be given to a future generation of Jews.* The word translated *nation* usually means Gentiles, but it can clearly mean a nation of people. This is the meaning in this passage, indicating a reference to the future people of Israel. This was a strong rebuke to the first century rulers of Israel. The Lord Jesus reiterated that the promises of the Kingdom would be fulfilled in a later generation.

The Apostle Paul taught the perpetuity of the land promise in Romans 9-11. Referring to a future for the nation of Israel Paul recorded, "God has not cast away His people whom He foreknew" (Rom. 11:2). Again, Paul proclaimed:

> For I do not desire, brethren, that you should be ignorant of this mystery, lest you should be wise in your own opinion, that blindness in part has happened to Israel until the fullness of the Gentiles has come in. And so all Israel will be saved, as it is written: *"The Deliverer will come out of Zion, and He will turn away ungodliness from Jacob; for this is My covenant with them, when I take away their sins"* (Rom. 11:25-27).

The deliverance of Israel at the Second Coming of Christ will usher in the fulfillment of the Kingdom promises of God, including the Land Covenant.

Revelation 19 reveals the Second Coming of Christ. Within this dramatic teaching we find that once more the Scriptures restate the coming Kingdom of Christ. Consider the powerful teaching of the Word of God:

> Now I saw heaven opened, and behold, a white horse. And He who sat on him was called Faithful and True, and in righteousness He judges and makes war. His eyes were like a flame of fire, and on His head were many crowns. He had a name written that no one knew except Himself. He was clothed with a robe dipped in blood, and His name is called The Word of God. And the armies in heaven, clothed in fine linen, white and clean, followed Him on white horses. Now out of His mouth goes a sharp sword, that with it He should strike the nations. And He Himself will rule them with a rod of iron. He Himself treads the winepress of the fierceness and wrath of Almighty God. And He has on His robe and on His thigh a name written: KING OF KINGS AND LORD OF LORDS (Rev. 19:11-16).

Notice that verse 11 specifically mentions a white horse.

This is not the first time the book of Revelation references a white horse. Revelation 6:1-8 contains the teaching of the four horsemen of the apocalypse, which make up the first four seal judgments. The first horseman of the apocalypse is on a white horse. Revelation 6:2 teaches, "And I looked, and behold, a white horse. He who sat on it had a bow; and a crown was given to him, and he went out conquering and to conquer." This is the Antichrist. The first seal judgment is the revelation of the Antichrist. This correlates with both 2 Thessalonians 2 and Daniel 9. 2 Thessalonians 2:3 teaches that the Antichrist will be revealed before the Day of the Lord. There are some startling contrasts that should be noted:

- The first rider of the white horse is an imposter (Rev. 6:2).
- The second rider is described as faithful and true (Rev. 19:11).
- The first rider, "went out conquering and to conquer" (Rev. 6:2). Nothing is said about righteousness.
- The second rider, "in righteousness He judges and makes war" (Rev. 19:11).

Christ will not return to this earth alone. We learn, "And the armies in heaven, clothed in fine linen, white and clean, followed Him on white horses" (Rev. 19:14). The Church Age saints will return to this earth with Christ, riding on white horses to usher in His Kingdom.

Revelation 19:11-16 is the culmination of the Great Day of the Lord's Wrath. It will begin in Revelation 6, and the people will cry out, "Hide us from the face of Him who sits on the throne and from the wrath of the Lamb!" (Rev. 6:16). The promise throughout the Old Testament is that one day God's wrath will be poured out against all the enemies of Yahweh and His people. Revelation describes the fulfillment of this wrath that will come from the eternal Son of God. But it is often missed that Revelation 19 is also directly referring to the ushering in of the Kingdom of Christ. The Lord Jesus Christ will rule the nations with a rod of iron (Rev. 19:15). This is a direct reference to an earthly Kingdom.

Each aspect of the Abrahamic Covenant (the land, seed, and blessing) reiterates the promise of the Land Covenant. The Promised Land is referenced in passages describing the New Covenant, the Davidic Covenant, the Abrahamic Covenant, as well as the Land Covenant.

The Present State of the Land of Promise

Understanding the present state of the land requires us to take a step back in time to the rise of the modern Zionist movement. A man by the name of Theodor Herzl wrote *The Jewish State* in 1896. Consider the historical reality at that time. Israel did not exist as a nation and to many people the idea of the rebirth of the nation of Israel was thought to be laughable. Herzl convened the First Zionist World Congress in 1897 in Basle, Switzerland. He put forward the Uganda Plan, which was to give Israel a homeland in Uganda. The problem with this line of thinking is that Uganda is not the Holy Land; it is the wrong land.

Herzl wrote in his personal diary on September 3, 1897, after the conference, "At Basel, I founded the Jewish State. If I said this out loud today, I would be answered by universal laughter. Perhaps in five years, certainly in fifty, everyone will know it." Roughly fifty years later, Israel became a nation.

Another historical development took place on November 2, 1917. A letter was sent from the United Kingdom's Foreign Secretary, Arthur James Balfour, to Baron Rothschild. At the time, Rothschild was a leader of the British Jewish community. The declaration stated:

> His Majesty's Government view with favour the establishment in Palestine of a national home for the Jewish people, and will use their best endeavors to facilitate the achievement of this object, it being clearly understood that nothing shall be done which may prejudice the civil and religious rights of existing non-Jewish communities in Palestine, or the rights and political status enjoyed by Jews in any other country.

This helped to crystallize the tension for decades to come. No one party is seen as having exclusive rights to the land.

World War II had a lasting impact on the course of direction for the Jewish people.[5] There was already a sizable population of Jewish people living in the land known as Palestine, but the Nazi Holocaust left a great number of homeless Jewish survivors longing for their homeland. Devout Jews looked to the promise of the Abrahamic Covenant as giving them the right to their land. This left the British government with a sizable problem. Their control of Palestine led to a push from Arab states to curb the immigration of Jewish people.

The conflicts and clashes between the Jews and the Arabs continued to escalate. Eventually, the situation was delegated to the United Nations. A historic vote was taken on November 29, 1947. On that day the United Nations voted to divide the land of Palestine into Jewish and Arab states. Jerusalem would become an international zone. The plan was rejected by the Arabs, but was accepted by the Jews. Many Arabs pledged to destroy Israel.

History was once again made on May 14, 1948, when the Jewish people signed their Declaration of Independence. The next day, May 15th, five Arab states: Egypt, Jordan, Syria, Lebanon, and Iraq simultaneously invaded Israel with the goal of destroying the Jewish state. As a result of their military victory, Israel annexed land that had been set aside for an

Arab Palestinian state. This left only East Jerusalem, the West Bank, and the Gaza Strip under the control of the Arabs.

In the summer of 1956, the government of Egypt decided to nationalize the Suez Canal. Israeli ships were blocked from passing through the canal. In response, on October 29th, Israeli troops entered the Sinai Peninsula and took control in one hundred hours. British and French troops then secured the Suez Canal. Negotiations with the United States allowed for Israeli shipping to resume, which resulted in the withdrawal of Israeli forces from the Sinai Peninsula.

On May 28-29, 1964, the Palestine Liberation Organization (PLO) was formed. The PLO explicitly denied Israel's right to exist and vowed to destroy Israel. Yasser Arafat was elected chairman of the PLO in 1969.

The Six Day War came on June 5-10, 1967. Syria had been shelling northern Israeli towns and threatening the destruction of Israel for years. Egypt was posturing for war with Israel. Because of the imminent threat of Arab invasion, Israel initiated an offensive against Egypt, Jordan, and Syria. Through this offensive Israel captured the West Bank, East Jerusalem, and Gaza. Israel also took the Sinai and the Golan Heights. The Six Day War was a defensive war launched for the very survival of the nation. Peace talks have centered on a return to the pre-1967 borders ever since.

A surprise attack by Egypt and Syria was launched on October 6th of 1973, to take back the Sinai and Golan Heights. This attack was timed to coincide with Yom Kippur (the Day of Atonement), which is why this has become known as the Yom Kippur War. A cease-fire was scheduled to take place on October 22nd but was not implemented until a few days later.

The United States was able to negotiate a peace agreement between Egypt and Israel on March 26, 1979. At this time Israel returned the Sinai to Egypt, but held on to the Gaza Strip. These are often referred to as the Camp David Accords.

Israel annexed the Golan Heights on December 14, 1981. This land had already been taken from Syria in 1967 during the Six Day War. This strategic location has been the source of considerable contention. Up until 1967, Syria used this land to shell northern Israel. Now, Israel uses it to monitor the movements of Syrian troops.

Another problem for Israel has been the nation of Lebanon, which has a history of being a safe-haven for terrorists. During the 1970's the PLO found refuge within the borders of Lebanon. From this location the PLO staged repeated terrorist attacks and shellings of Israeli towns.

As the deaths and injuries from these attacks mounted, Israel had the obligation to protect itself. In June of 1982 Israel responded by invading Lebanon. Israel withdrew in 1985, but kept a security zone along the border.

Officially, a peace agreement was reached on September 13, 1993. This document, known as the Oslo Accords, was signed in Washington D.C. This agreement between Israel and the PLO allows for limited Palestinian control in the West Bank and Gaza. Since this time the violence and tension has continued to surface.

Lebanon is now harboring the terrorist group Hezbollah. Their terrorist attacks on Israel led to another military conflict in 2006. Hezbollah continues to operate within Lebanon, amassing more arms for more attacks.

These conflicts will continue until the Tribulation, when the Antichrist signs a short-lived peace treaty. This treaty will guarantee the protection of Israel. Three and one-half years into the treaty the Antichrist will break it. He will defile the rebuilt Temple and demand worship of himself as god. It must be recognized that there will never be lasting peace until Christ returns to take the throne. He is the Prince of Peace (Isa. 9). The conflict over the land of Israel will not be settled until the Lord reigns. Only then will there be a complete fulfillment of everything that has been promised to Israel.

The Prophetic Implications of the Land Promise

In order for the Land Covenant to be fulfilled Israel must be converted as a nation. This does not mean every Jewish person on the earth will place his trust in Christ. During the future Tribulation period, many will take the mark of the Beast and reject the Messiah, Jesus. At the First Advent of Christ the prevailing attitude was against His acceptance as the Messiah. At the Second Advent the minority will become the majority, as the prevailing attitude will be trust in Jesus as the Messiah of Israel. As predicted, the nation of Israel will repent at the Second Coming of Christ. Zechariah foretold:

> And I will pour on the house of David and on the inhabitants of Jerusalem the Spirit of grace and supplication; then they will look on Me whom they pierced. Yes, they will mourn for Him as one mourns for his only son, and grieve for Him as one grieves for a firstborn. In

that day there shall be a great mourning in Jerusalem, like the mourning at Hadad Rimmon in the plain of Megiddo. And the land shall mourn, every family by itself (Zech. 12:10-12).

The intense persecution during the Tribulation will cause many Jews to scatter throughout the earth. Israel will be regathered from her world-wide dispersion and installed into her Promised Land. We already witnessed that the Lord instructed:

Then the sign of the Son of Man will appear in heaven, and then all the tribes of the earth will mourn, and they will see the Son of Man coming on the clouds of heaven with power and great glory. And He will send His angels with a great sound of a trumpet, and they will gather together His elect from the four winds, from one end of heaven to the other (Matt. 24:30-31).

This will be the regathering of Israel predicted throughout the Old Testament (Deut. 30:1-6; Isa. 11:11-12).[6]

The Land Promise Fulfilled

The nation of Israel must receive all of the blessings of the promised Kingdom. A central aspect of the coming Kingdom of Christ is the Land Covenant. Since these promises have yet to be fulfilled, the only true understanding we can arrive at (without violating the plain, normal meaning of the Word of God) is that these prophecies await a future fulfillment. Christians should hold fast to their faith in the imminent return of our Lord. Let us rejoice in the hope of Israel knowing that God's promises to His people will be fulfilled!

Discussion Questions

1. What important land struggle exists today?
2. Why are passages like Genesis 12 and 15 critical to understand when studying Israel's claim to land?
3. Who established the boundaries of Israel's Promised Land?
4. Has the Land Covenant been completely fulfilled? Which Bible passage proves this?

5. What must the children of Israel do to receive the blessings of land? Who will make this happen?
6. Where can we witness the priority of the land promise?
7. How is the promise of land to Israel reaffirmed throughout the New Testament?
8. Provide a brief timeline of the modern day events that describe the present state of the Promised Land.
9. Describe what must happen for Israel to receive all of the blessings of the land.
10. What should be the reaction of Christians in regard to the Land Covenant?

Endnotes

1. Charles L. Feinberg, *Israel: At the Center of History and Revelation*, 3rd ed. (Portland, OR: Multnomah Press, 1980), 168.
2. This same teaching is found in Deuteronomy, "And the LORD your God will drive out those nations before you little by little; you will be unable to destroy them at once, lest the beasts of the field become too numerous for you" (Deut. 7:22).
3. Amongst dispensationalists there are many different views of the timing of the Battle of Gog and Magog in Ezekiel 38-39. These are addressed in greater detail in chapter 14.
4. Arno C. Gaebelein, *The Annotated Bible, Volume 6: Matthew to The Acts*, 46-47.
5. The following summary of the recent conflicts over the land was partially adopted from "The Mideast conflict: A look at the region's history," http://www.usatoday.com/graphics/news/gra/gisrael2/flash.htm (accessed July 5, 2012). See also http://www.guardian.co.uk/flash/0,5860,720353,00.html
6. See also Isa. 43:5, 6; 49:12; Jer. 16:14, 15; Ezek. 34:13; 36:24; 37:21-23.

CHAPTER 7

The Promise of a King - The Davidic Covenant

And in the days of these kings the God of heaven will set up a kingdom which shall never be destroyed; and the kingdom shall not be left to other people; it shall break in pieces and consume all these kingdoms, and it shall stand forever.

- Daniel 2:44

THE FUTURE OF a kingdom depends on its king. This simple truth was well known to the people of Russia. At a time when succession to the throne was based on having a male heir, the Tsar of Russia had none to offer. Emperor Nicholas II and his wife, Alexandra, had been blessed with four daughters. As charming as they were, none of them could ever take their father's place by inheriting the throne.

The long awaited heir finally came in the summer of 1904. A gun salute from cannons announced the good news to the nation. The rejoicing literally spilled out into the streets, and bells were rung declaring the arrival of the long awaited heir to the throne. Prayers of thanksgiving were spoken in churches, and the night sky was lit up with fires of celebration. The name, Alexei, was given to the child that everyone in Russia thought would one day take the throne.

Six weeks into his life Alexei gave his parents great cause for concern. Alexei unexpectedly started to bleed from his navel. On the second day the doctors were finally able to bring the bleeding under control. The diagnosis was crippling to the family. Alexei had hemophilia; his blood simply would not clot like it was supposed to.

With no known cure, this put the heir to the throne in constant danger. The decision was made to keep this grim news a secret. The smallest cut could have jeopardized his life and brought instability to Russia. The people would not want an heir to the throne who was sick, weak, and always at risk of death. The future of the Russian Empire was certainly not secure. Yet, as it turned out, the concerns of the royal family were irrelevant. What they could not have known was that during the Russian Revolution the entire royal family would lose their lives. All of their efforts to secure a legitimate heir to the throne and to protect the life of young Alexei would come to a meaningless end.

The kingdoms of men are eventually toppled. Rulers come and go. Wars and revolutions eventually bring down the mightiest of nations, but one kingdom will stand for all of eternity. The coming Kingdom of Christ will not face the typical troubles and insecurities of earthly domains. The King of kings will reign in perfect justice and peace. His Kingdom will be without end.

The Guarantee

The Davidic Covenant guarantees that one day there will be an heir upon the throne of David. This unconditional promise was made to David in 2 Samuel 7. The Davidic Covenant has both an immediate promise and an eschatological promise. The immediate aspect can be found in verse 12, "When your days are fulfilled and you rest with your fathers, I will set up your seed after you, who will come from your body, and I will establish his kingdom" (2 Sam. 7:12). David would have a son, yet to be born, who would succeed him and establish his kingdom. David was also told, "Behold, a son shall be born to you, who shall be a man of rest; and I will give him rest from all his enemies all around. His name shall be Solomon, for I will give peace and quietness to Israel in his days" (2 Chron. 22:9).

The instruction to David continued, "He shall build a house for My name, and I will establish the throne of his kingdom forever" (2 Sam. 7:13). Solomon would build the Temple instead of David. Notice that the text is not suggesting that Solomon would live forever. Instead, God would establish the throne of Solomon's kingdom forever.

> I will be his Father, and he shall be My son. If he commits iniquity, I will chasten him with the rod of men and with the blows of the sons of men. But My mercy shall not depart from him, as I took it from Saul, whom I removed from before you. And your house and your kingdom shall be

established forever before you. Your throne shall be established forever
(2 Sam. 7:14-16).

Verses 14-15 reveal that Solomon's throne would not be removed even
though his sins would justify such discipline. Solomon, the imperfect,
sinful, human king in the line of David could not preempt what is
ultimately, unconditionally promised by Yahweh to His people. In verse
16 we learn that David's house, kingdom, and throne would be established
forever. It is once again clear from the context that these words were to be
taken literally.

The Messianic Psalms

The Old Testament contains other key passages regarding the Davidic
Covenant that specifically mention the future reign of Christ. These
include the Messianic Psalms.

Psalm 2 is a well-known passage of Scripture. The Word of God
teaches:

> Why do the nations rage, and the people plot a vain thing? The kings of
> the earth set themselves, and the rulers take counsel together, against the
> LORD and against His Anointed, saying, "Let us break Their bonds in
> pieces and cast away Their cords from us." He who sits in the heavens
> shall laugh; the LORD shall hold them in derision. Then He shall speak
> to them in His wrath, and distress them in His deep displeasure: "Yet I
> have set My King on My holy hill of Zion." "I will declare the decree: The
> LORD has said to Me, 'You are My Son, today I have begotten You. Ask
> of Me, and I will give You the nations for Your inheritance, and the ends
> of the earth for Your possession. You shall break them with a rod of iron;
> You shall dash them to pieces like a potter's vessel.'" Now therefore, be
> wise, O kings; be instructed, you judges of the earth. Serve the LORD
> with fear, and rejoice with trembling. Kiss the Son, lest He be angry, and
> you perish in the way, when His wrath is kindled but a little. Blessed are
> all those who put their trust in Him (Ps. 2:1-12).

It is important to remember that this was written about a thousand years
before the First Advent of Christ. This is a beautiful hymn describing the
time when the eternal Son of God will come and be installed as King. The
nations of the earth will be His inheritance. His second coming will be the
instrument of God's wrath. We remember that Revelation 19:15 teaches us,
"He Himself treads the winepress of the fierceness and wrath of Almighty

God." Psalm 2 is a parallel reference to the eschatological wrath of God. Christ will rule the nations with a rod of iron. Psalm 2 is a clear promise of the eternal Son of God coming and reigning on the earth.

Psalm 110 is another famous Messianic Psalm. Once again, consider the text:

> The LORD said to my Lord, "Sit at My right hand, till I make Your enemies Your footstool." The LORD shall send the rod of Your strength out of Zion. Rule in the midst of Your enemies! Your people shall be volunteers in the day of Your power; in the beauties of holiness, from the womb of the morning, You have the dew of Your youth. The LORD has sworn and will not relent, "You are a priest forever according to the order of Melchizedek." The Lord is at Your right hand; He shall execute kings in the day of His wrath. He shall judge among the nations, He shall fill the places with dead bodies, He shall execute the heads of many countries. He shall drink of the brook by the wayside; therefore He shall lift up the head (Ps. 110:1-7).

Melchizedek was an Old Testament priest who ministered to Abraham (Gen. 14:18-20). This took place hundreds of years before Aaron and his descendants became the priests of Israel. Even though Christ was of the lineage of David, and not Aaron, He is a priest after the order of Melchizedek (Heb. 5:5–11; 6:20; 7:1–28). His priesthood is by the decree of God, not based on being a descendant of Aaron. Just as Melchizedek predated the priests of Israel, Christ is eternal and supersedes the Aaronic priesthood. Psalm 110 is another testimony of the future outpouring of the wrath of God on the nations and the installment of Christ as King.

The New Testament provides the additional information about these events (which are covered in greater detail in later chapters of this book). The precursor to the Second Coming of Christ is a brief period of time known as the Seventieth Week of Daniel. Within God's program of the ages this period of seven years is but a brief moment in time within the history of mankind.

The Old Testament describes the Day of the Lord (referred to as the Day of the Lord's Wrath) as one climactic event, without much added detail. The New Testament reveals that this time begins after the Rapture. The Rapture rescues the Church from the Great Day of the Lord's Wrath because He has not appointed the Church to suffer wrath (1 Thess. 1:10). Then the outpouring of God's wrath begins (Rev. 6). The Antichrist will be revealed and the wrath of God will intensify through the seal, trumpet, and bowl judgments. The climax of His wrath will be with the coming of the King who will slay the unbelieving kings of the nations before Him. The people alive at that time will face the Sheep and Goats Judgment (Matt. 25:31-46). Christ will then take the throne and rule in perfect righteousness.

Psalm 132 also contains a passage that references the throne of David. Verses 11-12 record, "The LORD has sworn in truth to David; He will not turn from it: 'I will set upon your throne the fruit of your body. If your sons will keep My covenant and My testimony which I shall teach them, their sons also shall sit upon your throne forevermore.'" This is referencing God's covenant with David in 2 Samuel 7. Again, we remind ourselves that almost every time we see a reference in the Word of God to the Kingdom of Christ, it is described as an eternal kingdom.

Next on our list of Messianic Psalms is Psalm 89. Verses 20-29 teach:

I have found My servant David; with My holy oil I have anointed him, with whom My hand shall be established; also My arm shall strengthen him. The enemy shall not outwit him, nor the son of wickedness afflict him. I will beat down his foes before his face, and plague those who hate him. But My faithfulness and My mercy shall be with him, and in My name his horn shall be exalted. Also I will set his hand over the sea, and his right hand over the rivers. He shall cry to Me, "You are my Father, My God, and the rock of my salvation." Also I will make him My firstborn, the highest of the kings of the earth. My mercy I will keep for him forever, and My covenant shall stand firm with him. His seed also I will make to endure forever, and his throne as the days of heaven (Ps. 89:20-29).

God reaffirmed His covenant with David. The Davidic Throne will endure forever. Verse 36 also proclaims, "His seed shall endure forever, and his throne as the sun before Me" (Ps. 89:36). This is another reiteration of God's unconditional promise that through David Israel will have a king who will reign on the earth.

Psalm 45 also speaks of the coming Kingdom of Christ, "Your throne, O God, is forever and ever; a scepter of righteousness is the scepter of Your kingdom. You love righteousness and hate wickedness; therefore God, Your God, has anointed You with the oil of gladness more than Your companions" (Ps. 45:6-7). Here the King is addressed as God, but it is also God who has anointed Him. This indicates a clear reference to the Messianic King.

Psalm 46 takes on a different perspective when you properly understand Bible prophecy from a premillennial perspective. Recognizing that Christ is going to come back prior to the Millennium and set up His Kingdom on earth helps us to rightly divide this text. Amillennial and covenant theologians, because of their system of belief, are forced to spiritualize Psalm 46. The result is that Psalm 46 is said to teach the basic message that God is in control. Certainly God is in control, but Psalm 46 demonstrates that He is in control in a particular way.

Verse 1 of Psalm 46 teaches, "God is our refuge and strength, a very present help in trouble." The question that needs to be asked is, "In what way is He our helper?" Verse 2 records, "Therefore we will not fear, even though the earth be removed, and though the mountains be carried into the midst of the sea" (Ps. 46:2). This is a poetic way of testifying that no matter what calamity befalls us, we are going to trust in Him. Verses 3-7 continue to teach:

> Though its waters roar and be troubled, though the mountains shake with its swelling. Selah There is a river whose streams shall make glad the city of God, the holy place of the tabernacle of the Most High. God is in the midst of her, she shall not be moved; God shall help her, just at the break of dawn. The nations raged, the kingdoms were moved; He uttered His voice, the earth melted. The LORD of hosts is with us; the God of Jacob is our refuge (Ps. 46:3-7).

The expression *the Lord of hosts* contains a military connotation. The references to kingdoms and nations indicate national ramifications on earth.

Notice verses 8-9, "Come, behold the works of the LORD, who has made desolations in the earth. He makes wars cease to the end of the earth; He breaks the bow and cuts the spear in two; He burns the chariot in the fire" (Ps. 46:8-9). This is specifically referring to the time when the Prince of Peace will come and reign. Only at that time, will there be no more fighting. The Millennium will be a time of peace without the armies of men. Only when Satan is let loose at the very end, will he hastily gather together the unbelievers for one final, failed, and futile attempt to come against Christ.

Verse 10 of Psalm 46 is famous, "Be still, and know that I am God; I will be exalted among the nations, I will be exalted in the earth!" This verse has provided great comfort for God's people throughout the ages. Within the Church Age, we tend to commonly think that it means to be still and meditate or contemplate the Lord. The context reveals that this is not really the intended meaning of the text. The Hebrew term for *be still* means to stop fighting. The New American Standard Bible translates it as *cease striving*. This is an accurate representation of the intended meaning. Wars will cease when God is exalted among the nations. The Psalm is calling for us to recognize that God is sovereign over all of the earth, and ultimately, He is going to be the only one who can put an end to war.

Understanding the literal promises of the Bible regarding a kingdom on earth gives us greater insight into the Word of God and our faith in Jesus Christ. It is one thing for us to be able to hope, and believe by faith, that God is in control no matter the trials and tribulations that we are facing in life. It is a better understanding of His Word to recognize God's plan for His people, which bolsters our faith in Him. This includes the teaching that in the future the earth will look very different from what it is today. It will be an earth that is characterized by justice, not inequity. It will be a time when the people will be led by righteous leadership, not the unrighteous of our day. Peace and goodness will dominate the age. We have a very clear picture of a foreseeable future because we believe that Christ is going to come back.

The Old Testament Prophets

The Old Testament also contains other key passages regarding the Davidic Covenant, within the words of the prophets. We read in Amos:

> "For surely I will command, and will sift the house of Israel among all nations, as grain is sifted in a sieve; yet not the smallest grain shall fall to the ground. All the sinners of My people shall die by the sword, who say, 'The calamity shall not overtake nor confront us.'" "On that day I will raise up the tabernacle of David, which has fallen down, and repair its damages; I will raise up its ruins, and rebuild it as in the days of old; that they may possess the remnant of Edom, and all the Gentiles who are called by My name," Says the LORD who does this thing. "Behold, the days are coming," says the LORD, "When the plowman shall overtake the reaper, and the treader of grapes him who sows seed; the mountains shall drip with sweet wine, and all the hills shall flow with it. I will bring back the captives of My people Israel; they shall build the waste cities and inhabit them; they shall plant vineyards and drink wine from them; they shall also make gardens and eat fruit from them. I will plant them in their land, and no longer shall they be pulled up from the land I have given them," says the LORD your God (Amos 9:9-15).

James quoted from this passage at the Jerusalem council in Acts 15, which serves to highlight the importance of this text to the nation of Israel.

Verses 9-10 of Amos 9 are a reference to the Tribulation period. It is a testimony that the Tribulation will catch many Jews, in particular, off guard. Given the clear teaching about this time in both the Old and New Testaments, the coming deception will be remarkable. The entire Olivet Discourse, the book of Daniel, and the Minor Prophets talk about the Day of the Lord, but yet many Jews will be deceived. This helps us to understand why the Lord Jesus was so passionate about sounding the warning of not falling into deception within the Olivet Discourse. The deception during the seven-year Tribulation will be stifling. We are reminded that the First Advent of Christ was likewise predicted clearly in the Word of God (even down to the city of His birth, born of a virgin, etc.) and still most Jews missed it. The Devil is the great deceiver and will once again lead many Jews down the path of rejecting the true Messiah of Israel.

Verse 12 of Amos 9 reminds us, with a reference to the Gentiles, that the coming Kingdom of Christ will be a global kingdom, not just a Jewish kingdom. Verse 13 is a poetic way of talking about the incredible beauty and fruitfulness of the Kingdom when Christ is upon the throne. With verse 15, Yahweh was testifying to the nation of Israel that He will plant the people in their land, never to be removed by men again.

The entire passage in Amos is Messianic. The whole text is referring to the time when God will raise up the tabernacle of David. This is a reference to the coming of Christ to take the throne and the Messianic hope of Israel. This future time for the nation of Israel will be an unprecedented time of blessing.

Ezekiel also foretold this future Kingdom:

> Then say to them, "Thus says the Lord GOD: 'Surely I will take the children of Israel from among the nations, wherever they have gone, and will gather them from every side and bring them into their own land; and I will make them one nation in the land, on the mountains of Israel; and one king shall be king over them all; they shall no longer be two nations, nor shall they ever be divided into two kingdoms again. They shall not defile themselves anymore with their idols, nor with their detestable things, nor with any of their transgressions; but I will deliver them from all their dwelling places in which they have sinned, and will cleanse them. Then they shall be My people, and I will be their God. David My servant shall be king over them, and they shall all have one shepherd; they shall also walk in My judgments and observe My statutes, and do them. Then they shall dwell in the land that I have given

to Jacob My servant, where your fathers dwelt; and they shall dwell there, they, their children, and their children's children, forever; and My servant David shall be their prince forever'" (Ezek. 37:21-25).

Yet again, we see another powerful passage about the future Kingdom of Christ. Judah and Israel will never be divided again. Verse 23 highlights the sinless perfection of God's people in the Kingdom. At that time, "Then they shall be My people, and I will be their God" (Ezek. 37:23).

A familiar passage from Isaiah bears testimony of this Kingdom:

> For unto us a Child is born, unto us a Son is given; and the government will be upon His shoulder. And His name will be called Wonderful, Counselor, Mighty God, Everlasting Father, Prince of Peace. Of the increase of His government and peace there will be no end, upon the throne of David and over His kingdom, to order it and establish it with judgment and justice from that time forward, even forever. The zeal of the Lord of hosts will perform this (Isa. 9:6-7).

This is another example of an Old Testament prophecy being fulfilled in two parts. "For unto us a Child is born, unto us a Son is given" occurred at the First Advent of Christ (Isa. 9:6). Everything else within this passage awaits the Second Advent. The Lord of hosts once again references God's future military victory over the nations. The continued warfare by the nations of the world is pointless. Many great kingdoms have historically attempted to conquer the world, but their attempts have been rooted in futility. Ultimately, it is the Lord who is in control of His creation. Isaiah 9:6-7 is a strong testimony from God's Word about the Davidic Covenant.

The Scope of the Davidic Covenant

It should be self-evident that the Davidic Covenant is unconditional. This is apparent from the *I will* language that we see in both 2 Samuel 7:12-16 and Amos 9:11-15. Consider the record of the written Word of God:

- I will bring back the captives of My people Israel (Amos 9:14).
- I will plant them in their land (Amos 9:15).
- I will establish the throne of his kingdom forever (2 Sam. 7:13).

This is an eternal covenant (2 Sam. 7:13, 16; 23:5; Isa. 55:3; Ezek. 37:25). The Davidic Covenant amplifies the seed element of the Abrahamic Covenant, which is also clearly unconditional.

The promise of the Davidic Covenant is repeatedly stated in terms that convey its eternal nature. The Bible teaches:

- But King Solomon shall be blessed, and the throne of David shall be established before the LORD forever (1 Kings 2:45).
- Then I will establish the throne of your kingdom over Israel forever, as I promised David your father, saying, "You shall not fail to have a man on the throne of Israel" (1 Kings 9:5).
- And I will establish him in My house and in My kingdom forever; and his throne shall be established forever (1 Chron. 17:14).
- He shall build a house for My name, and he shall be My son, and I will be his Father; and I will establish the throne of his kingdom over Israel forever (1 Chron. 22:10).
- Yet the LORD would not destroy the house of David, because of the covenant that He had made with David, and since He had promised to give a lamp to him and to his sons forever (2 Chron. 21:7).
- Your throne, O God, is forever and ever; a scepter of righteousness is the scepter of Your kingdom (Ps. 45:6).

It is also important to note that the Davidic Covenant was made specifically with Israel. Scripture teaches, "Moreover I will appoint a place for My people Israel, and will plant them, that they may dwell in a place of their own and move no more; nor shall the sons of wickedness oppress them anymore, as previously" (2 Sam. 7:10). A normal plain reading of the text demands a literal fulfillment. This covenant was not made with the Church; it was made directly with the nation of Israel.

This is precisely how the original recipients of the covenant in 2 Samuel 7 would have understood the promise of God. The Davidic Covenant was even confirmed by a literal oath (Ps. 132:11; 89:3). The conviction of Solomon indicates that he understood the promise of the covenant literally. The Word of God proclaims:

And he said: "LORD God of Israel, there is no God in heaven or on earth like You, who keep Your covenant and mercy with Your servants who walk before You with all their hearts. You have kept what You promised Your servant David my father; You have both spoken with Your mouth and fulfilled it with Your hand, as it is this day. Therefore, LORD God of Israel, now keep what You promised Your servant David my father, saying, 'You shall not fail to have a man sit before Me on the throne of Israel, only if your sons take heed to their way, that they walk in My law as you have walked before Me.' And now, O LORD God of Israel, let Your word come true, which You have spoken to Your servant David" (2 Chron. 6:14-17).

This passage records Solomon's prayer of dedication and is central to the discussion at hand. Solomon was looking at the completed Temple of God. He even directly stated that the Temple was a fulfillment of God's promise. It should be obvious that Solomon saw this as a literal promise from God. When the Temple was destroyed, did this mean God changed His mind about His promises to the nation of Israel? Or, does it make more sense to believe in a future fulfillment of the Temple as promised in Ezekiel 40-48?

David likewise testified of a literal fulfillment of God's promises to Israel. Psalm 110 (a Psalm of David) teaches, "The LORD said to my Lord, 'Sit at My right hand, till I make Your enemies Your footstool'" (Ps. 110:1). This beautiful verse of Scripture describes a conversation between God the Father and the Messiah of Israel. David was proclaiming that there will be a time when the Messiah of Israel comes and takes the earthly throne.

We must consider the consistent testimony of Scripture. The phrase *throne of David* is repeatedly used in a literal sense in the Word of God (Jer. 17:25; 22:4; 29:16; 2 Sam. 3:10; 1 Kings 2:24). *It is never used symbolically.*

A careful examination of the Bible reveals that the Jews interpreted the covenant as a literal promise. John the Baptist and Jesus both said, "Repent, for the kingdom of heaven is at hand" (Matt. 3:2; 4:17). The disciples wanted to know, "Lord, will You at this time restore the kingdom to Israel?" (Acts 1:6). As Jesus sent out the twelve disciples, He told them to say, "The kingdom of heaven is at hand" (Matt. 10:7). These passages demonstrate the general understanding among the Jews that the promised Kingdom will have a literal fulfillment. It is also significant that the promises of God to Israel that have already been fulfilled, have been fulfilled literally.

The New Testament teaching on the Kingdom verifies the literal nature of the promise. Consider the words of Gabriel to Mary, "And behold, you will conceive in your womb and bring forth a Son, and shall call His name Jesus. He will be great, and will be called the Son of the Highest; and the Lord God will give Him the throne of His father David. And He will reign over the house of Jacob forever, and of His kingdom there will be no end" (Luke 1:31-33). This happened approximately a thousand years after the promise was made to David. Clearly there was something more than just Solomon that was a part of the fulfillment of this promise. It is self-evident that the promise to Israel is still in effect. This is why we see the testimony of Gabriel about the Christ, "and the Lord God will give Him the throne of His father David" (Luke 1:32).

We have already briefly touched on the parable of the minas in Luke 19. A more fitting title for this passage is the parable of delay because this is what it is truly about. Jesus began informing the disciples that His Kingdom was going to be delayed. Within the parable, a king went away to receive a kingdom. He would be gone for a while, but while he was away his servants were to be busy doing his business until the day of his return. When the king returned his people would give account of what they did while he was away. The parable is most certainly an allusion to the Church Age.

What makes this parable so intriguing is that it is one of the few occasions where the inspired author gives us a glimpse of why Jesus told the parable. Luke teaches, "Now as they heard these things, He spoke another parable, because He was near Jerusalem and *because they thought the kingdom of God would appear immediately*" (Luke 19:11, emphasis added). Jesus gave the parable to teach about the delay of His Kingdom. So far the Church Age has lasted approximately 2,000 years, but the King is certain to return. This is the promise of His Word. The point is to recognize that the New Testament verifies the belief of the early Church in a literal earthly kingdom (Matt. 25; Acts 1:6-11; 13:32-39; 15:13-17; Heb. 1-2).

The Standing of the Davidic Covenant

The Davidic Covenant relates to the Kingdom of God. It reiterates the seed aspects of the Abrahamic Covenant. The Kingdom program of God includes an establishment of an heir to the throne. God's eternal Son will, in fact, rule on earth someday.

The Seed Aspect of the Abrahamic Covenant

We are reminded that three elements of the Abrahamic Covenant are subsequently amplified with three more covenants (the land, seed, and blessing). The seed aspect is a key element of God's Kingdom program.

Many of the crucial issues in eschatology are clarified within the context of the Davidic Covenant. Three central features include the throne, the Temple, and the Kingdom. All three of these are literal. There is never a time in biblical history (or even human history) when one would interpret any of these spiritually, metaphorically, or symbolically. When kings talked about a throne, they meant a physical throne. A throne certainly can be a metonym for ones' rule, but there was always a literal throne. A throne simply meant a place to sit. A temple meant a place to dwell and rule from. A kingdom meant the boundaries of your domain. These are all clarified in the Davidic Covenant regarding the coming Kingdom of Christ.

The seed aspect of the Abrahamic Covenant is evident in the text of Scripture. God told Abraham, "I will make you a great nation" (Gen. 12:2). But we should also recognize that the seed element of the Abrahamic Covenant is witnessed in both the Land and the New Covenant.

The Seed and the Land Covenant

Genesis 26:4 instructs, "And I will make your descendants multiply as the stars of heaven; I will give to your descendants all these lands; and in your seed all the nations of the earth shall be blessed." This passage clearly emphasizes both the land and the seed aspect of the Abrahamic Covenant.

Genesis 28:14 teaches, "Also your descendants shall be as the dust of the earth; you shall spread abroad to the west and the east, to the north and the south; and in you and in your seed all the families of the earth shall be blessed." Possession of the Promised Land presupposes a ruler. This is why Scripture records, "Then the LORD your God will bring you to the land which your fathers possessed, and you shall possess it" (Deut. 30:5).

The Seed and the New Covenant

Quite frequently we witness in the Word of God that the seed aspect of the Abrahamic Covenant is mentioned in the New Covenant. Consider the words of Jeremiah 31:36-37, "'If those ordinances depart from before Me,' says the LORD, 'then the seed of Israel shall also cease from being a nation before Me forever.' Thus says the LORD: 'If heaven above can be measured, and the foundations of the earth searched out beneath, I will also cast off all the seed of Israel for all that they have done,' says the LORD." The context makes it clear that the ordinances departing are a reference to the sun, moon, and the stars. In other words, as long as the sun, moon, and stars exist God's covenant will come to pass. They are all tied to God's unconditional promise. This is a poetic description of the certainty of His unconditional covenant. Heaven cannot be measured and the foundations of the earth cannot be searched out beneath. Therefore, God will not cast off the seed of Israel.

Another New Covenant passage is Ezekiel 37:22-24. Here again we witness both the Davidic and New Covenant.

The Prophetic Significance of the Davidic Covenant

The Davidic Covenant has tangible implications for the future of the nation of Israel. Israel must be brought back to her Promised Land. David's seed, Jesus Christ, must return to the earth in bodily form to rule and reign, from the throne, over His Kingdom. His Kingdom will be an eternal kingdom.

The united testimony of the Word of God is that this will take place at the Second Coming of the Lord Jesus Christ (Rev. 19-20; Zech. 14:1-9; Isa. 66:14-16; Joel 2:30-32; Matt. 24:29-31; 25:31-46). See figure 7.1 below.

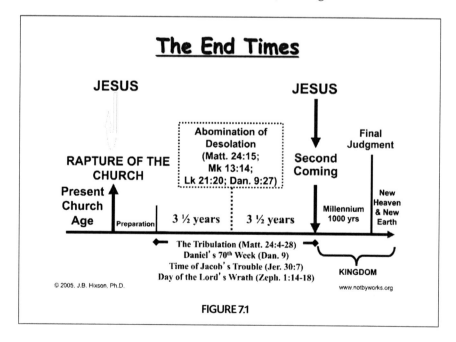

FIGURE 7.1

136

At the Rapture of the Church the Lord Jesus Christ will come to rescue the Bride of Christ. There is an unspecified period of preparation before the Antichrist will make a peace treaty with Israel. When he does, this will start the seven-year period of tribulation. The last half of this period is known as the Great Tribulation. At the midpoint of the seven-year tribulation period the Antichrist will set himself up as God and demand that people worship him. The situation on earth will get even worse with the seal, trumpet, and bowel judgments. At the Second Coming Christ will return to earth to establish His Kingdom.

The Davidic Covenant Fulfilled

The Davidic Covenant is the hope of a righteous King. As believers in Christ, we can rest on the promise of the Word of God that the Davidic Covenant will be fulfilled. There is only one person who has the right to the throne, and it is our responsibility to worship Him. Let us walk in obedience to the coming King and anticipate the day when His eternal Kingdom will be ushered in!

Discussion Questions

1. What does the Davidic Covenant guarantee?
2. Explain the importance of the Messianic Psalms. Give one specific example.
3. What role do the Old Testament prophets play in regard to the Davidic Covenant?
4. List three key words which describe the Davidic Covenant.
5. What are the three key elements of the Abrahamic Covenant? Why are each important?
6. What is the prophetic significance of the Davidic Covenant?
7. In light of the Davidic Covenant, what is the responsibility of Christians?

CHAPTER 8

Perfect Obedience - The New Covenant

No more shall every man teach his neighbor, and every man his brother, saying, "Know the LORD," for they all shall know Me, from the least of them to the greatest of them, says the LORD. For I will forgive their iniquity, and their sin I will remember no more.

- Jeremiah 31:34

MIKE HAD COME to trust in Jesus Christ as his Savior in a dirty, dim corner of a jail cell. The rusted bars that confined him could not contain Mike's joy now that he had found new life in Christ. He used his time behind bars to grow in his understanding of the Bible. He carefully studied Acts and the New Testament epistles. An image began to form in his mind of what the Church of Jesus Christ should look like.

After eight months of incarceration Mike was released, and he immediately started to visit local churches. This became a confusing time in the life of this new believer. Many of the doctrines being taught seemed out of place with the Word of God. Sin seemed to reign in the lives of the Christians he came into contact with. Very few people that he met in the local churches even seemed to have a desire to learn about Christ. Even more staggering was the amount of judgment that he faced from believers for his sins before salvation in Christ. Truthfully, Mike felt defeated.

It took time for Mike to realize that the Church of Jesus Christ is made up of imperfect men and women of faith. As he grew in his faith, he became more aware of his own sin and need for a better understanding of the doctrines of the Christian faith. Mike experienced the typical growing pains of a believer seeking to learn more about Christ.

Can you imagine a community of believers where obedience to Jesus Christ dominates the landscape? Is it possible to conceive of a community of people who know their Savior and His teachings? Will our minds allow us to comprehend a place and time where sin is completely unheard of? The promises of the New Covenant directly confront us with this future.

In chapter 5 we examined the chart shown in Figure 8.1. There we witnessed that the New Covenant amplifies the promise of spiritual blessing found within the Abrahamic Covenant. There will be a time of unprecedented and unequaled spiritual blessing over the face of the earth.

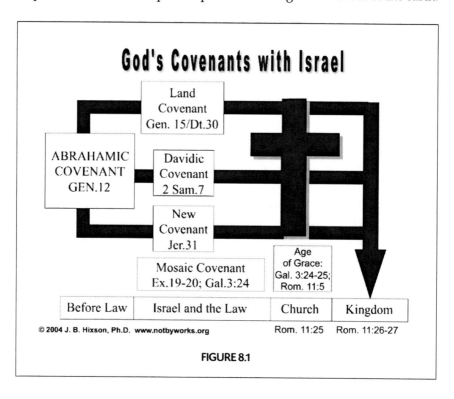

FIGURE 8.1

Four Dispensational Approaches

There are four dispensational approaches to the New Covenant. The tension exists because the plain normal literal-grammatical-historical reading of Jeremiah 31 and Ezekiel 36 reveals a different reality than what we see in the Church today. Despite this obvious truth, most Christians still believe the New Covenant is in force today. Four different views attempt to explain the differences between these texts and what the Church is experiencing in this present age.

The Classic Dispensational View

Originally, many dispensationalists held to the teaching that there are two new covenants. This view was held by Lewis Sperry Chafer, and at one time it was also held by John Walvoord.

One of the key components (one of the sine qua non) of dispensationalism is the distinction between God's program for Israel and His program for the Church. Because this point is so important, and recognizing the tension between the New Covenant passages in the New Testament and the plain obvious reading of the New Covenant in Jeremiah 31, many older dispensationalists suggested that the New Testament passages were referring to a different New Covenant. With this view, when Jesus mentioned the cup being the New Covenant of His blood, He is not said to be referring to the covenant of Jeremiah 31.

As much as we appreciate the men who have held to this position, there are some problems with this particular view. First, it creates a huge question as to when the New Covenant in Jeremiah 31 was actually made. If this position is correct, it leaves us no record of when this occurred. If Calvary was not the ratification of the covenant, then when was it? A second and larger problem is that it seems evident (especially in Hebrews) that the New Covenant referenced in the New Testament goes back to the one Jeremiah promised. Jeremiah contrasted the New Covenant with the Mosaic Covenant, and Hebrews also contrasts the New Covenant with the Mosaic Covenant. Therefore, this is not the best solution to solve the tension. This view is not widely held anymore.

Revised-Classic Dispensational View

The second view is the position that John Walvoord taught in the latter years of his ministry. This view teaches that there is only one New Covenant (which is for the nation of Israel) that was promised in the Old Testament, but the blessings spill over and impact the Church today. This is by far the most popular view. It leads many Christians to say that the New Covenant is partially fulfilled today, and that its blessings are here already for the Church, but it is not yet completely fulfilled. Unfortunately, this language has led people down the path to the third view (the progressive dispensational view).

The problem with the idea of a partial fulfillment is that there is absolutely nothing within the language of the New Covenant passages that indicates the Church participates in the blessings of the New Covenant today. This particular view appeals to a lot of people because it acknowledges the fact that textually the New Covenant belongs to Israel and the Kingdom, but yet it is a way of attempting to explain what the Spirit of God is doing today. The present work of the Spirit is assigned to the New Covenant. This view is like having your feet firmly planted in midair or attempting to straddle the fence.

It is much better to see what is happening today as purely foreshadowing. It is a separate event, totally distinct, that does foreshadow in part what will happen in complete later, but it is not tied to the New Covenant. The present ministry of the Holy Spirit is but a glimpse of what is to come, and is used to provoke Israel to jealousy (Rom. 11:11). This correlates directly to the purpose of the Church because it is a glimpse of what life will be like in the Kingdom. However, we do not have to tie the present work of the Spirit to the specifics of the New Covenant. It is better to understand that God is presently doing a unique and distinct work.

The Progressive Dispensational View

This controversial position teaches that there is one New Covenant, but with a two-fold fulfillment. There are real problems with this view. It teaches that there is a fulfillment for the Church and a fulfillment for Israel.

There are great inconsistencies within progressive dispensationalism. For example, progressive dispensationalists usually do not give much attention to the Land Covenant. The simple reason is that the Church could never fulfill any aspect of the Land Covenant because it would be nonsensical. As for the Davidic Covenant, it is considered to be already fulfilled in some ways, but not yet fulfilled in others. Christ is said to be upon the Davidic Throne today. This is a major weakness of this view. It equates the throne at the right hand of God with the Davidic Throne, but the Scripture is clear that the Davidic Throne is a literal, earthly throne, not a heavenly throne. The throne in heaven is not the Davidic Throne. Nevertheless, according to progressive dispensationalists, their entire hermeneutic is driven by the mantra *already, but not yet*. This leads them to the conclusion that the Davidic Covenant is already, but not yet completely fulfilled. Likewise, the New Covenant is also seen as already inaugurated, but not yet fully inaugurated.

It is worth noting that if you took this a step further and said that the Land Covenant also has a fulfillment today, then essentially you have amillennialism. To be sure, progressive dispensationalists still believe in a literal future kingdom on earth for Israel, and amillennialists do not. But other than this, they are almost identical positions. Progressive dispensationalism is essentially one step away from amillenialism. Those who hold to it believe Christ is upon the Davidic Throne today. They also believe the New Covenant is in force today, but they continue to hang on to the promise of a literal earthly kingdom for Israel. Why would two of the blessings of the Abrahamic Covenant already be fulfilled, but not the third?

Traditional Dispensational View

This view was held by John Nelson Darby. He is known for popularizing this view and systematizing dispensational theology.

The traditional dispensational view teaches that there is one New Covenant for Israel. Accordingly, the Church is unrelated to the New Covenant of Jeremiah 31. The Church comes between the ratification and inauguration of the New Covenant, but we are not the fulfillment of it. The Church and Israel are each independently connected to the Mediator of the New Covenant. We receive similar, but not identical blessings. The Church is a mystery; it is something previously undisclosed. This is a period of blindness for Israel, but someday at the end of the Church Age the Deliverer will come out of Zion and all Israel will be delivered (Rom. 11:26-27).

The traditional dispensational view is preferred. Christians need to recognize the differences between the plain descriptions of the New Covenant in the Old Testament compared to the lives of believers during the Church Age. The Church is not the fulfillment of the New Covenant. This awaits the coming Kingdom of Christ.

Examining the New Covenant

A central question surrounds the promise of the coming Kingdom of Christ. How will Israel ever be obedient enough to receive the Promised Land and all the other Kingdom promises? Even though the Abrahamic

Covenant is guaranteed and unconditional, the timing of the Kingdom coincides with Israel's obedience (Ps. 118:22-26; Isa. 32:15-17). We remember that Jesus specifically warned the leaders of Israel, "For I say to you, you shall see Me no more till you say, *'Blessed is He who comes in the name of the LORD!'"* (Matt. 23:39). The nation of Israel will not see their Messiah until they are living in obedience, returning to the land, and receiving Him as their King. If obedience is necessary, and yet the nation's history is marked by disobedience, how will God's covenant program ever be consummated?

Jeremiah 17:9 teaches, "The heart is deceitful above all things, and desperately wicked." It is for this very reason that Israel has been unable to fulfill the righteous requirements of the Law, despite the presence of the prophets, priests, kings, and judges. The only way the people of Israel will be able to walk in obedience to their Messiah is by the grace of God. The grace of God that brings individual salvation will also bring corporate deliverance of the people of Israel into the Kingdom. Complete obedience to Christ must be a work of God. The New Covenant is the key to this obedience.

It is essential to remember that the Word of God does not teach that obedience by Israel is necessary to receive the New Covenant because it is promised by God unconditionally. Instead, obedience is necessary regarding the timing of it. Because the history of Israel has been marked by continual disobedience to God, the question is how will God's covenant program ever be consummated? The guarantee of the Kingdom and the necessity of Israel's national obedience converge in the New Covenant of Jeremiah 31:31-34. The New Covenant answers the tension between the requirement of obedience to enter the land and the unconditionality of the promise. This covenant was *promised* in the Old Testament, but it will not be *fulfilled* until the arrival of the promised Messianic Kingdom.

Within Jeremiah 31 and Ezekiel 36-37 we witness powerful statements from God about the future obedience of the people of Israel:

- I will be the God of all the families of Israel, and they shall be My people (Jer. 31:1).
- I will put My law in their minds, and write it on their hearts; and I will be their God, and they shall be My people (Jer. 31:33).
- I will give you a new heart and put a new spirit within you; I will take the heart of stone out of your flesh and give you a heart of flesh. I will put My Spirit within you and cause you to walk in

My statutes, and you will keep My judgments and do them (Ezek. 36:26-27).
- I will put My Spirit in you, and you shall live, and I will place you in your own land. Then you shall know that I, the LORD, have spoken it and performed it (Ezek. 37:14).

The New Covenant teaches that God will be the one conducting the work within the people of Israel. He will put His Spirit within them. The people will become circumcised of heart, and the Spirit of God will be the source of their obedience to Christ (Deut. 30:6). We have already mentioned that the covenant program of God serves as the title deed to the land and as a guarantee of an heir to the throne of David. It also serves as a source of obedience for His people within the coming Kingdom of Christ. The source of obedience will be the Spirit of God within them. It will be the grace of God that enables and empowers His people to be righteous.

Certainly this will be a change in the role of the ministry of the Holy Spirit. Today, during the Church Age, the Spirit of God does not cause believers to directly obey Christ. If this were the case, every Christian would be living in perfect obedience. During this present dispensation, the sanctification process is a cooperative effort between our yielding to the Holy Spirit and the work of the Spirit in our lives. Obedience to Christ is not automatic and is not guaranteed. Believers should lead godly, righteous lives. We have the capacity to obey Christ because of the indwelling of the Spirit, but we continue to have a choice. Believers have the ability to quench the Spirit, grieve the Spirit, and to not walk in the Spirit (1 Thess. 5:19; Eph. 4:30; Gal. 5:16, 25).

Those who experience the benefit of the New Covenant will be those who survive the Tribulation in bodily form, believe the gospel, and enter into the Kingdom in their physical bodies. Even though they will have physical bodies they will not be able to sin. It should be self-evident that the redeemed with glorified bodies in the Kingdom will not sin because the old nature will no longer be present within them.

The New Covenant is not in effect at this time. After the Second Coming of Christ the covenant community (Jews and Gentiles alike) will receive the pouring out of the Spirit of God. These believers will obey Christ and will not fall into sin. The Spirit of God will be the source of obedience to the Lord. This is all for the glory of God. God will do the work in the lives of these believers and bring it all to completion.

Aspects of the New Covenant in the Old Testament

The focal passage of the New Covenant is Jeremiah 31:31-34. The backdrop of Jeremiah places us into the late seventh century B.C. (c. 605). It was written amidst a period of spiritual and moral decay among the people of Israel. The lack of response to Jeremiah's ministry has famously led to his characterization as the weeping prophet. The men and women of Israel did not turn back from their sin. Jeremiah contains the message of God's judgment on disobedience and Israel's future blessing. It is within this context that God told the nation of Israel that in spite of how bad things had become, as long as there is a sun, a moon, and stars in the heavens, He would be true to the covenant He made with Abraham. God will one day usher in a time of spiritual blessing.

Jeremiah 31:31 reveals, "Behold, the days are coming, says the LORD, when I will make a new covenant with the house of Israel and with the house of Judah." *This teaches us that this is a future covenant.* Notice the words, "I will make a new covenant." In Genesis 12, God *made* a covenant with Abraham that guarantees certain blessings. In Deuteronomy 30, God *made* a covenant with Israel that guarantees certain land blessings. In 2 Samuel 7, God *made* a covenant with Israel that guarantees certain seed blessings. But when we come to Jeremiah 31, we see that God did not *make* a covenant. *Instead, He promised to make a covenant.*

This leads us to an important question. If the New Covenant was only promised in Jeremiah 31, then when was it made? The New Covenant was made at Calvary. The night before He died our Savior said, "For this is My blood of the new covenant, which is shed for many for the remission of sins" (Matt. 26:28; also see Mark 14:24-25; Luke 22:17-20). This was the ratification of the New Covenant, but it has yet to be inaugurated.

A second point to be made in Jeremiah 31:31 is that the Scripture teaches us it is a Jewish covenant. Notice again the text reveals, "I will make a new covenant with the house of Israel and with the house of Judah." Covenants are legally binding agreements with specified parties involved. The parties to the New Covenant, like the parties to the other covenants in God's program, will be the nation of Israel and Yahweh.

The teaching in Jeremiah continues, "Not according to the covenant that I made with their fathers in the day that I took them by the hand to lead them out of the land of Egypt, My covenant which they broke, though I was a husband to them, says the LORD" (Jer. 31:32). This informs us that this is a *different covenant* than the Mosaic Covenant. It is a perfect contrast between the Mosaic Covenant and the New Covenant. The Mosaic Covenant was intended to be a rule of law, which if followed, would bring about obedience and righteousness. It was a conditional covenant that failed. This is the reason the Apostle Paul testified, "For Christ is the end of the law for righteousness to everyone who believes" (Rom. 10:4). Jesus Himself declared, "Do not think that I came to destroy the Law or the Prophets. I did not come to destroy but to fulfill" (Matt. 5:17). The New Covenant is a replacement of the failed Mosaic Covenant. Because this covenant replaces the Mosaic Covenant, its application must of necessity be limited to the same people with whom the original Mosaic Covenant had been made. Ezekiel 36:28 indicates that when this spiritual heart transplant takes place, Israel will be dwelling in the land. Thus, the promise of the New Covenant is tied to Israel's future kingdom blessings.

The Jews had a zeal for the Law, but they did not attain righteousness. Under the New Covenant, the righteousness that all of God's people have sought will be fulfilled only by the inner working of God through the indwelt Holy Spirit. It is obvious that this has not happened yet. The incorrect notion that the New Covenant is now in effect tends to denigrate the work of God. It testifies that He is presently doing this work within us, when we know as believers how imperfectly we live out the Christian faith.

Just as the Mosaic Covenant failed, the Church Age has also failed. Certainly, there have been pockets of revival and great heroes of the faith throughout the last 2,000 years. The goal for Church Age believers continues to be that we walk by faith and not by sight. We should trust the Lord daily, not get ahead of His will, not fall behind His will, seek to grow in our knowledge of Him, and seek to be conformed to His image by the renewing of our minds. We do this to varying levels of success and failure. Sometimes it is three steps forward and two steps back. But as a whole (thinking of the entire Body of Christ from Acts 2 until today) we are no better than the men and women of Israel in the Old Testament. The Church Age, in terms of righteous living by believers, is more akin to the Mosaic Covenant than it is a description of the New Covenant. The New Covenant is a replacement of the failed Mosaic Covenant. What the Law could not do, the New Covenant will accomplish in the Kingdom.

The New Covenant is also a spiritual covenant. This is where some of the confusion enters in for believers today. It is assumed by many that the present work of the Spirit of God in the lives of believers is the fulfillment (or partial fulfillment) of the New Covenant.

There are two basic reasons why Christians tend to believe the New Covenant is in force today. The first is directly related to the New Testament references to the New Covenant. In the upper room Jesus specifically referred to it (Matt. 26:28). Paul directly mentioned it in his teaching on the Lord's Supper (1 Cor. 11:25). The New Covenant is also referenced in Hebrews. The presence of these references to the New Covenant within the New Testament often gives believers the impression that the New Covenant must be in effect today. But these sparse and scattered references within the New Testament serve another purpose, and most certainly do not teach that the New Covenant is in effect in this present age.

The second reason believers assume the New Covenant is in force today is because of the similarity between the unique ministry of the Holy Spirit in the Church Age and the unique ministry of the Holy Spirit in the Kingdom. Let us remember that similarity does not equal identity. There are aspects of the present ministry of the Holy Spirit that are similar to the New Covenant, but they are clearly not the same.

Consider the events of Acts 2. Peter testified to the crowd at Jerusalem:

> But this is what was spoken by the prophet Joel: *"And it shall come to pass in the last days, says God, that I will pour out of My Spirit on all flesh; your sons and your daughters shall prophesy, your young men shall see visions, your old men shall dream dreams. And on My menservants and on My maidservants I will pour out My Spirit in those days; and they shall prophesy. I will show wonders in heaven above and signs in the earth beneath: Blood and fire and vapor of smoke. The sun shall be turned into darkness, and the moon into blood, before the coming of the great and awesome day of the LORD. And it shall come to pass that whoever calls on the name of the LORD shall be saved"* (Acts 2:16-21).

The prophetic events quoted by Peter, from Joel 2:28-32, clearly did not happen on the day of Pentecost. The events were similar, but not the same. There were no wonders in heaven. The sun was not turned into darkness. Peter was not testifying that the events on the day of Pentecost were the fulfillment of Joel 2. Instead, Peter was telling the crowd at Jerusalem, "Do not be surprised that God is moving in this way. Do not be surprised that the Spirit of God is being given because look at the promise from Joel that God will yet one day accomplish. This is not the fulfillment of it, but the teaching of Joel instructs us that this type of ministry of the Holy Spirit is possible."

Christians need to recognize that the ministry of the Holy Spirit in this present age is distinct from the ministry of the Holy Spirit in the Kingdom. The greatest similarity is the indwelling of the Spirit of God, but the promises of Joel will yet one day be fulfilled when, "it shall come to pass afterward that I will pour out My Spirit on all flesh; your sons and your daughters shall prophesy, your old men shall dream dreams, your young men shall see visions" (Joel 2:28).

The teaching in Jeremiah continues:

> But this is the covenant that I will make with the house of Israel after those days, says the LORD: I will put My law in their minds, and write it on their hearts; and I will be their God, and they shall be My people. No more shall every man teach his neighbor, and every man his brother, saying, "Know the LORD," for they all shall know Me, from the least of them to the greatest of them, says the LORD. For I will forgive their iniquity, and their sin I will remember no more (Jer. 31:33-34).

When God fulfills this covenant in the Kingdom, He will put His law in the minds of believers. Under the New Covenant they will have the desire and the ability to obey. This will clearly involve the work of the Holy Spirit.

This text from Jeremiah also informs us that the New Covenant is a revelatory covenant. There will be no need for witnessing about Christ because knowledge of the Messiah will be universal. In the truest sense, it will be an unveiling of God in perfect form. When Christ returns the people will all know of Him, from the least to the greatest. God will be able to be known, through His Son, to everybody at that time.

Verse 34 of Jeremiah 31 reveals that the New Covenant is an atoning covenant. That is, once its promises are fulfilled, it will lead to the forgiveness of sins for the recipients. Atonement is another reason that some people confuse the present age with the New Covenant. But the reality is, the central supreme event in all of human history that is necessary to ultimately ratify God's entire covenant program is also the central supreme event in human history that is necessary to redeem every individual being, from Adam to the end of the age. Christ died for sins past, present, and future. A great amount of theological truth is wrapped up in Calvary. Just because Calvary was necessary for the covenant program of God to come into being does not mean that the Church is the result of the covenant program of God. We (the Church) share in the supreme sacrifice of the New Covenant today because it was one event. The blood of Christ spilled on the Cross had a twofold purpose. The shed blood of Jesus ratified the New Covenant and made it possible to put into place at a later time. The shed blood of Christ also has an even greater purpose, which is to make redemption possible for every human being, from Adam forward.

There are several other Old Testament texts that complement the teaching on the New Covenant. Ezekiel 36:26-27 reveals, "I will give you a new heart and put a new spirit within you; I will take the heart of stone out of your flesh and give you a heart of flesh. I will put My Spirit within you and cause you to walk in My statutes, and you will keep My judgments and do them." Confusion, once more, enters the picture when believers assume this is describing the present ministry of the Holy Spirit within the Church. Instead, it should be understood that this is again describing the fulfillment of the New Covenant within the Kingdom. God will put His Spirit within believers, but only at that time will He cause His people to walk in His statutes. Once more, it should be self-evident that today the Spirit of God is not causing us to walk perfectly in His statutes.

Isaiah instructs, "Until the Spirit is poured upon us from on high, and the wilderness becomes a fruitful field, and the fruitful field is counted as a forest" (Isa. 32:15). Notice again the teaching of the future pouring out of the Spirit of God. Isaiah also records, "For I will pour water on him who is thirsty, and floods on the dry ground; I will pour My Spirit on your descendants, and My blessing on your offspring; they will spring up among the grass like willows by the watercourses" (Isa. 44:3-4). Remember, the New Covenant focuses on the blessing aspect of the Abrahamic Covenant. It will be a spiritual blessing that will be brought about by the Spirit of God.

Zechariah, likewise, reminds us of this future outpouring of the Spirit of God, "And I will pour on the house of David and on the inhabitants of Jerusalem the Spirit of grace and supplication; then they will look on Me whom they pierced" (Zech. 12:10). This text makes it clear that every Jew who turns to the Lord and enters the Kingdom will receive the Spirit of God.

The New Covenant community will be made up of believers. During the Millennium, there will eventually be a population on earth who will not be participating in the New Covenant community because they will not be saved. As unbelievers, the blessings of the New Covenant will not apply to them.

Analysis of the New Covenant in the New Testament

With an understanding of the New Covenant in its Old Testament context, what are we to make of the New Testament treatment of the New Covenant? How did the New Testament writers understand the New Covenant? Did they understand it in the same eschatological sense for Israel that a simple plain reading of the Old Testament passages suggests? Let us examine the New Covenant passages in the New Testament.

As mentioned, the New Covenant was ratified (or made) at Calvary when Christ was crucified. The New Testament presents Christ as the Mediator of the New Covenant. Yet, the ratification of a covenant does not mean that its blessings are in force. The mere ratification of a covenant does not mean that it is being fulfilled. There is a difference between the *ratification* of a covenant and the *fulfillment* of a covenant. A case in point would be the Abrahamic Covenant. God ratified the covenant with Abraham in Genesis 15, but He clearly has not fulfilled the specific land elements of that covenant yet.

Note that the institution of the Lord's Supper took place at a time prior to the establishment of the Church, and in a context with eschatological overtones. The Passover meal took place one day after Jesus had given His famous Olivet Discourse, in which He explained the details and circumstances surrounding the coming Messianic Kingdom.

This touches on another related New Testament teaching concerning the New Covenant. As Christians observe the Lord's Supper, the focus is typically on what Christ did for us at Calvary. An examination of the New Testament reveals that this should only be a part of the focus. The Gospels and the writings of Paul also focus on observing the Lord's Supper *until He comes* (Matt. 26:28-29; Mark 14:24-25; Luke 22:17-20; 1 Cor. 11:23-26). Mark instructs, "And He said to them, 'This is My blood of the new covenant, which is shed for many. Assuredly, I say to you, I will no longer drink of the fruit of the vine until that day when I drink it new in the kingdom of God'" (Mark 14:24-25). Our observance of the Lord's Supper is to be a time of remembrance as well as a time of *looking forward* to the return of Christ. It should be a time when Christians also look forward to the fulfillment of the New Covenant because the Lord's Supper demonstrates that it has been ratified, but will be fulfilled when Christ returns.

The New Covenant is certainly anticipated in Paul's instruction about the Lord's Supper in 1 Corinthians 11:25-26. Paul's teaching has a clear eschatological context. Believers are taught to observe the Lord's Supper, "till He comes" (1 Cor. 11:26). The Church, like Israel, looks forward to the blessings of the coming Kingdom (1 Cor. 11:25). In the context, Paul is giving instruction about how the memorial supper that Jesus commanded the disciples to observe is to be handled. He comments that by drinking the cup, which represents Christ's blood, the Church proclaims His death, "till He comes." Again, we notice the eschatological context. Paul says that by drinking the cup as part of the memorial meal, the Church also looks forward to the return of the Lord. Therefore, the Lord's Supper, far from being a celebration of the *fulfillment* of the New Covenant, is a celebration of the *promised fulfillment* of the New Covenant! The Lord's Supper looks both forward and backward. The bread looks back to His body representing His death. The cup, in that it symbolizes His blood, looks forward to the realization of New Covenant blessings that will come because of the blood of the New Covenant.

A great deal of confusion surrounds the book of Hebrews and its references to the New Covenant. Hebrews 9:15 is an example of this. It teaches, "And for this reason He is the Mediator of the new covenant, by means of death, for the redemption of the transgressions under the first covenant, that those who are called may receive the promise of the eternal inheritance" (Heb. 9:15). This text is easy to clear up if we remind ourselves that Hebrews has one overarching purpose: to remind the Jewish Christians in the late 60's A.D. that to abandon the Messiah (Jesus) who saved them is to go back to an inferior way of life. Jesus is far superior to anything and everything that Judaism had to offer in the first century. The author was simply making this case by reminding them that Jesus is the Mediator of the New Covenant. It does not mean that the New Covenant is in force, it simply means that Jesus is the Mediator of the New Covenant. That makes Him superior to first century Judaism. The Mediator of the New Covenant had come, and the supreme sacrifice had been given. Why would they want to turn back in their faith?

Rightly dividing the book of Hebrews requires that we understand that the entire epistle is about the world to come. It will be better because there will be a better King. Believers could know that even though they may go through physical sacrifices (maybe even martyred for their faith) they should continue to hold to their faith in Christ. They should remain steadfast in their faith without wavering because a better day is coming to the world. Consider a few examples:

- "For He has not put *the world to come, of which we speak,* in subjection to angels" (Heb. 2:5, emphasis added).
- Hebrews 10:11-17 speaks of the perfection (completion) of God's people. The emphasis of this passage is on the finality of Christ's work that will *perfect* believers *in the future Kingdom.* This is in keeping with the entire covenant program of God wherein the New Covenant blessings guarantee the obedience required to receive the land and seed blessings. Note the eschatological context in verse 13.
- Hebrews 12:18-29 reveals that the New Covenant blessings of the Kingdom have not yet been received, but we can look forward to them. Note the eschatological context, especially in verses 27-29.

The writer of Hebrews wrote about the world to come, not this present age. Therefore, it is understandable that the author would frequently refer to the New Covenant. The message of Hebrews is, "Hold on to Christ because a better day is coming."

Romans 11:26-27 teaches that the blessings of the New Covenant will be received in conjunction with the Second Coming and the establishment of the Messianic Kingdom. Note the reference to Jeremiah 31:33-34. This passage (Rom. 11:26-27) is often ignored in discussions of the relationship between the Church and the New Covenant, but it settles the issue. The entire argument lives or dies on this passage. Because, here, the New Covenant passage of Jeremiah 31 is directly quoted and connected unambiguously to the Second Coming.

The Apostle Paul referred to the New Covenant in 2 Corinthians 3 and explained that believers today are experiencing a new covenant-like ministry that is characterized by a dependence on the Holy Spirit (2 Cor. 3:6). Admittedly, this is a passage that needs careful examination. In context, Paul is defending the nature of his ministry, which emphasized grace, against the ministry of his legalistic accusers who emphasized law. Paul is *not* contrasting the Age of Grace with the Age of Law. He is contrasting ministry that is dependent on the Spirit with ministry that is dependent on the Law. The Apostle instructed, "And we have such trust through Christ toward God. Not that we are sufficient of ourselves to think of anything as being from ourselves, but our sufficiency is from God, who also made us sufficient as ministers of the new covenant, not of the letter but of the Spirit; for the letter kills, but the Spirit gives life" (2 Cor. 3:4-6). Paul contrasted a ministry that is based on the

Law versus a ministry that is based on the Spirit of God, which will characterize the New Covenant Age. Remember, the present ministry of the Spirit foreshadows the future ministry of the Holy Spirit under the New Covenant. So it can be correctly stated that the present ministry of believers is also based on the Spirit, in contrast with the Law.

Like Israel in the future Kingdom, the Church today is experiencing a spiritual administration that is completely unlike the administration that was characterized by the Mosaic Law. We are ministers of a ministry that is new covenant-like (note the anarthrous construction, not *the* New Covenant) in the sense that our ministry is not based on self-effort, but spiritual enablement. It is critical to note that Paul does not say we are *fulfillers* of the New Covenant. Nor does Paul say that the New Covenant is being fulfilled in us. Rather, we are servants of the New Covenant in that we demonstrate or foreshadow what life will be like when the whole world is under an administration characterized by dependence on the Spirit.

Clearly the Church is not experiencing the full effects of the New Covenant as described by Jeremiah. After all, believers still sin and the New Covenant promises that the indwelling Spirit will lead to righteousness and that sin will be judged swiftly and directly (cf. Ezek. 36:26-27; Isa. 32:15-16; 65:20). To the extent that this is obviously not happening today, it hardly seems appropriate to claim that the New Covenant promises are in effect. Furthermore, the New Covenant promises that no one will need a teacher (Jer. 31:34). If the New Covenant is being fulfilled today, how does one reconcile Jesus' Great Commission to go and teach? The even larger question that must be answered is, "If the New Covenant is being partially fulfilled today, in what sense is today any different from the Old Testament when, under the Mosaic Law, believers were partially obedient?" The New Covenant cannot be partially in effect today because, by definition, this covenant provides complete and total obedience where partial obedience already exists!

It is often argued that in order to be a minister of the New Covenant, believers must be currently participating in it. However, when the Apostle Paul states that we are ministers of the New Covenant, it is not necessary to conclude that this means the New Covenant is in place today. The same Christ that we serve today will one day take the throne in the Kingdom. The same Spirit that indwells us will also guarantee complete obedience within believers in the Kingdom. Since we share the

Mediator of the New Covenant, it is true that we are also ministers of the New Covenant. This does not mean that we are living in the fulfillment of the New Covenant today. Even though believers today may be ministers of this covenant, the specific promises of the New Covenant, as outlined by Jeremiah, are not being fulfilled today.

Jesus Christ is the Mediator of the New Covenant (Heb. 8:7-13; 9:15; 12:24). He is a priest according to the order of Melchizedek, but is not functioning in that role at the present time (Heb. 2:5-9; 7:1-28; 10:12-13). The author of Hebrews argues that just as the Mosaic Covenant and Aaronic priesthood are connected, so too are the New Covenant and the Melchizedekian priesthood. When there is a change in the priesthood, there must also be a change in the Law (or covenant; Heb. 7:12). When the New Covenant and the Melchizedekian priesthood begin to function, there will be no going back to the Mosaic and Aaronic era. *But notice that the writer of Hebrews does not teach that Jesus is currently functioning as the Melchizedekian High Priest. He simply states that his readers have such a High Priest (Heb. 8:1).* The person of the New Covenant (the Melchizedekian High Priest) has come, and one day at the appointed time He will take on that role and fulfill the New Covenant.

Remember the author's argument. Throughout the letter, he is trying to demonstrate the superiority of Christ to the old Mosaic Law. So naturally, he is going to highlight the fact that Jesus is the one who will fulfill the New Covenant blessings, which will one day accomplish everything that the Mosaic Covenant could not. Jesus is the Melchizedekian High Priest, but He is not functioning in the Melchizedekian role yet. The Melchizedekian priesthood relates to Israel. Christ's priestly ministry today relates to the Church. In fact, Hebrews 8:1 teaches, "We have such a high priest who is seated at the right hand of the throne of the Majesty in the heavens." What is Christ doing there? He is waiting for all things to be put under subjection to Him when He returns to take the Davidic Throne (Heb. 2:5-9; 10:12-13). To assume that He is presently functioning as the Melchizedekian High Priest is tantamount to putting Him upon the Davidic Throne now because all the covenants are interconnected.

The Old Testament saints came to the God of the Davidic Covenant, but this did not mean that the Davidic Covenant was being fulfilled at that time. In the same manner, to come to Jesus as the Mediator of the New Covenant does not demand that the covenant is presently being fulfilled.

A Better Covenant

The New Covenant was ratified at the death of Christ. The Word of God never testifies that it is being fulfilled today. With the exception of 2 Corinthians 3:6, the New Covenant is always mentioned in an eschatological context because it will be fulfilled at the Second Coming of Christ. Recognize God's sovereignty when it comes to His covenant plan. Remember that things are going to be a lot better!

Discussion Questions

1. What are the four dispensational approaches to the New Covenant?
2. Explain which of the four dispensational approaches is preferred. Why is it the best approach?
3. Who will cause Israel to be obedient to God and, thereby, cause the New Covenant to be consummated?
4. Compare the role of the Holy Spirit in the New Covenant to His role in the Church Age.
5. What is the focal passage of the New Covenant? How can its teaching be summarized?
6. How did the New Testament writers understand the New Covenant?
7. When will the New Covenant blessings be fulfilled? What is the proof text for this?
8. Describe the relationship that Christians have to the New Covenant.

CHAPTER 9

The Bride of Christ - The Church

Simon Peter answered and said, "You are the Christ, the Son of the living God." Jesus answered and said to him, "Blessed are you, Simon Bar-Jonah, for flesh and blood has not revealed this to you, but My Father who is in heaven. And I also say to you that you are Peter, and on this rock I will build My church, and the gates of Hades shall not prevail against it."

- Matthew 16:16-18

CIVILIZATION AFTER CIVILIZATION has climbed the ladder of knowledge and accomplishment to create the marvels of the modern world. Students of history recognize the different rungs of progress that have brought us to the level of development witnessed in the world today. An indispensable rung of this historical ladder includes the advancements of the Roman Empire.

The accomplishments of the Roman Empire forever changed the landscape of Western civilization. The vast empire needed an effective system of maintaining peace and control. An effective solution was developed. An extensive and well-built road system was created to assist with communication and the movement of troops. Widespread trade became the financial backbone of the empire. Aqueducts were built to bring water to farmland and cities. The discovery of concrete led to great advances in both architecture and the construction of buildings. Dams, bridges, and great amphitheaters were built. The presence of peace in the land gave writers the freedom to create literary masterpieces. It truly was a remarkable time in which to live.

The collapse of the Roman Empire ushered in the Dark Ages. Without the cohesiveness of the Roman Empire, the quality of life for people started to decline. The road systems and aqueducts began to decay. Shipping routes were no longer safe. Wars undermined the stability and peace. Scholars and artists no longer had the continued safety and freedom to pursue their endeavors. The Dark Ages left Western civilization longing for something better.

The dawn of the Renaissance brought an end to roughly 1,000 years of darkness. The return of learning brought about many new discoveries. New continents were identified by explorers. Science and art once again took center stage. The invention of the printing press led to the distribution of knowledge, and trade returned to being the backbone of the nations. Great architecture and literature flourished once more. The rebirth of learning had taken place.

The Church Age

History is full of surprises. The end of an age is the dawn of another. The last two thousand years have been a dark time for the nation of Israel, but a future time of restoration and revival is promised in God's Word. Right now the age we find ourselves living under is the Church Age. The Church Age is a time when God is doing something new on the earth. The birth of the Church is a new work, that was previously undisclosed. Paul labeled it, "this mystery among the Gentiles: which is Christ in you, the hope of glory" (Col. 1:27). This is a special dispensation in which Israel is set aside temporarily, not permanently. It is a delay in the fulfillment of the Kingdom promises, but not a forfeiture of them. During this delay we are living in the Church Age, which is an age of grace. At some point in the future the Church Age will end, and we will see the fulfillment of the Kingdom promises. God has a distinct plan for both Israel and the Church.

The Church Anticipated

As we think about the program of the Church, we see a glimpse of this time period allowed for in the Old Testament. It was never directly mentioned; it was never spelled out. But God anticipated that there would be this parenthesis, which is demonstrated in His prophecy to Daniel.

Daniel's ministry spanned a period of approximately seventy years, covering the entire time of the Babylonian exile (c. 605-536 B.C.). He prophesied in a time when Jerusalem and the Temple lay in ruins. He was living in the postexilic community. The book of Daniel emphasizes the sovereignty of God in working out His covenant program with Israel. Chapters 1-6 demonstrate God's sovereignty at work in the past. Chapters 7-12 show God's sovereignty at work in the future, in particular as it relates to that period of time Jesus would later call, "the times of the Gentiles" in Luke 21:24. There would come a time when the Gentiles would be on center stage in God's program. Through Daniel, God revealed a period of Gentile domination of Israel that would include four great world powers: Babylon, Medo-Persia, Greece, and Rome.

A critical section of prophecy is the Seventy Weeks of Daniel. Daniel 9 is the single, most significant passage in the Bible, when it comes to understanding biblical prophecy. Verse 1 gives us the time context: 538 B.C. Jeremiah had promised seventy years of captivity (Jer. 25:11-13). It should be noted that verse 2 reveals that Daniel understood Jeremiah's prophecy of seventy years literally; he did not attempt to spiritualize it. When the Word of God uses the term *years* in a prophetic context, the precedent is to always take that literally.

Jeremiah revealed that God would restore His people to their land when they prayed to Him wholeheartedly (Jer. 29:12-14). This revelation prompted Daniel to pray (Dan. 9:3). Daniel realized that the prophecy of seventy years from Jeremiah was coming to completion. Daniel poured out his heart to the Lord, requesting that God's people be allowed to return to their land (Dan. 9:3-19). In a remarkable turn of events, the Lord used His angel, Gabriel, to respond to Daniel's prayer (Dan. 9:20-23).

Within verses 24-27 of Daniel 9, God revealed a 490-year timetable for His future plan for Israel (Daniel's Seventy Weeks). Daniel was told, "Seventy weeks are determined for your people and for your holy city" (Dan. 9:24). God was revealing a new phase in His program. The word *week* in the Hebrew language refers to the *number seven*. Therefore, the text is literally referring to seventy periods of seven. The context of Daniel 9 indicates that these periods of seven must be periods of seven years. The result is that Daniel was being told of seventy periods of seven years that would affect the nation of Israel. This becomes a total of 490 years.

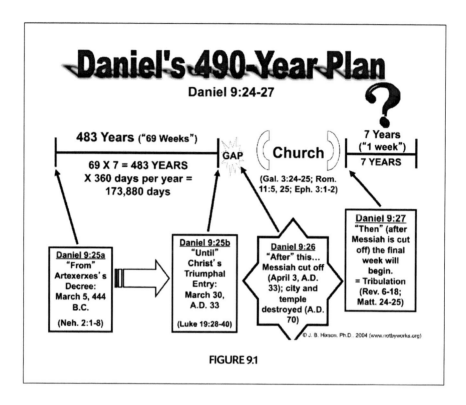

FIGURE 9.1

Pay close attention to the wording of verse 25, "Know therefore and understand, that from the going forth of the command to restore and build Jerusalem until Messiah the Prince, there shall be seven weeks and sixty-two weeks; the street shall be built again, and the wall, even in troublesome times." It is important to recognize the time markers in this passage. The beginning point would be *from* the decree to restore and rebuild Jerusalem. Historically, we know that Artaxerxes gave the decree on March 5, 444 B.C. (Neh. 2:1-8).[1]

The next marker of time in verse 25 is the word *until*. This text is revealing that from point A to point B there would be a total of sixty-nine weeks. The combination of seven and sixty-two equals sixty-nine weeks. The ending point is when Messiah the Prince has come. It is absolutely essential to understand that from point A until point B there would be 69 weeks, or 483 years.

The prophecy continues, "And after the sixty-two weeks Messiah shall be cut off, but not for Himself; and the people of the prince who is to come shall destroy the city and the sanctuary. The end of it shall be with a flood, and till the end of the war desolations are determined" (Dan. 9:26). It was revealed that after this initial period of 483 years some significant events would occur. The Messiah would be cut off, which is a reference to the crucifixion of Christ that took place on April 3, 33 A.D. The city of Jerusalem and the Temple would be destroyed, which historically took place in A.D. 70. Counting forward from March 5, 444 B.C. (the most widely accepted historical date for Artaxerxes' decree) a period of 173,880 days (which is 360 days in a Jewish year multiplied by 69 years) you arrive at March 30, 33 A.D. This happens to be the day of Christ's triumphal entry. Clearly the time of Christ fulfills the first 483 years of this promise of Daniel.[2]

Verse 27 continues, "Then he shall confirm a covenant with many for one week; but in the middle of the week He shall bring an end to sacrifice and offering. And on the wing of abominations shall be one who makes desolate, even until the consummation, which is determined, is poured out on the desolate." Note that in the sequence marked out in the prophecy, this is following the destruction of the Temple (notice the time marker *then*). There will be another seven-year period, which will begin with the signing of the peace treaty by the Antichrist. When the Antichrist signs the peace treaty confirming the covenant with Israel, the clock will start ticking on the final seven-year period. This is referred to as: the Tribulation, the Seventieth Week of Daniel, the Great Day of the Lord's Wrath, and the time of Jacob's trouble (Jer. 30:7). It is variously referred to throughout Scripture as a unique time. There is more information about these seven years than just about everything else in God's prophetic plan. All of Revelation 6-18 deals with this seven-year period.

This prophecy in Daniel, without even considering any New Testament references, indicates that Daniel foresaw a gap of time between the sixty-ninth and seventieth week. For some reason, clearly unknown to the original recipients of Daniel's prophecy, God chose to mark out the seventy weeks in three segments. The text gives no indication of a gap between the sixty-two weeks and the seven weeks. There is nothing in the wording that separates them. There is nothing in the wording that is described as taking place between the sixty-two weeks and the seven weeks, which tells us there is no gap. They are to be understood as taking place sequentially. After the initial sixty-nine weeks (sixty-two plus seven) there is a final week, or a seven-year segment. Between the initial sixty-nine weeks and the seventieth week the text indicates certain events would take place. Because this gap is already there (allowed for in Daniel), as

God began to unveil more of His plan in the New Testament, He revealed more information that would be included within this gap of time. This information relates directly to the Church.

The Church is a new program, a new work that God is doing with unique purposes, and a unique role to play. In the truest sense of the word, the Church Age is a parenthesis. This language has been frequently maligned by opponents of dispensationalism because they do not like the idea of this present age being relegated to a parenthesis. It is often misunderstood and thought that dispensationalism is teaching that the Church Age is an afterthought, but a parenthesis is not in any way an afterthought. It does not put an end to God's program for Israel, as revealed through Daniel, it simply interrupts it. The Church is an interruption in God's plan for Israel, not a replacement of it. In grammar, what is in a parenthesis can be more important than what is the main clause of the sentence. It indicates important additional information that is not the main subject of the sentence. Looking at it in a purely grammatical sense, the Church fits into the middle of the sentence, but it is not the end of the sentence. There is more to come. The sentence, to continue to use the grammatical metaphor, is God's plan for Israel. That plan includes 490 years, and only 483 of those years have occurred. There are seven more years yet to come.

This creates a problem for many interpreters of the Bible. The first 483 years were fulfilled literally. The decree took place on March 5, 444 B.C. and you can count forward 483 years on an actual calendar. What should be done with the last seven years that are yet to be fulfilled? Covenant theologians allegorize them, but this is inconsistent with the literal fulfillment of the first 483 years. Another approach, sometimes taken, is to attempt to force the final seven-year period into the historical record of the first century. This simply does not do justice to the text of Scripture. Others choose to simply ignore the last seven years. But to extend the metaphor even further, it is like a dangling participle. It leaves something missing in the sentence. Just as you would not end a sentence without a punctuation mark, this leaves the program of God incomplete. Sixty-nine weeks have already happened in the past. The present Church Age is a parenthesis, and there will be a future for national Israel when God completes the program. This is something covenant theologians must wrestle with.

It is significant that God predicted the Messiah would come 483 years after the decree to rebuild the city of Jerusalem. The Messiah would be cut off, and then the Temple would be destroyed. The literal fulfillment of these events should instill great confidence that the rest of the prophecy will one day be fulfilled when the Antichrist signs a covenant to confirm peace with Israel for a seven-year period.

The Concern of the Church Age

We have spent most of our time in the Old Testament looking at the covenants and laying the foundation for God's Kingdom program. As we shift gears, we move into the New Testament, which gives us all the information that we have about the Church Age. Everything we know about the Church comes from the New Testament. The Old Testament does not teach us about the Church, even though the Church Age is allowed for in Daniel 9. We need to clarify the distinction between God's purpose for Israel and His purpose for the Church.

God's Purpose for Israel

God's purpose for Israel was to be a witness to the unity of Yahweh in the midst of universal idolatry and paganism (Deut. 6:4; Isa. 43:10-12). The Shema (the basic confession of faith in Judaism) teaches, "Hear, O Israel: The LORD our God, the LORD is one!" (Deut. 6:4). The message that God wanted Israel to proclaim to the pagan nations was that their multiplicity of gods (their pagan gods) was not the real God. There is only one real and true God, the God of the Jews. Israel was to be a witness to the unity of God to the nations.

Another purpose of Israel was to be an example to the nations of the benefits of serving Yahweh (Deut. 33:26-29). Consider the blessings of Deuteronomy 30-33, those who followed God were blessed. God wanted Israel to show the pagan nations the benefits of following God's Word.

Another interesting purpose of Israel was to receive and record God's revelation (the Scriptures). We see this in Deuteronomy 4:5-8 and Romans 3:1-2. Almost the entire Bible was written by the hand of a Jew. God used His chosen nation to record the written revelation.

God also used the nation of Israel to produce a Savior (Gen. 3:15; 12:3; 22:18; Isa. 7:14; 9:6; Rom. 1:1-6). The Lord Jesus Himself testified, "For salvation is of the Jews" (John 4:22). We know the ultimate seed of Israel is Jesus, who provides salvation for mankind.

God's Purpose for the Church

We can contrast this directly with five purposes for the Church Age from the New Testament. First, according to Acts 15:14, God is calling out a people for His name (cf. Acts 11:26). The disciples were first called Christians (people who belonged to Christ) at Antioch. James, speaking before the Jerusalem council, testified, "Simon has declared how God at the first visited the Gentiles to take out of them a people for His name" (Acts 15:14).

A second purpose of the Church is to showcase the exceeding riches of God's grace and mercy (Eph. 2:7; Rom. 11:11-15, 31). It cannot be emphasized enough that the Church Age, the present age, is intended to be a microcosm of what life will be like in the glorious Kingdom of Christ. To whatever extent that we are following Christ, living for Him, walking in the Spirit, and honoring God, we are showcasing the exceeding riches of God's grace and mercy. This is not to say that God has not been functioning first, and foremost, as a God of grace throughout human history because He certainly has. Yahweh was clearly a God of grace in the Old Testament. If God had been primarily a God of retribution, He would have obliterated Israel from His plan. The very fact that God is still keeping His unconditional covenant with Israel demonstrates that He is a God of grace. In the New Testament His grace really began to be manifested more clearly. His grace became more obvious. It was highlighted most powerfully through the redemptive, atoning work of Christ on the Cross. The entire world can look to the fact that God was pouring out His grace. This is precisely what Paul taught when he testified, "But God demonstrates His own love toward us, in that while we were still sinners, Christ died for us" (Rom. 5:8).

Paul demonstrated this same point in a powerful way in Romans 11. The Apostle described the relationship between Israel and God's purpose for the Church. Paul was answering the question, "Is Israel's rejection by God final? Had God written them off entirely?" In verse 11 Paul said, "I say then, have they stumbled that they should fall?" In other words, has their rejection of the Messiah resulted in their utter fall? His answer was, "Certainly not! But through their fall, to provoke them to jealousy, salvation has come to the Gentiles" (Rom. 11:11). Notice this next part, "Now if their fall is riches for the world, and their failure riches for the Gentiles, how much more their fullness!" (Rom. 11:12). The riches of God's grace and mercy that are so obvious and manifest in the Church today, as the Spirit indwells believers, is nothing when compared to the fullness of the Kingdom someday. We are reminded that Hebrews testifies, "God, who at various times and in various ways spoke in time past to the fathers by the prophets, has in these last days spoken to us by His Son, whom He has appointed heir of all things, through whom also He made the worlds; who being the brightness of His glory and the express image of His person" (Heb. 1:1-3). God spoke to mankind through Christ, "the brightness of His glory and the express image of His person." Christ came as God's greatest showcase of His riches in grace and mercy. To the extent that we are like Christ, we also show forth God's riches in mercy and grace. Consider the wording of Ephesians:

> But God, who is rich in mercy, because of His great love with which He loved us, even when we were dead in trespasses, made us alive together with Christ (by grace you have been saved), and raised us up together, and made us sit together in the heavenly places in Christ Jesus, that in the ages to come He might show the exceeding riches of His grace in His kindness toward us in Christ Jesus (Eph. 2:4-7).

It is not that God's demonstration of His grace is new; it is just more emphasized today.

Back in Romans 11 we witness another purpose for the Church. The Apostle taught, "I say then, have they stumbled that they should fall? Certainly not! But through their fall, to provoke them to jealousy, salvation has come to the Gentiles" (Rom. 11:11). God is using the Church today to get Israel's attention. The Church is the Bride of Christ and plays a unique role in God's program, but Israel is still God's primary focus. Israel is His chosen nation, and He has not forsaken His people.

Ephesians 3:10 informs us that another purpose of the Church Age is to showcase God's wisdom. Ephesians 3 is where the Apostle Paul explained that, indeed, the Church is a mystery. It was previously undisclosed in the Old Testament and now has been revealed. Paul demonstrated great humility by teaching:

> To me, who am less than the least of all the saints, this grace was given, that I should preach among the Gentiles the unsearchable riches of Christ, and to make all see what is the fellowship of the mystery, which from the beginning of the ages has been hidden in God [not revealed] who created all things through Jesus Christ; to the intent that now [in this present age] the manifold wisdom of God might be made known by

the church to the principalities and powers in the heavenly places (Eph. 3:8-10).

Never before in human history has the message of the Creator of the universe been so widely disseminated. The nation of Israel was charged with this task, and had times of success, but never to the levels presently witnessed within the Church Age. Never before has the world seen the global expansion of the teaching of the Word of God. This is what Paul meant when he wrote that the wisdom of God is to be made known by the Church. It is one of the express purposes of the Church Age to continue to teach the wisdom of God.

Does this mean the Church must succeed in reaching every unreached people group prior to the Rapture? According to the Bible, we know that this is not going to happen. Certainly the Church should attempt to reach these people, but the reality is that it will not be until the Tribulation when every human being on the earth will hear the gospel. This will be due primarily to the ministry of the 144,000 witnesses. This does not deemphasize the evangelistic enterprise of the Church. We have an obligation to go into the entire world and showcase God's wisdom, but it is a misapplication of the Great Commission to believe that the Church must succeed prior to the implementation of Daniel's Seventieth Week (the Tribulation). The Rapture could happen at any time, even before unreached people have an opportunity to hear the gospel.

Finally, another key purpose of the Church is to prepare a body that will help rule the Messianic Kingdom (Matt. 19:28; Luke 19:11-27; 22:28-30; 2 Tim. 2:12; Rev. 20:4-6).[3] One of the recurring themes within the Epistles of the New Testament is the concept of rewards. A common reward mentioned in Scripture is the position of leadership or authority. Consider 2 Timothy 2:12, "If we endure, we shall also reign with Him. If we deny Him, He also will deny us." This is referring to the right to reign with Christ, but it is often misunderstood by believers today. Those people approaching this text with the false presupposition that believers can lose their salvation quote this verse and testify that if you deny Christ you are destined for hell. Others use this verse to promote Lordship Salvation by proposing that Paul was telling Timothy, "Believers who persevere give evidence of the genuineness of their faith. ... Those who so deny Christ give evidence that they never truly belonged to Him (1Jn 2:19) and face the fearful reality of one day being denied by Him (Mt 10:33)."[4] But notice carefully the context of the verse; it says nothing at all about hell or salvation. Instead, Paul was directly referring to the reward of believers reigning with Christ. Jesus had clearly promised throughout His own teaching that those who follow Him faithfully will reign with Him. We remember that Jesus testified, "Assuredly I say to you, that in the regeneration, when the Son of Man sits on the throne of His glory, you who have followed Me will also sit on twelve thrones, judging the twelve tribes of Israel" (Matt. 19:28). The Apostles of Christ will serve in positions of leadership.

Once again, we return to the teaching found within the parable of delay (minas) in Luke 19. Jesus gave this instruction shortly before His death. Our Savior clearly indicated that He would be leaving. During His absence, His servants are to be busy conducting His business. Within the parable, the person who served particularly faithfully was put in charge of ten cities. The one who served a little less effectively was put in charge of five cities. The individual who did nothing did not get assigned any responsibility, but was still in the Kingdom. When Christ returns at the Rapture, believers will give an account of how they used their time. The more responsibility taken by individual believers in this age will mean the more responsibility that will be given to them by Christ in His Kingdom.

The Kingdom Age involves a one-world government, with Christ upon the throne. Christians are going to rule and reign with Him. This is one of the unique purposes of the Bride of Christ.

It should be recognized that there are believers today who will be in the Kingdom, and ultimately in heaven, who will not have any positions of authority. 1 Corinthians 3 describes what will take place at the Judgment Seat of Christ. It allows for one whose works are judged and every bit of them are burned up. Yet, the text states, "If anyone's work is burned, he will suffer loss; but he himself will be saved, yet so as through fire" (1 Cor. 3:15). This person will enter the Kingdom, but will not be rewarded any position of leadership.

This is consistent with the teaching of Christ in Luke 19. There Jesus described the individual who did nothing of eternal value with his life. Because every servant is described as receiving the same thing (one mina), the implication is that a life of service is in view.[5] In other words, what did you do with your life to serve Christ? All three servants get into the Kingdom. The people who do not are the citizens who hated Him, which is a reference to unbelieving Israel. The teaching contained in Luke 19 should be a clear motivation for the Church to live in light of the future rewards and positions of service that will be handed out.

The Commencement of the Church Age

If the Church (as the Bible teaches) is a parenthesis in God's plan, it must have a beginning and an end. The commencement of the Church Age can be unequivocally proven to be Acts 2, on the day of Pentecost. There are six passages that help us to know with certainty that the Church, as an institution, began in Acts 2.

The first verse to look at is Matthew 16:18, "And I also say to you that you are Peter, and on this rock I will build My church, and the gates of Hades shall not prevail against it." The reason we start with this text is because we know that, as of this particular point in time, the Church was obviously not in existence yet because Jesus spoke of it in the future tense. He told Peter that on his statement of confession that Jesus is the Christ, the Son of the living God, He would build His Church (future tense). At the very least, we know that at this late date in Christ's earthly ministry the Church had not started yet. This eliminates the Old Testament as a starting point for the Church. Despite this, covenant theologians believe the Church was started in the Old Testament, even though it is never mentioned in it. It is difficult to see how they can reconcile this with Matthew 16:18.

Next our attention turns to the day of ascension in Acts 1:4-5, "And being assembled together with them, He commanded them not to depart from Jerusalem, but to wait for the Promise of the Father, 'which,' He said, 'you have heard from Me; for John truly baptized with water, but you shall be baptized with the Holy Spirit not many days from now.'" The disciples wanted to know if Christ was now going to usher in the Kingdom of God (Acts 1:6). Jesus promised the baptism of the Spirit in a few days.

Continuing in the book of Acts, we read in the second chapter, "And they were all filled with the Holy Spirit and began to speak with other tongues, as the Spirit gave them utterance" (Acts 2:4). This is where the baptism of the Spirit occurred, on the day of Pentecost. How do we know that this is the baptism Christ predicted? A survey of the following references demonstrates this to be true.

Our study takes us next to Acts 11:15-16. Acts 10 reveals the conversion of Cornelius, which was the conversion of a Gentile. This created quite a stir. Peter was called to explain the events that had transpired. We learn, "And when Peter came up to Jerusalem, those of the circumcision contended with him" (Acts 11:2). Peter explained the situation to Jewish leaders of the early Church, "And as I began to speak, the Holy Spirit fell upon them, as upon us at the beginning. Then I remembered the word of the Lord, how He said, 'John indeed baptized with water, but you shall be baptized with the Holy Spirit'" (Acts 11:15-16). Peter reflected back to the events on the day of Pentecost and referred to it as a beginning. This begs the question, "The beginning of what?" The Apostle Peter plainly believed that something began on the day of Pentecost. This is an important point to take notice of in understanding the start of the Church.

The next piece of information comes from the Apostle Paul, "For as the body is one and has many members, but all the members of that one body, being many, are one body, so also is Christ. For by one Spirit we were all baptized into one body— whether Jews or Greeks, whether slaves or free—and have all been made to drink into one Spirit" (1 Cor. 12:12-13). The baptism of the Spirit forms a body. Believers are baptized into one body.

The final piece in the argument is found in the later writings of Paul, in both Ephesians 1:22-23 and Colossians 1:18. There we witness that he refers to the body as the Church. For example, "And He [Jesus] put all things under His feet, and gave Him to be head over all things to the church, which is His body, the fullness of Him who fills all in all" (Eph. 1:22-23). Consider the progression:

- The Church did not yet exist in Matthew 16.
- The baptism of the Holy Spirit was promised by John the Baptist and by Christ in Acts 1.
- The baptism of the Spirit initially occurred in Acts 2.
- Peter believed something began on the day of Pentecost (Acts 11:15-16).
- The baptism of the Spirit that occurred in Acts 2 formed a body (1 Cor. 12:12-13).
- The body is called the Church (Eph. 1:22-23; Col. 1:18).
- Therefore, the Church began in Acts 2.

This is an illustrative example of the importance of synthesis, comparing Scripture with Scripture to build our doctrine.

The Character of the Church Age

There are some unique aspects of this present age. First, we learn that the Church Age is a mystery (Eph. 3:1-12; Col. 1:24-27). We have already examined Ephesians 3 where the Apostle Paul used the terms *mystery* and *dispensation,* but let us consider the teaching from Colossians 1:24-27:

> I now rejoice in my sufferings for you, and fill up in my flesh what is lacking in the afflictions of Christ, for the sake of His body, which is the church, of which I became a minister according to the stewardship from God which was given to me for you, to fulfill the word of God, the mystery which has been hidden from ages and from generations, but now has been revealed to His saints. To them God willed to make known what are the riches of the glory of this mystery among the Gentiles: which is Christ in you, the hope of glory.

The mystery is, "Christ in you, the hope of glory." It is the unique privilege of this age to have God the Son indwelling us. Again, this foreshadows the intimacy that will characterize the Kingdom.

During the Church Age, we are living in the last days (1 Pet. 1:5; Jude 18; 1 John 2:18; 1 Tim. 4:1; 2 Tim. 3:1; Heb. 1:2). This makes this present age a unique time.[6] After the Church Age is the Tribulation. This will be the final seven years from Daniel 9. Then the Kingdom of Christ is ushered in, which will be the fulfillment of God's prophecy to Israel. The Church Age is the final period before these events take place. It is the final age before the fulfillment of God's prophetic plan.

Scripture also teaches that the Church is an *evil age* (Gal. 1:4; 2 Cor. 4:4; Eph. 6:12; Titus 2:12; 2 Tim. 3:1). The present age is the greatest manifestation to date of God's glory and His presence through the coming of Christ and because His wisdom is on display through the Church. But as we see the cosmic battle between the Creator and the Devil throughout the ages, it is evident that the opposite extreme is also intensifying. Satan is the prince of this present age. He is unleashing his deception, which will increase. The Church Age is an escalation of the spiritual battle. This highlights the importance of the spiritual armor mentioned by the Apostle Paul in Ephesians 6. It also demonstrates the importance of prayer. The Bible teaches us that the deception during this present age will only continue to get worse and worse (2 Tim. 3:13).

The Evil Character of the Church Age

Some of the characteristics of this present evil age include a denial of God (2 Tim. 3:4-5). Certainly, this is not new. In fact, none of the wickedness present in our age is new. David testified, "The fool has said in his heart, 'There is no God'" (Ps. 14:1). But certainly in this age we see an intensification of the wickedness of man.

Scripture also instructs us that during this age we will witness the denial of Christ (1 John 4:3). Men will also deny the return of Christ. The Apostle Peter taught, "Knowing this first: that scoffers will come in the last days, walking according to their own lusts, and saying, 'Where is the promise of His coming? For since the fathers fell asleep, all things continue as they were from the beginning of creation'" (2 Pet. 3:3-4).

The denial of the faith is another characteristic of this evil age (1 Tim. 4:1-2; Heb. 10:35; 2 Tim. 2:13; Jude 3). It is hard to imagine a time in history when the denial of the faith was as widespread as it is today. In the Old Testament it was not as common for Jews to outright deny their heritage as the people of Yahweh. To be sure, at various periods throughout Israel's history the Jews were involved with pagan idolatry and were in open rebellion to the Lord. But did they deny that Yahweh exists? They were more inclined to mix their beliefs with pagan idolatry than they were to outright reject God. Unfortunately, the denial of the faith is widespread in our day. Some may even be true believers, if they have trusted in Christ for salvation. Various influences (false teaching, problems in life, or a crisis) lead weak believers to walk away from the Lord.

This was a unique problem in the early Church. The persecution by the Roman government increased when the Christians became scapegoats for upsetting the peace of Rome. Unbelieving Jews were worried that their special relationship with the Roman government would be threatened, so they caused great trouble for the early Christians (referred to as those of the Way). As a result, many Jewish Christians (those who had believed the gospel) abandoned the faith. This is what the book of Hebrews is about. In order to save their lives, and avoid martyrdom in some cases, Jewish Christians were denying the faith. Despite popular opinion, this does not mean they were lost.

Imagine that a Muslim terrorist bursts into the room as you are reading this. He holds a gun to your head and says, "Deny your faith in Jesus Christ!" What would you honestly do? Hopefully our faith would be strong enough to say, "Jesus is my Lord and Savior!" The truth is that nobody knows for sure until they are actually faced with such a difficult situation. What if the terrorist held a gun to your spouse's head or the head of your child? Then he says, "Deny Jesus! Curse Him or I am going to murder your child!" What would you do? Again, we hope our faith would be strong enough to say, "No matter what, I am going to serve

You Lord." But we truly do not know what we would do in a moment of crisis and weakness. None of this would have any bearing on the fact that we had already trusted in Christ as our Savior. Would a momentary weakness automatically negate our prior trust in Christ? Hardly, because later decisions (no matter how wrong and tragic they may be) cannot undo what took place at the moment of faith. The moment a person trusts in Jesus Christ for eternal life they are eternally secure; nothing can change this. At that moment they are united forever with the Lord. Christians backslide in their faith to varying degrees. Even if a believer backslides to the point of denying their faith, it does not undo their earlier trust in Christ for eternal life. The Scriptures warn of the consequences of believers denying Christ, both in the present life and at the Judgment Seat of Christ. Yet, none of these consequences includes the loss of salvation. As predicted in the Word of God, we are witnessing an increase, in the latter days, of those who deny the faith (1 Tim. 4:1).

The denial of sound doctrine is another distinctive of the Church Age (2 Tim. 4:3-4). In this postmodern age, doctrine is commonly seen as having no lasting value. Doctrine is said to be the, "stuff of divinity schools." It is often considered to be a waste for churches to spend their time on doctrine. Instead, the focus today is on experience. Believers who hold to the absolute truth of Scripture are considered to be divisive. The pluralistic view is seen as the only correct view. It is typical for churches to no longer post their doctrinal statements, especially on the Internet. Doctrine is simply no longer a priority. When you allow experience and programs to eclipse the centrality of the Word of God, it is a manifestation of the denial of sound doctrine that characterizes the present age.

A survey of New Testament teaching about the Church reveals a central focus on doctrine. This can be seen early on, "Then those who gladly received his word were baptized; and that day about three thousand souls were added to them. And they continued steadfastly in the apostles' doctrine and fellowship, in the breaking of bread, and in prayers" (Acts 2:41-42). The first thing that is mentioned in verse 42 is doctrine. Paul's counsel to Timothy was similar, "Let no one despise your youth, but be an example to the believers in word, in conduct, in love, in spirit, in faith, in purity. Till I come, give attention to reading, to exhortation, to doctrine" (1 Tim. 4:12-13). Just a few verses later Paul again admonished, "Take heed to yourself and to the doctrine" (1 Tim. 4:16). Tragically, this is precisely what the Church is failing to do.

The Close of the Church Age

Scripture is not silent about the end of the Church Age. Jesus promised in the Upper Room, "Let not your heart be troubled; you believe in God, believe also in Me. In My Father's house are many mansions; if it were not so, I would have told you. I go to prepare a place for you. And if I go and prepare a place for you, I will come again and receive you to Myself; that where I am, there you may be also" (John 14:1-3). This passage is the only clear reference to the Rapture in the Gospels. The Rapture was not revealed explicitly until 1 Thessalonians 4, which was one of the earliest epistles of Paul, written in A.D. 51.

This raises the issue of the Olivet Discourse. It is a misconception to assume that the Rapture was revealed in the Olivet Discourse, even though at times it may sound like it. The confusion usually surrounds Matthew 24:40-41, "Then two men will be in the field: one will be taken and the other left. Two women will be grinding at the mill: one will be taken and the other left." The context makes it clear that this is not a reference to the Rapture. The one taken is taken away in judgment. The one left behind is left to inherit the Kingdom. The Rapture is just the opposite, where the one taken is rescued and the one left behind will have to suffer the Tribulation. Therefore, John 14:1-3 is the only reference in the Gospels to the Rapture.

The Apostle Paul taught that believers could look forward to a sudden future time when they are, "caught up together with them in the clouds to meet the Lord in the air" (1 Thess. 4:13-18; 1 Cor. 15:50-58). The reality is that there is a generation of Christians who will never see death. It is indeed troubling that many Christians do not live in light of the truth that Christ could return for us at any moment. We need to practice what we believe. Like the early Church, we have become so complacent in this promise of the imminent return of the Lord Jesus that it has become a doctrine to which we ascribe, but not a belief to which we live by and look for. Do we believe what we say? According to the Apostle Paul, there is a special reward for those who long for His appearing (2 Tim. 4:8). We are to wait for Jesus to return and rescue us, "from the wrath to come" (1 Thess. 1:10).

Immediately after the Rapture, there will not be any more Christians on earth. Certainly as time marches forward there will be Tribulation saints, but the Church will not exist on earth. Remember, the Seventieth Week of Daniel is God interacting with the nation of Israel, not the Church.

It will be the responsibility of the tribes of Israel to lead the people of the nations to saving faith in the Christ (Rev. 7:1-17). The close of the Church Age is the Rapture of the Bride of Christ.

The Commands of the Church Age

As we walk by faith in obedience to the teachings of Christ, we must recognize that the New Testament contains commands for Church Age believers. These include:

- make disciples (Matt. 28:19-20)
- be faithful to our calling (1 Cor. 4:1-5; 1 John 2:28)
- walk worthy of our calling (Eph. 4:1)
- be watchful for the appearing of our Lord (2 Tim. 4:8)
- prepare to serve in the Kingdom (John 12:26; Luke 19:17)

The Importance of the Church Age

Our service to the Lord does not end at the Rapture. During the Church Age, our Lord is preparing a body of believers to rule and reign with Him in the Kingdom. God is also using this temporary interruption in His covenant program with Israel to showcase His mercy, grace, and wisdom to the Gentiles. This foreshadows the mercy and grace that God will demonstrate in His Kingdom. The Scriptures teach that the next prophetic event to take place is the rescue of the Church at the Rapture.

Discussion Questions

1. What is the Church Age? When does it take place?
2. What allowance does the Old Testament make for the Church?
3. Explain the concept of Daniel's Seventy Weeks. Where in Daniel is this concept explained?
4. What is the evidence that proves that the prophecy given to Daniel should be taken literally?
5. Describe God's purpose for the Church. How does this contrast with His purpose for Israel?

6. Define the role of Christians during the Kingdom.
7. Provide a brief summary of the description of the Church found in Ephesians.
8. When is the beginning and end of the Church Age?
9. How is the Church Age characterized?
10. In what way should Christians be living during the Church Age?

Endnotes

1. This date is based on one of the most standard, accepted, and authoritative datings of Jewish and apostolic history, which is from Harold Hoehner. There are some scholars who suggest an alternate date of March 14, 445 B.C. for this decree. Either date does not alter the discussion in a significant manner. The intention is not to be dogmatic about the exact date on the calendar. Rather, the intention is to show that there was a definite beginning point sometime during the reign of Artaxerxes in Persia, with his decree to restore and rebuild Jerusalem.

2. There is some disagreement to the exact event in the ministry of Christ that the prophecy corresponds to. Either way, the point is that 483 years after Artaxerxes' decree we arrive at the time of Christ. Whether that was His baptism, the Upper Room discourse, or the Triumphal Entry is beside the point. Clearly the time of Christ fulfills the first 483 years of this promise of Daniel.

3. This is examined in greater detail in the section on the Judgment Seat of Christ.

4. John F. MacArthur, Jr., *The MacArthur Study Bible: New American Standard Bible.* (Nashville, TN: Thomas Nelson Publishers, 2006), 2 Tim. 2:12.

5. It should be noted that the parable of the minas is completely different from the parable of the talents. The context and details are considerably different. In the parable of the talents each servant received different amounts. Furthermore, the one that is the subject of God's displeasure in the parable of the talents does not get into the Kingdom, but is instead cast into outer darkness. In Matthew 25 two of the three servants get into the Kingdom, but one does not. In Luke 19, all three servants enter the Kingdom. Matthew 25 is referring to Israel, and Luke 19 is referring to the Church. This is covered in greater detail in chapter 13.

6. For more information on the last days see Dr. Hixson's book, *The Great Last Days Deception.*

CHAPTER 10

The Greatest Rescue - The Rapture

---

*And to wait for His Son from heaven, whom He raised from
the dead, even Jesus who delivers us from the wrath to come.*

- 1 Thessalonians 1:10

A FEROCIOUS NIGHTMARE confronted the crew of the fishing vessel,
Alaska Ranger, in the frigid waters of the Bering Sea. On March 23rd
of 2008, the *Alaska Ranger* began to take on water at approximately 2:20
a.m. The nearly 200 foot ship had also lost control of its rudder, which
meant reaching the safety of Dutch Harbor, 120 miles to the east, was an
insurmountable task. A distress call was received from the sinking ship
by the Coast Guard at 2:52 a.m. The *Alaska Ranger* then transmitted its
position to the Coast Guard. Forty-seven people onboard the *Ranger* now
waited to see if help could reach them in time.

Ships that venture into the perilous waters of the Bering Sea are
fitted with life rafts. The sailors are also given survival suits, designed
to keep their bodies dry if the unthinkable should happen. In a perfect
world the combination of the two extends the chances for survival, but
life in the Bering Sea is anything but ideal. With an air temperature of
twelve degrees Fahrenheit, and a water temperature of thirty-two degrees
Fahrenheit, the deck of the *Ranger* was slick with ice. When the order was
finally given to abandon ship, the *Ranger* was already listing to one side.
This movement caused the life rafts to float away, beyond the reach of
much of the crew.

Attempting to rescue forty-seven people in the dark of night from the
Bering Sea is a sizable task. Helicopters have weight limits, and the great

distance involved meant it would take time to get back and forth from the site. This was time that they simply did not have.

Two Coast Guard helicopters were dispatched to the site. When the first helicopter arrived on the scene, the strobe lights from the survival suits pierced through the night sky. They also revealed that the fishermen were scattered in the icy waters below. Twenty-five mile an hour winds and six to eight foot waves made the rescue even more daunting. One by one the helicopter crews plucked the men out of the water. Fortunately, the fishing vessel, *Alaska Warrior*, was close by and was able to rescue twenty-two of the men. The Coast Guard lifted twenty men out of the frigid waters alive. Only five men perished in this tragedy at sea. This is a testament to the dedication of the Coast Guard to rescue people from certain death.[1]

Our Rescue

A powerful storm of end time events is gathering on the horizon, and it is the plan of God to remove His people from the danger that is to come. Believers can know with certainty that Jesus Christ will rescue them before the Tribulation. We are, "to wait for His Son from heaven, whom He raised from the dead, even Jesus who delivers us from the wrath to come" (1 Thess. 1:10). This is the teaching known as the Rapture of the Church. It will be a time when Church Age believers are caught up to meet the Lord in the air (1 Thess. 4:17). We will be lifted up from the earth to escape the wrath of the Lamb (Rev. 6:15-17). Christians will be rescued from the peril that will befall the unredeemed men and women of the world.

The Rapture Presented in Scripture

The Rapture refers to the sudden catching up of Church Age believers to meet the Lord in the air when He returns at the close of the present age. Critics of the biblical doctrine of the Rapture unfortunately tend to focus on the fact that the term *rapture* is never mentioned in the Bible. It should be recognized that there are a lot of terms never mentioned in the Bible, such as the Trinity, that are used by believers to identify a doctrine which is taught in the Word of God. The doctrine of the Rapture is unambiguously revealed in Scripture, as we shall see in the pages that follow.

The term *rapture* comes from the Latin Vulgate translation of the New Testament. Notice the wording of 1 Thessalonians 4:17, "Then we who are alive and remain shall be caught up together with them in the clouds to meet the Lord in the air." The English words *caught up* are a translation of the original Greek word *harpazo*. When Jerome translated the Bible into Latin in late 4th-century, he chose the Latin word *rapio* (*rapere, raptus*) to translate *harpazo*. This is where this phrase comes from.

Like the Church Age, the Rapture is described in the New Testament as a mystery. We have already witnessed in Ephesians 1 that the Apostle Paul defined the Church Age as a mystery, as something new and previously undisclosed. Paul used the same language to describe the special blessing for the Church, which is the Rapture. Scripture reveals, "Behold, I tell you a mystery: We shall not all sleep, but we shall all be changed" (1 Cor. 15:51). Sleep is a euphemism for die. The mystery that was revealed is that we shall not all die. This is a wonderful promise that gives hope to every believer living in the Church Age. There will be a group of believers who will not face death. This is the mystery that was revealed through Paul. Universally, death has befallen mankind. With two exceptions (Enoch and Elijah), everyone has previously faced death. At some point during the Church Age, believers will not face death. Instead, they will be caught up to meet the Lord!

Paul described that the Rapture will happen:

> in a moment, in the twinkling of an eye, at the last trumpet. For the trumpet will sound, and the dead will be raised incorruptible, and we shall be changed. For this corruptible must put on incorruption, and this mortal must put on immortality. So when this corruptible has put on incorruption, and this mortal has put on immortality, then shall be brought to pass the saying that is written: *"Death is swallowed up in victory." "O Death, where is your sting? O Hades, where is your victory?"* The sting of death is sin, and the strength of sin is the law. But thanks be to God, who gives us the victory through our Lord Jesus Christ (1 Cor. 15:52-57).

The dead in Christ will receive their incorruptible glorified bodies. Their souls are already in the presence of the Lord, but right now their bodies are in the grave. Those corrupt and decayed bodies will be resurrected. Those believers alive at the Rapture shall be changed as they receive their immortal bodies.

It is interesting to note that the four key passages that teach on the Rapture in the New Testament (1 Thess. 4:13-18; 1 Cor. 15:50-58; John 14:1-3; 2 Thess. 2:1-10) all end with an exhortation of encouragement.

Believers should look forward to the day that they receive these glorified bodies.

The Rapture is the next great prophetic event to which the world looks forward. Nothing prophetically must precede the Rapture. It is imminent, which means that it could happen at any time. This does not necessarily mean soon, it means that it could take place at any moment.

Imagine that your parents are coming for a visit. They call to tell you that they are a few hours away, but then they shut their cellphone off. You have no way of communicating with them. Did they stop for another break? Did they have a flat tire or get lost? Your kids sit and watch out the front window waiting for them to pull up. It might be thirty minutes, or a few hours. You are expecting them at any time. Their arrival is imminent, but you do not really know if it is soon. Likewise, the Rapture is imminent, but it might not happen for another thousand years. It could take place at any moment, but it may or may not be soon.

A Note about Imminency

Quite often the doctrine of the imminency of the Rapture is taught, by well-intentioned believers, by referring to passages that mention the importance of watchfulness. A word of caution is in order because these types of texts do not explicitly teach the imminent return of the Lord for His Church. The reason is simple; the same exact terminology about being watchful is used of the Second Coming, which is not imminent (e.g. Matt. 24:42; Rev. 16:15). The presence of a command to be watchful does not, in and of itself, prove that the Rapture is imminent. In other words, an exhortation to watch for the Lord's return is not necessarily an explicit indication of the imminency of the Rapture, since believers during the Tribulation are likewise exhorted to watch, and the Second Coming is obviously not imminent.

Imminency is not a primary exegetical proof of pretribulationism. To state it another way, people often proclaim that they believe in the pretribulational Rapture of the Church because of the commands of Scripture to watch for the Lord's return. The problem is that Scripture also instructs people to watch for His second coming, which is not imminent. Imminency is derived from theological conclusions regarding the order of end time events. That is, imminency does not prove pretribulationism; pretribulationism demands imminency. Once it is established from Scripture that the Rapture must occur before the Tribulation, then there is no other conclusion that can be made except for the simple truth that the Rapture can happen at any moment in time because nothing else must take place before it. There are several passages that indicate the imminent return of the Lord for His Bride (1 Cor. 15:51-52; Phil. 3:20; 4:5; Titus 2:13; James 5:7-9; 1 John 2:28; Rev. 3:11; 22:7, 12, 17, 20). Notice that this list *does not* include passages that teach believers to be watchful (e.g. 1 Thess. 5:2).

The Purpose of the Rapture

A central purpose of the Rapture is to bring an end to the Church Age. On figure 10.1 the Rapture is the right hand parenthesis of the Church Age.

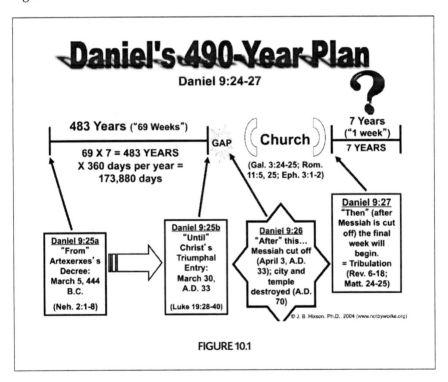

FIGURE 10.1

Anyone who gets saved after the Rapture is not a part of the Body of Christ. By definition, they are not a part of the Church. These believers will still be in the Kingdom of Christ, but they will have a different role to play. Matthew 25:31-46 clearly reveals that there will be believers (sheep) alive on earth at the Second Coming of Christ who will inhabit the Kingdom.

These are the believers who will come to faith in Christ after the Rapture and survive the Tribulation. Revelation 7 instructs that people of every nation, tribe, and tongue will come out of the Tribulation as believers.

We remember from the previous chapter that a part of the purpose of the Church Age is that this is a time when God is calling out a people for His name (Acts 15:14; cf. 11:26). When the Rapture occurs there will not be any more believers added to the Church. During the Church Age, Christ is preparing a body that will help rule the Messianic Kingdom.

A second purpose for the Rapture is that it provides certain blessings for the Body of Christ. These special blessings for the Church include:

- Glorified bodies (1 Cor.15:51; Rom. 8:23-25). As we await the consummation of our adoption through Christ, our bodies groan as they await their redemption. The Apostle Paul instructed, "Even we ourselves groan within ourselves, eagerly waiting for the adoption, the redemption of our body" (Rom. 8:23).
- Meeting the Lord (1 Thess. 4:17). It will be an incredible day when we get to see our Lord face to face.
- A reunion with loved ones (1 Thess. 4:16-17). Right now we are experiencing a temporary separation from our loved ones who are redeemed in Christ. The Rapture will lead to a reunion with them.
- Rewards that believers will receive (Rev. 22:12).
- The Marriage of the Lamb (Rev. 19:6-8). The Church is the Bride of Christ and will be united to Him for all of eternity.

A third purpose of the Rapture is that it rescues the Church from the wrath to come (1 Thess. 1:10; 1 Thess. 5:9; Rev. 3:10). The Scriptures teach of a great eschatological wrath of God. Zephaniah refers to this coming time as, "the great day of the Lord" and "the day of the Lord's wrath" (Zeph. 1:14, 18). The Rapture protects the Church from this time of Jacob's trouble on earth.

The Portrayal of the Rapture

The preeminent passage in the New Testament concerning the Rapture of the Church is 1 Thessalonians 4:13-18. Verse 13 teaches, "But I do not want you to be ignorant, brethren, concerning those who have fallen asleep, lest you sorrow as others who have no hope." Once more, we are reminded that *fallen asleep* is a euphemism for death. Paul presented a remarkable contrast between the death of believers and unbelievers. When unbelievers die there is no hope. No hope of ever seeing them again. No hope that they are in a better place because they are in torment. There is no hope at all for people who die without the Lord. Notice that Paul did not deny the reality of the sorrow over the loss of a loved one in Christ. There is a reality to the sorrow we experience when a believer dies, and Paul did not rebuke them for this. Instead, Paul was testifying that it is a different type of sorrow that we have when a Christian dies.

The teaching continues, "For if we believe that Jesus died and rose again, even so God will bring with Him those who sleep in Jesus" (1 Thess. 4:14). In the original Greek text, the idea behind the words, "for if we believe" is *since we believe*. Therefore, Paul was stating that just as we believe Jesus died and rose again, God will bring with Him those who die in Christ.

Verse 15 begins with an interesting statement, "For this we say to you by the word of the Lord." We are left wondering when this revelation was given. Was more detail given by Jesus in the Upper Room than what is recorded in John 14? Was this directly revealed from the Lord to Paul? We do not have the answer, but we can rest assured that this is a promise from the Lord Himself. This teaching came with the authority of the Lord, "That we who are alive and remain until the coming of the Lord will by no means precede those who are asleep" (1 Thess. 4:15). Those who are dead in Christ will be the first to experience this event.

Paul explained how this event will take place, "For the Lord Himself will descend from heaven with a shout, with the voice of an archangel, and with the trumpet of God. And the dead in Christ will rise first. Then we who are alive and remain shall be caught up together with them in the clouds to meet the Lord in the air. And thus we shall always be with the Lord" (1 Thess. 4:16-17). The expression *in Christ* is a reference to Church Age believers. It is important to remember that Old Testament believers are not resurrected at the Rapture. Daniel 12 and Isaiah 26 tell us that they will be resurrected at the Second Coming. At that time they will receive their glorified bodies. At the Rapture the dead in Christ (Church Age believers) will rise first, and then the rest of the Church that is alive. We see the teaching end with a note of comfort again, "Therefore comfort one another with these words" (1 Thess. 4:18).

Certain questions arise from the teaching of the Rapture of the Church. It is asked, "Does the Bible support the alleged doctrine of soul sleep?"

Soul sleep is the idea that when believers die they go into an unconscious state for centuries until the Lord comes back, and then He awakens them. Most certainly the Bible does not teach this. When believers die they are immediately in the presence of the Lord. To be absent from the body is to be present with the Lord (2 Cor. 5:8).

Another related question asked about the Rapture is, "What about cremation, people lost at sea, or people whose bodies are never found?" The bottom line is that when the Rapture takes place the bodies of Church Age believers (regardless of the method of their death) will be reconstituted into glorified bodies because, "this mortal must put on immortality" (1 Cor. 15:53). The Creator of the world is surely capable of raising the dead, in whatever state their decayed bodies are in. This powerful and loving God has promised us glorified bodies.

The certainty of the Rapture is connected to the historical reality of the Resurrection of Jesus (1 Thess. 4:14). This should instill comfort. To deny the Rapture is tantamount to denying the Resurrection of Jesus Christ. Since we believe that He died and rose again, even so we also believe in the Rapture. This is a very important point that people who deny the Rapture (e.g. those who hold to covenant theology) should wrestle with. The Lord will return during the earthly lives of some believers (1 Thess. 4:15). At that time, "the Lord Himself will descend from heaven with a shout, with the voice of an archangel, and with the trumpet of God. And the dead in Christ will rise first" (1 Thess. 4:16). The bodies of dead believers will be resurrected and glorified. Living believers will be translated into their glorified bodies in the twinkling of an eye (1 Cor. 15:51-52). Translation is the term used to refer to the glorification of the bodies of living people. Resurrection is the glorification of the bodies of dead people. Believers alive at the day of the Rapture will be translated. Translated believers will be caught up to meet the Lord in the air, when their eternity with Christ begins (1 Thess. 4:17).

A Comparison of John 14 and 1 Thessalonians 4

A remarkable consistency is found by comparing the teachings of the Rapture in John 14 and 1 Thessalonians 4. Consider the following:

- In John 14:1 Jesus said, "Let not your heart be troubled." Paul stated in 1 Thess. 4:13, "lest you sorrow as others who have no hope."

- Both passages begin with a similar context. Jesus testified in John 14:1, "You believe in God, believe also in Me." In 1 Thess. 4:14 Paul wrote, "We believe that Jesus died and rose again." Both texts refer to our sustaining faith.
- In John 14:1 the Lord Jesus referenced God and Himself when He said, "You believe in God, believe also in Me." Paul also referenced God and Jesus by testifying, "We believe that Jesus died and rose again, even so God will bring with Him those who sleep in Jesus" (1 Thess. 4:14).
- Jesus stated in John 14:2, "If it were not so, I would have told you." Paul said, "For this we say to you by the word of the Lord" (1 Thess. 4:15).
- Jesus taught in John 14:3, "I will come again." In verse 15 of 1 Thessalonians 4 Paul referred to, "the coming of the Lord."
- In John 14 Jesus said in verse 3, "I will come again and receive you." Paul mentioned in verse 17 of 1 Thessalonians 4 that believers will, "be caught up" to meet Him.
- Jesus specifically taught that He would, "receive you to Myself" (John 14:3). Paul taught that we will, "meet the Lord in the air" (1 Thess. 4:17).
- In verse 3 of John 14 Jesus promised the disciples, "that where I am, there you may be also." Paul stated that believers will, "always be with the Lord" (1 Thess. 4:17).

When you compare the teaching, point by point, of both of these sections of Scripture, it is self-evident that John 14 is a reference to the Rapture. This also demonstrates the unity of the Word of God. There is no other passage in the Gospels that directly mentions the Rapture of the Church.[2]

Contrasting the Rapture and the Second Coming

The denial of a future literal Kingdom for Israel, and the failure to see the distinction between Israel and the Church, has led to the improper merging of passages that speak of the Rapture and the Second Coming. A careful examination of Scripture clearly reveals that they are not the same event. This is demonstrated by observing the contrasts between 1 Thessalonians 4:13-18 and Revelation 19:11-21. This can be seen in figure 10.2.

At the Rapture Christ will come in the air and believers will be called up to meet Him. At the Second Coming Christ will come all the way to the earth. In fact, His feet will touch the Mount of Olives (Zech. 14:4). At the Rapture only the redeemed in Christ from the Church Age are included. It is the rescue of the Church, not the judgment of the lost. At the Second Coming both the saved and unsaved are included. Never is this more clearly seen than in the Sheep and Goats Judgment of Matthew 25. Jesus undoubtedly had both believers and unbelievers in view. The redeemed will enter the Kingdom and the lost will go into the everlasting fire. At the Rapture the dead in Christ receive their resurrected bodies, but at the Second Coming unbelievers are sent to their death (eternal separation from God). At the Rapture believers will go from earth to heaven. At the Second Coming believers from the Church Age will return from heaven to earth. Revelation 19 teaches that the Church (armies in heaven) will ride with Christ upon white horses to return to earth (Rev. 19:14; cf. 19:8).

Contrasts between the Rapture in First Thessalonians 4 and the Second Coming in Revelation 19

1 Thess. 4:13-18	Revelation 19:11-21
Christ comes in the air	Christ comes to the earth
Only saved are in view	Saved/unsaved are in view
Dead are raised to life	Living are sent to death
Believers go from earth to heaven	Believers come from heaven to earth

© 2005, J. B. Hixson, Ph.D.   www.notbyworks.org

FIGURE 10.2

As we broaden our focus to examine the entire New Testament teaching on the Rapture and the Second Coming, we certainly see more differences between the two. This is demonstrated in figure 10.3.

The Rapture is followed by the Tribulation, and the Second Coming is followed by the Millennium. The Rapture is imminent, but the Second Coming is preceded by numerous signs. In fact, the entire purpose of the Olivet Discourse was to give signs of His second coming. This was the question that the disciples asked, "What will be the sign of Your coming, and of the end of the age?" (Matt. 24:3). There will be many signs that lead up to the Second Coming of Christ. It is truly astonishing that people will not be prepared for it, but it is not imminent. The Second Coming could not take place today because, according to Scripture, many things must take place first:

- The Temple must be rebuilt (Matt. 24:15; 2 Thess. 2:4).
- The Antichrist has to be revealed (2 Thess. 2:3, 8).
- The peace treaty has to be signed (Dan. 9:27).
- The Abomination of Desolation has yet to happen (Matt. 24:15).
- Armageddon must take place (Rev. 16:14-16).
- The two witnesses will die and be resurrected (Rev. 11:3-13).
- The ministry of the 144,000 witnesses has yet to occur (Rev. 7:1-17).
- The seal, trumpet, and bowl judgments have to be unveiled (Rev. 6; 8-9; 16).

Many things must yet occur before the Second Coming, but nothing must happen before the Rapture.

The Rapture is a mystery (1 Cor. 15:51); it is never revealed in the Old Testament. Daniel 9 allowed for the Rapture by revealing a clear gap in time between the sixty-ninth and seventieth week, but it is never mentioned. The Second Coming, however, is repeatedly predicted in the Old Testament.

The coming of Christ is often merged in the Old Testament prophets as one event. When we compare the additional details provided in the New Testament, we see that some verses refer to His first advent, and some refer to His second coming. Isaiah 9 illustrates this well:

> For unto us a Child is born, unto us a Son is given; and the government will be upon His shoulder. And His name will be called Wonderful, Counselor, Mighty God, Everlasting Father, Prince of Peace. Of the increase of His government and peace there will be no end, upon the throne of David and over His kingdom, to order it and establish it with judgment and justice from that time forward, even forever. The zeal of the Lord of hosts will perform this (Isa. 9:6-7).

The first part of verse 6 was fulfilled at the First Advent of Christ, when He was born at Bethlehem. The rest, however, refers to the government and peace that Christ will establish at His second advent. This same situation is witnessed in Isaiah 61:1-2, where part of the prophecy refers to His first advent and part refers to His second advent. The point to be recognized is that the Old Testament clearly predicts the Second Coming of Christ.

The purpose of the Rapture is to rescue the Bride of Christ, but the purpose of the Second Coming is to judge the nations (Matt. 25:32). Likewise, the Rapture is a message of comfort, but the Second Coming is a message of warning and judgment. The Rapture is a joyful reunion for believers in Christ (1 Thess. 4:13-18). Revelation 19:11-16 describes a time of terror for the unbelievers living on earth at the Second Coming.

Additional Contrasts between the Rapture and the Second Coming

Rapture	Second Coming
Is followed immediately by the tribulation	Is followed immediately by the millennium
Is imminent	Is preceded by numerous signs
Is a mystery	Is predicted in the OT
Purpose is to rescue	Purpose is to judge
Is a message of comfort	Is a message of warning and judgment

© 2005, J. B. Hixson, Ph.D.

www.notbyworks.org

FIGURE 10.3

The Placement of the Rapture

Before we can definitively place the timing of the Rapture, it is helpful to clarify and review a few terms. Premillennial, postmillennial, and amillennial all relate to the timing of the Second Coming of Christ relative to the Millennium. Amillennial is the belief that Christ will return, but there is no Millennium (a- simply means no). Postmillennial teaches that Christ will return after the Millennium. Premillennial refers to the teaching that the Second Coming of Christ will take place before the Millennium. Christ will return to establish a literal Kingdom on earth for Israel. A literal interpretation of the Word of God reveals that Christ's second coming will take place prior to the Millennium. At that time, Christ will establish His Kingdom.

Pretribulation, midtribulation, and post-tribulation refer to the timing of the Rapture relative to the Tribulation. It is imperative to recognize that these terms are referring to the timing of the Rapture, not the Second Coming. Pretribulation simply means that Christ will rapture the Church before the Tribulation. Midtribulation teaches that the Rapture will happen in the middle of the Tribulation. Post-tribulation is the belief that the Rapture will take place after the Tribulation.

Amillennial and postmillennial theology do not debate the timing of the Rapture simply because neither position even teaches that the Rapture will take place. Without the understanding from Scripture of the distinction between the Church and Israel, and without the understanding that Christ will return to establish His earthly Kingdom for Israel, the belief is that somehow we are living in the Kingdom today. If this is the Kingdom now, then there is no need seen for the Rapture.[3] Pretribulation, midtribulation, and post-tribulation are all premillennial positions. Within premillennialism, these are the predominant schools of thought.

The Post-tribulation Rapture View

The post-tribulation Rapture view is illustrated in figure 10.4. This position teaches that, at some point, the Tribulation will start with the signing of the peace treaty by the Antichrist. It is recognized that this period of Tribulation will last for seven years. The midpoint of the Tribulation is correctly seen as the Abomination of Desolation. According to this position, the Rapture and the Second Coming happen simultaneously at the end of the Tribulation. Afterwards, the Kingdom begins. This position does hold to the belief in a future literal Kingdom and the distinction between Israel and the Church. However, it is believed that the Church goes through the Tribulation.

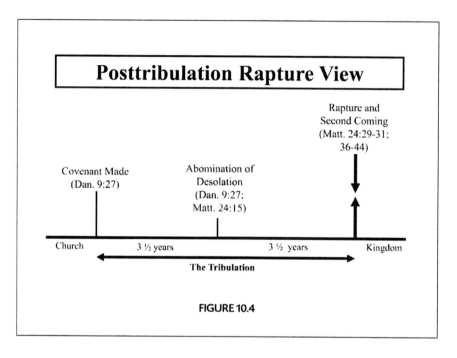

Posttribulation Rapture View

Rapture and
Second Coming
(Matt. 24:29-31;
36-44)

Covenant Made
(Dan. 9:27)

Abomination of
Desolation
(Dan. 9:27;
Matt. 24:15)

Church   3 ½ years   3 ½ years   Kingdom

The Tribulation

FIGURE 10.4

Quite often it is argued by proponents of this particular view that the teaching of the Rapture occurring prior to the Tribulation was not taught until more recent times. Therefore, the idea of the Church escaping the Tribulation is presented as a more recent invention in Church history. The evidence demands a different verdict. The Apostle Paul clearly taught in Scripture that the Rapture would precede the Tribulation. A two-phased return of the Lord was also taught throughout Church history. Certainly the predominance of false teachings throughout the Church Age has obscured the teaching of the Rapture, but it is a mistake to assert that it was not taught. A closer examination of the historical records reveals theologians throughout the Church Age who held to a two-phased return of the Lord.

Exegetical errors also lead some Christians to believe that the Rapture will take place after the Tribulation. Matthew 13 contains the parable of the wheat and tares. It is believed this text reveals that the Church and unbelievers will all grow together until the final harvest at the end of the age. Therefore, accordingly, the Church would be present during the Tribulation. However, it should be noted that nothing in this text precludes the Rapture of the Church before God once again turns His attention to the nation of Israel during the Tribulation and the end of the age. Because Jesus was speaking to a Jewish audience, we should expect the focus of the teaching to be on God's future interaction with the nation of Israel. It should not be a surprise that this chapter does not contain a detailed exposition of the Rapture of the Church.

In John 16:33 Jesus told the disciples, "In the world you will have tribulation." The word, "tribulation is literally 'pressure,' and figuratively means 'affliction' or 'distress.'"[4] Jesus was simply teaching that believers would face affliction and distress. Church history has proven these words to be true. There is no reason to suggest that this means the Church is promised to go through the seven years of tribulation. There is a vast difference between *tribulation* and *the Tribulation*.

Perhaps the biggest problem with the view that the Rapture takes place after the Tribulation is that it creates tension with the teaching in Scripture concerning the millennial phase of the Kingdom. Remember, the Kingdom of Christ will be established on earth after the Second Coming. Matthew 25 reveals that unbelievers will be cast into the everlasting fire. 1 Corinthians 15 teaches that at the Rapture of the Church believers will receive their glorified bodies (which will not have the ability to procreate). If it were true that the Rapture and the Second Coming happen at the same time, then who would be left in the Kingdom to repopulate the earth? Unbelievers would be in the lake of fire and believers would not have the ability to procreate, so how would the Kingdom of Christ repopulate the earth? No unbelievers would be left at the beginning of the Kingdom of Christ. No babies would be born, but Revelation 20 teaches that after the Millennium there will be enough unbelievers living at that time for Satan to attempt one final battle against God. Logically, this view is inconsistent with the teaching of the Word of God.

The Midtribulation Rapture View

The midtribulation Rapture view is illustrated in figure 10.5. This position teaches that the Rapture takes place midway through the Tribulation.

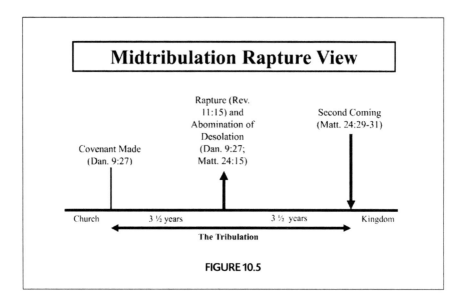

FIGURE 10.5

This particular view is based upon an incorrect cross-reference of Scripture. The seventh trumpet during the Tribulation (Rev. 11:15) is correlated with the last trumpet mentioned in 1 Corinthians 15:52 and 1 Thessalonians 4:16. It is argued that Revelation 11:15 is referring to the Rapture. It is correct that in both 1 Corinthians and 1 Thessalonians Paul referred to a trumpet at the Rapture, but this does not mean that it should randomly be assigned to the trumpet of Revelation 11:15. There are many trumpets mentioned in the Bible. Why not connect this to the trumpets of Jericho, or any other trumpet mentioned in Scripture? There is no justification for assuming the seventh trumpet, in the trumpet judgments of Revelation 11, is in fact the same as the last trumpet that will end the Church Age. Notice that 1 Corinthians 15:52 does not state that this will be the last trumpet ever. Instead, it is referring to the last trumpet of the Church Age.

The Partial Rapture View

The partial Rapture view is represented in figure 10.6. This particular viewpoint is rare. The general idea is that when a believer is spiritually mature enough they will be caught up to meet the Lord. At first, it will be a host of believers, who will be eagerly waiting and watching for the Lord, that are said to be caught up all at once. Then the rest of the believers will be caught up throughout the Tribulation as they mature in their faith.

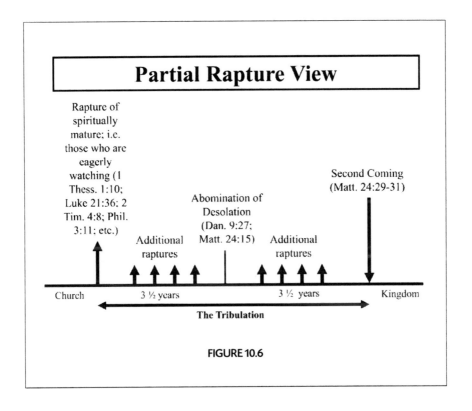

FIGURE 10.6

This view is based on a misunderstanding of passages that seem to make watchfulness a condition for being raptured. The passages that are said to teach this include Luke 21:34-36; Matt. 24:36-44; Heb. 9:28; Phil. 3:11; 2 Tim. 4:8; 1 Thess. 1:10. A careful examination of these texts demonstrates that some of them are referring to the Second Coming and not the Rapture (Luke 21:34-36; Matt. 24:36-44). Even the passages that do refer to the Rapture are not teaching that if you fail to watch you will not be caught up to meet the Lord. These verses are simply challenging believers to watch for the return of the Lord for His people. To say otherwise is to read more into the text than what is written.

The Prewrath Rapture View

The prewrath Rapture view was popularized by Marvin Rosenthal in 1990, which is illustrated in figure 10.7. Rosenthal's book *The Prewrath Rapture of the Church* provides the defense of this view.

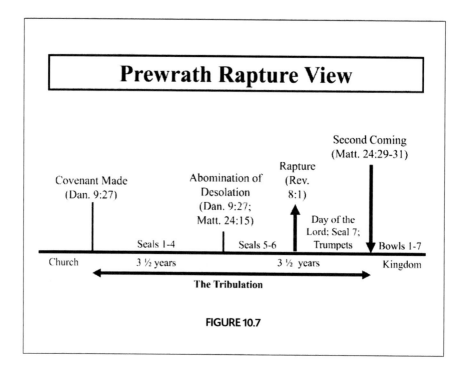

FIGURE 10.7

This position hinges on the assumption that the Day of the Lord is limited to the last eighteen months of the Tribulation. Therefore, the Rapture is said to not occur until the middle of the second half of the Tribulation. Truthfully, this is a modification of the midtribulation Rapture view. The Church is seen as being raptured out before the wrath of God, but the wrath of God is not seen as taking place until the second half of the Tribulation. This view has no cohesiveness and does not take into account the clear benchmarks in Scripture of the distinction between Israel and the Church. It leaves the question of why the Church would be left to go through a portion of the Tribulation.

The Pretribulation Rapture View

The Rapture is before the Tribulation. This is represented in figure 10.8.

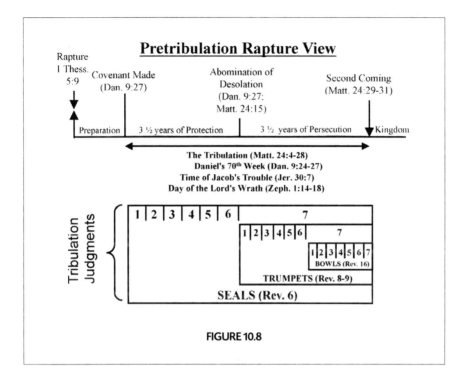

FIGURE 10.8

The Rapture takes place at the close of the Church Age. This is followed by an unspecified time of preparation, which is followed by the official start of the Tribulation, including the seal, trumpet, and bowl judgments outlined in Revelation. The Tribulation is variously referred to as Daniel's Seventieth Week, the time of Jacob's trouble, and the Great Day of the Lord's Wrath.

Five Proofs of Pretribulationism

The proof for the pretribulational Rapture of the Church eliminates the other views. The number one proof is that the Church must be rescued *before* the Day of the Lord's Wrath. 1 Thessalonians 1:10; 5:9, and Revelation 3:10 all indicate that the Church will be rescued before the Day of the Lord's Wrath. Therefore, identifying when the Day of the Lord's Wrath begins identifies when the Rapture will take place sequentially.

The Day of the Lord's Wrath encompasses the entire Seventieth Week of Daniel (Zeph. 1:14-18; Hos. 5:10; Ezek. 7:19; Luke 21:23). We come to this conclusion by carefully examining and comparing the related passages in Scripture. Revelation 6 begins with the seal judgments. The first seal judgment reveals the imposter upon the white horse, the Antichrist, who will go out to conquer the world. Daniel 9:27 informs us that the unveiling of the Antichrist is the beginning of the Tribulation, so we can safely conclude that the seal judgments of Revelation commence the Tribulation. By comparing these texts we learn that the seal judgments of Revelation 6 begin at the start of the seven-year Tribulation. This does not necessarily mean that we have yet proven that the seal judgments are the prophetic wrath of God. All that we have established at this point is that the seal judgments begin the Tribulation.

Revelation chapters 4-5 contain an extended theodicy which demonstrates that the Lamb is worthy and justified to open the seals on the scroll. Revelation 6:8 alludes to Ezekiel 14:21, which has a clear eschatological wrath context. The key to knowing that the opening of the seals is the unleashing of the wrath of God is found in Revelation 6:16-17. We witness that the men of the earth will cry out, "Fall on us and hide us from the face of Him who sits on the throne and from the wrath of the Lamb! For the great day of His wrath has come, and who is able to stand?" The wrath of the Lamb is already present at this point. The men of the earth will already be hiding from the wrath, as six of the seals will have been opened. Therefore, there can be no question that the seal judgments are the beginning of the prophetic wrath of God. Because the Church is promised to be rescued before the Day of the Lord's Wrath, this places the Rapture before the seal judgments, or before the Tribulation begins.

Furthermore, the Olivet Discourse gives a chronological account of the entire Seventieth Week of Daniel, if you note the references to time throughout it (cf. Matt. 24:15). A comparison of the seal judgments of Revelation 6 with the Olivet Discourse in Matthew 24 indicates that the seals take place at the start of the Seventieth Week of Daniel 9. This is demonstrated in figure 10.9.

In Matthew 24, the disciples wanted to know the sign of Lord's coming (Matt. 24:3). Jesus responded, "Take heed that no one deceives you. For many will come in My name, saying, 'I am the Christ,' and will deceive many" (Matt. 24:4-5). In Revelation 6 the first seal judgment is the unveiling of the preeminent false christ (Rev. 6:1-2).

A Comparison of the Olivet Discourse and the Seal Judgments	
Olivet Discourse (Matt. 24; Mark 13; Luke 21)	Seal Judgments (Rev. 6)
1. FALSE CHRISTS (Matt. 24:4-5, 23-26; Mark 13:6, 21-23; Luke 21:8)	1. The Antichrist unveiled (Rev. 6:1-2)
2. WAR (Matt. 24:6-7; Mark 13:7-8; Luke 21:9-10)	2. People kill one another (Rev. 6:3-4)
3. FAMINE (Matt. 24:7; Mark 13:8; Luke 21:11)	3. Scarcity of food (Rev. 6:5-6)
4. DEATH (Matt. 24:9, 22, 28; Mark 13:12, 20; Luke 21:16)	4. ¼ of population dies (Rev. 6:7-8)
5. MARTYRDOM (Matt. 24:9-13; Mark 13:9-13; Luke 21:12-19)	5. Martyrs cry out for justice (Rev. 6:9-11)
6. COSMIC SIGNS (Matt. 24:29; Mark 13:24-25; Luke 21:11)	6. Cosmic disturbances (Rev. 6:12-17) www.hottyworks.org

FIGURE 10.9

Jesus warned of, "wars and rumors of wars" (Matt. 24:6). At the second seal judgment peace will be taken from the earth, "Another horse, fiery red, went out. And it was granted to the one who sat on it to take peace from the earth, and that people should kill one another; and there was given to him a great sword" (Rev. 6:4). It is noteworthy, in verse 6 of Matthew 24, that Jesus told the disciples, "The end is not yet." This suggests that this passage refers to the entire seven-year period and not just the first half. There will still be a few more years of tribulation.

In the Olivet Discourse, Jesus then warned of famines in that day (Matt. 24:7). Revelation 6:5-6 informs us that the third seal judgment will be a famine.

Verse 8 of Matthew 24 contains a critical piece of information. Jesus instructed, "All these are the beginning of sorrows." The New American Standard Bible translates this text, "But all these things are merely the beginning of birth pangs."[5] The birth pangs are characteristically used in Scripture to describe the period of trouble that immediately precedes the Messianic Age (cf. Isa. 13:8; 26:17; Jer. 4:31; 6:24; Mic. 4:9-10). The troubling events that Jesus had predicted up until this point are merely the beginning of the Day of the Lord.

In the Olivet Discourse, Jesus then warned of the death that would ensue, "Then they will deliver you up to tribulation and kill you, and you will be hated by all nations for My name's sake" (Matt. 24:9). In the second half of the Tribulation, the protection that the Antichrist will provide for Israel will be removed. Many Jews will lose their lives. Revelation 6:7-8 teaches that the fourth seal judgment will lead to the death of one-quarter of the population.

Jesus continued by teaching of the martyrdom that will come (Matt. 24:9-13). Specifically, Jesus warned, "Then they will deliver you up to tribulation and kill you, and you will be hated by all nations for My name's sake" (Matt. 24:9). As we look once again to Revelation 6, we see that the fifth seal judgment is the plea for justice from the martyrs that have been killed during the Tribulation (Rev. 6:9-11).

In Matthew 24:29 Jesus taught, "Immediately after the tribulation of those days the sun will be darkened, and the moon will not give its light; the stars will fall from heaven, and the powers of the heavens will be shaken." These are the cosmic signs that will immediately precede the coming of Christ. The sixth seal judgment will be earthquakes and cosmic disturbances. The Apostle John instructed:

> I looked when He opened the sixth seal, and behold, there was a great earthquake; and the sun became black as sackcloth of hair, and the moon became like blood. And the stars of heaven fell to the earth, as a fig tree drops its late figs when it is shaken by a mighty wind. Then the sky receded as a scroll when it is rolled up, and every mountain and island was moved out of its place (Rev. 6:12-14).

The point of the comparison between Revelation 6 and Matthew 24 is to recognize that both texts are undoubtedly referring to the same events. Together, they demonstrate remarkable unity in the Word of God. Further, they help us to identify the timing of the Rapture by providing additional evidence that the seal judgments begin at the start of the Tribulation. Revelation 6:16 demonstrates that the opening of the seals is the prophetic Day of the Lord's Wrath. Therefore, this wrath must begin at the start of the Tribulation. Because the Church is to be rescued from this wrath, the Church will be raptured before the Tribulation begins.

The second proof of the pretribulation Rapture of the Church is related directly to the Jewish nature of the Tribulation. The critical distinction between the Church and the nation of Israel must not be forgotten. The Church did not participate in the first sixty-nine weeks of years for the nation of Israel (Dan. 9:24-25). Why would the Church then participate in the seventieth week? Remember, this period of time is referred to as, "Jacob's trouble" (Jer. 30:7). Even in Daniel 9:24 we witness the distinct references to the Jewish people as Daniel was told, "Seventy weeks are determined for your people and for your holy city." The 144,000 witnesses will be of, "the tribes of the children of Israel" (Rev. 7:4). There will be 12,000 from each of the 12 tribes (Rev. 7:5-8). The Olivet Discourse itself is Jewish in nature. Regarding the Olivet Discourse in Matthew, "The church is not present in any sense in chapters 24 and 25. The disciples' questions related to Jerusalem, Israel, and the Lord's second coming in glory to establish His kingdom."[6] Further, even the Old Testament descriptions of this period are clearly Jewish in nature (Zech. 12:8-9).

A third argument for pretribulationism is that the literary structure of the book of Revelation indicates that the Church is not present on earth once the seal judgments begin. An overview of Revelation in figure 10.10 demonstrates this truth.

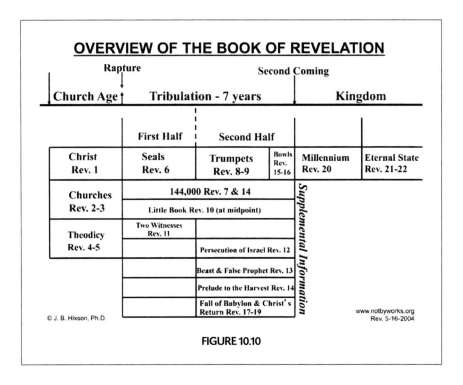

FIGURE 10.10

The book of Revelation is actually quite easy to outline if the eschatological context is kept in mind. The first three chapters are directly related to the Church. Chapter 1 presents Jesus Christ, the Revelation. It is a common mistake to refer to the final book of the Bible as Revelations. Chapter 1 demonstrates that the correct title is Revelation because it is the Revelation of Jesus Christ. Chapters 2 and 3 are letters to the literal historical churches in the first century. Chapters 4 and 5 are a theodicy demonstrating the worthiness of the Lamb to pour out the wrath of God.

As previously demonstrated, chapter 6 begins the Tribulation period. The seal judgments of Revelation 6 will take place in the first half of the Tribulation. The trumpet and bowl judgments take place in the second half. Based on the nature of the bowl judgments, they probably take place in the final hours before the Second Coming. These judgments are preparation for Armageddon (Rev. 16:16). Chapter 19 details the Second Coming of Christ. The Millennium is revealed in chapter 20, and the Eternal State is mentioned in chapters 21 and 22. Both the Millennium and the Eternal State comprise the Kingdom.

Certainly the book of Revelation gives us supplemental information about additional activities that will take place during the Tribulation. It is generally understood that the ministry of the 144,000 witnesses will span the entire 7 years. The intense persecution of Israel will primarily take place in the second half of the Tribulation. The discussion of the Beast and the False Prophet relates to the second half. This additional information further describes the activities taking place during this seven-year period.

The point is to recognize that the Church is never mentioned in Revelation 4-18. If the Church is to take part in some of the judgments of the Tribulation, why is it never mentioned? Therefore, the literary structure of Revelation is a strong argument for the Rapture of the Church taking place before the Tribulation.

A fourth argument relates directly to the mystery concept of the Church. This makes the pretribulation Rapture a necessity. The Church is a temporary interruption in God's program with Israel, which was not brought into existence until after the sixty-ninth week of Daniel 9. Historically, the Church had no place in the first sixty-nine weeks, and so it follows that the Church has no place in the seventieth week either.

The strongest exegetical proof for the pretribulation Rapture comes from 2 Thessalonians 2. This is the direct exegetical evidence that the

Rapture occurs before the Tribulation. Verse 1 teaches, "Now, brethren, concerning the coming of our Lord Jesus Christ and our gathering together to Him." The reference to the Church being "gathered together" to meet the Lord is an undisputable reference to the Rapture, which Paul had previously referenced in his first letter to the Thessalonians (cf. 1 Thess. 4:13-18 and 2 Thess. 2:5).

Paul continued, "We ask you, not to be soon shaken in mind or troubled, either by spirit or by word or by letter, as if from us, as though the day of Christ had come" (2 Thess. 2:1-2). This is Paul's second letter to the church at Thessalonica. He had already taught them about this reunion in the sky in 1 Thessalonians 4. In 2 Thessalonians 2, Paul was now referring back to his previous teaching and instructing them to not be shaken or troubled. Evidently, someone had written a forged letter in Paul's name telling the believers that the Day of the Lord had come.[7] The issue at hand resulted in the question, "Are we in the Day of the Lord, or not?" The early Church had a large percentage of Jewish believers who were well acquainted with the Day of the Lord. They understood the eschatological Day of the Lord as being the outpouring of God's wrath and the final age before the Kingdom. For this reason, they were deeply troubled by this false report that had taught they were already in the Day of the Lord. Any persecution that they faced made their concerns grow stronger.

Paul answered, "Let no one deceive you by any means; for that Day will not come unless the falling away comes first, and the man of sin is revealed, the son of perdition, who opposes and exalts himself above all that is called God or that is worshiped, so that he sits as God in the temple of God, showing himself that he is God" (2 Thess. 2:3-4). Paul insisted two things must happen first. In other words, two things must take place before it can be said that someone is living in the Day of the Lord. The bottom line is whether or not these two things have occurred. If the answer is yes, then the Day of the Lord is at hand. If not, you cannot possibly be in the Day of the Lord.

What are these two things that must take place *before* the Day of the Lord? These include the falling away and the revelation of the man of sin. Paul assured them that the Day of the Lord is not here because the falling away has not happened and the man of sin has not been revealed (v. 3). The man of sin is the Antichrist. So you cannot be in the Day of the Lord unless the Antichrist has been revealed and this falling away has occurred.

Historically, the term *falling away*, which is the Greek word *apostasia*, has been understood as a spiritual falling away, but the actual word simply means *departure*. Context, as it does with all words, has to determine whether it means spiritual departure or a physical geographic departure. There is nothing inherent in the Greek word *apostasia* that implies spiritual apostasy.

Amillennial theologians do not distinguish between the Rapture and the Second Coming of Christ. Therefore, they have historically used this passage to teach that prior to the end of the age there is going to be a great end times spiritual apostasy. This is their interpretation of this passage.

The New Testament does reveal that within the Church there will be a clear worsening of the spiritual condition of believers. In 2 Timothy 3:13 Paul testified, "But evil men and impostors will grow worse and worse, deceiving and being deceived." It is also true that the further we progress into the Church Age, Satan's impact on the world will spill over into the Church (2 Tim. 4:3-4). However, this is not the subject at hand in 2 Thessalonians 2:3-4.

We have no indication contextually that Paul was referring to a spiritual apostasy. Quite the contrary, an examination of the immediate context indicates that a physical departure is in mind. Verse 1 states, "concerning the coming of our Lord Jesus Christ and our gathering together to Him" (2 Thess. 2:1). This refers to a physical movement from point A to point B. This is a reference to a physical departure at the coming of the Lord Jesus and our gathering to meet Him in the air. Moreover, verse 7 also mentions the removal of the restraining influence from the earth. The end of this restraining influence coincides with the unveiling of the antichrist. These references to geographic movement make it more natural to see the term *apostasia*, in verse 3, is a reference to the Rapture—the physical departure of Christians from the earth to meet the Lord in the air. With this in mind, Paul was testifying that the Thessalonians could not be in the Day of the Lord (the Tribulation) because the Rapture had not taken place and the Antichrist had not been revealed.

The conclusion is that the departure of the Church to meet the Lord in the air (the Rapture) must precede the arrival of the Day of the Lord's Wrath.

The Blessed Hope of the Early Church

We need to be aware that as we read through the New Testament, especially the Epistles, the Rapture is beneath the surface of much of the text. It was the blessed hope of the early Church.

The Apostle Paul first introduced the doctrine of the Rapture, under the inspiration of the Holy Spirit, in one of his earliest epistles. 1 Thessalonians was the second epistle recorded by Paul, in A.D. 51. The Church was not even twenty years old at this time, and yet the Christians had already begun to learn about this concept of the catching up of believers to meet the Lord in the air to rescue them from the day of wrath that is to come.

The four primary passages from the New Testament that teach on the Rapture (1 Thessalonians 4:13-18; John 14; 1 Corinthians 15; 2 Thessalonians 2) are the texts that give us the instruction to build our understanding of the doctrine of the Rapture. But once we take into account the numerous allusions to the Rapture in the New Testament, it is truly astounding how pervasive the teaching is.

Titus 2:13 teaches, "Looking for the blessed hope and glorious appearing of our great God and Savior Jesus Christ." The phrase *appearing* is unique to verses that refer to the Rapture because the Second Coming typically mentions Christ coming all the way to the earth and events that are associated with the Second Coming. The Rapture is an event that takes place in the air. Titus 2:13 is a reference to the Rapture.

1 Thessalonians contains an indirect reference to the Rapture. It states, "and to wait for His Son from heaven, whom He raised from the dead, even Jesus who delivers us from the wrath to come" (1 Thess. 1:10). This is a promise to rescue the Church from the eschatological wrath of God. The means of rescue is the Rapture.

Philippians 3:20-21 also refers to the Rapture. Paul wrote, "For our citizenship is in heaven, from which we also eagerly wait for the Savior, the Lord Jesus Christ, who will transform our lowly body that it may be conformed to His glorious body, according to the working by which He is able even to subdue all things to Himself." A simple observation of the text demonstrates that Paul, as a Church Age believer, included himself in this discussion. The instruction of what will take place with the transformation of our bodies is consistent with the unified testimony in the New Testament of the Rapture (cf. 1 Cor. 15:51-54; 1 Thess. 4:16-17). This is yet another reference to the return of Christ for the Church.

The Provocation of the Rapture

The doctrine of the Rapture of the Church provokes believers to respond to the hope of being caught up to meet the Lord in the air. First, the Scriptures instruct us not to be troubled (John 14:1; cf. 2 Thess. 2:2). Christ will return for us and reunite us with the dead in Christ. Therefore, we should comfort one another with this truth (1 Thess. 4:18). The return of our Lord should be a motivation for us to be, "steadfast, immovable, always abounding in the work of the Lord, knowing that your labor is not in vain in the Lord" (1 Cor. 15:58).

Believers are also instructed to remain in close fellowship with Christ, so that we are not ashamed when He comes (1 John 2:28). We should live our lives in such a way that we will be rewarded at the Judgment Seat of Christ (1 Cor. 3:10-15; 2 Cor. 5:9-11; Col. 3:23-24; 2 John 8; Rev. 22:12). The Bema Judgment will be the first order of business once believers are raptured, and we want to be found faithful. We want to hear the words, "Well done good and faithful servant." We want to be rewarded and receive positions of leadership in the Kingdom that will help us to serve and reign. It is wise to redeem the time because there is no guarantee of tomorrow (cf. James 4:14; Eph. 5:15-16).

The doctrine of the Rapture of the Church also means we can anticipate and be comforted by the prospect of being reunited with believers who have died (1 Thess. 4:13-18). The anticipation of the Rapture should give us hope during difficult times (Col. 1:27; Titus 2:13). It should cause us to look up and be watchful because the return of our Lord could happen at any moment.

Our Hope for Rescue

The doctrine of the Rapture of the Church is intended to bring us hope (Titus 2:13). The Lord Jesus Christ wants us to realize that our rescue is certain. The Church will not face the eschatological wrath of the Lamb of God (1 Thess. 1:10). The Rapture brings the Church Age to an end, and it is a time when we are reunited with the dead in Christ to receive our glorified bodies (1 Thess. 4:13-17). Believers will be lifted up to be united forever with Christ. May these be the words that bring us comfort in times of distress, as we look to the day of our glorious reunion with Jesus Christ!

Discussion Questions

1. Define the Rapture.
2. What will take place at the Rapture?
3. When will the Rapture happen?
4. Describe the purpose of the Rapture.
5. What is the key Bible passage concerning the Rapture? How does it portray the Rapture?
6. Explain the differences between the Rapture and the Second Coming.
7. Name the correct view in regard to the timing of the Rapture. Why is this the correct view?
8. The Rapture should provoke Christians to do what?
9. Why is the Rapture a doctrine of hope for believers?

Endnotes

1. Kalee Thompson, "Inside the Coast Guard's Most Extreme Rescue," http://www.popularmechanics.com/technology/aviation/crashes/4267469 (accessed September 27, 2012); Kalee Thompson, "Alaska Ranger: Lessons from Coast Guard's most challenging rescue," http://coastguard.dodlive.mil/2011/01/alaska-ranger-lessons-from-coast-guards-most-challenging-rescue/ (accessed September 27, 2012).
2. Luke 19 is an allusion to an event that will take place in conjunction with the Rapture (the Judgment Seat of Christ), but there is no other passage in the Gospels that directly mentions the Rapture.
3. For a greater discussion on amillennial and postmillennial theology see chapters 3-4.
4. Earl D. Radmacher, Ronald Barclay Allen, and H. Wayne House, *Nelson's New Illustrated Bible Commentary* (Nashville, TN: Thomas Nelson Publishers, 1999), John 16:33.
5. *New American Standard Bible: 1995 Update* (LaHabra, CA: The Lockman Foundation, 1995), Matt. 24:8.
6. Louis A. Barbieri, Jr., *Matthew in The Bible Knowledge Commentary: An Exposition of the Scriptures Vol. 2* (Wheaton, IL: Victor Books, 1985), 76.
7. The reading of the Greek text in 2 Thessalonians 2:2 depends on which manuscript you are reading from. The M-Text reads, "the Day of Christ." The NU-Text reads, "the Day of the Lord."

CHAPTER 11

Rejoice and Give Glory - The Bema Judgment and Marriage of the Lamb

Let us be glad and rejoice and give Him glory, for the
marriage of the Lamb has come, and His wife has made
herself ready

- Revelation 19:7

THE AUDITORIUM WAS filled with the hopes and dreams of the next generation. Graduation day had finally arrived for the senior class at Meteor Hill High School. With it came the individual stories of the young men and women who hoped to tackle the world.

Susan had long dreamed of medical school. She knew that four more years of college were ahead of her, before she would even get there. Still, this was a day to celebrate. Susan's strong academic record had put her at the head of the class, and this would be the next step in her path to becoming a pediatrician. Her hard work was rewarded with scholarships for college.

Chuck had taken a much different route through high school. His future was never his focus. Chuck spent his free time with his friends, seemingly, without a care in the world. This changed his junior year when a guidance counselor finally sat him down. Chuck was not on course to graduate, which meant that getting into a trade program to become a mechanic would have been out of the question. The final two years of high school Chuck had buckled down and pulled his grades up. He was not proud of his grades throughout the years, but he was relieved that he had made it to graduation day.

A terrible event in his life led Bret and his family to celebrate this day. A year earlier, he had been involved in a car accident with some of his classmates. Bret was the only one with serious injuries. The smashed car collapsed on him and crushed his bones. He had always been a good student and planned to attend college, but now rehabilitating his body took priority. It was a testimony of his determination to see him walk again. His parents were thankful that Bret was even alive and able to graduate.

A Fitting Comparison

It has been correctly observed that the Judgment Seat of Christ can be compared to a graduation ceremony. Samuel Hoyt summarized the great teaching of the Judgment Seat of Christ in a way that is exceptionally clear:

> The Judgment Seat of Christ might be compared to a commencement ceremony. At graduation there is some measure of disappointment and remorse that one did not do better and work harder. However, at such an event the overwhelming emotion is joy, not remorse. The graduates do not leave the auditorium weeping because they did not earn better grades. Rather, they are thankful that they have been graduated, and they are grateful for what they did achieve. To overdo the sorrow aspect of the Judgment Seat of Christ is to make heaven hell. To underdo the sorrow aspect is to make faithfulness inconsequential.[1]

It is the goal of this study to accurately present the Judgment Seat of Christ in the same balance that is portrayed within the Scriptures.

The phrase *judgment seat* comes from the Greek word *bema*. It is used a total of twelve times in the New Testament, and literally means a step or raised place mounted by steps. In the ancient world of the Roman Empire, the word *bema* generally referred to the official seat of the judge. One of these ancient seats of judgment can still be seen in the remnants of the city of Corinth. In the New Testament the word is used this way in several passages, usually in reference to the Roman Governor or of the Emperor (Matt. 27:19; John 19:13; Acts 18:12, 16-17; 25:6, 10, 17). This is also the term that Paul used to describe the spiritual judgment of believers in Christ. At the Judgment Seat of Christ, believers of the Church Age will be rewarded for their acts of service that were accomplished during their lives on earth.

The Certainty of Eternal Rewards

The certainty of eternal rewards was presented in our Lord's teaching. Even though these passages do not deal directly with the Church, we can witness that our Lord did present the teaching of future rewards to His disciples. This was demonstrated in the Sermon on the Mount when Jesus testified, "Lay up for yourselves treasures in heaven, where neither moth nor rust destroys and where thieves do not break in and steal. For where your treasure is, there your heart will be also" (Matt. 6:20-21). The Lord was instructing that believers' actions can pay dividends later when they will be rewarded for their faithful service.

Further into Matthew we once again see the Lord teaching on the future rewards. Jesus instructed:

> He who receives you receives Me, and he who receives Me receives Him who sent Me. He who receives a prophet in the name of a prophet shall receive a prophet's reward. And he who receives a righteous man in the name of a righteous man shall receive a righteous man's reward. And whoever gives one of these little ones only a cup of cold water in the name of a disciple, assuredly, I say to you, he shall by no means lose his reward (Matt. 10:42).

The context reveals that Jesus was sending out His disciples. The expression *little ones* is simply a figure of speech that Jesus used to refer to the disciples. We note that at the very end of verse 42, Jesus directly mentioned the term *reward*. Jesus wanted the disciples to know that the individuals who faithfully received them would receive a future reward.

We have already examined the teaching of the Lord in Luke 19 and the parable of the minas. It is there that Jesus clearly instructed the disciples on the importance of a life of service while the King is away. The definite implication is that believers will give an account to the King when He returns to inaugurate His Kingdom. Those who were faithful stewards will be rewarded in His Kingdom. Those who fail to redeem the time will be without rewards in the Kingdom. These individuals will still enter the Kingdom, but they will definitely experience a loss of rewards. In great contrast, those who reject the King altogether and never believe in Him will most certainly not inherit the Kingdom of God. Luke 19 has a direct application to the Church today.

Our Savior also mentioned His return in Revelation 22. There we are told, "And behold, I am coming quickly, and My reward is with Me, to give to every one according to his work" (Rev. 22:12). The reward in this specific verse cannot be a reference to merely ushering believers into heaven. The rewards believers will receive are based on their works (2 Cor. 5:10). The Bible excludes works as a determining factor in whether we end up in heaven or hell (Eph. 2:8-9). Therefore, we can safely conclude this verse is not a direct teaching about eternal salvation. Jesus was stating that He is coming back for His Church and will reward His believers accordingly.

The Consistent Teaching of Paul

As an Apostle of Christ, it should not surprise us that Paul also taught about the Judgment Seat of Christ and believers' future rewards. By far, the most detailed teaching we have about these future rewards comes from the Apostle Paul. This takes us first to the book of Romans. Before we can focus on a key teaching about the Judgment Seat of Christ, we need to set the broader context. Chapters 12-16 contain Paul's practical admonitions for believers. It is within this section of Romans that we find Paul's instruction about the Judgment Seat of Christ.

The immediate context of Romans 14 reveals that Paul taught that it is wrong to judge our fellow Christians who relate to amoral activities (meaning preference type issues) differently from the way we do. We all live and die to the Lord (cf. 2 Cor. 5:9). Further, the Lord is the judge of the living and the dead (cf. Acts 10:42; 2 Tim. 4:1; 1 Pet. 4:5).

It is within this context that Paul instructed, "But why do you judge your brother? Or why do you show contempt for your brother? For we shall all stand before the judgment seat of Christ. For it is written: *As I live, says the LORD, every knee shall bow to Me, and every tongue shall confess to God.'* So then each of us shall give account of himself to God" (Rom. 14:10-12). Judging others is out of order because it is not our place. One day every knee will bow before the Lord. Church Age believers will bow before the Lord at the Judgment Seat of Christ, Old Testament believers at the Second Coming, and unbelievers at the Great White Throne Judgment. Each person will one day give an individual account to the Lord.

1 Corinthians 3 is also a foundational passage concerning the Judgment Seat of Christ. There Paul told the believers at Corinth:

> Now he who plants and he who waters are one, and each one will receive his own reward according to his own labor. For we are God's

fellow workers; you are God's field, you are God's building. According to the grace of God which was given to me, as a wise master builder I have laid the foundation, and another builds on it. But let each one take heed how he builds on it. For no other foundation can anyone lay than that which is laid, which is Jesus Christ. Now if anyone builds on this foundation with gold, silver, precious stones, wood, hay, straw, each one's work will become clear; for the Day will declare it, because it will be revealed by fire; and the fire will test each one's work, of what sort it is. If anyone's work which he has built on it endures, he will receive a reward. If anyone's work is burned, he will suffer loss; but he himself will be saved, yet so as through fire (1 Cor. 3:8-15).

It is imperative to notice in this foundational passage on the Judgment Seat of Christ that what will take place will be about rewards and loss of rewards, but not about punishment. There is no reference in this text to punitive penalties. Rewards will be given to faithful believers, but those who do not receive them are not punished.

Christ will not merely judge the outward works of men. Instead He will, "both bring to light the hidden things of darkness and reveal the counsels of the hearts" (1 Cor. 4:5). Christ will examine the inward motives of believers that only God Himself can know. It is not simply a matter of performing good works that leads to rewards; they must be done with the right motive. Christ wants us to perform good works because of our love for Him and His people. This type of attitude can only come from abiding in Christ. The Judgment Seat of Christ will be based on the counsels of the heart. We can take great confidence that our Judge will be fair because He is, "the righteous Judge" (2 Tim. 4:8).

In Paul's second letter to the church at Corinth we witness a parallel passage. The beloved Apostle had been writing about our future glorified bodies that await us. Right now believers are to, "walk by faith, not by sight" (2 Cor. 5:7).[2] Paul then testified, "We are confident, yes, well pleased rather to be absent from the body and to be present with the Lord. Therefore, we make it our aim, whether present or absent, to be well pleasing to Him. For we must all appear before the judgment seat of Christ, that each one may receive the things done in the body, according to what he has done, whether good or bad" (2 Cor. 5:8-10). Our life is about more than what we can see, feel, and touch. Our life is about so much more than this earthly realm. As Paul addressed the goal of being well pleasing to Christ, this takes us back to the attitudes of the heart. Paul was motivated by the firm commitment and conviction that he would one day stand before Christ to give an account for what he had done. This should be a sobering and powerful motivator for every believer in Christ. This is where faith comes in. The reality of someday standing before Christ gives us cause to live our lives diligently, faithfully, openly, and honestly before the Lord.

Nestled into the third chapter of Colossians we once again find the Apostle Paul teaching about the Judgment Seat of Christ. This time Paul taught, "And whatever you do, do it heartily, as to the Lord and not to men, knowing that from the Lord you will receive the reward of the inheritance; for you serve the Lord Christ. But he who does wrong will be repaid for what he has done, and there is no partiality" (Col. 3:23-25). As we witnessed in 1 Corinthians 3, some of our works are compared to gold, silver, and precious stones. Others are compared to wood, hay, and straw which will be consumed by the fire of Christ's judgment (1 Cor. 3:12-15). Only those works that stand up to His judgment will be rewarded. This again is the focus in Colossians 3. Believers will either be rewarded, or they will suffer a loss of rewards. Christians who fail to serve Christ will be repaid. This repayment will come with the loss of rewards.

The Concise Teaching of John

The Apostle John certainly did not elaborate nearly as much as Paul did about the Judgment Seat of Christ. This, however, does not mean that John did not teach about this glorious event.

In 2 John 8 we read, "Look to yourselves, that we do not lose those things we worked for, but that we may receive a full reward." This once again is another example of works being tied to receiving something in the future. Because the Bible explicitly disconnects works from eternal salvation in a number of places, we know that this cannot be a reference to getting into heaven. If John was saying that it is possible to lose your salvation because of your lack of good works, then the Bible would contradict itself. This leads us to safely conclude that this must be a reference to future rewards. John was urging the believers to guard against the deception of false teachers. By yielding to the deception, believers could be lead astray and end up missing out on their full reward.

John also taught on the concept of rewards in his first epistle. 1 John 2:28 teaches, "And now, little children, abide in Him, that when He appears, we may have confidence and not be ashamed before Him at His coming." We know that there will be shame at the Judgment Seat of

Christ for those who squandered their opportunities to serve Christ. This is where we must be careful to not take this to mean something that is not supported by the text. Truthfully, we do not have a lot of details about this, but clearly the text speaks of the prospect of remorse at the Judgment Seat of Christ. John was warning of the prospect of not abiding in (or remaining in fellowship with) Christ when He returns for the Church. No believer should want to be found walking in darkness at His return.

Hebrews and Rewards

Because we cannot say with certainty who wrote Hebrews, we will address it as a category by itself. In Hebrews 10, the author was challenging believers to walk in steadfast faith and confidence in Christ. These Jewish believers were not to abandon their relationship with Him in favor of the temporary and earthly safety found in Judaism. Many of these believers were being persecuted, were suffering, and were being called on to make sacrifices for their faith. The writer exhorts, "Therefore do not cast away your confidence, which has great reward" (Heb. 10:35). The term translated *cast away* carries the idea of carelessly flinging something away. The word is used in other Greek literature of a ring slipping off a finger. It carries the basic idea of carelessness. It would have been careless for these believers to renounce their Christian faith in a moment of weakness, only to embrace Judaism and their former way of life.

Imagine a man walking behind his self-propelled lawn mower. As he looks ahead at the grass, he sees something shiny, so he stops the mower. The shiny object is a washer. Thinking that he does not want to run the mower over this and have it go flying through a window, the man flings it into the woods behind his house. Five minutes later one of the wheels comes off the mower. The washer, along with the nut, had been part of securing the wheel to the mower. Finding the washer was a warning sign of what was to come. Now the man wished he had the washer back. This is the idea of carelessly not thinking something through. In much the same manner, the author was instructing the believers to not carelessly cast away their confidence because it would also mean the loss of a future reward.

Notice the context that begins in the next verse, "For you have need of endurance, so that after you have done the will of God, you may receive the promise: *'For yet a little while, and He who is coming will come and will not tarry. Now the just shall live by faith; but if anyone draws back, My soul has no pleasure in him.'* But we are not of those who draw back to perdition, but of those who believe to the saving of the soul." (Heb. 10:36-39). Again, this cannot be a reference to receiving the gift of eternal life because we do not receive it by enduring. The idea of drawing back to perdition simply means judgment. It is not a statement that these individuals who had believed the gospel were now in danger of facing hell.

Notice in verse 39 the writer said these believers are, "of those who believe to the saving of the soul." The word *soul* does not simply mean the immaterial part of man. The word *soul* is *psychē*, and it means life. The context determines the proper meaning, and in this case the reference is to physical life. It is just as vital to remember that the word *saving* is not always a reference to eternal life. The word is *peripoiēsis* and carries the general meaning of keeping safe or delivering. The writer is admonishing the believers to not draw back in their faith and thereby face negative consequences or a loss of rewards.

Any believer in Christ who denies the Lord is in danger of facing the serious consequences that this will bring. Earlier in the chapter the writer testified, "Of how much worse punishment, do you suppose, will he be thought worthy who has trampled the Son of God underfoot, counted the blood of the covenant by which he was sanctified a common thing, and insulted the Spirit of grace?" (Heb. 10:29). It was the intention of the author, under the inspiration of the Holy Spirit, to encourage the Jewish believers to continue to be confident and steadfast in their faith. This would deliver them from the consequences of the sin of turning back on their faith in Christ. By comparing Hebrews 10 with 1 Corinthians 3, it becomes evident that the deliverance the author had in mind, in Hebrews 10:39, is a reference to deliverance at the Judgment Seat of Christ. Paul testified believers' works would be examined by saying, "If anyone's work which he has built on it endures, he will receive a reward. If anyone's work is burned, he will suffer loss; but he himself will be saved, yet so as through fire" (1 Cor. 3:14-15). Hebrews 10 is yet another example from the New Testament of the concept of the rewards that will come.

Earning Rewards

Now that it has been established from Scripture that believers will receive rewards at the Judgment Seat of Christ, a natural question follows, "What types of behavior will lead to these rewards?"

Before we answer this question it is imperative that we set the stage by remembering two basic facts. Eternal life is a free gift received by faith

(Eph. 2:8-9; Titus 3:5; Rev. 22:17). Eternal rewards are a wage earned by good works (1 Cor. 3:8; Col. 3:23-24; 2 John 8; Rev. 22:12).

Enduring Trials

James taught, "Blessed is the man who endures temptation [trials]; for when he has been approved, he will receive the crown of life which the Lord has promised to those who love Him" (James 1:12). The word translated *temptations* is the same word that is translated in verse 2 as *trials*. It should also be translated *trials* in verse 12. The trials of life are to be endured, not temptations. Temptations are to be resisted.

Consider what James had already written, "My brethren, count it all joy when you fall into various trials, knowing that the testing of your faith produces patience" (James 1:2-3). The trials of life are designed to bring growth in our walk with Christ. Believers should embrace their trials as an opportunity to depend more on God.

James wrote in verse 12, "for when he has been approved." This phrase was used of the testing of coins and metals. The idea given is that our trials may not seem necessary to us, but God uses them as a part of His plan for our lives. The expression *for when he has been approved* refers back to verses 3-4 and the growth that God is looking for in your life. The testing of our faith is designed to produce maturity in Christ. This is what God desires. It should remind us of the words of the Apostle Paul when he wrote, "And not only that, but we also glory in tribulations, knowing that tribulation produces perseverance; and perseverance, character; and character, hope" (Rom. 5:3-4).

It is not the intention of James to suggest that the trials we face, and how we handle them, is the proof or evidence of whether or not we truly belong to God. Instead, James is testifying that believers who have the right attitude toward their trials (welcoming the trial as an opportunity to grow in their faith) can look forward to the crown of life.

Believers in Christ have already received eternal life. Christians have already escaped eternal death, eternal condemnation. Eternal life is a free gift (Rom. 3:24; 6:23). So this crown of life must be something more than the gift of eternal life. At the Judgment Seat of Christ believers who have endured trials in life, and have responded the way that God intends them to respond, will receive the crown of life. This is a promise from God to all who love the Lord Jesus Christ.

The only other place in Scripture that mentions this crown of life is found in Revelation 2:10, which was written well after the book of James.

Referring to the Christians at the church of Smyrna Revelation records, "Do not fear any of those things which you are about to suffer. Indeed, the devil is about to throw some of you into prison, that you may be tested, and you will have tribulation ten days. Be faithful until death, and I will give you the crown of life." There is a clear focus on suffering. The crown of life is the reward for those who are found faithful. It cannot be something that is received in this life because verse 10 teaches that if the believers were faithful unto death, they would receive the crown of life.

If believers endure trials and allow these tough moments to bring them closer to God, this will be their reward at the Judgment Seat of Christ.

Diligently Seeking God

The writer of Hebrews mentions the promise of reward for those who diligently seek God. Hebrews instructs, "But without faith it is impossible to please Him, for he who comes to God must believe that He is, and that He is a rewarder of those who diligently seek Him" (Heb. 11:6). The words *diligently seek* are in the Greek present tense. The original audience of the letter to the Hebrews was tempted to abandon the hope that we have in Christ. They were told that God would reward those believers who continue to seek after Him. These Jewish Christians were to continue to walk by faith.

Perseverance

It should not be a surprise to read of rewards for believers in the book of Revelation. To the church of Thyatira Jesus said, "And he who overcomes, and keeps My works until the end, to him I will give power over the nations—'He shall rule them with a rod of iron; they shall be dashed to pieces like the potter's vessels'— as I also have received from My Father" (Rev. 2:26-27). The difficulty with this text deals with the phrase *he who overcomes.* Considerable debate exists as to the identity of the overcomers in Revelation.

Regarding the overcomer in Revelation 2:7, Robert Thomas explains, "This promise to the overcomer (as well as those in the other six messages) entails participation in eternal blessings that belong to all the saved. For example, eating of the tree of life is synonymous with possessing eternal life (cf. Rev. 22:2, 14)."[3] Thomas also warns about the, "failure to note that *nikaō* in John's writings is synonymous with saving faith in Christ (cf. 1 John 5:4-5)."[4] The overcomers refer to believers in Christ. It is a description of the position of every believer in Christ, and their identification with Jesus Christ.[5]

But notice that verse 26 of Revelation 2 is not just referring to overcomers. It contains a promise to the overcomer (believer) who keeps, "My works until the end." The *works of Christ* is faithful obedience to Him. The works belong to Christ, which means that even in difficult times we represent Him. Christ promised a reward to believers who are faithful to Him. It will be the privilege of reigning with Christ in His Messianic Kingdom.

The reference, in verse 27, to Psalm 2:9 is a prophecy of the coming rule of Christ. It is the Kingdom of Christ that is in view. The smashing of the brittle clay vessels, or the potter's vessel, is a metaphor for this climax in history. The point is that the nations of the earth will be broken when Christ comes to establish His Kingdom. The nations of men oppose Jesus Christ, but they will be shattered when Christ sets up His Kingdom. Only believers who persevere and remain faithful to Christ will have the honor of reigning with Him in His Kingdom. In the same manner Paul taught, "If we endure, we shall also reign with Him. If we deny Him, He also will deny us" (2 Tim. 2:12). When Christ takes possession of His Kingdom, He will deal with His enemies and establish His reign. Those Church Age believers who were faithful to Christ will be rewarded with the responsibility of sharing in His reign.

Faithful in Ministry

1 Peter chapter 5 begins by testifying, "The elders who are among you I exhort" (1 Pet. 5:1). The specific instruction to the elders was, "Shepherd the flock of God which is among you, serving as overseers, not by compulsion but willingly, not for dishonest gain but eagerly; nor as being lords over those entrusted to you, but being examples to the flock; and when the Chief Shepherd appears, you will receive the crown of glory that does not fade away" (1 Pet. 5:2-4). Verse 4 reveals the reward for elders who are faithful to the ministry to which they have been called. When Jesus Christ appears, the Chief Shepherd of the Church, they will receive the crown of glory.

Longing for Christ's Appearing

As the Apostle Paul wrote his last epistle, he knew that his time left on earth was short. He had just stated, "For I am already being poured out as a drink offering, and the time of my departure is at hand" (2 Tim. 4:6). Still, with great confidence the Apostle could proclaim, "Finally, there is laid up for me the crown of righteousness, which the Lord, the righteous Judge, will give to me on that Day, and not to me only but also to all who have loved His appearing" (2 Tim. 4:8). Paul's faithful service to Christ meant that he was not ashamed of meeting his Lord. He could testify that he had kept the faith (2 Tim. 4:7). He knew that on the day of Christ's return he would receive a reward. It should be the desire of believers in Christ to walk faithfully with Him so that they are not ashamed at His return (1 John 2:28).

Leading Others to Christ

Most believers consider it a great privilege to lead another person to salvation in Christ. The Apostle Paul certainly did. He told the church at Thessalonica, "For what is our hope, or joy, or crown of rejoicing? Is it not even you in the presence of our Lord Jesus Christ at His coming?" (1 Thess. 2:19). Paul was so thankful for the great work God had done in the lives of these believers he testified that at the Judgment Seat of Christ they would be his joy and crown of rejoicing.

Faithfulness to Christ

The Apostle Paul saw himself as a servant of Christ and a steward of the mysteries of God (1 Cor. 4:1). A servant and a steward held different degrees of responsibility. A steward was also a servant, but he was charged with the responsibility of managing the affairs of his master. Joseph held the position of a steward in Potiphar's house (Gen. 39:2-19). This considerable responsibility is why Paul testified, "Moreover it is required in stewards that one be found faithful" (1 Cor. 4:2). Paul further instructed that a steward is responsible to his master. This caused Paul to conclude, "Therefore judge nothing before the time, until the Lord comes, who will both bring to light the hidden things of darkness and reveal the counsels of the hearts. Then each one's praise will come from God" (1 Cor. 4:5). Those who have been found faithful to Christ will receive their praise from Him.

Diligence in the Christian Walk

There are several passages that refer to a diligent Christian walk being rewarded by Christ (1 Cor. 9:24-27; Heb. 6:11-12; 2 Pet. 1:10-11). In 1 Corinthians 9, we notice Paul referred to disciplining his body and running to win the race. Paul did these things to obtain an imperishable crown (1 Cor. 9:25). In the same manner, the writer of Hebrews called for the Christians to show diligence in their faith until the end (Heb. 6:11).

Stewardship of what Has Been Entrusted to Us

Certainly the Lord has entrusted to His people different gifts, talents, and abilities. Again, by appealing to the parable of the minas in Luke 19, we witness that there will be different positions of service rewarded in the Kingdom of Christ to those are found faithful to the gifts that Christ has entrusted to them (Luke 19:11-27). It is unfortunate that altogether too many believers squander their time before the return of the King.

Enduring Persecution

The New Testament teaches repeatedly about believers who endure persecution (Matt. 5:11-12; 2 Tim. 2:12-13; Heb. 10:36). 2 Timothy is of special interest regarding this subject. Paul told Timothy, "If we endure, we shall also reign with Him. If we deny Him, He also will deny us. If we are faithless, He remains faithful; He cannot deny Himself" (2 Tim. 2:12-13). This text is often taken to mean believers must persevere (keep trusting Christ and be faithful to Him) in order to demonstrate we are truly saved. Those who endure in the Christian life and endure in good works are thought to be those who have eternal life, but those who deny Christ are said to be proving that they never truly believed in Christ to begin with.

It should be noted that nothing in this text refers to being denied entrance to eternal life with Christ. Paul had just proclaimed his confidence in God to secure his eternal salvation (2 Tim. 1:12). Paul now included himself in the discussion in chapter 2, which would be at odds with what he had previously stated in chapter 1, if his own eternal security was at stake.

2 Timothy 2:12-13 is a parallel contrast, which is why it is set apart in many study Bibles. As previously mentioned, Paul was writing near the end of his life and was facing his own persecution for the faith. The very real prospect existed that Timothy may also face persecution, so Paul was challenging him to endure. Paul wanted Timothy to know that denying Christ meant he would not receive the special privilege of reigning with Christ in the Kingdom. It was a reminder to keep his eyes on the things above, to keep his focus on his citizenship in heaven. Believers who endure persecution will receive a special position of authority in the Kingdom. If we deny Christ as we face persecution (much like Peter did on the night

of Christ's arrest), then we will be denied the privilege of reigning with Christ. But even if we are faithless in a time of trial, Christ remains faithful because He cannot deny those that belong to Him. It is very similar to the description Jesus gave in Luke 19 of the one who did nothing with the mina entrusted to him. The man still got into the kingdom, but did not have as much of a reward.

Remaining in Close Fellowship with Christ

John encouraged believers to, "abide in Him, that when He appears, we may have confidence and not be ashamed before Him at His coming" (1 John 2:28). Believers that continue to abide in Christ can have confidence at His return for the Church. No believer should want to be ashamed before Him.

Benevolence toward the Poor

Benevolence toward the poor was certainly a part of the Lord's teaching (Mark 10:21; Luke 12:32-33). Jesus taught that men and women should lay up treasures in heaven, rather than here on earth. Once again demonstrating the remarkable unity of the Word of God, the Apostle Paul taught, "Command those who are rich in this present age not to be haughty, nor to trust in uncertain riches but in the living God, who gives us richly all things to enjoy. Let them do good, that they be rich in good works, ready to give, willing to share, storing up for themselves a good foundation for the time to come, that they may lay hold on eternal life" (1 Tim. 6:17-19).

Wholehearted Service to Christ

In John 12, we see that Jesus promised honor from the Father. What could lead to this? Jesus testified, "If anyone serves Me, let him follow Me; and where I am, there My servant will be also. If anyone serves Me, him My Father will honor" (John 12:26). Wholehearted service to Christ will lead to this honor.

Ministering to the Saints

It is a wonderful promise of Scripture that our actions do not escape the notice of God. The writer of Hebrews reminds us, "For God is not unjust to forget your work and labor of love which you have shown toward His name, in that you have ministered to the saints, and do minister" (Heb. 6:10). We can have confidence that our Lord remembers and will reward our ministering to the saints.

Types of Rewards at the Judgment Seat of Christ

Crowns

The most common reward that believers think of are the crowns mentioned repeatedly in the Word of God (James 1:12; 1 Pet. 5:4; 1 Cor. 9:25; 2 Tim. 4:8; 1 Thess. 2:19; Rev. 2:10; 3:11). These eternal rewards are not mere synonyms with salvation. Salvation is a gift (Rom. 6:23), but each of these passages demonstrates that these are rewards for the works believers have done.

Reigning with Christ in the Kingdom

The New Testament teaches repeatedly about believers reigning with Christ in the Kingdom (2 Tim. 2:12; Matt. 19:28-30; 24:45-51; Luke 19:11-27; 22:28-30; Rev. 2:26-27; 20:4-6). Again, it must be stated that a significant purpose of the Church Age is to prepare a body of believers that will help to rule and reign in the Kingdom. Some believers will be rewarded with the responsibility of reigning with Christ, but not all. Christ's global Kingdom will necessitate numerous positions of responsibility, service, and authority. Those Church Age believers found faithful at the Judgment Seat of Christ will be rewarded with these positions.

Praise from God

Even though Scripture does not specifically state that this is a reward, we must recognize that receiving praise from God at the Judgment Seat will be very rewarding for believers. At that time, "each one's praise will come from God" (1 Cor. 4:5).

An Inheritance in the Kingdom

The New Testament confronts us with the teaching of an inheritance in the Kingdom of God for believers in Christ. The vast majority of the passages that teach on this inheritance equate it with our eternal life in Christ (Heb.1:14; 9:15; 1 Pet. 1:4; Rev. 21:7; Gal. 5:19-21; 1 Cor. 6:9-10;

Eph. 5:3-5; James 2:5). One text stands alone in distinction. Paul taught the believers at Colossae, "And whatever you do, do it heartily, as to the Lord and not to men, knowing that from the Lord you will receive the reward of the inheritance; for you serve the Lord Christ" (Col. 3:23-24). This instruction was given to the slaves (Col. 3:22). Paul encouraged them to do their work unto the Lord, knowing that they will be richly rewarded by Jesus Christ.

The Timing of the Judgment Seat

The precise timing of the Judgment Seat is not directly revealed to us in Scripture. Still, it can be narrowed down to a timeframe between the Rapture and the Second Coming. It is certain that it will occur after the Rapture, when the Church is removed from the earth to meet the Lord in the air. It also must be concluded by the Second Coming because at that time the Church will return to earth with Him (Rev. 19:14), and many of the rewards involve positions of service in the Kingdom.

The Impact of the Judgment Seat on Believers

The reality of the Judgment Seat of Christ should have a direct and lasting impact on the lives of believers. The prospect of eternal rewards should motivate believers to live out their faith in Christ by doing the very things that Scripture says will be rewarded (Rev. 22:12; 2 John 8; Col. 3:23-24). It should also encourage believers to have a heavenly perspective (Col. 3:1-4; Phil. 3:20-21).

God has created mankind with the desire to work. The prospect of eternal rewards answers the natural desire within believers to earn a wage based on works (1 Cor. 3:8; 2 John 8; Col. 3:23-24).

The prospect of eternal rewards also fills the gap created by the simplistic heaven/hell view of theology, which is common in many evangelical churches. It is a mistake to think that everything about the Christian faith can be reduced to a discussion about heaven or hell. This is a contributing factor for some Christians to teach that if a believer is living in consistent sin, they must not be saved. It is not recognized by many Christians that a believer can behave like an unbeliever, if they are catering to the flesh. The Bible makes it clear that there is a very real category of believers known as carnal Christians (1 Cor. 3:1). These believers need to be encouraged to put on a heavenly mindset and live for the day when they will stand before the Lord Jesus Christ.

Reasons the Prospect of Rewards is Seldom Taught

There are a number of reasons that cause the prospect of rewards for believers to be seldom taught in the Church today:

- Some people neglect it because most evangelical churches are not premillennial. A failure to see the distinction between Israel and the Church, and a lack of understanding of eschatology, means that they fail to even contemplate issues such as the Judgment Seat of Christ.
- Some people mistakenly assume that the doctrine of eternal rewards contradicts salvation by faith alone.
- Some people feel that the doctrine of eternal rewards promotes a selfish motivation.
- Some people believe that all believers will be equally rewarded.
- Some people assert that differing rewards in eternity will lead to jealousy. The absence of the sin nature for believers in the Kingdom of God should eliminate this concern. Believers will have different rewards, and jealously will not be an issue.
- Some people claim Jesus taught that we are all merely servants who deserve no rewards.
- Some people mistakenly believe that emphasizing eternal rewards is pointless, since believers are thought to ultimately give all of their rewards back to Christ. This comes from a misunderstanding of Revelation 4:9-10. The elders spoken of, in verses 9-10, are portrayed in the text as repeatedly casting their crowns before Christ throughout eternity. This is not a one-time event, as it is often taken to be.

There are many motives presented in the Word of God for believers to do good works.[6] Certainly our love for God should be a primary motivation. Yet, it should be recognized that the concept of rewards is a biblical motivation for Christians to carry out good works that goes hand in hand with our other motivations to serve Christ. Everything we do should be done for the glory of God, out of our love for Him. But let it also be recognized that the Judgment Seat of Christ addresses a longing within the heart of man to work for some aspect of our eternal future. Because our works have no part in our eternal salvation (Eph. 2:8-9), God has instituted a plan in which our works will be rewarded. This fulfills the longing of man to earn, or work, toward some aspect of our future. One of the ways that the Lord motivates us to trust Him and to yield to the Holy Spirit is by the recognition that this world is not our home. Someday, we will be at our eternal home in the Kingdom. How we use our time, and the manner in which we live in the present, will dramatically affect the way that we live in the Kingdom. It will have a direct impact on the role that we will have in serving our Savior for all of eternity. The Judgment Seat of Christ is the ultimate reminder that our citizenship is in heaven and we eagerly await our Savior (Phil. 3:20).

We should not underestimate the significance of countless believers in Christ failing to recognize and understand the promise of rewards in the New Testament. This doctrine of Scripture is intended to have a profound impact on our lives and change the way we view our faith. These promised future rewards are a common theme and an integral part of the teaching of the New Testament. A failure to clearly identify and understand these teachings can lead to confusion. All too often, passages teaching on future rewards are taken to be texts that teach on eternal salvation. The end result is disastrous, as Christians are led to believe that we must work to keep from losing our salvation, instead of to earn rewards. The vital teaching on the Judgment Seat of Christ and the rewards offered to believers is a future promise that is intended to be a special blessing for the Church.

The Marriage of the Lamb

Another scriptural doctrine that is neglected in churches today is the Marriage of the Lamb. Again, this is another teaching that is interwoven throughout the New Testament.

In his letter to the believers at Rome Paul taught, "Therefore, my brethren, you also have become dead to the law through the body of Christ, that you may be married to another—to Him who was raised from the dead, that we should bear fruit to God" (Rom. 7:4). Because of Christ's death on the Cross, believers are now considered to be dead to the Law, which allows us to be married to another, Jesus Christ.

This future marriage of the Church to the Lamb should have a defining impact on the way in which we live. It is for this reason Paul warned the church at Corinth, "For I am jealous for you with godly jealousy. For I have betrothed you to one husband, that I may present you as a chaste virgin to Christ" (2 Cor. 11:2). The Church is considered to be betrothed to Christ. During this time Paul wanted nothing more than the Church to remain faithful to her heavenly Bridegroom.

Ephesians 5:25-33 contains extended teaching on the Bride of Christ. This text highlights our relationship with the Lord Jesus as believers in the Body of Christ.

Revelation contains direct teaching on the Marriage of the Lamb. The Bible records, "'Let us be glad and rejoice and give Him glory, for the marriage of the Lamb has come, and His wife has made herself ready.' And to her it was granted to be arrayed in fine linen, clean and bright, for the fine linen is the righteous acts of the saints" (Rev. 19:7-8). It should be noted that the actual marriage ceremony will take place in heaven. The marriage feast (the wedding feast) will take place on earth when Christ returns to reign (Luke 16:15-24). We will return with Him at the Second Coming (Rev. 19:14).

The Time of the Marriage

The Marriage of the Lamb must occur sometime *after* the Rapture, when the entire Body of Christ is united in heaven, having been caught up to meet the Lord (2 Cor. 5:10; 1 John 2:28). The Church will be refined and tested at the Judgment Seat of Christ and ready to be married to the Lord. But the Scriptures also indicate that the Marriage of the Lamb must *precede* the Second Coming. This is ascertained by a careful examination of Revelation 19:7. There the wording states, "for the marriage of the Lamb has come." The Greek (aorist tense and indicative mood) indicates a completed past act. In other words, the Church is seen in Revelation 19:7 as already married to Christ. This is before the Second Coming (Rev. 19:11-16).

The Place of the Marriage

Given the time frame of the wedding, the marriage must take place in heaven. The earth will be undergoing the intense tribulation of the Day of the Lord's Wrath. We are reminded that the Church will return from heaven with Christ (Rev. 19:14).

The Participants in the Marriage

The saints that participate in the Marriage of the Lamb must be limited to the Church. The Old Testament saints will not be included because they will not be resurrected until the Second Coming (Dan. 12:1-3; Isa. 26:19-21). As we previously noted, the Marriage of the Lamb will take place before the Second Coming. Therefore, this excludes the Old Testament saints. It also cannot include the Tribulation saints martyred for their faith because they too will not be resurrected until the Second Coming (Rev. 20:4-6).

The Scriptures we have already examined clearly state that the Church is the Bride of Christ. The Marriage of the Lamb will be a unique blessing for Church Age believers

.

The Marriage versus the Marriage Supper

The Marriage Supper and the Marriage of the Lamb are related, but are not the same event. As mentioned, the Marriage of the Lamb relates only to the Church, the Bride of Christ. The Marriage Supper includes Israel and all the citizens of the Kingdom of Christ. It will take place at the beginning of the Millennium.

We have already examined the healing of the centurion's servant in Matthew 8:5-13.[7] Jesus marveled at the great faith of the centurion. Then He said, "Assuredly, I say to you, I have not found such great faith, not even in Israel! And I say to you that many will come from east and west, and sit down with Abraham, Isaac, and Jacob in the kingdom of heaven. But the sons of the kingdom will be cast out into outer darkness. There will be weeping and gnashing of teeth" (Matt. 8:10-12). The wording *sit down* is actually a reference to *reclining to eat*, as they would do at a banquet table. This is referring to the actual Marriage Supper.

The great faith demonstrated by the centurion caused Jesus to mention that in the Kingdom there will be many Gentiles at the Marriage Supper. The sons of the Kingdom (unbelieving Israel) will be cast into outer darkness, where there will be weeping and gnashing of teeth. In chapter 4 we saw that this simply means they will be left out in the dark, which is what outer darkness means. It is not a technical term that refers to some special place that some people will go to. Unbelievers will be left out of the Kingdom.

When the Kingdom begins, the Marriage Supper will take place. According to Jewish customs, these feasts would always take place at night. The picture given is of the unbelieving Jews left out in dark because they will be in hell.

The presence of Abraham, Isaac, and Jacob at this feast reveals that all the citizens of the Kingdom will be invited (Matt. 8:11). Certainly the Church (the Bride of Christ) will be at this feast. Tribulation and Old Testament saints will be the invited guests (Rev. 19:9). Other New Testament passages that teach about this feast include: Matthew 22:1-14; 25:1-13; Luke 14:16-24).

The End of the Age

The close of the Church Age will be a unique time on the stage of world history. With the shifting of the spotlight once again to the nation of Israel for the Seventieth Week of Daniel, Christ will return for His Bride. Christians alive at that time will be translated. The dead in Christ will have their bodies resurrected at the Rapture, and we will all stand before the Lord and give an account to Him at the Judgment Seat. The Church will then be presented to Christ, as His Bride, in heaven.

Christians should recognize and appreciate the unique place we have in God's program, as a part of the Bride of Christ. It is our privilege to be able to eagerly look forward to the moment when we will be united formally to the Bridegroom. Until then, let us strive to represent Christ with honor as we look for, "the blessed hope and glorious appearing of our great God and Savior Jesus Christ" (Titus 2:13).

Discussion Questions

1. What can the Judgment Seat of Christ be compared to? What is the main point of this comparison?
2. Describe what will take place at the Judgment Seat of Christ.
3. Provide some examples of key passages that reveal the certainty of eternal rewards, and a summary of their teaching.
4. What is the difference between eternal life and eternal rewards?
5. List the types of behavior that will lead to the eternal rewards given at the Judgment Seat of Christ.

6. Explain the different types of rewards that believers will be able to obtain.
7. When will the Judgment Seat of Christ occur and what impact should it have on believers?
8. Give an overview of the Marriage of the Lamb including what it is, who is involved, and when and where it will take place.
9. What is the Marriage Supper? Who will take part and who will not?
10. As the Bride of Christ, what should Christians look forward to?

Endnotes

1. Samuel L. Hoyt, "The Negative Aspects of the Christian's Judgment," *Bibliotheca Sacra* 137 (April–June 1980): 131.
2. This is a key principle for living the Christian faith. When Jesus Christ was physically present on the earth, believers walked by sight. Jesus was here and people could physically see and touch Him. They literally followed Him and obeyed His verbal instructions. Now that He is gone, the entire Christian life is about living by faith in Him and His Word.
3. Robert L. Thomas, *Revelation 1-7: An Exegetical Commentary* (Chicago, IL: Moody Publishers, 1992), 152.
4. Ibid.
5. For more information see: J.B. Hixson, et al. *Freely By His Grace: Classical Free Grace Theology* (Duluth, MN: Grace Gospel Press, 2012), 463-68.
6. See Dr. Hixson's article *Reasons for the Christian to do Good Works* at www.NotByWorks.org.
7. See chapter 3.

CHAPTER 12

Perilous Times -
The Antichrist and Day of the Lord

And then the lawless one will be revealed, whom the Lord will consume with the breath of His mouth and destroy with the brightness of His coming.

- 2 Thessalonians 2:8

UNCERTAIN TIMES CREATE open doors for men who crave power. The early 1930's found Germany in a desperate situation. An economic collapse left millions of people unemployed. Political infighting led to a lack of progress in adopting solutions for the German people. The average German was tired of the misery and suffering. Starvation and homelessness were realistic concerns for many Germans.

Little by little the Nazi party began to rise to power. Desperation had set in, and the German people were willing to elect anyone who seemed capable of leading them out of their hopeless situation. The nation was ready to accept a new type of leader.

Adolf Hitler played the part of a leader who could usher in stability and offer hope to the people. His promises were short on details, and his campaign repeated short catchphrases to indoctrinate the Germans. Hitler's appearances were carefully staged to have a maximum effect on the people. Banners, swastikas, music, lighting, and even his speeches were all carefully choreographed. The intention was to appeal to the emotions of the German people to create loyalty to the cause.

These types of leaders usually come promising much more than they can deliver. Hitler was no exception. His promises included stability of the nation, work for the unemployed, economic prosperity, and a stronger nation. Hitler used these vague promises to manipulate the masses, and the Nazi party was seen as the wave of the future. After years of political maneuvering, Adolf Hitler became the Chancellor of Germany on January 30, 1933. Within a short time he would become the dictator of Germany, which would result in the outbreak of the Second World War and the deaths of millions of people.

The Antichrist Revealed

Immediately after the Rapture, there will be no more Christians on earth. It will be a time of unprecedented chaos, as world leaders scramble to explain the disappearance of millions of people. Social unrest and economic concerns are certain to ensue. One man will rise to the surface with what will seem to be a plausible explanation and a plan to reestablish order. Allegiance to this man will bring about much more than the destruction of Europe; it will cost men their eternal destiny. His deception will enthrall the masses of humanity and, eventually, lead the armies of the world to do battle with Jesus Christ. The Bible calls this man the Antichrist.

The Identity of the Antichrist

Christians have frequently attempted to identify the Antichrist by examining the global leaders of our day. Comparisons are then made with the characteristics of the Antichrist presented in the Scriptures. This type of speculation tends to create more questions than answers. We do know that he will deceive the nations with persuasive language. His global appeal will be massive, as he promises the world peace. It is also certain that he will forsake the god of his fathers (Dan. 11:37-38). But truthfully, we do not know the specific identity of the Antichrist, and it is foolish to attempt to label an individual as the fulfillment of the prophetic Antichrist.

In every age Satan must have a man ready to take on the role of the Antichrist. Because Satan is not omniscient, he cannot know when the Rapture is going to happen. It is a total mystery to him because he is not privy to the plan of God, as it relates to the timing of the Rapture. So he must always have somebody ready in every generation to seize the moment after the Rapture of the Church. Therefore, throughout history, many of these men have been alive and present on the stage of world events. If the Rapture would have occurred, it could have been Hitler, Mussolini, or any number of world leaders throughout the last 2,000 years. We cannot say with certainty that the Antichrist, who will fulfill the prophecies of Scripture, is alive today. However, it seems reasonable to assume that one whom Satan would select to empower to be the Antichrist is alive today.

It also seems logical to assume that such a candidate has worked himself into a position of power somewhere in the world. The Antichrist will be someone with some political clout or standing in the world scene. He will be someone able to bring the chaos under control after the Rapture.

The identity of the Antichrist will not be known with certainty until he signs the treaty, guaranteeing peace for the nation of Israel (Dan. 9:27). This is when he will be revealed (2 Thess. 2:3, 6).

The Title Antichrist

What does it mean theologically that this man, who will rule before the Second Coming of Christ, is the Antichrist? Two meanings are usually associated with the prefix *anti*. The first carries the idea of a fake (opposite) substitute, which would mean a false christ. The second meaning is against. Therefore, it would be a person whose agenda and schemes are against Christ. Both of these are appropriate definitions of the Antichrist. Certainly, he will be empowered by Satan and claim to be God (2 Thess. 2:4, 9), but his actions will also demonstrate his opposition to Christ. Revelation 19:20 teaches us that when Christ returns, He will cast the Antichrist into the lake of fire.

The Antichrist in the Word of God

The specific term *antichrist* is used in the epistles of John. One of the locations that John uses this terminology is 1 John 2:18. The context of the passage is the recognition or the rejection of Jesus as the Messiah. The Apostle John was referring to the many antichrists that had already been on the scene, but he contrasted them with the one yet to come. Because the surrounding context discusses the identity of the Messiah, it becomes clear that the future Antichrist must also be a person. 1 John 2 contrasts the personal reality of Christ with the personal reality of the future Antichrist.

By John identifying this age as the last hour, in verse 18, he wasn't necessarily talking about the generation living in the first century. The Church Age is the final period of time before God unfolds His eschatological program. There will be the seven years of Tribulation, and then the Kingdom will come. The false teachers present in John's day indicated that the last hour was upon the Church. This was not intended to signify a specific time, but rather, "the beginning of the end of all things."[1] Many antichrists had already come, and so the Church could witness the beginning of deception. The spirit of the Antichrist was already at work in the world (1 John 4:3). This deception will peak under the reign of the Antichrist.

The Bible gives us many different designations for the Antichrist, including:

- the little horn (Dan. 7)
- prince who is to come (Dan. 9:26)
- the willful king (Dan. 11:36)
- one who makes desolate (Dan. 9:27)
- the man of sin (2 Thess. 2:3)
- the son of perdition (2 Thess. 2:3)
- the lawless one (2 Thess. 2:8)
- the beast (Rev. 11:7; 19:19-20; 20:10)
- the beast out of the sea (Rev. 13:1-8)

Daniel 7

From this list above, let us first turn our attention specifically to Daniel 7, where the Antichrist is referred to as the little horn. The ten horns represent ten kings (v. 24). The little horn (the Antichrist) will uproot three of the kings in this final world empire of men (v. 8).

We are able to discern from the teaching of Daniel that the Antichrist will be a man. The little horn is represented as having, "eyes like the eyes of a man" (Dan. 7:8). This focuses on the humanity of this individual in contrast to the eyes of the Spirit possessed by the Lamb of God (Rev. 5:6). Daniel also presents the Antichrist as having, "a mouth speaking pompous words" (Dan. 7:8). These words will be spoken against God (v. 25).

There can be no doubt that the Antichrist will have authority on earth. He will be allowed to wage war against the saints and prevail against them (Dan. 7:21). He will seek to establish his own system of law (v. 25). The kingdom established by the Antichrist will be destroyed when the Son of Man receives His Kingdom from the Ancient of Days (vv. 9-14). The revelation contained in Daniel informs us that the Antichrist will be judged by God in burning fire (Dan. 7:9-11; cf. Rev. 19:20).

Daniel 11

Daniel 11 contains the teaching of the willful king, which is another description of the Antichrist. Verse 36 teaches, "Then the king shall do according to his own will: he shall exalt and magnify himself above every god, shall speak blasphemies against the God of gods, and shall prosper till the wrath has been accomplished; for what has been determined shall be done." Notice the direct rebellion against God. The Antichrist will exalt and magnify himself above all gods and speak against the true God. He will be allowed to prosper for a time until the prophetic wrath of God is completed.

Daniel continues, "He shall regard neither the God of his fathers nor the desire of women, nor regard any god; for he shall exalt himself above them all" (Dan. 11:37). First we are told that he will reject the god of his fathers. It is not that he will convert from one religion to another; he will not regard any god. Someone who will not align himself with any one god will be more readily acceptable to people with a pluralistic worldview. Much discussion has been made about the phrase, "nor the desire of women." This suggests the possibility that the Antichrist will be a homosexual, but the wording does not demand it.

The Antichrist will have a focus on political and military power (vv. 38-39). He will set out to conquer. This power will lead him to acquire great wealth. The Antichrist will battle against the king of the North and the king of the South (vv. 40-44).

This section of text in Daniel deals with the formation of a Western alliance, probably led by the future Antichrist, that invades Egypt (Dan. 11:40-43). It is important to note that this is after the Rapture, but shortly before the Antichrist will be unveiled (See Appendix).

A common misconception is that the Tribulation begins immediately after the Rapture. There must be an intervening time because there are different events associated with the end of the Church Age and the beginning of the Tribulation. The Church Age ends with the Rapture, and the Tribulation begins with the covenant made by the Antichrist with Israel (Dan. 9:27). Since these two events are not identical, there must be at least a minimum sequence of time between them. This is illustrated in figure 12.1.

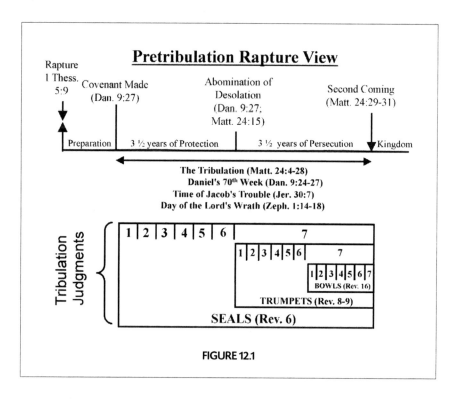

FIGURE 12.1

We are not told exactly how long this time of preparation will be. The general sense of Scripture is that it will be a limited period of time. This is when the Battle of Gog and Magog ensues (Ezek. 38-39). A Northern alliance will be formed to invade Israel (Ezek. 38). The Western alliance, led by the Antichrist, will protest and come to Israel's defense (Dan. 11:44). God will supernaturally intervene, allowing the Western alliance to defeat the Northern alliance (Ezek. 38:21-39:7). The Antichrist will take credit for it, which is certain to give him notoriety and pave the way for his reign of terror (Dan. 9:27). Then the Antichrist will be unveiled (2 Thess. 2:3) when he signs the peace treaty with Israel. This will constitute the official beginning of the Tribulation.

2 Thessalonians 2

The Antichrist, in 2 Thessalonians 2:3, is referred to as the man of sin. He must be revealed before the Day of the Lord arrives (v. 3). This should be self-evident from simple deduction. The Day of the Lord begins with the signing of the peace treaty. The man of sin is the one who signs that peace treaty. Therefore, he must be revealed before the Day of the Lord arrives.

The Apostle Paul also labeled him as the son of perdition (destruction). This is intended to point to his ultimate doom. As mentioned before, he will set himself up as God (2 Thess. 2:4).

The program of Satan is currently being restrained (2 Thess. 2:6-7). It is the ministry of the Holy Spirit in the lives of Church Age believers that is restraining the work of Satan. Although during this present age many people, including many believers in Jesus Christ, will turn away from the truth (1 Tim. 4:1-3), once the Church is removed at the Rapture, the situation will become much worse.

The Church is in place for a purpose. Our purpose is to glorify God, to showcase His grace and wisdom, and to be a people for His name. The Holy Spirit, working in and through the Church, is restraining the evil in the world today (2 Thess. 2:6). No matter how wicked the world may seem today, always remember that it would be considerably worse without the Church.

Regarding the present ministry of the Holy Spirit, Paul explained, "He who now restrains will do so until He is taken out of the way" (2 Thess. 2:7). Paul was not teaching that the Spirit of God will be completely gone during the Tribulation. The Holy Spirit is omnipresent, which means that He will not be leaving altogether. Even though He will not leave when the Church departs at the Rapture, His influence through the Church will be gone. Lawlessness and open rebellion against God will abound during the Tribulation.

After the Church is removed, "the lawless one will be revealed" (2 Thess. 2:8). He will view himself as above the laws of God. Empowered by Satan, the Antichrist will perform signs and false wonders (v. 9). He will lead men and women into unrighteous deception because they did not believe the Gospel of Christ (vv. 10-12).

Revelation 13

We get more details about the future activity of the Antichrist from Revelation 13 than from anywhere else in the Bible. Revelation 13:1

teaches, "Then I stood on the sand of the sea. And I saw a beast rising up out of the sea, having seven heads and ten horns, and on his horns ten crowns, and on his heads a blasphemous name." The Beast rising up out of the sea is John's apocalyptic description of the Antichrist and his kingdom (v. 1). The ten horns refer back to the ten horns or kingdoms/ kings which constitute the fourth world empire in Daniel 7. Therefore, he is identified as coming out of the revived Roman Empire. The seven heads are clarified later in Revelation 17. They represent five fallen kingdoms/kings, one that existed at the time of the writing of Revelation, and one that is yet to come (Rev. 17:10). The five fallen kingdoms/kings are Egypt, Assyria, Babylon, Persia, and Greece. The one who is (from the first century point of view) can only be the Roman Empire. The one who is to come is the Beast and his kingdom (a revived Roman Empire).

Over the centuries, different pagan nations have come against God and His people (Israel). It has all been a part of Satan's plan to thwart God's purpose in the world. The Tribulation is the culmination of the cosmic struggle between good and evil that has existed since the serpent first approached Eve. The Beast will epitomize the evil that has existed in the kingdoms arrayed against Israel throughout history.

The Beast will be like a leopard, bear, and lion (Rev. 13:2). These are representative of Greece, Medo-Persia, and Babylon in Daniel's vision of the four world kingdoms (Dan. 7). The Beast sums up all of the characterizations of the kingdoms/kings that preceded him. His power and authority will come from Satan (v. 2).

The Beast will also receive a mortal wound and be healed (Rev. 13:3). This will cause the people of the world to marvel and follow the Beast, which in turn will lead men to worship him (vv. 3-4).

The arrogance of the Antichrist will lead him to boast and blaspheme (Rev. 13:5). He will make war for a period of forty-two months, which is a reference to the last three and a half years of the Tribulation (v. 5). The Antichrist will actively work to oppose the God of the Jews (v. 6). His opposition will extend to the saints of God, and he will be victorious for a time. The Antichrist will rule the entire world (v. 7). We are also told, "All who dwell on the earth will worship him, whose names have not been written in the Book of Life of the Lamb slain from the foundation of the world" (Rev. 13:8).

The Antichrist will not act alone. His assistant is presented as the second Beast (the False Prophet) who will preside over a one-world religion that is centered on the worship of the Antichrist (Rev. 13:11-15).

The False Prophet will perform great signs in order to lead people to worship the Antichrist (v. 13). His deception will truly be great (v. 14).

One of the striking scenes in Daniel is of the image created by Nebuchadnezzar to be worshipped (Dan. 3). In much the same way, the False Prophet will instruct people to create an image of the Antichrist to be worshipped (Rev. 13:14-15). This image will both speak and, "cause as many as would not worship the image of the beast to be killed" (v. 15).

The False Prophet will require all people who want to buy and sell to have a mark on their foreheads or on their right hands (Rev. 13:16-17). The number that is the mark of the Beast is 666 (v. 18).[2]

The Nationality of the Antichrist

The Antichrist will come out of the last (fourth) pagan world empire in the same way that the prior leaders emerged (Dan. 7). This could mean that he will be European, rather than from the Middle East. Either way, he certainly will have a relationship with the Middle East. The parallel with Antiochus Epiphanes (Dan. 8) implies that he will be a Gentile world leader. Even Daniel 11:37 seems to indicate that he will not be Jewish.[3]

The Downfall of the Antichrist

As terrifying as the end time events will be, two points must be kept in mind. First, the Church of Christ will not be here to experience the wrath of the Lamb. Second, the time of the reign of the Antichrist is limited by God. Throughout all of these events, God will still be in control of His end times program. The Beast, the False Prophet, and all other earthly forces of evil will be captured and cast into the lake of fire. This will take place when Christ returns with His Bride at the Second Coming (Rev. 19:17-21).

The Day of the Lord

The Day of the Lord is the culmination of God's justice, righteousness, and holiness. He will bring His judgment, the Great Day of the Lord's Wrath, on mankind because of their sin. This study should be a somber reminder of how bad things will become.

The Day of the Lord is mentioned in the following passages: Isa. 2:12; 13:6, 9; Ezek. 13:5; 30:3; Joel 1:15; 2:1, 11, 31; 3:14; Amos 5:18 (twice), 20;

Obad. 15; Zeph. 1:7, 14 (twice); Zech.14:1; Mal. 4:5; Acts 2:20; 1 Thess. 5:2; 2 Thess. 2:2; 2 Pet. 3:10. In addition, the phrases *that day, the day,* or *the great day* occur more than seventy-five times in the Old Testament. A survey of these passages clearly indicates that the idea of judgment is central in all of them (see especially Zeph.1:14-18).

Defining the Day of the Lord

A general definition of the Day of the Lord is that period of time when God intervenes directly in the affairs of mankind in power and great glory to accomplish a specific or divine purpose. It does not always have eschatological implications, especially in the Old Testament. Theologically, in its broadest sense, it refers to that period of time in the eschaton beginning with the Rapture and continuing until the creation of the new heavens and new earth.

The context determines the specific meaning in the Bible. Depending on the context, the phrase may be limited to:

- the Tribulation period, also known as the Seventieth Week of Daniel
- the Second Coming - Even though the Second Coming will usher in the Kingdom (which will be a kingdom of peace, hope, righteousness, and justice), Christ will be coming with a sword preceding out of His mouth to execute judgment and to tread the winepress of the wrath of almighty God (Rev. 19:15).
- the Millennium - the first 1,000 years of the Kingdom
- the entire period between the Rapture and the new heavens and new earth

There are many different terms used in Scripture to describe the nature of the Day of the Lord. Identifying them gives us a better picture of this coming time. They include:

- wrath (Zeph. 1:15; Zech. 14:1-9)
- judgment (Rev. 14:7)
- indignation (Isa. 26:20-21)
- trial (Rev. 3:10)
- trouble (Jer. 30:7)
- destruction (Joel 1:15)

- darkness (Amos 5:18)
- desolation (Dan. 9:27)
- overturning (Isa. 24:1-4, 19-21)
- punishment (Isa. 24:20-21)

Primary Elements of the Day of the Lord

A primary element of the Day of the Lord will be the judgment and persecution of the nation of Israel. Israel will be presented with one final chance to receive the Messiah during the Tribulation. This is why the Olivet Discourse is so powerful and important in our study of the end times. It is filled with reminders, cautions, and warnings to that future generation to not be deceived and to be ready. We will take a closer look at the Olivet Discourse in the next chapter.

A second element is the judgment of the Gentile nations. The coming judgment is broader than Israel. It is judgment on all of mankind, and the culmination of human history. Human history must be seen through the lens of Jewish history. Salvation has always been of the Jews; they are His chosen people. God temporarily set them aside during the present age, but this is not a permanent situation. Israel will return to center stage and play a major role in God's eschatological program. When the Kingdom starts, the promises of Scripture will be fulfilled. The end times program of God will funnel through Israel, but affect all the people of the world. This will be especially true at the Sheep and Goats Judgment of Matthew 25:31-46.

The Scope of the Day of the Lord

The Day of the Lord includes the Tribulation (Zeph. 1:14-18). It also includes events related to the Second Coming (Zech. 14:1-4) and the Millennial Age (2 Pet. 3:10). The Day of the Lord is imminent (1 Thess. 5:2; 2 Pet. 3:10). This is because from the broadest perspective, it begins after the Rapture and ends with the new heavens and new earth. Because the Rapture is imminent, the Day of the Lord is also imminent. Once the Day of the Lord has begun, God's eschatological program will continue to unfold.

Paul told the church at Thessalonica, "For you yourselves know perfectly that the day of the Lord so comes as a thief in the night" (1

Thess. 5:2). Paul could make this statement because the Day of the Lord begins after the Rapture. He then proceeded to warn them about the destruction that would come upon the people of the world. Paul had already told them that Jesus would deliver believers from the wrath to come (1 Thess. 1:10). Paul again proclaimed, "For God did not appoint us to wrath, but to obtain salvation through our Lord Jesus Christ" (1 Thess. 5:9). This salvation is not a reference to individual redemption, but rather deliverance from the Great Day of God's Wrath.

Peter also referred to the sudden arrival of the Day of the Lord. In 2 Peter 3:10 he wrote, "But the day of the Lord will come as a thief in the night, in which the heavens will pass away with a great noise, and the elements will melt with fervent heat; both the earth and the works that are in it will be burned up." Just as a thief comes without warning, so it will be that this day of judgment will overtake the unredeemed without warning. This is yet another example of the Day of the Lord being used in a broader context to describe events between the Rapture and the new heavens and new earth.

Events within the Day of the Lord

The Day of the Lord encompasses many events that are yet to occur, including:

- The formation of a federation of nations into a revived Roman Empire (Dan. 2; 7).
- The rise of the Antichrist (Dan. 9:27; Rev. 13:1-10).
- The formation of a one-world religion (Rev. 13:11-18).
- The seal judgments (Rev. 6).
- The commissioning of the 144,000 Jewish witnesses (Rev. 7; Matt. 24:14).
- The trumpet judgments (Rev. 8-11).
- The two witnesses (Rev. 11).
- The persecution of Israel (Rev. 12).
- The bowl judgments (Rev. 16).
- The rise and fall of Babylon (Rev. 17-18).
- The campaign of Armageddon (Ezek. 38-39; Rev. 16:16; 19:17-21).
- The Second Coming (Matt. 24:29-30).
- The resurrection of Old Testament and Tribulation believers (John 6:39-40; Rev. 20:4).

- The Beast and the False Prophet cast into the lake of fire (Rev. 19:11-21).
- The Sheep and Goats Judgment (Matt. 25).
- The regathering of Israel into the land (Ezek. 37:1-14; Matt. 24:31).
- The restoration of Israel to the land (Amos 9:15).
- The binding of Satan for 1,000 years (Rev. 20:2-3).
- The Millennium (Rev. 20).
- The final rebellion of Satan (Rev. 20).
- The Great White Throne Judgment (Rev. 20).
- The purging of the heavens and the earth (2 Pet. 3:10-13).

There is considerable overlap between the study of the Day of the Lord and the Tribulation. For this reason, many of the events listed will be addressed in greater detail in our examination of the Tribulation.

The Antichrist and the Day of the Lord in Review

The Antichrist is a future individual who will be the central world figure during the period of time known as Daniel's Seventieth Week. The Antichrist will play a pivotal role as an instrument of Satan in the battle between good and evil.

His wickedness will show no bounds. He will be empowered by Satan (possibly even indwelt by him), glorify himself as God, and oppose Christ, the Jews, and Gentile believers. His attack is certain to be on all of national Israel, regardless of whether they are believers or not. Another specific target will be Gentile believers who are saved during the Tribulation. It seems probable that the Antichrist is going to be a Gentile ruler who arises out of a revived Roman Empire and attempts to control the world, along with its religious institutions.

The Day of the Lord is generally defined as a period of time when God intervenes directly in the affairs of mankind in power and great glory to accomplish a specific or divine purpose. Theologically, in its broadest sense, it refers to that period of time in the eschaton beginning with the Rapture and continuing until the creation of the new heavens and new earth. The Tribulation and the Second Coming will be times of great judgment for Israel and the Gentile nations of the world.

Be thankful that we, as part of the Church, will be rescued before that great and awful Day of the Lord, when the Antichrist will wreak havoc on the world.

Discussion Questions

1. When will the Antichrist be revealed?
2. What do we know about the identity of the Antichrist?
3. Define what the title, Antichrist, means.
4. How is the Antichrist described throughout the Bible?
5. Describe the activities of the Antichrist.
6. What is the Day of the Lord?
7. How can the nature of the Day of the Lord be described?
8. When will the Day of the Lord occur?
9. Explain some of the events that will take place during the Day of the Lord.
10. Do Christians need to fear the Day of the Lord? Why or why not?

Endnotes

1. Earl D. Radmacher, Ronald Barclay Allen, and H. Wayne House, *Nelson's New Illustrated Bible Commentary* (Nashville, TN: Thomas Nelson Publishers, 1999), 1 John 2:18.
2. There are textual variants that have it being a different number. The vast majority of the manuscripts have the number as 666. Either way, the number is not the issue. It is the fact that there will be a number that is the mark of the Beast.
3. Daniel 11:37 would be better translated, "neither shall he regard the gods of his fathers."

CHAPTER 13

When will be the End of the Age? - The Olivet Discourse

Now as He sat on the Mount of Olives, the disciples came to Him privately, saying, "Tell us, when will these things be? And what will be the sign of Your coming, and of the end of the age?"

- Matthew 24:3

G O BACK IN time a few hundred years. In 1782, a man by the name of William Miller was born in Pittsfield, Massachusetts. As a young man he was a farmer in Vermont, and during the War of 1812 he served as a captain in the United States Army.

Up until 1816, Miller was a Deist. Now, he was determined to search the Scriptures for the truth and provide answers for the skeptics. After only two years of study, in 1818, he came to the conclusion that Christ would return around the year 1843. This interpretation was based on a misunderstanding of Daniel 8:14 which teaches, "For two thousand three hundred days; then the sanctuary shall be cleansed." Miller made several mistakes with this text. He assumed that the cleansing of the sanctuary referred to the purification of the earth by fire. Miller also understood a day to equal a prophetic year. The 2,300 days were thought to begin with the decree of Artaxerxes to rebuild Jerusalem.[1]

Miller was convinced that the end of the world was soon at hand. He stated, "I was thus brought to the solemn conclusion that in about 25 years from that time all the affairs of our present state would be wound up."[2] At first, Miller kept quiet about his conclusions, but by the early 1830's he was preaching his message in churches. In 1833, he was licensed by a Baptist church. His audience was starting to grow.

Several developments led to an explosive growth of his ministry. In 1838, he published *Evidence from Scripture and History of the Second Coming of Christ, About the Year 1843*. Miller took his message on the road to the larger cities of New England and took on a manager and publicity agent. The largest tent in the country was purchased for meetings. The Millerite Movement was born; speaking tours were launched, and tracts, pamphlets, and books were published. As the crowds grew, more than 50,000 people believed his message, with millions of others curious about what would transpire. In January of 1843, he announced that the return of the Lord would take place between March 21, 1843 and March 21, 1844.[3]

Men and women changed their entire lives in anticipation of the return of the Lord Jesus Christ. Men quit their jobs. Families gave away everything they owned, and many even sold their homes. March 21, 1844 came and went, and nothing happened. The disappointment felt was overwhelming. Then, hope once again sprang to life:

> One of his followers pointed to other verses (Hab. 2:3, Lev. 25:9) and explained there must be a "tarrying time" of seven months and ten days.
>
> So October 22, 1844, became the new day of Christ's return, and people were rallied again with the slogan: "The Tenth Day of the Seventh Month." Miller was finally converted to the new date. "I see a glory in the seventh month," he said. "Thank the Lord, O my soul! ... I am almost home." The excitement revived, and the number living on the edge of eternity seemed to be greater than ever.[4]

People gathered in churches and upon mountaintops. Normal life seemed to come to a standstill on the morning of October 22, 1844, as much of New England awaited the end of the world. When the second date came and went, disillusionment set in. This second failure became known as *The Great Disappointment*.

Some of his followers held to the date of October 22, 1844, even though it had come and gone. They explained that on that date, "Jesus moved from His seat at God's right hand into the holy place to begin an 'investigative judgment' of all professing believers, many of whom will be blotted out of the book of Life. This remnant of Millerites eventually founded the Seventh-day Adventist Church."[5]

The united testimony of the Word of God is that the day and time of Christ's return is something that God the Father has not revealed to us. We remember in Acts 1, the disciples asked Jesus after His resurrection, "Lord, will You at this time restore the kingdom to Israel?" (Acts 1:6). The answer from Christ should guide us. He told them, "It is not for you to know times or seasons which the Father has put in His own authority" (Acts 1:7). It was this same type of questioning that led to the teaching found in the Olivet Discourse. The disciples wanted to know when Christ would return and usher in His Kingdom (Matt. 24:3).

What is the Olivet Discourse?

This is the title given to Jesus' teaching from atop the Mount of Olives just two days before He was crucified. The synoptic accounts give us a clear picture of the teaching from Christ. It is recorded in Matthew 24-25, Mark 13:1-37, and Luke 21:5-36.

Significance

The Olivet Discourse is arguably the most important eschatological passage in the entire New Testament. There are at least three reasons for this:

1. It is the most comprehensive eschatological passage in the New Testament.
2. It contributes significantly to the systematization of eschatology.
3. It contributes to a chronological unity of end time events.

Matthew's Purpose

Before we embark on our study of the Olivet Discourse, it is imperative to remember the purpose of the Gospel of Matthew. Matthew selected and included events from the life and ministry of the Lord, in order to convince his Jewish audience that Jesus of Nazareth is, in fact, the long awaited Messiah. Jesus is the Christ, the Savior of the world, the one who will take the throne of David as King and rule and reign over the Kingdom of Israel. This is what Matthew sought to demonstrate from the life of Christ.

The Big Picture

Matthew 1-2

Keeping the Olivet Discourse in its proper context is also important. Matthew organized his thoughts and arguments around particular themes. Chapters 1-2 record the genealogy and childhood of Jesus. Matthew began by establishing the genealogy of Jesus from the line of David. He then referenced several prophecies. These include Isaiah's prophecy of the virgin birth of Christ (Isa. 7:14), Micah's prophecy that the Messiah would be born in Bethlehem (Mic. 5:2), and Hosea's prophecy about Egypt (Hos. 11:1). Matthew was pointing out to his Jewish audience that Jesus is unique. He is the long awaited Seed of Israel.

Matthew 3

Matthew chapter 3 presents the authentication of Jesus as the Messiah. This is seen in several different ways. First, we witness that the forerunner of the King (John the Baptist) came preparing the way for the Christ. This is supported by the reference to Isaiah 40:3. Next, is the baptism of Jesus, which was a pivotal moment. God the Father spoke from heaven saying, "This is My beloved Son, in whom I am well pleased" (Matt. 3:17). The Gospels record three occasions of the Father speaking audibly from heaven (Matt. 3:17; 17:5; John 12:28). At the baptism of Christ and the transfiguration it was the same message from the Father, which was to authenticate Jesus as the Son of God (Matt. 3:17; 17:5). Steeped in their own history through the Old Testament, the importance of this would not be lost on the Jewish people. When God spoke it was a significant event (Exod. 19-24), and Matthew sought to make the connection to Christ.

Matthew 4

The fourth chapter of Matthew presents the beginning of Jesus' ministry and the call of the first disciples. Matthew also records the temptation of Christ for a period of forty days in the wilderness, which provides an analogy. Israel wandered in the desert for forty years because of their failure to trust the Lord. The Messiah of Israel was tempted for a period of forty days in the wilderness and demonstrated His faithfulness.

Matthew 5-7

The first major sermon that Matthew includes is the Sermon on the Mount (Matt. 5-7). It appears to have taken place about a year into the Lord's ministry. The purpose for the Sermon on the Mount was to bring conviction to the Jews living in the first century. The men and women of Israel needed to know that getting into the Kingdom of God was much different from what they thought it would be. It is not through keeping the letter of the Law, and it certainly is not through being self-righteous. It boils down to a heart issue.

The righteousness that the Kingdom demands is perfect righteousness. This is why Jesus taught, "For I say to you, that unless your righteousness exceeds the righteousness of the scribes and Pharisees, you will by no means enter the kingdom of heaven" (Matt. 5:20). Again, He instructed, "Therefore you shall be perfect, just as your Father in heaven is perfect" (Matt. 5:48). The only way to obtain perfect righteousness is by faith (Rom. 3:21-26). The Sermon on the Mount presents Jesus demonstrating the need for faith righteousness.

Matthew 8-9

One of the first things that Matthew included in chapter 8, after the Sermon on the Mount, is the interaction between Jesus and a leading Gentile, the centurion. Matthew highlighted the fact that the centurion said, "Lord, I am not worthy" (Matt. 8:8). This is a repeated theme throughout the Gospel of Matthew; mankind is not worthy (Rom. 3:10). As mentioned, the only way to be worthy is to gain the righteousness of Christ by faith (Rom. 3:21-26). Jesus immediately commended the centurion and said, "Assuredly, I say to you, I have not found such great faith, not even in Israel!" (Matt. 8:10). Faith righteousness is the unmistakable message of the Gospel of Matthew. This section of Scripture also records the display of Christ's power to heal the sick.

Matthew 10-12

Several events from the ministry of Christ were selected and recorded in Matthew 10-12. Chapter 10 presents the commissioning of the disciples. In Matthew 11, we find John the Baptist questioning the identity of Jesus. This foreshadows the rejection to come by the Jews. Chapter 12 shows the intensification of the conflict between Jesus and the religious leaders of the Jews.

Matthew 13

Matthew 13 showcases the formal rejection of the Kingdom by Israel, as well as the mysteries of the Kingdom. All of the parables of the Kingdom in Matthew 13 relate to Israel. Sometimes it is taught that Matthew 13 presents a veiled illusion to the Church Age. Instead, it should be recognized that the parables contained in Matthew 13 give additional information about the Kingdom (Matt. 13:11). Consider an example:

> Another parable He put forth to them, saying: "The kingdom of heaven is like a mustard seed, which a man took and sowed in his field, which indeed is the least of all the seeds; but when it is grown it is greater than the herbs and becomes a tree, so that the birds of the air come and nest in its branches" (Matt. 13:31-32).

Jesus directly stated that this was a parable about the Kingdom of Heaven. The mustard seed indicates that the Kingdom will start out small and then grow. With the completed revelation of the Word of God, we know that at the end of the Tribulation, when Christ comes back to usher in the Kingdom, there will be a comparatively small group of people on earth that survive and enter the Kingdom. After 1,000 years the earth will be flourishing with people. This is the teaching of the parable of the mustard seed.

Another example is found in the parable of the leaven. Matthew records, "Another parable He spoke to them: 'The kingdom of heaven is like leaven, which a woman took and hid in three measures of meal till it was all leavened'" (Matt. 13:33). Again, we witness that Jesus mentioned the Kingdom of Heaven within the parable. He was simply teaching that within the first 1,000 years of the Kingdom, there will be some unbelievers present (Rev. 20:7-8).

The rest of the Gospel of Matthew shows the continued escalation of the hostility toward Christ by the Jewish leaders. Because of this, Jesus shifted His message from the proclamation of the Kingdom to the inter-advent age.

Matthew 14-15

Matthew 14-15 demonstrates additional reactions to Jesus' Kingdom message. Within these chapters we witness continued instruction by Christ, healings, and rising opposition.

Matthew 16-18

At the time of Matthew 16-18, Jesus was ministering in the area of Galilee. It is within this section of Scripture that Peter made his confession that Jesus is the Christ (Matt. 16:16). Once again, Jesus also predicted His own death (Matt. 16:21).

Matthew 19-20

Matthew 19 opens by informing the reader that Jesus had departed from Galilee and had traveled to the region of Judea (Matt. 19:1). It is there that Jesus continued to instruct His disciples, which is detailed in Matthew 19-20. The varied topics included marriage, children, wealth, and service to Christ.

Matthew 21-22

The Triumphal Entry of Christ is recorded in Matthew 21. Once more, we see that Matthew quoted from the Old Testament prophets (Matt. 21:5). The Triumphal Entry of Christ fulfilled the prophecy of Zechariah 9:9. Matthew 21-22 illustrates the official rejection of Christ by the religious leaders of Israel. The events recorded within these chapters took place in the final week before the Cross.

Matthew 23

Jesus issued a scathing rebuke of the scribes and Pharisees in Matthew 23. He was speaking to the multitudes and the disciples (v. 1). This is an important point in understanding the increased and dramatic tension that was present on that particular day. Jesus was not merely talking to His disciples; this was public teaching to the multitudes. It is not hard to imagine that some of the scribes and Pharisees were within the sound of His voice. Notice the wording of some of the *woe* statements contained in Matthew 23:

> But woe to you, scribes and Pharisees, hypocrites! For you shut up the kingdom of heaven against men; for you neither go in yourselves, nor do you allow those who are entering to go in. Woe to you, scribes and Pharisees, hypocrites! For you devour widows' houses, and for a pretense make long prayers. Therefore you will receive greater condemnation. Woe to you, scribes and Pharisees, hypocrites! For you

travel land and sea to win one proselyte, and when he is won, you make him twice as much a son of hell as yourselves. Woe to you, blind guides, who say, "Whoever swears by the temple, it is nothing; but whoever swears by the gold of the temple, he is obliged to perform it." Fools and blind! For which is greater, the gold or the temple that sanctifies the gold? (Matt. 23:13-17).

This was not a pleasant conversation. The words of Christ, in Matthew 23, give us a small glimpse of God's wrath. Jesus was criticizing their entire way of life. It was a condemnation of the rules and regulations that they had imposed on the people, as the religious leaders.

Again, consider more of His words from this rebuke, "Woe to you, scribes and Pharisees, hypocrites! For you pay tithe of mint and anise and cummin, and have neglected the weightier matters of the law: justice and mercy and faith. These you ought to have done, without leaving the others undone" (Matt. 23:23). This underscores the truth that the New Testament teaching of grace and mercy is not new. It is highlighted through the Cross and through the lives of believers today. The grace and mercy of God is more manifest in the Church Age, but it is not new. Noah found, "grace in the eyes of the Lord" (Gen. 6:7). Moses could also testify that he found grace in the sight of the Lord (Exod. 33:12).

In verse 13, we already witnessed that Jesus said, "But woe to you, scribes and Pharisees, hypocrites! For you shut up the kingdom of heaven against men; for you neither go in yourselves, nor do you allow those who are entering to go in" (Matt. 23:13). Jesus stated that the scribes and Pharisees would not be entering the Kingdom of Heaven. Then, in verse 14, Jesus spoke of their condemnation. Still addressing the scribes and Pharisees, in verse 33 Jesus rebuked them by testifying, "Serpents, brood of vipers! How can you escape the condemnation of hell?" (Matt. 23:33). Take note that Jesus equated failure to get into the Kingdom with hell. This is an important theological point that is often overlooked or missed. In the coming pages we will witness that the Olivet Discourse reveals that those who do not get into the Kingdom are cast into the everlasting fire prepared for the Devil and his angels. Exclusion from the Kingdom means an eternity in hell.

Jesus ended His scathing rebuke of the scribes and the Pharisees by explaining, "Assuredly, I say to you, all these things will come upon this generation" (Matt. 23:36). The chapter closes with Jesus lamenting the condition of His people:

O Jerusalem, Jerusalem, the one who kills the prophets and stones those who are sent to her! How often I wanted to gather your children together, as a hen gathers her chicks under her wings, but you were not willing! See! Your house is left to you desolate; for I say to you, you shall see Me no more till you say, *"Blessed is He who comes in the name of the LORD!"* (Matt. 23:37-39).

Jesus was heartbroken over the rejection and opposition He encountered, and lamented the future that Jerusalem was facing. Repetition of a name (Jerusalem, Jerusalem) is an indication of strong emotion (Matt. 27:46; 2 Sam. 18:33; Acts 9:4). The key to understanding these last three verses of Matthew 23 are the words, "you shall see Me no more till you say" (v. 39). Then Jesus went on to quote Psalm 118 verse 26, which is a Messianic passage.

Israel as a nation has never called on the name of the Lord, but individuals have come to faith in Jesus. Even in Jesus' day there were some who cried out Hosanna! Hosanna! (Matt. 21:9). But the multitudes wanted Jesus crucified (Matt. 27:22-23). When Christ returns at the Second Coming, those Jewish believers who have believed the message of the 144,000 witnesses will be regathered into the land (Matt. 24:30-31). At that time, there will be a vast chorus of, *"Blessed is He who comes in the name of the LORD!"* (Matt. 23:39). The men and women of Israel will cry out to their Savior, the Messiah, Jesus.

The Connection

The opening words of Matthew 24 record, "Then Jesus went out and departed from the temple, and His disciples came up to show Him the buildings of the temple" (Matt. 24:1). It is significant that the original text did not have chapter divisions. Verse 1 actually begins with the connective word *kai*. This Greek word is translated as *then* in the New King James Version. The King James Version starts verse 1 with the word *and*. Both of these translations show the connection to the preceding section, where Jesus had denounced the Jews for rejecting Him and had lamented over Jerusalem for what she would face in the future.

The Disciples' Misplaced Focus (24:1-2)

As Jesus left the Temple complex, some of the His disciples began to brag about the buildings of the Temple (Matt. 24:1; cf. Luke 21:5). Try to imagine their confusion. Remember what they had just heard. Jesus had publicly rebuked the Pharisees and the scribes. When Jesus was lamenting over Jerusalem He had said, "Your house is left to you desolate" (Matt. 23:38). The disciples were constantly focused on the ushering in of the Kingdom of God, but Jesus was warning about what would come upon that generation (Matt. 23:36). The words of Jesus, from Matthew 23, left them with questions. The Temple was in the process of being renovated. It was a massive and beautiful complex. The Temple was the pride of the Jewish people. Its existence was considered to be the evidence of the blessing of God on His people and Jerusalem. Pointing to the Temple afforded them the opportunity of getting clarification about the teaching they had just heard.

By examining the different Gospels we obtain additional information. Luke recorded in his account, "Some spoke of the temple, how it was adorned with beautiful stones" (Luke 21:5). Mark teaches us, "One of His disciples said to Him, 'Teacher, see what manner of stones and what buildings are here!'" (Mark 13:1).

Verse 2 of Matthew 24 reveals that Jesus responded to the attention given to the Temple by bluntly predicting the destruction of it. Jesus said to the disciples, "Do you not see all these things? Assuredly, I say to you, not one stone shall be left here upon another, that shall not be thrown down" (Matt. 24:2). The context demonstrates that this prediction is eschatological.

Most dispensationalists believe that verse 2 refers to the fall of Jerusalem in A.D. 70. However, the implications of Jesus' statement imply total destruction. Many of the huge stones of the Temple Mount still stand to this day. The Lord's statement is more in keeping with the nature of the events described in Revelation 6-18, with the destruction of the Tribulation Temple, than the events that occurred in A.D. 70 (cf. Rev. 11:1-2; Zech. 12:1-2; 13:8-9; 14:1-2).

The Disciples' Questions (24:3)

The Mount of Olives is directly to the east of where the Temple stood. The Kidron Valley separates the Mount of Olives and Jerusalem.

The location of where this discourse took place has given Matthew 24-25 the name, *The Olivet Discourse*. It is doubtful that there could have been a more fitting place for Jesus to teach about His return. The Lord ascended into heaven from the Mount of Olives (Acts 1:9-12), and the Lord will return to the Mount of Olives at His second coming (Zech. 14:4). As Jesus sat upon this mountain, which overlooks Jerusalem, He began to teach His disciples.

The disciples had asked, "Tell us, when will these things be? And what will be the sign of Your coming, and of the end of the age?" (Matt. 24:3). We find out in Mark's account that Peter, James, John, and Andrew were the ones who questioned Jesus (Mark 13:4). The Lord's teaching was in response to the questions from the disciples.

A common dispensational understanding of verse 3 is that the disciples were asking two questions. The first had to do with the destruction of Jerusalem. The second dealt with the Second Coming and the end times. It is assumed, by those that hold to this view, that Jesus ignored the first question entirely and only answered the second question. Other dispensationalists see three subjects addressed by the disciples' questions:

- the destruction of Jerusalem
- the signs of Christ's coming
- the end of the present age

A more preferred understanding is to take the questions as expressing one unified eschatological concern. When would all of this happen: the judgment of Jerusalem, His coming, and the end of the age? In light of the Lord's response, this seems to be the plain understanding of the text. Jesus had just predicted an attack upon Jerusalem (Matt. 24:2). His disciples associated the destruction of Jerusalem with His return, based on what He had said in Matthew 23:39. This led them to ask when all of this would take place. Separating the disciples' questions into two (or three) completely distinct questions stretches the natural flow of the narrative beyond its boundaries. Furthermore, to assume that Matthew and Mark would ignore Jesus' answer to the question about the destruction of Jerusalem without comment seems unwarranted.

Viewing Matthew 24:3 as three separate questions has led some to outline the Olivet Discourse in three different sections. There is no grammatical evidence that the Olivet Discourse was intended to be broken apart in that manner. The flow of thought does not support such artificial divisions.

General Signs Relating to the Entire Tribulation Period (24:4-14)

When would all of this happen? Starting in verse 4, Jesus began to answer that question. The entire Olivet Discourse is focused on answering this question. What could they expect just prior to His return?

This raises a curious issue. If the disciples would not be around when all of this happened, why did Jesus bother telling them? God has historically given His revelation to a current generation, even though it is predicting what will occur in a future generation. The Old Testament is filled with examples. Daniel's prophecy of the signing of the peace treaty demonstrates this reality (Dan. 9:27).

We remember from our earlier study that the Church was not in existence yet. The disciples at this point were representatives of the believing remnant of Israel. The scribes and Pharisees had been rebuked by Christ for their lack of faith (Matt. 23). It is those with faith who will inherit the Kingdom, and so this message was given to the disciples as representatives of national Israel. The Kingdom has been delayed at least 2,000 years, but at some point there will be a future generation of Jewish leaders for whom this text will have an immediate and direct application. We recognize that the truth contained in the Olivet Discourse has profound significance for believers living in the Church Age, but for the generation that will experience the Tribulation, it becomes a matter of life and death. Deception will lead many to take the mark of the Beast. The truth contained in the Olivet Discourse is intended to be a guide for national Israel during the Tribulation. It will be a roadmap for survival during this time.

Outline of the Olivet Discourse

Matthew 24:4-14 contains general signs of the entire Tribulation period. Verses 4-8 relate to the first half of the Tribulation and verses 9-14 refer to the second half. After this, Jesus gave more specific signs that relate to the second half of the Tribulation (Matt. 24:15-26). From there, Jesus gave detailed signs that will immediately accompany His second coming (cosmic signs, lightning from east to west, etc.) (Matt. 24:27-31).

The rest of the Olivet Discourse is direct application for how national Israel should respond during this time (Matt. 24:32-25:46). This includes being watchful, ready, and prepared for the Sheep and Goats Judgment.

A Popular Dispensational Outline of the Olivet Discourse

A popular dispensational outline charts a much different understanding of the Olivet Discourse. The prediction of the destruction of the Temple is seen as having been fulfilled in A.D. 70 (Matt. 24:1-2). Verse 3 contains the questions from the disciples. The next section is viewed as referring to general events that will characterize the Church Age (Matt. 24:4-8). Then it is said that Jesus' discussion of the Tribulation begins in verse 9 and continues through verse 14. Specifically, it is taught that verses 9-14 refer to the first half of the Tribulation.[6] The Great Tribulation (the second half of the Tribulation) is seen in verses 15-28, with verse 29 beginning a discussion of the Second Coming (vv. 29-31). This supposed outline is represented as follows:

- Matthew 24:1-2 (A.D. 70)
- Matthew 24:3 (The Disciples' questions)
- Matthew 24:4-8 (Church Age)
- Matthew 24:9-14 (First half of the Tribulation)
- Matthew 24:15-28 (Second half of the Tribulation)
- Matthew 24:29-31 (Second Coming)

However, there are some problems with this outline. It is preferable to view verses 4-14 as comprising one complete section, in which Jesus gave a general description of the entire seven-year Tribulation. This conclusion is based on the following:

- The phrase *birth pains* is used routinely in the Old Testament to describe the period of distress preceding the Messianic Kingdom, specifically the Tribulation (cf. Isa. 13:8; 26:17; Jer. 4:31; 6:24; Mic. 4:9-10).[7]
- There are several similarities between the events described in this section and the seal judgments in Revelation 6. These similarities are found in both Matthew 24:4-8, as well as Matthew 24:9-14. Since the seals clearly take place in the Tribulation, it would seem odd to see the Church Age referenced in Matthew 24 (see figure 10.9 in chapter 10).

- Verses 13-14 refer to the *end* which can only refer, in context, to the end of the Tribulation. That is, to Christ's second coming (cf. *endure to the end* and *then the end will come*). Thus, it seems out of place to mark verse 14 as the midpoint of the Tribulation.
- The description in this section is not particularly striking. There have always been wars, earthquakes, famines, etc. What distinguishes Jesus' description here is its connection with the Old Testament prediction of a time of severe world judgment. In the Old Testament this time of worldwide trouble is given various names: the time of Jacob's trouble, that day, the Day of the Lord, and the Tribulation. Against this Old Testament background, the disciples would quickly identify the time of which Jesus spoke.

Matthew 24:4-14

As mentioned, verses 4-14 should be seen as referencing the entire Tribulation period. Verses 4-8 relate to the first half of the Tribulation and verses 9-14 refer to the second half. It must be kept in mind that Jesus was speaking in the context of national Israel, and God's future dealings with the people as a nation. The questions which stimulated this discourse were asked from an Old Testament frame of reference. In the Olivet Discourse Jesus affirmed that the glorious kingdom which Israel expected will surely come.

The deception during the Tribulation will be stifling. The very first thing we read in Matthew about this time is the unmistakable deception that will come. Matthew teaches, "And Jesus answered and said to them: 'Take heed that no one deceives you. For many will come in My name, saying, "I am the Christ," and will deceive many'" (Matt. 24:4-5; cf. 24:23-28). The Jewish people will need to be careful about being tricked into following a false christ, and confusing the coming of the Antichrist with the arrival of Christ, the true Messiah of Israel. The revelation of the Antichrist is the first seal judgment (Rev. 6:1-2). This great deceiver will pass himself off as the hero of the time. He will be seen as the one able to solve the chaos in the world related to the Rapture and the Battle of Gog and Magog.

The Tribulation will be a period marked by, "wars and rumors of wars" (Matt. 24:6; cf. Ezek. 38-39; Rev. 13:7; Dan. 7:23-27). Jews living in that day should not assume that talk of war means Christ's return is imminent because, "the end is not yet" (Matt. 24:6).

Throughout the seven years of Tribulation there will be various calamities on the face of the earth (Matt. 24:7-8). This will include wars, famine, pestilences, and earthquakes. These are, "the beginning of sorrows" (Matt. 24:8). It is clear at this point in the text that the Tribulation is underway.

When verses 4-8 are taken to be references to the Church Age, it has a notable effect. Large earthquakes and wars are said to be a fulfillment of verse 7, but let it be recognized that there will be an intensification of these calamities after the Rapture, when Christians are gone. It will be a time of total chaos. Rogue nations will attack other countries, and the Battle of Gog and Magog will ensue. There is no merit for inserting the Church Age into Matthew 24:4-8. It is eschatological and Jewish in nature. These beginnings of sorrows should be taken as general signs referring to the first half of the Tribulation.

Starting in verse 9, Jesus began to give general signs of the second half of the Tribulation. Consider the teaching found in verses 9-14:

> Then they will deliver you up to tribulation and kill you, and you will be hated by all nations for My name's sake. And then many will be offended, will betray one another, and will hate one another. Then many false prophets will rise up and deceive many. And because lawlessness will abound, the love of many will grow cold. But he who endures to the end shall be saved. And this gospel of the kingdom will be preached in all the world as a witness to all the nations, and then the end will come (Matt. 24:9-14).

There will be an intensification of the persecution of Israel after the midpoint. This is noticeable in verse 9 with the reference to the hatred of the nations. We must remember that only the first three and a half years of the Tribulation provide relative protection for Israel. Once the treaty is broken at the midpoint (the Abomination of Desolation) Israel becomes a target. Again, this points to the Tribulation starting in verse 4. If the Tribulation is being introduced in verse 9, as is often taught, it is difficult to reconcile why the discussion would be introduced with persecution, tribulation, and martyrdom when those events are not prevalent for Israel in the first three and a half years.

The Bible speaks of one individual that will be the Antichrist. The same is true of the False Prophet. However, their regime will include many false christs, deceivers, and false prophets that will go throughout the world performing the bidding of the Antichrist.

Take another look at verse 13, "But he who endures to the end shall be saved." Unfortunately, this is one of the most misused verses in the New Testament, particularly by those from a Reformed perspective. It is not referring to individual perseverance and good works in order to prove that you are really a Christian. Such a concept is completely foreign to the flow of thought and the Jewish nature of the book of Matthew. To insert, in this context, some type of general statement about individual believers persevering to avoid ending up in hell is completely out of place with the rest of the teaching of the Olivet Discourse. We remember that the word *saved* simply means *delivered*.

Notice again the subject matter of verse 14, "And this gospel of the kingdom will be preached in all the world as a witness to all the nations, and then the end will come." This is the answer to what the disciples wanted to know. The disciples had asked, "What will be the sign of Your coming, and of the end of the age?" (Matt. 24:3). Jesus answered in verse 14 by proclaiming that it would happen when the Gospel of the Kingdom is preached to the entire world. Those future believers who endure this great time of tribulation, those who physically survive it, will be delivered into the Kingdom (v. 13). Individuals who take the mark of the Beast will not be delivered into the Kingdom; they will be excluded.

Detailed Signs Relating to the Second Half of the Tribulation (24:15-26)

Starting in verse 15, there is a shift in emphasis. Jesus began to give the disciples specific signs of the second half of the Tribulation. This is when the situation on earth will become especially troublesome. The wording in verses 15-16 demonstrate this, "'Therefore when you see the *"abomination of desolation,"* spoken of by Daniel the prophet, standing in the holy place' (whoever reads, let him understand), 'then let those who are in Judea flee to the mountains.'" When the Antichrist breaks his covenant with the Jews, sets himself up as God, and demands worship, then the men and women of Israel will be in for a terrible plight. Jesus began to demonstrate the urgency of this future time.

We notice in verse 15 that Jesus referenced the Abomination of Desolation (cf. Mark 13:14). Jesus directly linked this with Daniel's prophecy. Understanding what the Abomination of Desolation refers to is central to the meaning of this passage. The word *abomination* refers generally to things that are detestable by God and rejected by Him (cf. Rev.17:4-5; 21:8, 27). Daniel 11:31 used the phrase *Abomination of Desolation* in predicting the events of 168 B.C. when Antiochus Epiphanes erected an image of Zeus and sacrificed a pig in the Temple. In Daniel 9:27 and Daniel 12:11 it refers to a similar performance by the Antichrist that will occur at the midpoint of the Tribulation. Both 2 Thessalonians 2:3-4 and Revelation 13:12-15, even though the phrase itself is not used, give us a description of this future event. The disciples requested a sign of the return of Christ. The Abomination of Desolation becomes the most significant sign that signals the nearness of the Kingdom.

The Abomination of Desolation will be so repugnant that those who are in Judea at that time (the Jews) will not be able to miss it. When the Jewish people witness this event, they should find the fastest route out of Jerusalem possible. God will be about to pour out His judgment like never before (Matt. 24:21; cf. Rev. 12:14; Luke 17:20-37; 21:20-24; Mark 13:15-16). They should not waste any time retrieving possessions (Matt. 24:17). Neither should they return to their homes to get clothes (v. 18). Time spent gathering belongings could mean the difference between life and death. Pregnant and nursing women will have a harder time as they try to escape (v. 19). A Sabbath's day journey may not be enough to take someone out of harm's way (v. 20). This again demonstrates the Jewish nature of this teaching. The Church is not under the Sabbath law, showing that this cannot be referring to the Church Age.

The time of tribulation that follows the Abomination of Desolation will be unprecedented in human history. Jesus referred to it as, "great tribulation" (v. 21). Notice the wording, "For then there will be great tribulation, such as has not been since the beginning of the world until this time, no, nor ever shall be." The atrocities this world has already seen are unfathomable. But Jesus testified that the tribulation that will be experienced at this time will be unlike anything the world has ever seen.

Verse 22 reveals, "And unless those days were shortened, no flesh would be saved; but for the elect's sake those days will be shortened." The Greek word for *shortened* is *ekolobōthēsan*; it means to *terminate* or to *cut off*. This time of trouble will be so severe that if God did not end it, all the inhabitants of the earth would be destroyed (v. 22). Compare the trumpet and bowl judgments of Revelation, found in chapters 8-9 and 16.

The Second Coming of Christ will be the climax of the Tribulation (vv. 23-26). As the judgments of the Tribulation intensify, so too will false sightings of the Christ. In this section Jesus warned those living during the future Tribulation period not to be deceived by these empty claims.

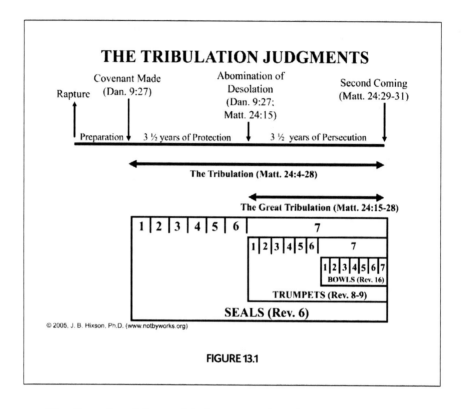

FIGURE 13.1

The first six of the seal judgments take place during the first half of the Tribulation. The second half of the Tribulation, described in Matthew 24:15-28, coincides with the seventh seal judgment, the trumpet judgments, and the bowl judgments (Rev. 6; 8-9; 16). This can be seen in figure 13.1.

The seal judgments include (Rev. 6):

1. White horse - the introduction of the Antichrist.
2. Red horse - the Antichrist will take peace from the earth.
3. Black horse - the Antichrist will bring a famine upon the land.
4. Pale horse - the Antichrist will bring death to one-quarter of the world's population.
5. Pleas for justice by early Tribulation martyrs.
6. A great earthquake and cosmic disturbances.
7. Seven more judgments revealed that are called trumpets.

Revelation 8-9 describes the trumpet judgments. During this time of judgment:

1. One-third of the earth will be burned.
2. One-third of the sea will turn to blood.
3. One-third of the fresh water will be poisoned.
4. One-third of the sun, moon, and stars will be darkened.
5. A huge swarm of locusts will invade the earth (the first woe).
6. Four special demons will be sent to kill one-third of the earth's population (second woe).
7. Seven more judgments will be revealed called *bowls* (third woe).

The bowl judgments are described in Revelation 16:

1. Ugly and painful sores will break out on people.
2. All sea life will be destroyed.
3. All fresh water will be destroyed.
4. The world's climate will be altered so that the sun will scorch people.
5. Unusual darkness will come over the earth.
6. The Euphrates River will dry up in preparation for Armageddon.
7. The worst earthquake in the history of mankind will occur.

Signs Immediately Accompanying the Second Coming (24:27-31)

When Christ returns to establish His Kingdom, it will be obvious (cf. Matt. 24:27, 29-31; Zech. 9:14; Luke 17:24; 21:27; Mark 13:24-26). Jesus said, "For as the lightning comes from the east and flashes to the west, so also will the coming of the Son of Man be" (Matt. 24:27). The point is to recognize that the Second Coming of Christ will be unmistakable; there will be no doubt. No one living at that time will have to wonder, "Has He come yet?" Christ's return and the precise location of it will be apparent (cf. Matt. 24:27-28; Luke 17:37). The Lord told the disciples, "For wherever the carcass is, there the eagles [vultures] will be gathered together" (v. 28). Scavenger birds will gather to consume the dead bodies of all those slain by Christ at the Battle of Armageddon. Just as surely as vultures gather around a carcass, so too at a time when devastation and destruction have set in (Armageddon; cf. Rev.19:17-21; 14:17-20; Ezek. 39:17-20), Christ will return.

Beginning in verse 29, Matthew records:

> Immediately after the tribulation of those days the sun will be
> darkened, and the moon will not give its light; the stars will fall from
> heaven, and the powers of the heavens will be shaken. Then the sign of
> the Son of Man will appear in heaven, and then all the tribes of the earth
> will mourn, and they will see the Son of Man coming on the clouds of
> heaven with power and great glory (Matt. 24:29-30).

Note the time marker in verse 29. The events described will take place
immediately after the Tribulation (cf. Joel 2:30-32; Acts 2:20; 3:15; Isa.
13:9-10; 34:4; Ezek. 32:7; Amos 8:9). Following the cosmic signs, everyone
on earth will see Jesus when He returns with His Bride, the Church (Rev.
19:11-16).

A great deal of speculation exists as to the identification of the sign of
the Son of Man in verse 30. Suggestions include that it might be a cross,
clouds, or Jesus Himself. It seems likely that a literal sign of some sort is
in view. The important point to remember is that whatever it is, it will
clearly point to Christ. Whoever sees the sign will know beyond any
doubt that Christ is coming. This is the clear teaching of the rest of verse
30, "all the tribes of the earth will mourn, and they will see the Son of
Man coming on the clouds of heaven with power and great glory."

Verse 31 contains great theological significance. Jesus proclaimed,
"And He will send His angels with a great sound of a trumpet, and
they will gather together His elect from the four winds, from one end
of heaven to the other." The Lord will gather His elect from the globe
and usher them into the long awaited Kingdom of Christ. Certainly it is
true that all believers alive at the end of the Tribulation will enter into the
Kingdom, not just the Jewish believers. However, the elect, in the context
of verse 31, refers to Israel (Isa. 27:12-13; cf. 42:1; 45:4; 65:9, 22; Matt.
24:22, 24). This will be the fulfillment of the regathering of the nation of
Israel into the land that was predicted throughout the Old Testament.
Specifically, we read in Deuteronomy 30:3, "The LORD your God will
bring you back from captivity, and have compassion on you, and gather
you again from all the nations where the LORD your God has scattered
you."

The Parable of the Fig Tree: Signs Indicating the Nearness of Christ's Return (24:32-35)

Jesus began to make an application through the use of a parable. He had already given all kinds of signs to watch for. Now, He wanted them to learn the parable of the fig tree. Jesus taught, "Now learn this parable from the fig tree: When its branch has already become tender and puts forth leaves, you know that summer is near. So you also, when you see all these things, know that it is near—at the doors!" (Matt. 24:32-33). This parable is actually rather simple and straightforward. Just as the budding of leaves on a fig tree indicate that summer is near, likewise, all the signs Jesus had discussed will indicate that His return is near. The signs that take place in the Tribulation will indicate the soon return of the Lord at the Second Coming.

The next verse has engendered quite a bit of controversy over the years. Matthew teaches, "Assuredly, I say to you, this generation will by no means pass away till all these things take place" (Matt. 24:34). This has become the proof text for Preterists. The entire Preterist view rises or falls on this one verse because it is taught that it means everything prophesied by Christ in the Olivet Discourse needed to be fulfilled within the generation living at that time. Everything Jesus prophesied is seen as fulfilled by A.D. 70. Because of this, it becomes necessary to spiritualize many specific prophecies. For example, according to Preterists, verse 27 of Matthew 24 is taken to refer to the smoke billowing up over Jerusalem in A.D. 70, after it was attacked by Rome. Yet, let it be recognized that there is a significant difference between smoke from a burning Temple and lightning from the East to the West!

This is also a key passage for covenant theologians who, likewise, interpret verse 34 as indicating that the teaching from Jesus in the Olivet Discourse had to be fulfilled within that generation. They interpret the words *this generation* to mean the *first century generation*, which is not what it means in context.

The problem centers on the English translation of the text. At first glance, it seems like a reasonable assumption that Jesus was referring to the generation to whom He had been speaking. A closer look reveals that Jesus was referring to the generation He had been speaking about, the generation alive during the Tribulation. It is the generation who sees all these things that will witness the fulfillment of the words of Christ.

Generation is the Greek word *genea*. It can mean either *a literal generation (forty years)* or *a nation (race)*. The most natural meaning in verse 34 is of a literal generation. The context mandates that it refers to the generation alive at the time when, "all these things take place" (cf. v. 33). Again, He was talking to the generation who will be alive when the Tribulation and Second Coming take place.

This can be further demonstrated by another look at verse 33. Notice once more the wording of this verse, "So you also, when you see all these things." Two times in verse 33 Jesus said the word *you*. Who was He addressing? He could not have meant the disciples, which was His immediate audience, because they did not see His second coming, or any of the events of the Tribulation which He had just discussed. Throughout the Olivet Discourse Jesus used the word *you* with the meaning of *you who are alive at the time these signs take place*. He was prophetically speaking to this future generation (cf. Isa. 33:17-24; 66:10-14; Zech. 2:11; 9:9; 14:1; Isa. 27:12-13; Ezek. 38-39; Joel 2:28-29). The entire message is meant to be a warning to Israel regarding the events immediately preceding Christ's return at the Second Coming. Within the Olivet Discourse, *this generation* refers prophetically to *that future generation*. The generation who witnesses the beginning of the signs will also see the end of the signs. The generation who sees the beginning of the signs will witness the return of Christ. Because the beginning of the signs has not occurred yet, we know that we cannot claim this promise.

Notice also, that verse 33 refers to that future generation *seeing*, "all these things." This looks back to the wording of verse 30, when that generation *sees* the return of the Son of Man. The signs that we have examined so far in the Olivet Discourse point to the Second Coming of Christ. The generation that witnesses the signs will not pass away until all these events take place.

Then Jesus declared, "Heaven and earth will pass away, but My words will by no means pass away" (Matt. 24:35). This verse is a profound statement of the authority, veracity, and indestructibility of Jesus' words (cf. 1 Pet. 1:23-25).[8]

The Analogy of the Flood: The Second Coming will Occur Unexpectedly (24:36-44)

Matthew 24:36 is a transitional verse within the Olivet Discourse. Christ next taught the disciples, "But of that day and hour no one knows, not even the angels of heaven, but My Father only." This is the springboard from which Matthew 24:37-25:30 arises. The parables and general teaching that follow verse 36 expand on the theme of watchfulness. They also point back to verse 33, where Jesus had said that when all of the signs He described are visible, then His return is, "near-at the doors!"

The Analogy of Noah

The purpose of the illustration about Noah was to demonstrate that for many individuals living in the Tribulation, the Second Coming will be completely unexpected (Matt. 24:37-44). In spite of the tremendous upheaval and chaos that will characterize life during the Tribulation, there will be those who are deceived and fail to prepare for the return of Christ and His coming Kingdom.

A Comparison from Luke 17:26-37

Luke provides us with additional teaching from our Lord about the illustration of Noah (Luke 17:26-37). The emphasis of this passage is not so much on the moral condition of the day, as it is the routine experiences. That is, people will be going through their normal routines when suddenly and unexpectedly judgment will come.

A key detail for correctly interpreting the illustration of Noah in Matthew 24:37-44 is found in Luke 17. Jesus introduced the illustration by saying, "But as the days of Noah were, so also will the coming of the Son of Man be" (Matt. 24:37). He described the typical activities taking place before the flood, "For as in the days before the flood, they were eating and drinking, marrying and giving in marriage, until the day that Noah entered the ark, and did not know until the flood came and took them all away" (Matt. 24:38-39). The English translations are not as direct or specific as they could be, which has led many to misidentify the word *them* in verse 39. Unfortunately, it is common for Christians to think *them* refers to the people in the ark being rescued. Because of this, the erroneous conclusion is made that this is referring to the Rapture.

Fortunately, Jesus used this same analogy of Noah in His teaching in Luke 17. Even though Luke 17 is not the Olivet Discourse, it is the same analogy used by Jesus. Comparing Matthew's account with Luke 17 provides clarity. What did Jesus mean that they were taken away by the flood? Luke 17:26-27 has the answer, "And as it was in the days of Noah, so it will be also in the days of the Son of Man: They ate, they drank, they married wives, they were given in marriage, until the day that Noah entered the ark, and the flood came and *destroyed them all* (emphasis added)." Jesus directly said that the flood came and destroyed them all. The flood was an instrument of judgment.

This informs us that in Matthew 24:39, when Christ spoke of the flood taking them all away, He was referring to how the flood took them away *in judgment*. Those left behind were Noah and his family, who were saved and left to inhabit the earth. Those taken from the earth were the unrighteous, who were swept away by the flood. The same thing will be true at the Second Coming. Those taken away will be taken away in judgment (the goats). Those left behind will be left behind to enter the Kingdom (the sheep).

Luke 17:31-33 also teaches us that Lot's wife serves as a historical example of one who misjudged the seriousness of God's judgment and failed to seek refuge in a timely manner. During the Tribulation, people will do well to take the impending judgment seriously, rather than focusing on their earthly treasures (Luke 17:33).

The Analogy Continued from Matthew

In Noah's day the flood came and destroyed the people, except for Noah and his family. Jesus taught, "For as in the days before the flood, they were eating and drinking, marrying and giving in marriage, until the day that Noah entered the ark, and did not know until the flood came and took them all away, so also will the coming of the Son of Man be" (Matt. 24:38-39). The people were oblivious to the fact that time was short. Those taken away in the day of Noah were taken away in judgment. The righteous were left behind. The antecedent *them* is talking about the people Christ had just described in great detail. It was those who were, "eating and drinking, marrying and giving in marriage." The flood came and took them all away to their death and eternal separation from God. Then Jesus specifically mentioned it will be the same with the coming of the Son of Man (the Second Coming of Christ).

Verses 40-41 of Matthew continue to teach, "Then two men will be in the field: one will be taken and the other left. Two women will be grinding at the mill: one will be taken and the other left." It is imperative to recognize that the individuals taken will be taken away in judgment, not raptured. A casual reading of these verses has led many to believe that they refer to the Rapture. Yet, contextually, we know that this is not the intended teaching by Christ because verses 38-39 explain that in the days of Noah the ones taken were taken away in judgment. Christ then taught that it will be the same at the Second Coming. Those who will not be expecting the Second Coming of Christ (unbelievers marrying and eating like in the days of Noah) will also be taken away in judgment. It is almost inconceivable, given the destruction, incredible signs, and direct intervention of God on earth during the Tribulation, that many Jews will still reject their Messiah. This shows how strong the deception will be.

Jesus then said, "Watch therefore, for you do not know what hour your Lord is coming" (Matt. 24:42). This is a warning to the future generation of the nation of Israel to be alert for the return of Christ at the Second Coming. Those prepared for the return of the Lord will remain on earth to inherit the Messianic Kingdom.

If verses 40-41 are referencing the Rapture, as it is often claimed, it is difficult to see where the Lord introduced the Church within the Olivet Discourse. The entire discourse is Jewish in nature. The context is of watching out for the horrible things that will come, which indicates He was addressing individuals that will be present during the Tribulation. Further, it would be strange indeed for Christ to use the same analogy on two separate occasions with two completely opposite applications. If the Rapture is being referenced in Matthew 24, we are left to conclude that in one instance Jesus taught that the ones taken away are (indisputably) the unrighteous being judged (Luke 17:27), and in the other instance the ones taken away are Christians being rescued by the Rapture (Matt. 24)!

The message of Matthew 24:42-44 is to be ready. The generation alive when Christ returns will need to be watchful so that they are not left unprepared for the Lord's return. Jesus then used a different analogy in verses 43-44 to once again challenge this future generation to be watchful. He warned, "Therefore you also be ready, for the Son of Man is coming at an hour you do not expect" (v. 44).

The Parable of the Faithful and Evil Servants: The Second Coming May Occur Sooner Than Expected (24:45-51)

The parable of the faithful and evil servants is intended to communicate a simple truth. This section of the Olivet Discourse continues Jesus' exhortation to be watchful. The Lord told this parable to demonstrate that for many in the Tribulation, the Second Coming will occur sooner than expected. The faithful wise servant during the

Tribulation will be watching and prepared for Jesus' return. The Church is given a similar exhortation in 1 John 2:28 with regard to the Rapture, but this does not mean that the Church is in view in verses 45-51.

Strangely, some misguided Bible students suggest that this parable teaches that some believers from the present Church Age (i.e. "the really bad ones") will be sent to a place of punishment (a sort of Christian purgatory) for a thousand years, where there will be weeping and gnashing of teeth. This erroneous teaching, often referred to as the *Kingdom Exclusion* view, is an example of faulty hermeneutics and an agenda-driven interpretive process. Nowhere does the New Testament teach that believers will face any punitive consequences, either at death or at the Rapture. In truth, this parable, like the rest of the Olivet Discourse, relates to the nation of Israel.

Notice that once more we see the use of the word *hypocrite* (v. 51). In Matthew's Gospel we witness that Jesus used this word on numerous occasions when dealing with the religious leaders of Israel. This parable exposes the danger for the Jews living in the Tribulation who are not prepared for the Kingdom. The Second Coming of Christ will catch them off guard. Unbelieving Jews will be cast out because of their lack of faith.

The Parable of the Wise and Foolish Virgins: The Second Coming May Occur Later Than Expected (25:1-13)

An attempt to identify the various elements within the parable of the ten virgins has led to numerous creative, though unwarranted, interpretations. When seeking to interpret parables in Scripture, it is important to keep certain hermeneutical principles in mind.

Interpreting Parables

The Greek word *parabole* is a noun, and *paraballo* is the verb meaning *to throw beside*. The noun means *a placing of one thing by the side of another, juxtaposition, as of ships in a battle*. Metaphorically it means *a comparing, comparison of one thing with another, likeness, similitude*. Interpreting parables involves understanding the historical and cultural setting in which they were given. The interpreter should always set out to study the immediate context of the passage. The primary goal in interpreting a parable is to identify the main idea or principle being taught. It is a mistake to become overly obsessed with the details.

The context of the parable of the ten virgins is in the midst of a discussion about the unexpected nature of Christ's return. The Second Coming will occur at a time when, for many, it is least expected. When Christ returns, those who are unprepared will not be allowed to enter the Kingdom. To be denied access to the Kingdom at Christ's second coming will mean spending eternity in hell.

Jewish Weddings

The historical background for this parable involves a typical Jewish wedding ceremony. In Israel, as well as in most other parts of the ancient Near East, a wedding was one of the most significant social events. Almost everyone in the village or community would be involved as either a participant or guest. The point of Jesus' analogy with the Jewish wedding is not to give details about what Christ will do when He returns. Rather, it is to illustrate the difference between being watchful and being unprepared.

Jewish marriages consisted of three parts:

1. The engagement: The engagement consisted of a formal agreement between the father of the bride and the father of the groom.
2. The betrothal: The betrothal was the marriage ceremony at which the bride and groom exchanged vows in the presence of family and friends. After the betrothal, the couple was considered to be married, even though the marriage was not physically consummated and the two did not live together until after the betrothal period. Their relationship during this time could be broken only by a formal divorce. If the husband died during the betrothal, the bride was considered a widow. If the bride was found to be with child during this time, the husband could divorce her (cf. Matt. 19:1-10). The betrothal could last for many months, sometimes a year, during which time the groom would establish himself in a business, trade, or farming and would make provision for a place for the couple to live.
3. The wedding feast: At the end of the betrothal period the wedding feast would be held. This festivity could last an entire week. It began when the groom, along with his groomsmen, traveled to the bride's home, where the bride and her bridesmaids would be waiting. The bride, groom, and their attendants would then all parade through the streets announcing the start of the wedding feast. The procession was

usually held at night. Lamps or torches were used by the wedding party to light the way, which also attracted attention to this event. After the wedding supper, the couple would be left alone together for the first time. The marriage would be consummated and the couple would begin living together in their new home. It was this third part of the marriage ritual that Jesus used as the basis for His analogy.

The Parable Explained

Matthew 25 opens with the words, "Then the kingdom of heaven shall be likened to ten virgins who took their lamps and went out to meet the bridegroom" (Matt. 25:1). Notice the similarity to the parables of the Kingdom in Matthew 13. In this parable, and the one that follows it, Jesus gave certain truths that relate to the coming Messianic Kingdom.

The parable begins with the bridesmaids (virgins) assembling and waiting for the groom's arrival. Jesus then told His disciples that five of the bridesmaids were foolish, and five were wise (v. 2). The foolish virgins were unprepared. Those alive on the earth at Christ's return should imitate the behavior of the wise virgins (vv. 3-4). Verse 5 teaches us that they all slept. For the foolish virgins it was a sleep of carelessness. For the wise it was a sleep of contentment (cf. Prov. 3:21-26).

Notice the teaching of verse 6, "And at midnight a cry was heard: 'Behold, the bridegroom is coming; go out to meet him!'" The *cry* announcing the arrival of the groom corresponds to the *sign of the Son of Man* in Matthew 24:30. After awaking, the foolish bridesmaids realized they did not have enough oil in their lamps. It is completely unnecessary to assign a particular meaning to the oil. This is beyond Jesus' point. All that He wanted the disciples to notice was that the foolish bridesmaids were unprepared.

While the foolish bridesmaids were busy trying to obtain oil, the bridegroom arrived (vv. 8-10). The teaching contained in verses 10-12 is especially important. It is there that Christ taught, "The bridegroom came, and those who were ready went in with him to the wedding; and the door was shut. Afterward the other virgins came also, saying, 'Lord, Lord, open to us!' But he answered and said, 'Assuredly, I say to you, I do not know you'" (cf. Matt. 7:21-23).

Jesus summarized the lesson of this parable in verse 13 by teaching, "Watch therefore, for you know neither the day nor the hour in which the Son of Man is coming." In light of the experience of the foolish virgins, those alive during the Tribulation should be alert because Jesus could come at an hour later than expected. The key to this passage is being ready for the arrival of Christ at the Second Coming.

The Rapture is never mentioned in the Gospel of Matthew. The references in the Olivet Discourse to the arrival of Christ are always referring to the Second Coming. Jesus was continuing to answer the question, "What are the signs of the end of the age?" Contextually, we do not even see the Church mentioned or referenced in the Olivet Discourse. The disciples had asked about the Kingdom, and the Lord's answers were all about the Kingdom. Notice again the opening words of chapter 25, "Then the kingdom of heaven shall be" (Matt. 25:1). This is yet another clear reference to the Messianic Kingdom.

The Parable of the Talents (25:14-30)

The parable of the talents begins with Christ stating, "For the kingdom of heaven is like a man traveling to a far country, who called his own servants and delivered his goods to them" (Matt. 25:14). In the Greek manuscripts the phrase *the Kingdom of Heaven* is not in the text. However, Jesus strung together a series of parables about the Kingdom, much like He did in Matthew 13. In other words, the meaning is implied. Jesus was continuing to speak about the Kingdom, from the perspective of the talents.

It needs to be noted that this parable is not the same as the parable of the minas in Luke 19. Notice in verse 14 Jesus referred to a man who called, "his own servants." This is a clear reference to Israel.

The parable of the minas is different for a number of reasons:

- Contextually, the parable of the minas is referring to the Church Age. Luke directly records that Jesus taught the parable of the minas because the disciples thought that Christ would usher in the Kingdom right away (Luke19:11). Jesus then taught them that there would be an inter-advent age (the Church Age).
- In the parable of the minas every individual received one mina, or the same amount. In the Church Age every believer has one life of stewardship that he will be accountable for at the Judgment Seat of Christ. The talents in Matthew 25 were given in different amounts to each person. This alone should teach us that these parables have different meanings.

- In Luke 19, the one who did nothing with his minas still got into the Kingdom. In the parable of the talents the end result is much different. The one who did nothing with his talent did not get into the Kingdom. Instead, he was cast into the outer darkness.
- The parable of the minas presents the ones that reject the Master as unbelieving Israel (the citizens who hated him in Luke 19:14, 27). The parable of the minas presented both unbelieving Israel and the Church. In Matthew 25, Jesus was continuing to teach about the Kingdom of Heaven and was addressing only Israel.

The parable of the talents is teaching that the people of Israel will have one final opportunity to do something with the privileged station that they have held amongst all the people of the earth. Throughout the course of Israel's history the nation has had varying degrees of blessing from the Lord. At times they had prophets, priests, and kings. Throughout their history the responsibility has remained to be faithful to the message that had been entrusted to them. The parable of the talents teaches that the nation of Israel will have one last opportunity to receive the message of Christ and the Gospel of the Kingdom.

Remember the context of Matthew 25. This parable is in the midst of a discussion about the unexpected nature of Christ's return. It is linked grammatically with the parable of the virgins. Both parables are intended to teach truths about the Kingdom. Unlike the shorter parables about the timing of Christ's return, this extended parable focuses on the rewards and the consequences that will be disbursed when Christ returns.

The parable of the talents relates directly to Israel and the degree to which individual Jews will be prepared (qualified) to enter the Kingdom. All three servants represent Israel (cf. Isa. 41:8; Luke 1:54). In view of Israel's incredible privilege as the chosen nation of God, the talents stand for all of the resources and benefits that are hers (cf. Rom. 9). Those believers who respond appropriately to the gospel message during the Tribulation will be rewarded with positions of rulership and authority in the Kingdom. Those who do not receive the gospel message will be excluded from the Kingdom. The same principle is true for believers of the present Church Age, but we do not get this teaching from this passage. Rather, it comes from passages such as: Heb. 1:14; 6:11; 9:15; Col. 3:24; 1 Pet. 3:9; Gal. 5:19-21; 1 Cor. 6:9-10; Eph. 5:3-5; James 2:5; 2 Tim. 2:12; Rev. 2:26-27; Rev. 3:21; Luke 19:11-27.

The fact that this parable is dealing specifically with the Kingdom, and not with heaven in general, is indicated by the phrase, "enter into the joy of your Lord" (Matt. 25:21, 23). It is further indicated by the statement that the unprofitable servant is cast into, "outer darkness" (v. 30). This is a reference to exclusion from the Messianic Kingdom.

Outer Darkness

We have already examined this phrase *outer darkness* in chapter 4. Because of the considerable attention that has been drawn to this expression, and the misunderstandings that have arisen, let us make some further observations. The English words translated *outer darkness* come from the Greek words *to skotos to exōteron* (Matt. 25:30).

Outer

The word *outer* is the Greek word *exōteron*. This term appears nowhere else in the New Testament outside of Matthew 8:5-13; 22:1-14; and 25:14-30. However, it does occur twenty-three times in the Septuagint (Greek translation of the Old Testament) and always in relation to the Tabernacle, Temple of God, or the palace of a king. Most significantly, the term is used fifteen times in Ezekiel to describe the outer court of the Temple (Ezek. 10:5; 40:19, 20; 41:15, 17; 42:1, 3, 6, 7, 8, 9, 14; 44:19; 46:20, 21). In one instance it describes the outer gate of the Temple (Ezek. 44:1). BDAG points to its use in the Septuagint of Exodus 26:4 and gives it the nuance of the, "farthest, extreme."[9] This passage describes the curtains used to make the Tabernacle.

Darkness

The other term that we need to define is *darkness*. As mentioned, this is the Greek word *skotos*. Our attention turns to several Greek lexicons and their definition of *skotos*:

- Strong's: 1. darkness. 1a. of night darkness. 1b. of darkened eyesight or blindness. 2. metaph. 2a. of ignorance respecting divine things and human duties, and the accompanying ungodliness and immorality, together with their consequent misery in hell. 2b. persons in whom darkness becomes visible and holds sway.[10]
- Vine's: (a) of "physical darkness," Matt. 27:45; 2 Cor. 4:6; (b) of "intellectual darkness," Rom. 2:19 (cf. C, No. 1); (c) of "blindness,"

Acts 13:11; (d) by metonymy, of the "place of punishment," e.g., Matt. 8:12; 2 Pet. 2:17; Jude 13; (e) metaphorically, of "moral and spiritual darkness," e.g., Matt. 6:23; Luke 1:79; 11:35; John 3:19; Acts 26:18; 2 Cor. 6:14; Eph. 6:12; Col. 1:13; 1 Thess. 5:4-5; 1 Pet. 2:9; 1 John 1:6; (f) by metonymy, of "those who are in moral or spiritual darkness," Eph. 5:8; (g) of "evil works," Rom. 13:12; Eph. 5:11, (h) of the "evil powers that dominate the world," Luke 22:53.[11]

- Excerpts from the entry in BDAG include: "Of the darkness of the place of punishment far removed from the heavenly kingdom" and "of death."[12]

The Meaning of Outer Darkness

With these definitions as a range of meanings, we seek to accurately define *outer darkness*. Based on the history of its usage, this phrase is best understood as a reference to exclusion from the festivities that will accompany the Marriage Supper of the Lamb at the beginning of the Millennium (cf. Rev. 19:6-9). Outer darkness is a metonym for not entering the Kingdom. Those servants who respond appropriately to the talent they are given will be granted entrance into the wedding feast (and by extension the Kingdom). Those servants who are unprofitable will be left out in the dark where they will experience intense remorse. The "weeping and gnashing of teeth" is a reference to the sorrow, grief, and agony of hell (Matt. 25:30).

The Meaning of the Parable of the Talents

The central message, therefore, of this parable is to do something with what you have been given. Jesus was instructing the nation of Israel that during the Tribulation the people will have one last occasion to do something with the opportunity afforded them. The nation of Israel is surely a blessed people, but when confronted with the Gospel of the Kingdom how will they respond? Some will bury this final opportunity. Others will respond and inherit the Kingdom, with varying levels of rewards and responsibilities entrusted to them.

This interpretation is confirmed by the usage of the expression, "enter into the joy of your lord" (Matt. 25:21, 23). This is a distinctly Messianic Kingdom phrase. Joy is a key word that is often used in the Old Testament to describe the Kingdom. The concept of entering should make us ask the question, "Enter what?" The answer is the Kingdom of Christ. Jesus directly mentioned that the servants who are allowed to enter are those who have been found faithful. The unprofitable (unfaithful) servants will be cast into outer darkness (v. 30).

The parable of the talents is often drawn upon to provide motivating instruction for believers of the Church Age. Reference is usually made to the Judgment Seat of Christ, and believers are challenged to be faithful with what they have been given. However, as the context makes clear, this passage is not dealing with the Church Age.

The New Testament teaching of the importance of Church Age believers being good stewards of their lives, and the reality of believers standing before Christ to give an account at the Judgment Seat, remains a central doctrine of eschatology. Yet, it is unfortunate that the parable of the talents has been misidentified as a text that is teaching about the Church.

Summary of the Parable of the Talents

The watchfulness parables are intended to teach this future generation of Jews (those living during the Tribulation) about the importance of being ready for the Second Coming of Christ. The parable of the talents is intended to teach the nation of Israel that they will have one last opportunity to come to faith in their Messiah. This parable also provides the third of the three outer darkness references in Matthew. The Tribulation period will provide the Jews with one final chance to do something with the *talent* they have been offered repeatedly throughout history. Jews who trust in the Gospel of the Kingdom will enter the joy of the Lord (the Kingdom). Jews who squander their last opportunity will be cast into outer darkness (excluded from the Kingdom).

The Judgment of the Nations and the Establishment of the Messianic Kingdom (25:31-46)

Let it be recognized that the entire Olivet Discourse reaches its climax in verses 31-46. It is there we see that Jesus taught about the Sheep and Goats Judgment.

Sheep and Goats Judgment

After the parable of the talents Jesus then said, "When the Son of Man comes in His glory, and all the holy angels with Him, then He will sit on the throne of His glory" (Matt. 25:31). This is the second time in the Olivet Discourse we see the expression, "When the Son of Man comes in His glory." Similar words were spoken by Christ in Matthew 24:30.

Immediately after the Second Coming of Christ and the Battle of Armageddon, the Lord will divide the nations like a shepherd dividing his sheep from the Goats. This is the great end times harvest. Matthew records, "All the nations will be gathered before Him, and He will separate them one from another, as a shepherd divides his sheep from the goats. And He will set the sheep on His right hand, but the goats on the left" (Matt. 25:32-33). Remember, the Kingdom will start with the believers who are alive at the end of the Tribulation.

This judgment is distinct from the Great White Throne Judgment (Rev. 20:11-15), which occurs at the end of the Millennium. The purpose of the Sheep and Goats Judgment is to determine who will enter the long awaited Kingdom, and who will not. The sheep represent those who are saved (thus qualified to enter the Kingdom). The goats represent those who are unsaved (thus excluded from the Kingdom and cast into hell).

Jesus first addressed His future response to the believers after the Second Coming:

> Then the King will say to those on His right hand, "Come, you blessed of My Father, inherit the kingdom prepared for you from the foundation of the world: for I was hungry and you gave Me food; I was thirsty and you gave Me drink; I was a stranger and you took Me in; I was naked and you clothed Me; I was sick and you visited Me; I was in prison and you came to Me." Then the righteous will answer Him, saying, "Lord, when did we see You hungry and feed You, or thirsty and give You drink? When did we see You a stranger and take You in, or naked and clothe You? Or when did we see You sick, or in prison, and come to You?" And the King will answer and say to them, "Assuredly, I say to you, inasmuch as you did it to one of the least of these My brethren, you did it to Me" (Matt. 25:34-40).

Verse 40 ends with a reference to the *brethren* of Christ. This is a reference to Jewish believers. Specifically, this is a reference to the Jewish missionaries who spread the Gospel of the Kingdom during the preceding seven-year Tribulation (Rev. 7:1-8). The basis for entrance into the Kingdom, then, is how one treated these *brethren*. The treatment of the brethren serves as a metonym for how one received the message of the Kingdom. The sheep responded favorably to the Gospel of the Kingdom by trusting in the coming King for the forgiveness of sins. The goats rejected the Gospel of the Kingdom and mistreated those who heralded this Gospel.

The term *righteous* is also significant (v. 37). These individuals will truly be righteous. We already witnessed that the Sermon on the Mount presents Jesus demonstrating the need for faith righteousness. The only way to obtain perfect righteousness is by faith (Rom. 3:21-26).

It should be obvious that Jesus was not teaching that you have to give the hungry food in order to get into the Kingdom. This would be a violation of everything Scripture teaches about getting into the Kingdom. Eternal life (entrance to the Kingdom) is not obtained by works (Eph. 2:8-9).

We need to remember that in the Tribulation the 144,000 witnesses will be sent out to preach the Gospel of the Kingdom (Rev. 7:1-8). Jesus had testified, "And this gospel of the kingdom will be preached in all the world as a witness to all the nations, and then the end will come" (Matt. 24:14). The behavior of the righteous that Jesus described in Matthew 25:34-40 is of individuals who will welcome the message of the envoys of Christ, as they go throughout the world witnessing. Welcoming the messengers (providing for their needs) will represent acceptance of their message. This will be especially true during the intense persecution of the Tribulation. In this case, the message is the Gospel of the Kingdom.

Jesus was not testifying that our entrance into heaven is dependent on our social actions (being nice to people, feeding the hungry, helping the poor, or being socially conscious). If this were true, then this passage would run contrary to the entire teaching of the Bible that justification is by faith. Therefore, it must be teaching that the manner in which people respond to His *brethren* during the Tribulation will be an indicator of their faith. Those individuals who respond favorably (symbolized by giving them food, water, and clothing) will thereby indicate an acceptance of the message. The end result for this group of individuals will be that Jesus will say to them, "Come, you blessed of My Father, inherit the kingdom prepared for you from the foundation of the world" (Matt. 25:34). The behavior of welcoming Christ's representatives during the Tribulation is indicative of the fact that they have trusted in Christ because no one will get into the Kingdom who did not believe; it is all about faith in Christ. Responding unfavorably will mean a rejection of the message. To reject the message of the Gospel of the Kingdom in that day, will be to seal your fate in the everlasting fire prepared for the Devil and his angels.

Regrettably, this passage is often used by evangelicals to teach that this type of outreach should be the main emphasis of the Church today. It leads to a social gospel, that the message of Christ is all about improving the physical lives of people, and helping them to overcome oppression. The Bible does teach that the love of Christ should compel us to reach out to meet the needs of others, but whether or not we show compassion to the less fortunate has no bearing on whether or not we get into heaven. The only factor on whether we get into heaven or not is faith righteousness.

Christ intended this teaching to go beyond the treatment of the 144,000 witnesses during the Tribulation. This was also an indictment on the same group of people He was speaking to moments earlier, in the sense that the Jewish leaders looked down on the less fortunate. There is a clear parallel here to the early parts of chapter 23, where Jesus painted a picture of the Jewish leaders as not being compassionate toward the lower echelon of the Jewish culture. Instead, the leaders actually put more burdens on them. Jesus was sending them the message that their pride and self-righteousness kept them out of the Kingdom. Instead of humbling themselves and welcoming the message of faith, their pride led them down the path of self-righteousness.

Keep in mind that Jesus had two audiences in view as He taught the Olivet Discourse. The first was the generation of leaders living in that day who were unbelievers, and for whom He had already spoken strong words of condemnation. It should be noted that the disciples represented the opposite end of the spectrum. They were a part of the believing remnant of Jews in the first century who did have faith.

Prophetically, His second audience was the future generation of national Israel. Prophets could only speak to the generation that was present, with the record of the prophecy preserved in the Word of God for the future generation that will be alive at the time of its fulfillment. Jesus was providing prophetic instruction in the Olivet Discourse for this future generation. The message is to watch out, be ready, and believe in the Messiah.

Historically, dispensationalists have referred to this section of Scripture as the Judgment of the Nations. The sheep and goats are all thought to be Gentiles, who will be judged on the way they treated Israel. However, it seems best not to take this passage as referring exclusively to a judgment of the Gentile nations. This is the climax of the entire Olivet Discourse. It is the Second Coming judgment that includes Israel and Gentiles alike. Verse 32 teaches that, "All the nations will be gathered before Him." There is no reason to assume that Israel will not be gathered before Him as well. There are places in Scripture where we do see Israel referred to as one of the nations (Matt. 28:18-20). The word *nations* by itself in Scripture would normally indicate Gentiles in contrast to the Jews. The addition of the qualifier *all*, as well as the surrounding context, indicates that Jews and Gentiles alike are in view. The word *nations* never refers to the dead anywhere in Scripture. Therefore, the ones gathered for this great judgment include all who are alive on the earth at the time of Christ's return. This will be the final judgment before the Millennium of those who get into the Kingdom, and of those who do not. It is preferable to recognize that everyone alive on earth at this time will be included in this judgment (Jews and Gentiles, believers and unbelievers).

To those on His left Christ will say:

> "Depart from Me, you cursed, into the everlasting fire prepared for the devil and his angels: for I was hungry and you gave Me no food; I was thirsty and you gave Me no drink; I was a stranger and you did not take Me in, naked and you did not clothe Me, sick and in prison and you did not visit Me." Then they also will answer Him, saying, "Lord, when did we see You hungry or thirsty or a stranger or naked or sick or in prison, and did not minister to You?" Then He will answer them, saying, "Assuredly, I say to you, inasmuch as you did not do it to one of the least of these, you did not do it to Me." And these will go away into everlasting punishment, but the righteous into eternal life (Matt. 25:41-46).

Judgment has been a primary theme throughout the Olivet Discourse. Jesus concluded this discourse by giving specific details about the judgment that will immediately precede the inauguration of the Kingdom.

This final section of the Olivet Discourse serves as a solemn warning to those who will be alive during the Tribulation, "Receive the gospel and you will be rewarded with entrance into the Kingdom (and ultimately heaven). Reject the gospel and you will spend eternity in hell."

Lessons from the Olivet Discourse

There are many lessons to be taken out of the Olivet Discourse. This would include the teaching that the King is more important than the King's house (Matt. 24:1-2). We learn that Satan's attempts to deceive the world will intensify during Daniel's Seventieth Week (Matt. 24:4-6). The Tribulation period will be marked by the intense persecution of believers (Matt. 24:9-14). One day, the good news about Jesus Christ will reach every corner of the earth (Matt. 24:14). The signs of the end times are clearly foretold by Jesus. No one in the final generation will be able to plead ignorance (Matt. 24:4-26). When Jesus returns to establish His earthly Kingdom, it will be obvious, and there will be no doubt about His return (Matt. 24:29-31).

The return of Christ will be the most awesome display of power the world has ever seen (Matt. 24:30). The prophecies of Christ are authoritative and guaranteed to come true (Matt. 24:35). Notwithstanding the clear outline of future events given in Scripture, the Second Coming will occur at a time when many are not expecting it (Matt. 24:36-44). In spite of the tremendous upheaval and chaos that will characterize life during the Tribulation, there will be those who are deceived and fail to prepare for the return of Christ and His coming Kingdom (Matt. 24:36-25:13). God, who is rich in mercy, will give His chosen people, Israel, one final chance to receive the gospel before Christ returns (Matt. 25:14-30). When Christ finally returns, all of humanity will fall into one of two categories, those who received the gospel and those who did not (Matt. 25:31-46). The consummation of God's Kingdom program will occur at the Second Coming of Christ.

Discussion Questions

1. What is the Olivet Discourse?
2. Why is the Olivet Discourse significant?
3. Describe the purpose of the Gospel of Matthew.
4. Give a brief summary of the overall teaching found in Matthew chapters 1-23.
5. What was the disciples' focus throughout the Olivet Discourse? What question did they ask?
6. What is the preferred dispensational outline of the Olivet Discourse? Provide three proofs that support this position.
7. List some of the signs that Jesus provided in response to the disciples' question.
8. How did Jesus provide application and understanding of His teaching? Name the parables He told and summarize the overall teaching of each.
9. Explain the Sheep and Goats Judgment found in the climax of the Olivet Discourse.
10. What lessons should we take away from the teaching found in the Olivet Discourse?

Endnotes

1. Daniel G. Reid, Robert Dean Linder, Bruce L. Shelley, and Harry S. Stout, *Dictionary of Christianity in America* (Downers Grove, IL: InterVarsity Press, 1990).

2. Mark Galli and Ted Olsen, *131 Christians Everyone Should Know* (Nashville, TN: Broadman & Holman Publishers, 2000), 191.

3. Ibid., 191-192.

4. Ibid., 192.

5. Ted Cabal, Chad Owen Brand, E. Ray Clendenen et al., *The Apologetics Study Bible: Real Questions, Straight Answers, Stronger Faith* (Nashville, TN: Holman Bible Publishers, 2007), 1284.

6. An alternative dispensational view teaches that Matthew 24:4-14 refers to the first half of the Tribulation.

7. See also 1 Thessalonians 5:3.

8. For a detailed discussion of "this generation" in Matthew 24:34 see Dr. Hixson's article, "The Meaning of 'This Generation' in Matthew 24:34" available at www.NotByWorks.org.

9. William Arndt, Frederick W. Danker, and Walter Bauer, *A Greek-English Lexicon of the New Testament and Other Early Christian Literature*, 3rd ed. (Chicago, IL: University of Chicago Press, 2000), 355.

10. James Strong, *Enhanced Strong's Lexicon*.

11. W. E. Vine, Merrill F. Unger, and William White, Jr., vol. 2, *Vine's Complete Expository Dictionary of Old and New Testament Words* (Nashville, TN: Thomas Nelson Publishers, 1996), 145.

12. William Arndt, Frederick W. Danker, and Walter Bauer, *A Greek-English Lexicon of the New Testament and Other Early Christian Literature*, 3rd ed. (Chicago, IL: University of Chicago Press, 2000), 932.

CHAPTER 14

The Seventieth Week - The Tribulation

And unless those days were shortened, no flesh would be saved; but for the elect's sake those days will be shortened.

- Matthew 24:22

HISTORY HAS ADEQUATELY demonstrated that some men never lack confidence, no matter how enormous the task that lies before them. Henry Winstanley was a living illustration of such a man. Born in England in 1644, Winstanley was an interesting character who made his money as an inventor, architect, engraver, and operator of a theatre. Eventually, he invested his money in ships, seeking to earn a profit from the lucrative trade business of England.

Fourteen miles off the coast of Cornwall was a deadly threat to the shipping business. There lay the Eddystone Reef, which had brought many vessels to their watery grave. Most of this reef only sticks out of the water a few feet, but it is deadly enough to the strongest of ships. Situated in the middle of the western end of the English Channel, the Eddystone Reef was a danger to any ship passing through. Many crews went far out of their way to avoid the threat.

Winstanley had lost one ship, and then he lost another. Something clearly needed to be done, and he was just the man to do it. Building a lighthouse on an outcropping of rocks, fourteen miles out from the coast, in the late seventeenth century was not an easy task. Nevertheless, Winstanley drew up his plans and set to work.

As the foundation was being built, a new problem arose: England and France were at war. Frenchmen took Winstanley and his men as prisoners and destroyed their initial work on the lighthouse. Thankfully, the King of France intervened and had them released, and the work started up once again.

In 1698, the lighthouse was complete. It was a testimony to one man's determination. Built on a stone base, the structure was mostly wood that was held together by metal, and it stood eighty feet above its foundation. It was able to survive the first winter, but it was severely damaged. The tower was rebuilt and strengthened, with the top of the structure removed and replaced. This newer lighthouse was completed in 1699.

As one can imagine, it is said that maintaining this lighthouse was not an easy task. Out in the English Channel the tower would rock back and forth during storms. The wood structure would creak and moan. Large waves would crash upon the building, instilling fear into the men. Publically, Winstanley's confidence was not shaken. He announced his wish to be in the lighthouse during the greatest storm that ever was.

In November of 1703, he got his wish. A North Atlantic hurricane reached the Eddystone rocks, and Winstanley was at the lighthouse when the storm hit. Just as he had wanted, it was one of the greatest storms ever recorded to have hit England. Thousands of people lost their lives, but first among them was Winstanley and his men. When ships arrived after the storm to survey the damage, the lighthouse was gone. Years of hard work had been leveled by the powerful storm. Eighty feet of wood, iron, and masonry were smashed to pieces and taken away. This tower had only stood upon the rocks of the Eddystone Reef for five short years. Winstanley and his men were never seen again.

The Nature of Men

Mankind continues to believe the lie that the civilization we have created will last forever. This mindset certainly is not new. Men once testified with this same type of arrogance, "Let us build ourselves a city, and a tower whose top is in the heavens; let us make a name for ourselves" (Gen. 11:4). Ever since the Tower of Babel man has tried to demonstrate his confidence, wisdom, and ability to shape his own destiny.

God is set to directly intervene in the affairs of men. When He does, billions of people will lose their lives, and the monuments of men will be in ruins. The pride of men will be completely destroyed. We turn our attention to this future time known as the Tribulation.

The People of the Tribulation

In the beginning, the Tribulation will be made up of two groups of people. There will be those who had never heard the Gospel of Christ, and those who rejected the Gospel in the Church Age. This raises an interesting question, "Can those who reject the gospel in the Church Age come to eternal life through faith in Christ after the Rapture?" The answer from Scripture should be a somber warning to anyone who would foolishly reject the good news of eternal life in Christ.

According to the Bible, those who had the opportunity to get saved prior to the Rapture, but rejected the gospel, will believe the lie and take the mark of the Beast. They will not have a second opportunity to receive eternal redemption in Christ. The focus of the mission work in the Tribulation will be on the unreached people groups, and people who were somehow never confronted with the gospel. It is not difficult to conceive of such people, even in the United States of America. Our inner cities are filled with completely different cultures, where some people have never seen a gospel tract, or a Bible, and are never told the glorious message of redemption in Christ.

This teaching about those who reject Christ before the Rapture is based on 2 Thessalonians 2:9-12. The Apostle Paul taught:

> The coming of the lawless one is according to the working of Satan, with all power, signs, and lying wonders, and with all unrighteous deception among those who perish, because they did not receive the love of the truth, that they might be saved. And for this reason God will send them strong delusion, that they should believe the lie, that they all may be condemned who did not believe the truth but had pleasure in unrighteousness.

The lawless one is referring to the Antichrist. The love of the truth is a metonym for the gospel message. For this reason, because they did not receive the saving message when they had the opportunity, they will be condemned. Paul was referring to a future time, when people living in the Church Age reject the gospel. When the Rapture happens, these people will find themselves in the Tribulation, but will not have a second opportunity to receive Christ.

There is no question that there will be untold multitudes of every nation, tribe, tongue, and language who come to salvation in the Tribulation (Rev. 7:9-17; Matt. 24:14). Yet, this does not include those who rejected Christ before the Rapture. Instead, they will be led astray by the Antichrist. God will send strong delusion in order that they believe the lie of the Antichrist (2 Thess. 2:11). This underscores the importance of unbelievers not putting off the decision to trust in Christ. Today is the day of salvation!

Key Old Testament Teaching on the Tribulation

There are several passages from the Old Testament that provide key teaching about the Tribulation. These include Isaiah 13:6-13; 24-27; Jeremiah 30:1-11; Joel 1-3; Zephaniah 1; Daniel 9:24-27; and Daniel 11:36-12:3. Many Christians are unfamiliar with these Old Testament texts, but they provide a wealth of information about God's plan for mankind.

Old Testament Designations of the Tribulation

A careful examination of the Scriptures results in twenty-three Old Testament designations of the Tribulation. Understanding the terminology used in the Bible to describe the Tribulation helps us to build our theology. With this in mind, we observe the designations used in the Old Testament for this period of time:

1. birth pangs (Isa. 21:3; 26:17-18; 66:7; Jer. 4:31; Mic. 4:10)
2. the Day of the Lord (Obad. 15; Joel 1:15; 2:1, 11, 31; 3:14; Amos 5:18, 20; Isa. 2:12; 13:6, 9; Zeph. 1:7, 14; Ezek. 13:5; 30:3; Zech. 14:1)
3. great and terrible day of the Lord (Septuagint Mal. 4:5)
4. day of wrath (Zeph. 1:15)
5. day of the Lord's wrath (Zeph. 1:18)
6. day of distress (Zeph. 1:15)
7. day of trouble (Zeph. 1:15)
8. day of desolation (Zeph. 1:15)
9. day of vengeance (Isa. 34:8; 35:4; 61:2; 63:4)
10. time of Jacob's trouble (Jer. 30:7)
11. day of darkness and gloom (Zeph. 1:15; Amos 5:18, 20; Joel 2:2)
12. day of clouds and thick darkness (Zeph. 1:15; Joel 2:2)
13. day of trumpet and battle cry (Zeph. 1:16)
14. day of alarm (Zeph. 1:16)
15. day of the Lord's anger (Zeph. 2:2-3)
16. destruction and ruin from the Almighty (Joel 1:15)

17. day of calamity and distress (Deut. 32:35; Obad. 12-14)
18. trouble/tribulation (Deut. 4:30)
19. one week of years (Dan. 9:27)
20. time of trouble/distress (Dan. 12:1; Zeph. 1:15)
21. the indignation (Isa. 26:20)
22. the overflowing scourge (Isa. 28:15, 18)
23. the fire of His jealousy (Zeph. 1:18)

These designations underscore the severity of this time of judgment. God will pour out His wrath on the world, causing men to cry out, "Fall on us and hide us from the face of Him who sits on the throne and from the wrath of the Lamb!" (Rev. 6:16).

Key New Testament Teaching on the Tribulation

The New Testament also has several passages that provide key teaching about the Tribulation. These are Matthew 24-25; Revelation 4-19; 2 Thessalonians 2; and 1 Thessalonians 5. It is on these texts that we base our New Testament doctrinal foundation regarding the Seventieth Week of Daniel.

New Testament Designations of the Tribulation

A survey of the New Testament provides us with thirteen designations for the Tribulation. These descriptions reveal the trials, wrath, and judgment that will dominate this period of time. Again, understanding the terminology used in the Bible helps us to recognize the intensity of God's judgment. The New Testament designations are:

1. the day (1 Thess. 5:4)
2. those days (Matt. 24:22; Mark 13:20)
3. the Day of the Lord (1 Thess. 5:2)
4. the wrath (1Thess. 5:9; Rev. 11:18)
5. the wrath to come (1 Thess. 1:10)
6. the great day of His wrath (Rev. 6:17)
7. the wrath of God (Rev. 15:1, 7; 14:10, 19; 16:1)
8. the wrath of the Lamb (Rev. 6:16)
9. the hour of trial (Rev. 3:10)
10. the Tribulation (Matt. 24:29; Mark 13:19, 24)

11. the Great Tribulation (Matt. 24:21; Rev. 2:22; 7:14)
12. the hour of judgment (Rev. 14:7)
13. birth pangs (Matt. 24:8)

It should be noted that some of these designations are taken from the Old Testament and repeated in the New Testament. The men who authored the written revelation of God described a coming time that will directly impact every living being on earth.

Purpose of the Tribulation

The greatest amount of material in the New Testament related to the eschaton focuses on the Tribulation. This coming time of judgment is not without purpose. There are at least six biblical reasons for the coming Tribulation. First, it will complete the decreed period of Israel's hardening as punishment for her rejection of the Messianic program (Isa. 6:8-13; 24:1-6; John 12:37-41; Rom. 11:7-10). There will be a definite focus on Israel during the Tribulation.

Secondly, the Tribulation will be a time of judgment for the Gentiles (Rev. 14:7; Matt. 25:31-46). It will be the global judgment of sin.

Third, the Tribulation will engender a Messianic revival among Jews scattered throughout the world (Deut. 4:27-30; Rev. 7:1-4; Matt. 24:14). A fourth purpose for the Tribulation is to prompt a complete return of the Jews to the land of Israel (Zech. 8:7-8; Ezek. 36:24; 37:21).

The Tribulation will also serve to end the time of the Gentiles (Isa. 24:21-23; 59:16-20; Luke 21:24; Rom. 11:25). This fifth reason for this period reminds us that the time of the Gentiles is broader in definition than the Church Age. The Church Age spans the period of time from the day of Pentecost, in Acts 2, until the Rapture. The time of the Gentiles is the present stage of Gentile domination of Israel, which will continue into the Tribulation. It will not be until after the Second Coming of Christ that Israel will finally reign over the world, when the Messiah will be ruling with a rod of iron.

Finally, we note that the Tribulation will serve to purge the earth of the wicked, in order to establish the Messianic Kingdom in righteousness (Isa. 11:9; 13:9; 24:19-20; Ezek. 20:33-38; 37:23; Zech. 13:2; 14:9; Matt. 25:31-46). No one who rejects Christ will be allowed to enter the Kingdom at the Second Coming. Because of the fulfillment of the New Covenant, believers living in the Kingdom will be without sin.

Three Key Events that Follow the Rapture

There are three key events identified in the Word of God that follow the Rapture (See Appendix):

1. A Western alliance, probably led by the future Antichrist, forms and invades Egypt (Dan. 11:40-43).
2. The Battle of Gog/Magog ensues (Ezek. 38-39).
3. The Antichrist is unveiled (2 Thess. 2). This must take place after the Rapture and shortly before the beginning of the Tribulation. We remember the Apostle Paul taught that before the Day of the Lord could take place, two things must happen first: the Rapture and the unveiling of the Antichrist (2 Thess. 2:3).

The Identification of Gog and Magog in Ezekiel

The identification of Gog and Magog in Ezekiel requires us to examine two passages in Scripture. First, we read in Genesis 10:2, "The sons of Japheth were Gomer, Magog, Madai, Javan, Tubal, Meshech, and Tiras." Japheth was the son of Noah (Gen. 10:1), and Magog was the son of Japheth. This genealogy gives us insight into the origin of the person Magog.

Ezekiel 38:2 is the key verse for identifying Gog and Magog. The Bible teaches, "Son of man, set your face against Gog, of the land of Magog, the prince of Rosh, Meshech, and Tubal, and prophesy against him." Ezekiel wrote about a ruler in his time identified as Gog. The prophecy from Scripture is of a future individual, named or titled Gog, who will arise from out of the land that Magog originally settled.

Josephus (d. 420) identified the *Magogites* as *Scythians* who lived north of the Caucasus Mountains by the Caspian Sea.[1] Tom Constable notes:

> The land of Magog probably refers to the former domain of the Scythians, who lived in the mountains around the Black and Caspian seas (modern southern Russia). Gog will also have authority over Rosh, Meshech, and Tubal. Rosh (lit. "head" or "chief") has not been identified either by biblical or extrabiblical references.[2]

Classical Greek writers used the designation of *Moschoi* for the people of *Meshech*. The Assyrians referred to the people of *Meschech* as *Muski*.

This people group settled in Armenia where Russia, Iran, and Turkey now come together. Tubal refers to the people that settled in central Turkey. The land of Magog will witness the rise of Gog, who will lead the Northern alliance against Israel.

The Allies of Gog and Magog in Ezekiel

Ezekiel also teaches us about the nations that will be involved as allies in the Battle of Gog and Magog (Ezek. 38:5-6). These include:

- Persia (modern Iran)
- Ethiopia (modern Sudan)
- Put (modern Libya)
- Gomer (probably eastern Turkey)
- Togarmah (Turkey/Syrian border)

Different Views on the Timing of the Battle of Gog and Magog

At the Battle of Gog and Magog the Northern alliance will come against Israel. The Western alliance will intervene to protect Israel. There are, however, several different views as to when this battle will take place.

Before the Rapture

The Battle of Gog and Magog is often thought to occur before the Rapture. This position was popularized in the *Left Behind* series by Tim LaHaye and Jerry Jenkins.

Yet, the doctrine of the imminency of the Rapture precludes this view. If the Battle of Gog and Magog must occur before the Rapture, then we could determine that the Rapture would not happen today. It is typically suggested by proponents of this viewpoint that the world will not know it is the Battle of Gog and Magog until we look back on it. Therefore, the Rapture is still said to be imminent.

The problem is that the nature and description of the Battle of Gog and Magog in Ezekiel 38-39 are so specific and all-encompassing that it seems inconceivable that it could take place without it being identified.

After the Rapture and Before the Tribulation

The second view is that the Battle of Gog and Magog will occur after the Rapture and before the official start of the Tribulation. This is a preferable position because:

- It accounts for the transition between the Church Age and Daniel's Seventieth Week.
- It accounts for the rise in the prominence and notoriety of the Antichrist. He will be seen as a hero for preventing this all-out war from taking place, which would cause Israel to be destroyed.
- It provides a logical reason for the peace treaty of Daniel 9:27.

First Half or Midpoint of Tribulation

The third and fourth views are closely related. Many dispensationalists hold to the third view and believe that this great battle will take place in the first half of the Tribulation. A fourth point of view is that the Battle of Gog and Magog will occur in the middle of the Tribulation. This is the position that J. Dwight Pentecost taught in his book *Things to Come*.

The Word of God presents Israel as experiencing a time of relative peace during the first half of the Tribulation. The seal judgments will take place, but Israel will be under divine protection. Further, the peace treaty with Israel will be honored during the first half of the Tribulation. During this time nations will not be rising up against Israel. Therefore, it seems difficult to imagine such a massive battle taking place at that time.

Second Half of the Tribulation

Another viewpoint is that the Battle of Gog and Magog will occur in the last half of the Tribulation. The second half of the Tribulation should be ruled out since it will be a time of great trouble and difficulty for Israel (Rev. 11-13; Dan. 9:24-27). Ezekiel 38-39 presents Israel as winning the battle and protected by God, but in the second half of the Tribulation Israel will be fleeing the wrath of God and driven out of her land. At that time, the Antichrist will have taken over the Temple. The Battle of Gog and Magog does not seem to fit into the latter part of the Tribulation.

Beginning of the Millennium

Some past dispensationalists placed the timing of the battle at the beginning of the Millennium. This was the position held by Arno Gaebelein. It is difficult to see how this fits into Scripture. The start of the Millennium can be ruled out because of its peaceful nature (Isa. 9:6-7; Mic. 4:3-4). The Millennium will be a time of peace with the Prince of Peace upon the throne. There will not even be any unbelievers at the beginning of the Millennium.

After the Millennium

Some people equate the Battle of Gog and Magog in Ezekiel 38-39 with the Battle of Gog and Magog after the Millennium in Revelation 20. We recognize that the Millennium itself (Rev. 20) is precluded because of the peaceful nature of this time. But the description of the Battle of Gog and Magog in Ezekiel 38-39 also does not fit the description in Revelation 20:7-10. Namely, Ezekiel describes the battle as preceding the Millennium (Ezek. 40-48), whereas Revelation has the battle following the Millennium (Rev. 20). These must be two different battles.

The Bible uses certain terms metaphorically. Some of the enemies within the historical life of Israel became so profound that they took on an identity of their own. Then, in the later revelation of Scripture, the Lord metaphorically referred to a new person or location by a prior name. Jezebel in Revelation 2:20, and Babylon used throughout Revelation, are representative examples of this. The usage of Gog and Magog in Revelation 20:8 falls into this category.

Chapters 40-48 of Ezekiel are clearly teaching about the Millennium. This broader context of Ezekiel dictates that chapters 38-39 are referring to a time prior to the Millennium, but the precise timing is not directly stated. The imminency of the Rapture contradicts the idea that this battle would take place before the Church Age believers are taken up to be with Christ. This places it into a timeframe of taking place after the Rapture, but before the Second Coming of Christ. It appears to be most congruent with the totality of Scripture to take the Battle of Gog and Magog in Ezekiel 38-39 as occurring just prior to the Tribulation (after the Rapture and before the signing of the peace treaty of Daniel 9:27). This would place this battle during the time of preparation, as seen in figure 14.1.

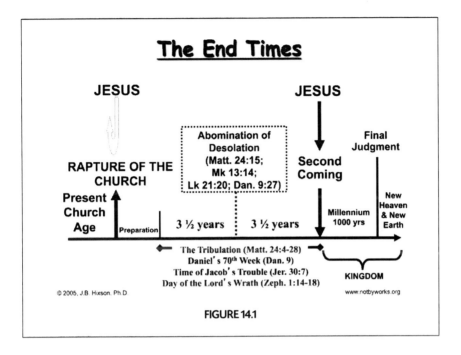

FIGURE 14.1

The Battle of Gog and Magog

The Bible teaches us that a Northern alliance will form (Ezek. 38-39). This will include Gog and Magog (modern Russia, Ukraine, and Kazakhstan). According to Ezekiel 38:5-6, nations from the South will join them. The allies from the South will include Persia (modern Iran), Ethiopia (modern Sudan), Put (modern Libya), Gomer (probably eastern Turkey), and Togarmah (Turkey/Syrian border). The Northern alliance of Russia and its Islamic neighbors will invade Israel (Ezek. 38:16). The Western alliance, headed by the Antichrist, will protest (Dan. 11:44), and God will supernaturally intervene to defeat the Northern alliance (Ezek. 38:21-39:7). The Antichrist will take credit for protecting Israel, which will give him notoriety and a stage to take over the world.

Key Events of the Tribulation

As we have seen, the unveiling of the Antichrist will take place after the Rapture (2 Thess. 2). He will then proceed to sign a treaty guaranteeing peace for Israel (Dan. 9:27). The signing of this treaty signals the official commencement of the Tribulation. At this same time, the seal judgments will begin (Rev. 6).

Description of the Seal Judgments

The seal judgments cover the entire seven years of the Tribulation. They start at the beginning, but their effects cover the whole period. This is illustrated in figure 14.2.

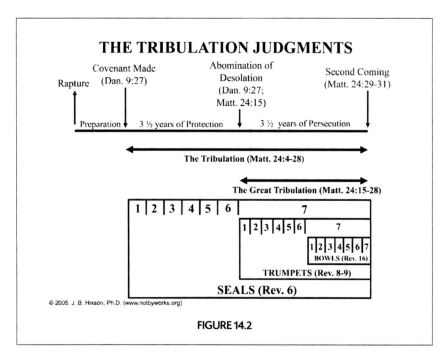

FIGURE 14.2

The first six of the seven seal judgments are described for us in Revelation 6. The white horse is the introduction of the Antichrist (v. 2). With the red horse, we witness the Antichrist taking peace from the earth (v. 4). The third seal is the black horse and the Antichrist bringing famine (vv. 5-6). The pale horse, and the fourth seal, is the Antichrist bringing death to one-quarter of the world's population (vv. 7-8). Do not underestimate the great amount of death that will be present on the earth at this time.

These four seals are often referred to, in popular literature, as the Four Horsemen of the Apocalypse. The English word *apocalypse* is the Greek word for *Revelation* (apokalypsis). These are the four horsemen mentioned in Revelation.

The fifth seal consists of the pleas for justice by the early Tribulation martyrs (Rev. 6:9-11). We know that a large number of martyrs will die in the Tribulation. John recorded, "After these things I looked, and behold, a great multitude which no one could number, of all nations, tribes, peoples, and tongues, standing before the throne and before the Lamb, clothed with white robes, with palm branches in their hands, and crying out with a loud voice, saying, 'Salvation belongs to our God who sits on the throne, and to the Lamb!'" (Rev. 7:9-10). These are the Tribulation saints who will die for their faith (v. 14). John used a figure of speech (a hyperbole) to clearly indicate a large number of people.

The sixth seal will bring a great earthquake and cosmic disturbances. John warned, "I looked when He opened the sixth seal, and behold, there was a great earthquake; and the sun became black as sackcloth of hair, and the moon became like blood. And the stars of heaven fell to the earth, as a fig tree drops its late figs when it is shaken by a mighty wind. Then the sky receded as a scroll when it is rolled up, and every mountain and island was moved out of its place" (Rev. 6:12-14).

The opening of the seventh seal is found in Revelation 8. To underscore the significance of this seal, verse 1 records, "When He opened the seventh seal, there was silence in heaven for about half an hour." The opening of the seventh seal will usher in seven more judgments called *trumpets*. These additional seven judgments will be introduced with a trumpet and will take place in the second half of the Tribulation. These will be examined in greater detail later in this chapter.

Ministry of the 144,000

Revelation 7 records the sealing of the 144,000 witnesses, where we learn that 12,000 from each of the 12 tribes of Israel will be set apart for this ministry. This will begin at the outset of the Tribulation (Rev. 7, 14; cf. Matt 24:14; 13:47-50).

Ministry of the Two Witnesses

Differing opinions exist in regard to the timing of the two witnesses (Rev. 11). Their ministry is identified as beginning at the start of the Tribulation, at the midpoint, or in the second half. It seems preferable to place their ministry as beginning at the start of the Tribulation, though this is not a point worth contending over.

Revelation 11:7 reveals that the Antichrist will kill the two witnesses and the people of the world will celebrate their death. At that time, "those who dwell on the earth will rejoice over them, make merry, and send gifts to one another, because these two prophets tormented those who dwell on the earth" (Rev. 11:10). Much to the astonishment of the world, they will be resurrected (v. 11). This will all take place at the midpoint of the Tribulation.

Reign of Terror Intensifies

The reign of terror by the Antichrist will intensify at the midpoint of the Tribulation. He will set himself up as God and demand to be worshipped (Dan. 9:27; Rev. 13; Matt. 24:15). This is the Abomination of Desolation that both Daniel and Jesus referred to.

The Trumpet Judgments

The timing of the trumpet judgments is the second half of the Tribulation (Rev. 8-9). This can be seen in figure 14.3.

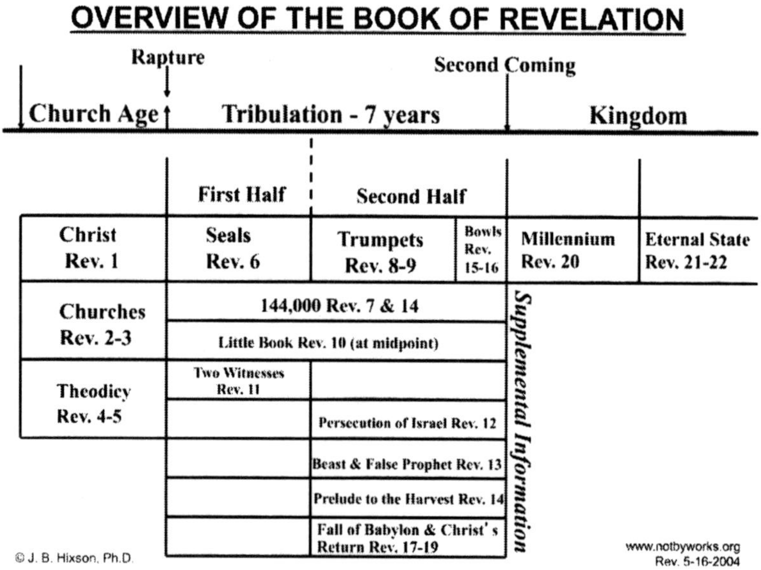

OVERVIEW OF THE BOOK OF REVELATION

	Rapture			Second Coming	
Church Age ↑	Tribulation - 7 years				Kingdom
	First Half	Second Half			
Christ Rev. 1	Seals Rev. 6	Trumpets Rev. 8-9	Bowls Rev. 15-16	Millennium Rev. 20	Eternal State Rev. 21-22
Churches Rev. 2-3	144,000 Rev. 7 & 14				
	Little Book Rev. 10 (at midpoint)				
Theodicy Rev. 4-5	Two Witnesses Rev. 11				
		Persecution of Israel Rev. 12			
		Beast & False Prophet Rev. 13			
		Prelude to the Harvest Rev. 14			
		Fall of Babylon & Christ's Return Rev. 17-19			

Supplemental Information

© J. B. Hixson, Ph.D.

www.notbyworks.org
Rev. 5-16-2004

FIGURE 14.3

This chart provides an overview of the book of Revelation. Chapter 1 begins with the revelation of the Christ. Chapters 2-3 are letters to first century churches. Chapters 4-5 contain a theodicy, which is justification for the wrath of God. In other words, what gives God the right to pour out His wrath? His holiness and justice give Him the right to judge mankind. The Lamb is worthy to open the scroll (the seals) because His blood was shed on the Cross (Rev. 5:7).

Starting in Revelation 6, the Tribulation begins. The seal judgments take place in the first half of the Tribulation. Then the trumpet and bowl judgments take place in the second half.

The trumpet judgments will bring massive destruction and death to the earth. One-third of the earth (the physical land) will be burned (Rev. 8:7). With the second trumpet judgment one-third of the sea will turn into blood (Rev. 8:8). The third trumpet judgment will poison one-third of the fresh water, which will kill many people. When the fourth of these judgments strikes it will be devastating, "A third of the sun was struck, a third of the moon, and a third of the stars, so that a third of them were darkened. A third of the day did not shine, and likewise the night" (Rev. 8:12).

The fifth trumpet judgment will bring a huge swarm of locusts that will invade the earth (Rev. 9:3-6). This is the first of three *woes* (Rev. 9:12). Then four special demons will be sent to kill one-third of the earth's population (Rev. 9:14-15). This is the sixth trumpet judgment and the second *woe*. A majority of the people on earth will have been killed by this time. The seventh and final trumpet will then be revealed (Rev. 11:15-19), which will bring seven more judgments, referred to as *bowls*. This will be the third *woe*.

The False Prophet

In Revelation 13, we witness that the False Prophet (second in command to the Antichrist) will take on an increased role. The commerce of the world will be controlled by the False Prophet. He will cause all, "both small and great, rich and poor, free and slave, to receive a mark on their right hand or on their foreheads, and that no one may buy or sell except one who has the mark or the name of the beast, or the number of his name" (Rev. 13:16-17).

Severe Persecution

The second half of the Tribulation will be a time of severe persecution for the Jewish people, as well as for all (Jewish and Gentile) believers (Rev. 12-13). There will be people from every nation, tribe, tongue, and language that come to faith in Christ. From the Antichrist's perspective, believers will simply be aligning themselves with Israel.

Babylon

Babylon is mentioned in Revelation 14, 16, 17, and 18. Geographically, it refers to the headquarters of the Beast during the Tribulation (Rev. 14:18; 16:19). Religiously, it refers to the one world religion, including the apostate church, which the Beast will use to deceive the world (Rev. 17). Politically, it refers to the center of world commerce and power during the Tribulation (Rev. 18).

Bowl Judgments

The bowl judgments take place at the very end of the Tribulation (Rev. 15-16). They are immediately followed by the Second Coming of Christ (Rev. 19:6-21). They take place in the final hours before the Second Coming. As a result of the bowl judgments:

1. Ugly and painful sores will break out on people.
2. All sea life will be destroyed.
3. All fresh water will be destroyed.
4. The world's climate will be altered so that the sun scorches people.
5. Unusual darkness will come over the earth.
6. The Euphrates River will dry up in preparation for Armageddon.
7. The worst earthquake in the history of mankind will occur.

This is an indication of the significance of the cosmic struggle that has been taking place since the Garden of Eden, but it will be heightened in the seven-year Tribulation. This will be the Day of the Lord's Wrath, when God will directly intervene in the affairs of His creation.

Nations from the East

As the Antichrist proceeds with his program, nations from the East (the Orient) will unite and attempt to stop him (Rev. 16:12-16).

Armageddon

The armies from the East and West will face off in a series of battles in an area around the mountains of Megiddo. This campaign is called Armageddon (Rev. 16:14; 19:17). There are at least three reasons for the campaign of Armageddon, which include:

- The Gentiles have scattered Israel and apportioned Israel's land (Joel 3:2).
- The wickedness of the Gentiles (Rev. 16:14; 19:15).
- The Gentiles' failure to glorify the One true God (Rev. 16:9).

The timing of the Battle of Armageddon is detailed for us in Scripture. It begins with the pouring out of the sixth bowl judgment (Rev. 16:12). We also know that it occurs in conjunction with Christ's Second Coming (Rev. 19:11-16; Zech. 14:4; Joel 3:15-16). This battle will end with Israel's regathering into the land/kingdom (Joel 3:1; Zeph. 3:20). Jeremiah prophesied, "'For behold, the days are coming,' says the LORD, 'that I will bring back from captivity My people Israel and Judah,' says the LORD. 'And I will cause them to return to the land that I gave to their fathers, and they shall possess it'" (Jer. 30:3).

The results of Armageddon promise to be dramatic. The armies of the earth will face defeat (Rev. 19:17-21). The Word of God also teaches us that the Antichrist and the False Prophet will be cast into the lake of fire (Rev. 19:20). In addition, Satan will be bound for 1,000 years (Rev. 20:1-3).

The Return of Christ

The climax of the campaign of Armageddon is when Christ returns to judge the nations, and establish His Kingdom (Zech. 14:4; Matt. 25; Rev. 19:11-21).

The Lord will take the throne and reign over the entire earth. This will usher in an entirely new era in human history, where everyone from the least to the greatest on earth will know about Christ. This becomes the subject at hand in chapter 15.

Discussion Questions

1. What is the time when God will directly intervene in the affairs of men known as? Describe the overall outcome of this time.
2. Who will be included in the Tribulation?
3. What will happen to people who reject the gospel during the Church Age?
4. What is the purpose of the Tribulation?
5. Name three events that occur after the Rapture.
6. Identify Gog, Magog, and their allies.
7. When will the Battle of Gog and Magog occur? Give three reasons that support this timing.
8. Create a timeline that identifies the progression of key events in the Tribulation.
9. How would you describe the events of the Tribulation?
10. What is the climax of the Tribulation?

Endnotes

1. Flavius Josephus and William Whiston, *The Works of Josephus: Complete and Unabridged* (Peabody, MA: Hendrickson Publishers, 1987).
2. Tom Constable, *Tom Constable's Expository Notes on the Bible* (2003), Ezek. 38:1.

CHAPTER 15

Arrival of the Messianic Kingdom - The Second Coming and Millennium

And behold, One like the Son of Man, coming with the clouds of heaven! He came to the Ancient of Days, and they brought Him near before Him. Then to Him was given dominion and glory and a kingdom, that all peoples, nations, and languages should serve Him. His dominion is an everlasting dominion, which shall not pass away, and His kingdom the one which shall not be destroyed.

- Daniel 7:13-14

THE BEST OF intentions, coupled with a wrong focus, can often lead to monuments of absurdity. This is the history behind the Millennium Manor Castle.

William Nicholson was convinced that the end times were at hand. Nicholson believed that if he and his family could survive Armageddon, they would need a place to live in the Millennium. Therefore, he set out to build a house that could survive Armageddon and a thousand years beyond.

Work started in 1938, and it would take until 1946 to build this home in Alcoa, Tennessee. The architecture was based on the building techniques used in the Roman Empire, much of which can still be seen standing 2,000 years later.

The first step was to build a wooden form for the building. Next, a rubber tarp was placed over the form. Large blocks of stone were stacked to build the home. Cement was then poured through the stacked stones. Over 4,000 bags of cement were used. Once it hardened, the forms were then taken away.

The end result of this massive project was a large stone castle that was built to stand the test of time. It boasts 3,000 square feet that includes 14 rooms and a two-car garage. All of the exterior walls are at least 25 inches thick, and all of the interior walls are at least 19 inches. The roof is a solid 3 feet of rock and concrete, which weighs an estimated 423 tons. The only wood used in the home was for doors, windows, and trim. Even the floor was built to last; it is more than 4 feet thick.

Nicholson's dreams faded in 1950, when his wife died of cancer at age 72. Fifteen years later, at age 88, William Nicholson passed away. His fortress still stands as a testimony to his misguided preparations for the return of Christ and the Millennium.[1]

The Arrival of the Kingdom of Our Lord

Very few Christians have a biblical understanding of what will take place when Christ establishes His Kingdom, and ushers in the Millennium. There are a few key points that are often missed:

- It is certain that Christ will return to establish a literal Messianic Kingdom. The Old Testament promises a kingdom (2 Sam. 7:12-16; Ps. 72:8-11; Isa. 2:3-4; 11:2-5). This same promise was reiterated in the New Testament (Acts 1:6-7; Rev. 20:4-6) and by Christ Himself (Matt. 19:28; 25:31). There is never even the slightest indication in the Scriptures that this kingdom will be anything other than a literal kingdom. Christ will return prior to the Millennium to establish His reign.
- The Messianic Kingdom is eternal. Dispensationalists have historically labeled the first 1,000 years as the *Millennial Kingdom*. However, the Eternal State is simply a continuation of the Kingdom of Christ. The Eternal State will be located in the new heavens and new earth, but it will be a part of the same Kingdom ushered in by Christ at the Second Coming. Therefore, it is more accurate to refer to the Messianic Kingdom with its two distinct phases: the millennial phase and the eternal phase.

Figure 15.1 shows that after the Second Coming of Christ, the Millennium begins. The end of the Millennium is not the end of the Kingdom. After the final judgment, the Kingdom of Christ will continue on in the Eternal State. It is for this reason that figure 15.1 shows an arrow representing the Kingdom continuing on into eternity.

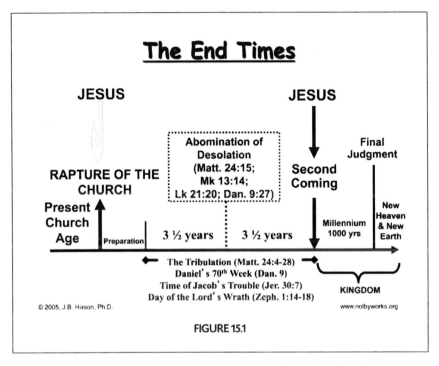

FIGURE 15.1

There are a significant number of texts in the Bible that demonstrate this teaching:

- Amos 9:11-15 refers to the ultimate restoration of Israel to the land. It does not indicate any limit of time for this Kingdom.
- Isaiah 9:6-7 clearly indicates that there will be no end to the reign of Christ. This coming Kingdom, therefore, should not be limited to 1,000 years.
- Daniel 2:44 makes another strong statement about the eternal nature of the Kingdom. There we are told, "The God of heaven will set up a kingdom which shall never be destroyed ... and it shall stand forever."
- Daniel 7:13-14, 18, 22, and 27 testify about the return of Christ and His eternal Kingdom.
- Luke 1:30-35 reveals that Gabriel told Mary that one day Jesus would reign, "over the house of Jacob forever, and of His kingdom there will be no end" (v. 33).
- Revelation 22:5 indicates this Kingdom will continue forever.

The references cited serve as representative passages. Both the Old and New Testaments have frequent references to the eternal nature of the Kingdom.

The Characteristics of the Future Kingdom

The future Messianic Kingdom will be governed by the theocratic rule of Christ (Dan. 7:14). This will be a time of worldwide allegiance (Rev. 19:15) and of Jewish centrality (Zech. 1:14-17). As noted, it will be an eternal kingdom (Dan. 7:14; Ps. 145:13; Mic. 4:7).

The Citizens of the Future Kingdom

Before we can consider the future citizens of the Kingdom of Christ, we need to examine what happens to individuals when they die. Figure 15.2 shows the different categories of people throughout the ages and what takes place at their death.

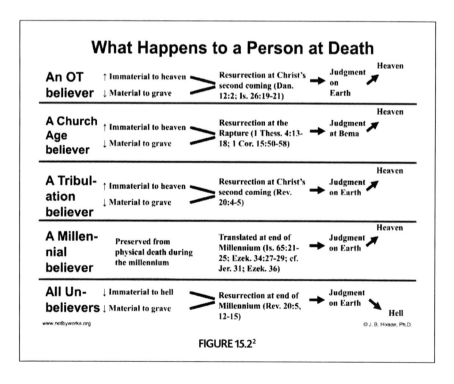

FIGURE 15.2[2]

When any believer of any age dies, the immaterial part of their body goes to heaven. For the purpose of figure 15.2 we are using heaven as a metonym for the dwelling place of God, with the understanding of the different terms used in the Bible for it (Paradise, Abraham's Bosom, etc.). When Old Testament believers died, they went to heaven and their body was put into the grave. As Church Age believers die, they also go to heaven, with their body going to the grave. Likewise, Tribulation believers (Jew and Gentile alike) who die will immediately go to heaven, with their bodies heading to the grave. All unbelievers, of every age, go to hell.

When are the physical bodies of believers resurrected? This is where the differences come into the picture. For Old Testament believers it will take place at the Second Coming (Dan. 12:2; Isa. 26:19-21). The resurrection for Church Age believers will take place at the Rapture (1 Thess. 4:13-18). This, once again, demonstrates the unique nature of the Church in God's plan. Tribulation believers who die will be resurrected at the Second Coming of Christ (Rev. 20:4-5).

Participants in the Kingdom with Glorified Bodies

Citizens of the future Kingdom will include all believers with glorified bodies who have died before the Second Coming of Christ. Specifically, believers who died before the Church Age even began will be resurrected at the Second Coming and will take part in the Kingdom. Church Age saints who die will be resurrected at the Rapture. Church Age believers alive at the Rapture will also receive their glorified bodies at that time (1 Cor. 15:51-58). Tribulation saints who either die or are martyred for their faith will be resurrected at the Second Coming. All of these groups of believers will take part in the Millennium in their glorified bodies. It should be obvious that believers living in glorified bodies will never again experience physical death.

Participants in the Kingdom with Earthly Bodies

Not everyone who enters the Kingdom will have glorified bodies. Both Jewish and Gentile believers, who are saved after the Rapture and survive the Tribulation, will enter the Kingdom in their earthly, physical bodies (Matt. 24:13). Because of this, procreation will result in offspring who are born in sin (Rom. 5:12). Individually, those children will still need to accept Christ someday. Those who reject Christ will result in a large population of unbelievers at the end of the Millennium.

Believers who enter into the Millennium in physical bodies will be preserved from death. This is based on Isaiah 65, which indicates death in the Millennium will always be punitive for those sins that are worthy of capital punishment.

Since death will only affect sinners, the question is, "Who can sin in the Millennium?" Jeremiah 31 and Ezekiel 36 teach that when the New Covenant is in force, believers will not be able to sin. Therefore, the conclusion is that believers will not die because they will not sin. A survey of the relevant biblical passages indicates that only unbelievers will experience death in the Millennium. In the Millennium the curse of sin will be removed from God's people. There will be divine protection of life for them. Even though many will still be in their physical bodies during the Millennium, the blessings of the New Covenant will keep them from sin and, therefore, death. Remember, during this time there will also be no accidental death.

Again, believers living in their physical bodies will not die because they will not sin. Yet, we know these believers must eventually receive glorified bodies (1 Cor. 15:50). There will be a translation for these Millennium believers from life on earth to life in the new heavens and new earth at some point in the future. It seems logical, and consistent with Scripture, that they will receive their glorified bodies at the end of the Millennium.[3]

The Citizens of the Future Kingdom

Kingdom citizens will be predominately saved, Spirit-filled (Isa. 32:15; Joel 2:28-29), and characterized by righteousness, justice, and peace (Ps. 72:1-4; Hag. 2:9; Isa. 11:1-9; Mic. 4:1-7). Believers living in the Kingdom will be joyful, prosperous (Jer. 31:12-14), and will have good health and long lives (Isa. 65:18-23; 35:5-7).

Differences Between the Millennium and the Eternal State

Acknowledging the distinction between the Millennium and the Eternal State helps us to better comprehend the teaching of the coming Kingdom. With this in mind, we set out to make some contrasts between the two:

Millennium	Eternal State
Exactly 1,000 Years	No End of Years
Old Heaven and Earth	New Heaven and Earth
Presence of Sin	No Sin
Presence of Unglorified Men	All Men Glorified
Presence of Unsaved Men	All Men Saved
Presence of Death	No Death
Jewish Temple	No Jewish Temple
Personal Presence of Messiah	Personal Presence of Triune God

Purpose of the Millennium

The purpose of the Millennium is to demonstrate the utter depravity of man because many people will choose to reject Christ. It is not as though they will be asked to trust in someone who lived 2,000 years ago that they have never seen. Jeremiah 31 teaches us that they will all know of Him, from the least to the greatest. Even under the most ideal conditions, with no injustice in the world, people will still reject Christ. Mankind will receive one final chance to trust in Christ under ideal conditions.

Characteristics of the Millennium

Geographical Characteristics of the Millennium

There are a number of geographical changes that will occur. Israel will increase her territory (Gen. 15:18; Isa. 26:15; Obad. 17-21), and there are also noticeable topographical changes that will take place (Ezek. 47:8-12; Isa. 2:2; Zech. 14:4-10).

The land of Israel will be considerably different from what it is today. The city of Jerusalem will be enlarged (Ezek. 48:35; Jer. 3:17), and its name will be changed (Isa. 62:2-4). The Jewish people will be regathered into the land (Ezek. 36:24; 37:25), with the land healed of its desolate condition (Ezek. 36:33-36; Isa. 62:4).

Social Characteristics of the Millennium

The Millennium will be a time of universal knowledge of the Lord (Isa. 11:9; 54:13; Hab. 2:14). Those present in earthly bodies will continue to naturally reproduce (Isa. 65:23; Ezek. 47:21-22; Zech. 10:8). The labor of men will be unimpaired (Ezek. 48:18-19; Isa. 62:8-9; 65:21-23). Even the confusion of language will come to an end. There will be one universal language so that, "they all may call on the name of the Lord, to serve Him with one accord" (Zeph. 3:9).

During the Millennium, no more wars and conflicts between the nations will exist (Isa. 2:4; 14:3-7; Zech. 9:8; 14:10-11; Amos 9:15). Christ will rule with a rod of iron. At first, the nations will not even have armies. Eventually, they will conjure up a hastily thrown together army to try to come against Christ when Satan is released. The Millennium will feature a peaceful society (Isa. 11:6-9; 65:21; Hos. 2:18; Zech. 9:10). This unprecedented peace will exist because the Prince of Peace will be upon His throne. The Millennium will also experience true and unprecedented justice because Christ will be the Judge of mankind (Isa. 9:6-7; 32:16; Jer. 30:9; Ezek. 34:23; Hos. 3:5).

Spiritual Characteristics of the Millennium

Universal worship of Christ will be present in the Millennium (Isa. 19:21; 52:1-10; Mal. 1:11; Zech. 8:22). The center of the world's worship will be in Jerusalem (Isa. 2:2-3; Mic. 4:1-2; Zech. 8:3; 14:16-21). This will feature a rebuilt Temple (Ezek. 37:26-28; 40-48; Hag. 2:7-9; Joel 3:18), and a return of the Shekinah glory (Ezek. 43:1-7; 48:35; Zech. 2:10-13; Jer. 3:17). With the rebuilt Temple will come a revival of the sacrificial system (Ezek. 43:13-27; 45:13-25; Isa. 56:7). This highlights the importance of recognizing that God is not done with the nation of Israel. When God's program shifts once again to Israel being center stage, the sacrificial system will be restored. The sacrifices will look back, in remembrance, to the finished work of Christ on the Cross.

There will also be a restoration of the Sabbath and the ritual feasts during the Millennium (Ezek. 44:24; Zech. 14:16). Believers, because of the New Covenant, will live in perfect obedience (Ezek. 36:25-28; 37; Jer. 31:31-34). Ezekiel records, "I will give you a new heart and put a new spirit within you; I will take the heart of stone out of your flesh and give you a heart of flesh. I will put My Spirit within you and cause you to walk in My statutes, and you will keep My judgments and do them" (Ezek. 36:26-27). Because Satan will be bound during this time, there will not be widespread spiritual deception like there is today (Rev. 20:1-3).

Other Characteristics of the Millennium

Righteousness will prevail during the Millennium (Isa. 1:26-27; 35:8-10; Zeph. 3:11). The effects of sin will still be present, but they will largely be held in check and dealt with in perfect justice. The curse of sin on the creation of the earth will not yet be entirely removed. However, as mentioned, there will be no accidental death during this time. No tornadoes, hurricanes, or other disasters will take the lives of believers and unbelievers living at that time.

It should be noted that during the millennial aspect of the Kingdom, life on earth will not be perfect. Perfection will not be ushered in until the earth is re-created. Remember, the New Covenant will be in place for believers throughout the Millennium, but there is nothing in it that promises there will not be trials and tribulations for those living during that time. The New Covenant promises knowledge of Christ and the ministry of the Spirit of God that will enable believers to obey Christ. In the Eternal State the curse of sin will be completely removed.

During the Millennium, many of the conditions of the original creation will be restored (Isa.11:6-9; 65:25). Even the harmful effects of the environment will be removed (Isa. 33:24; 35:5-7; Zeph. 3:19). This future time will include the restoration of longevity (Isa. 65:20). Isaiah 65 indicates that a child who dies at the age of one hundred will be considered young. There will even be an increase in daylight (Isa. 4:5-6; 30:26; 60:19-20; Zech. 2:5). Economic prosperity will be commonplace (Isa. 30:23-25; 35:1-7; Amos 9:13-15; Joel 2:21-27), and the people of the world will have universal access to Israel (Isa. 2:2-3; 11:16; 56:6; Jer. 3:14-15).

What does a Promise of a Future Messianic Kingdom Mean for us Today?

The Comfort of the Future Kingdom

Believers in Christ should be filled with hope for the future. We should maintain a Kingdom perspective no matter how difficult life may be. It is our task to live in light of eternity, recognizing that a better day is coming. Satan is currently the prince of this world, but we must live for the day when Christ will rule as King. The people of the earth continue to rebel against Him, but we must remember that His perfect judgment will come. Even though we live in a time when the days are evil, our focus and our hope needs to be in that day!

Discussion Questions

1. What are two key points that many Christians fail to understand about the Kingdom of Christ?
2. Name the two distinct phases of the Messianic Kingdom.
3. Describe the citizens of the future Kingdom. How many groups are there and what is unique about each of them?
4. List some of the differences between the Millennium and the Eternal State.
5. What is the purpose of the Millennium?
6. How is the Millennium described in the Bible?
7. What perspective should believers today have toward the future Kingdom?

Endnotes

1. D. J. Fontaine, "Millennium Manor Castle," http://www.blountweb.com/millenniummanor/ (accessed December 25, 2012).
2. Adapted from Thomas Constable's class notes at Dallas Seminary c. 1991.
3. See Dr. Hixson's article *Death in the Millennium* available at www.NotByWorks.org.

CHAPTER 16

Perfect Righteousness - The Eternal State

Nevertheless we, according to His promise, look for new heavens and a new earth in which righteousness dwells.

- 2 Peter 3:13

THE SINKING OF the *Titanic* is, perhaps, the most notable tragedy at sea in modern times, but hidden in this disaster is a remarkable story of hope. In 1912, Moody Church had called a man by the name of John Harper, from Scotland, to become their next pastor. His journey to Chicago, Illinois included a ticket aboard what was considered to be the greatest ship ever built. No one could have known that a few days into her maiden voyage, the *Titanic* would be on the bottom of Atlantic Ocean.

The scene on board the *Titanic* that fateful night was terrifying. A powerful jolt was felt by the passengers when the massive ship struck an iceberg, which tore a 300 foot long gash in its starboard side. Panic set in as the unthinkable happened. The *Titanic* was sinking, and it only had enough life boats for roughly half of the passengers on board.

Families were ripped apart, as men loaded their wives and children onto the lifeboats. Some of the women chose to stay with their husbands. Children cried as they were torn from their parents' arms, hoping they would see them again. Harper loaded his six-year-old daughter, Nana, into a lifeboat and kissed her goodbye.

Harper then joined the other souls left onboard the sinking ship. Little by little, the ship headed toward its final destination. The deck of the *Titanic* fell to a steep angle, as the front end of the ship sank beneath the water. Harper was seen on the deck of the ship yelling, "Women, children, and unsaved into the lifeboats!" He used his final moments aboard the *Titanic* to proclaim the lifesaving gospel message. Eventually, the hull broke into two pieces, sending the passengers into the frigid waters of the Atlantic Ocean.

Well over a thousand souls thrashed in the frigid water grasping for life. One by one, the dark and cold water began to claim its dead. The struggle for life started to fade as death set in. Out of the few fortunate souls plucked from the water alive that night, one man survived with a testimony that would span the ages.

It started when Harper saw the man drifting in the dark night on a piece of wreckage. Harper yelled out to him, "Are you saved?" The man responded that he was not saved. Quoting Acts 16:31, Harper then replied, "Believe on the Lord Jesus Christ and ye shall be saved!" The waves of the ocean caused the men to drift apart, but Harper could still be heard calling on others to place their trust in Christ. Eventually, the ocean current brought the men back together again. At this point, Harper was weak and exhausted from the cold. Still, he was able to ask once more, "Are you saved?" Again, the man responded that he was not. Before Harper slid down to his watery grave, he pleaded one final time, "Believe on the Lord Jesus Christ and ye shall be saved." The man was rescued by the *S.S. Carpathia*, but not before he placed his faith in Jesus Christ for eternal life. He lived to tell the world that he was John Harper's last convert.

Harper was a man who was focused on the eternal destiny of men. He lived and died proclaiming his faith in Jesus Christ. This type of commitment begins with a solid understanding of Christ and the life freely offered to men, which includes a place in the eternal Kingdom of Christ. In this final chapter we set out to explore the teaching of the Word of God regarding the Eternal State of those who find redemption in the Lord Jesus Christ.

Prelude to the Eternal State

Sin will not be present in the Eternal State. Therefore, before the Eternal State can be ushered in, four significant events must transpire. These will prepare the way for the new heavens and new earth.

Final Judgment of Satan and the Fallen Angels

Satan and his fallen angels will face a final judgment. At Calvary, his judgment was sealed; he was defeated (John 19:30). This was the mortal blow predicted in Genesis 3:15. Still, his defeat does not mean that he is done wreaking havoc in the world.

Imagine a missionary who arrives back at his hut only to find an enormous python, which had made its way into his home. Not knowing what else to do, the missionary shoots the snake in the head, hoping to kill it. Immediately after the fatal gunshot, the python begins to thrash around. The missionary steps out of the hut and watches as the walls shake. He continues to hear the noise of the massive creature banging into things within his home. Eventually, after several moments, all is finally still inside of the hut. He walks in to see everything in shambles from the thrashing of the snake, but the python is no longer a danger to him.

This provides us with a picture of what happened to Satan at Calvary. Christ has already issued the fatal blow to Satan at the Cross. Yet, throughout the entire Church Age, Satan is thrashing about as the prince of this world trying to take as many people with him to his ultimate demise. At some point, Satan will be done deceiving the nations of the world. He will no longer be a danger because he will be cast into the lake of fire for all of eternity, even though he was already defeated at Calvary.

In addition to his judgment at Calvary, Satan will be confined to the earth during the second half of the Tribulation (Rev. 12:7-12). A temporary judgment awaits Satan at the Second Coming of Christ. John informs us:

> Then I saw an angel coming down from heaven, having the key to the bottomless pit and a great chain in his hand. He laid hold of the dragon, that serpent of old, who is the Devil and Satan, and bound him for a thousand years; and he cast him into the bottomless pit, and shut him up, and set a seal on him, so that he should deceive the nations no more till the thousand years were finished. But after these things he must be released for a little while (Rev. 20:1-3).

Satan will be unable to deceive the nations for 1,000 years.

At the end of the Millennium Satan will face a final judgment, when his last rebellion is crushed (Rev. 20:7-10; 1 Cor. 6:3; Matt. 25:41). This is also detailed for us in Revelation 20:

> Now when the thousand years have expired, Satan will be released from his prison and will go out to deceive the nations which are in the four corners of the earth, Gog and Magog, to gather them together to battle, whose number is as the sand of the sea. They went up on the breadth of the earth and surrounded the camp of the saints and the beloved city. And fire came down from God out of heaven and devoured them. The devil, who deceived them, was cast into the lake of fire and brimstone where the beast and the false prophet are. And they will be tormented day and night forever and ever (Rev. 20:7-10).

This will be Satan's last stand. Right as he is about to implement his final plan, fire will come down from heaven and devour the enemies of Christ.

Why must there be this final battle with Satan? To ask this question, is to ask why there will be a millennial component to the eternal Kingdom. Why not usher in the Eternal State at the Second Coming? Why allow Satan to be loose again after he is confined for 1,000 years? The answer rests ultimately in the sovereign plan of God. The Millennium and the final rebellion of Satan demonstrate that even under ideal circumstances, when outward conformity to the Law will be mandated by the presence of the King ruling with a rod of iron, the heart of unregenerate man is wicked. Tragically, there will still be unbelievers who will rebel against God, but they will be without excuse. The Millennium will provide one final test for mankind, and one final manifestation of God's grace.

Old Heavens and Earth will Pass Away

A second preparatory judgment prior to the Eternal State will be the melting of the old heavens and earth by fire. Christ predicted this would come when He testified, "Heaven and earth will pass away, but My words will by no means pass away" (Matt. 24:35). Jesus also said in the Sermon on the Mount, "For assuredly, I say to you, till heaven and earth pass away, one jot or one tittle will by no means pass from the law till all is fulfilled" (Matt. 5:18). Christ taught that one day the heaven and earth will pass away.

This same teaching is echoed in several other places within the New Testament. John taught in Revelation, "Then I saw a great white throne and Him who sat on it, from whose face the earth and the heaven fled away. And there was found no place for them" (Rev. 20:11). Peter explicitly stated:

> But the heavens and the earth which are now preserved by the same word, are reserved for fire until the day of judgment and perdition of ungodly men. ... But the day of the Lord will come as a thief in the night, in which the heavens will pass away with a great noise, and the elements will melt with fervent heat; both the earth and the works that are in it will be burned up. Therefore, since all these things will be dissolved, what manner of persons ought you to be in holy conduct and godliness, looking for and hastening the coming of the day of God, because of which the heavens will be dissolved, being on fire, and the elements will melt with fervent heat? Nevertheless we, according to His promise, look for new heavens and a new earth in which righteousness dwells (2 Pet. 3:7, 10-13).

Revelation 21:1 and Hebrews 1:10-12 also testify that the old heavens and earth will be removed before the new heavens and new earth are put in place by God. The first century Church understood the temporary nature of the earth in which we live.

This teaching directly impacts our understanding and role as stewards of God's creation. The curse of sin affects the entire globe: the soil, the weather, the plants, the skies, etc. This earth is falling apart because of the curse of sin. We have a responsibility to be good stewards of the creation that God has entrusted to us. However, to worship the earth instead of the Creator is misguided. It is foolishness to believe that mankind will bring about the end of the earth. The earth will end when God wants it to end.

Why must the old heavens and earth be destroyed? The presence of sin in the universe, and the residual effects of the curse on creation (Gen. 3:17-18), means that this earth cannot be merely renovated enough to make it meet God's standard of righteousness for the Eternal State. It must all be completely destroyed and re-created. This takes us, once again, to God's purposes in human history, as demonstrated in figure 16.1.

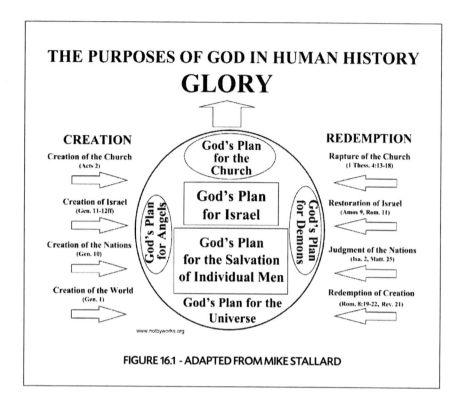

FIGURE 16.1 - ADAPTED FROM MIKE STALLARD

In Christ believers are a new creation. Paul taught the church of Corinth, "Therefore, if anyone is in Christ, he is a new creation; old things have passed away; behold, all things have become new" (2 Cor. 5:17). What happens individually in the life of every believer is a microcosm of what will happen globally for all of redeemed humanity and creation. The ultimate plan of God is to bring Himself glory. He will do this by redeeming the Church, Israel, and all of creation. The new heavens and new earth are one of the final pieces in His plan.

Great White Throne Judgment

The teaching about the Great White Throne Judgment is found in Revelation 20:

Then I saw a great white throne and Him who sat on it, from whose face the earth and the heaven fled away. And there was found no place for them. And I saw the dead, small and great, standing before God, and books were opened. And another book was opened, which is the Book of Life. And the dead were judged according to their works, by the things which were written in the books. The sea gave up the dead who were in it, and Death and Hades delivered up the dead who were in them. And they were judged, each one according to his works. Then Death and Hades were cast into the lake of fire. This is the second death. And anyone not found written in the Book of Life was cast into the lake of fire (Rev. 20:11-15).

Every unbeliever, from every age, will be resurrected at this time to be judged before the great white throne (v. 12). This will include unbelievers from the Old Testament, the Church Age, the Tribulation, and the Millennium. This judgment is only for unbelievers. Notice that, "the sea gave up the dead who were in it, and Death and Hades delivered up the dead who were in them" (v. 13). Wherever the dead bodies of these unbelievers are, from all of human history, they will be reconstituted in order for these people to face God's final judgment.

This is a terrifying description of unbelievers faced with an eternity of torment and separation from God. Warren Wiersbe reminds us, "The White Throne Judgment will be nothing like our modern court cases. At the White Throne, there will be a Judge but no jury, a prosecution but no defense, a sentence but no appeal. No one will be able to defend himself or accuse God of unrighteousness. What an awesome scene it will be!"[1]

Mankind has continually sought to overcome the problem of sin and separation from God with good works, but no matter how many good works a person has done, it will never be enough. No one is capable of being justified before God by his good works. Paul instructed, "Therefore by the deeds [works] of the law no flesh will be justified in His sight" (Rom. 3:20). Because these souls did not receive the free gift of eternal life, their sentence will be handed out at the Great White Throne Judgment. Each person's works will be judged and found unworthy (Rev. 20:12-13). It is important to recognize that the sentence of eternal separation from God is not because of a lack of good works, but rather it is because their names are not found in the Book of Life (Rev. 20:15). However, unbelievers will be judged according to their works (Rev. 20:13), indicating that even their own works will demonstrate that they deserve eternal punishment. Good works are incapable of justifying men before God. The result of not receiving Christ will be an eternity in the lake of fire (Rev. 20:14). This is called the, "second death" (Rev. 20:14). Anyone not found in the Book of

Life will be given an eternal body to face judgment and then God will cast them into the lake of fire (Rev. 20:15).

Translation of Millennial Believers

As previously stated, there will be believers with physical bodies during the Millennium. This involves two different groups of people:

1. Those who come to faith during the Tribulation and survive will enter the millennial phase of the Kingdom in physical, mortal bodies.
2. Those who are born during the Millennium to this previous group, and come to faith in Jesus Christ, will also have physical, mortal bodies.

These believers will experience the full blessings of the New Covenant and live throughout the Millennium in physical bodies. Prior to their entrance into the Eternal State they must put on immortality. This is referred to as the translation of millennial believers, and it must occur before the Eternal State (Rev. 21:1-5).

Paul taught on this principle for Church Age believers when he stated:

> Now this I say, brethren, that flesh and blood cannot inherit the kingdom of God; nor does corruption inherit incorruption. Behold, I tell you a mystery: We shall not all sleep, but we shall all be changed— in a moment, in the twinkling of an eye, at the last trumpet. For the trumpet will sound, and the dead will be raised incorruptible, and we shall be changed. For this corruptible must put on incorruption, and this mortal must put on immortality (1 Cor. 15:50-53).

Even though Paul's teaching relates directly to the Church, the principles can be applied to the millennial believers. Believers in Christ living in the Millennium must receive their glorified bodies prior to entering the Eternal State. Their mortal must put on immortality and their corruptible must put on incorruption (1 Cor. 15:53). Paul also taught that, "flesh and blood cannot inherit the kingdom of God" (1 Cor. 15:50). This is consistent with the teaching of John that all things will be made new in the Eternal State (Rev. 21:5).

It should be noted that in 1 Corinthians 15:50, even though Paul was teaching about the Rapture of the Church, he was using the expression

Kingdom of God to refer to the *Eternal State*. Sometimes the Scriptures refer to the Kingdom as both the Millennium and the Eternal State. At other times, it refers to only the Eternal State, which is how Paul used this expression in 1 Corinthians 15:50. This helps us to understand how other passages from the Word of God teach that flesh and blood will enter the Millennium, but will not inherit the final form of the Kingdom.

Flesh and blood are factors of time and space. It is the dwelling place of humanity in the world today, but when the old earth is destroyed, we will have glorified bodies for all of eternity. Even though it is not directly stated in Scripture, the inference from the New Testament is that believers from the Millennium who are still in physical bodies will be translated. This must occur prior to the Eternal State.

The Eternal State: Revelation 21-22

Revelation 21 and 22 have the distinction of being the last two chapters of the Bible. They also discuss the last elements of God's program, which is the Eternal State.

New Heaven and New Earth

Chapter 21 begins with the Apostle John testifying, "Now I saw" (Rev. 21:1). There is a clear progression revealed in chapters 20-21. The events now described will take place after the Millennium and the Great White Throne Judgment. This follows the destruction of the old heaven and earth, when there will be no more sea (v. 1). The Eternal State is a complete and utter change of life as we know it. This is represented in the strong contrast between the new heaven and new earth with the old (v. 1). Just as spiritual regeneration brings newness (2 Cor. 5:17) for redeemed individuals, physical regeneration will bring newness for the redeemed universe. The Millennium will represent a foreshadowing of the Eternal State. What will be renovated in Revelation 20 will become completely re-created in Revelation 21-22. God will make all things new (Rev. 21:5).

New Jerusalem

The New Jerusalem represents the eternal dwelling place of redeemed mankind (Rev. 21:3, 9-10; cf. Heb. 12:22-24). This is the central point to remember about the New Jerusalem.

It is helpful to recognize that a debate exists about this future city. Will the New Jerusalem be present during the Millennium? Quite a few prominent dispensationalists have stated that they believe it will be, including Darby, Gaebelein, Ironside, Ryrie, Walvoord, and Pentecost. During the Millennium, it is said that the Church will reside within the city, the New Jerusalem. The city is believed to hover over the earth, much like a satellite city. Jewish and Gentile believers who are not a part of the Church are thought to be the ones who will live on the earth during the Millennium. There are, however, some problems with this particular view. Those that have taken the opposite position, that the New Jerusalem will not be present during the Millennium, include Larkin, Newell, and many contemporary dispensationalists.

Reasons the New Jerusalem is not Present during the Millennium

The characteristics of the New Jerusalem are distinct from the characteristics of the millennial Jerusalem. The New Jerusalem will have no Temple in it. John testified, "But I saw no temple in it, for the Lord God Almighty and the Lamb are its temple" (Rev. 21:22). Yet, the revelation provided to Ezekiel demonstrates a Temple in Jerusalem during the Millennium (Ezek. 40-48).

The New Jerusalem will have no night (Rev. 21:25; 22:5; cf. Isa. 30:26; 60:19-20), the curse of sin will be removed (Rev. 22:3), and the reign from this city will be eternal (Rev. 22:5), whereas the millennial reign is 1,000 years (Rev. 20:4). It should also be noted that in Revelation 21:1-8 the new nature of the Eternal State presupposes the dissolution of the old. Two co-existing cities will not be possible (cf. Rev. 21:4).

The flow of thought in Revelation 20-22 makes it incongruous for the vision in Revelation 21:9-22:7 to be a retrogression to millennial conditions, after having introduced the final judgment of the earth in Revelation 21:1-8.

The view that the New Jerusalem will be the residence of believers during the Millennium would require that the city be removed during the destruction of the earth, and then return to take up its abode with the new earth for eternity. This is where the concept of the New Jerusalem being a satellite (that is a part of the heavens and not the earth) comes from, but Revelation 21:1-5 informs us that even the heavens will be re-created. This re-creation will be all-inclusive; all things will become new.

John Walvoord admits, "The possibility of Jerusalem being a satellite city over the earth during the millennium is not specifically taught in any scripture and at best is an inference based on the implication that it has been in existence prior to its introduction in Revelation 21."[2] However, it should be recognized that even though the New Testament references the New Jerusalem, in Hebrews 12, it does not mean it is already in existence.

The writer of Hebrews referred to the New Jerusalem as a motivation for the Jewish Christians in the first century to keep on persevering, in spite of great difficulty (Heb. 12:22-24). This text provides a running description of this future city that will include, "an innumerable company of angels, to the general assembly and church of the firstborn who are registered in heaven, to God the Judge of all, to the spirits of just men made perfect" (Heb. 12:22-23). The New Jerusalem will include many more individuals besides Church Age believers.

Revelation 21:3 testifies that during the Eternal State the, "tabernacle of God" will be with men. This should not be taken as a reference to a Temple. Rather, it is a general reference indicating that God will dwell with men.

The context of Revelation 21:1-5 indicates that the New Jerusalem will be a new creation, just like the new heaven and new earth. The New Jerusalem can only come into existence when the old Jerusalem is destroyed and, "former things have passed away" (Rev. 21:4).

Description of the New Jerusalem

The Apostle John was given additional revelation about the New Jerusalem. Revelation 21 records that this holy city will have:

- splendor: like a stone of crystal - clear jasper (v. 11)
- walls seventy-two yards high (v. 17)
- gates with giant pearls named for the twelve tribes of Israel (vv. 12, 21)
- twelve foundations with names of the twelve Apostles (v. 14)
- dimensions of a 1,500 mile cube or pyramid (v. 16)
- construction of pure gold, like clear glass (v. 18)
- streets of pure gold, like transparent glass (v. 21)
- God and the Lamb as the Temple (v. 22)
- light that shall be the glory of God the Lamb (v. 23)
- the nations present with the Church and Israel (v. 24)

- gates that never close (v. 25)
- no night (v. 25)
- purity, with no defilement present (v. 27)

Life in the Eternal State

The Millennium will provide a foretaste of life in the Eternal State. What will be present in part during the Millennium will be present completely and perfectly for all of eternity.

The mediatorial aspect of the Kingdom will be surrendered by Christ at the end of the Millennium (cf. 1 Cor. 15:24-28). During the Eternal State, He will no longer be mediating over the Kingdom ruling with a rod of iron. 1 Corinthians 15:24-26 teaches, "Then comes the end, when He delivers the kingdom to God the Father, when He puts an end to all rule and all authority and power. For He must reign till He has put all enemies under His feet. The last enemy that will be destroyed is death." During the Millennium, not all of the enemies of Christ are, "under His feet" (v. 25). There will still be the final rebellion against Him at the end of the Millennium. The Apostle Paul was teaching about the ultimate finality. Even though the eternal Kingdom of Christ begins after the Second Coming, there will be a definite shift in the nature of it when the old heavens and earth pass away. It will, however, continue to be the Kingdom of Christ.

Revelation also teaches us that the Eternal State will include unprecedented fellowship with God (Rev. 21:3; 22:4). Sin will have no place in the Eternal State; there will be complete holiness. John instructed, "But there shall by no means enter it anything that defiles, or causes an abomination or a lie, but only those who are written in the Lamb's Book of Life" (Rev. 21:27).

The unbelieving world has often portrayed the eternal destination of Christians in an unflattering manner. In truth, the Eternal State will be unprecedented joy. Again, we are told from Revelation, "And God will wipe away every tear from their eyes; there shall be no more death, nor sorrow, nor crying. There shall be no more pain, for the former things have passed away" (Rev. 21:4). It is difficult to imagine life in such an ideal state. We will continue to serve our God as He continues to reign throughout eternity! (Rev. 22:3; 22:5).

Discussion Questions

1. What four events must transpire before the Eternal State can be ushered in?
2. Describe the final judgment of Satan and his angels.
3. Why must the old heavens and earth be destroyed?
4. Where do the new heavens and new earth fit into the plan and purpose of God in human history?
5. What will occur at the Great White Throne Judgment?
6. Explain what will happen to the physical bodies of millennial believers.
7. How do we know that the New Jerusalem is not present during the Millennium?
8. Provide a brief description of what the New Jerusalem will look like.
9. In what way should life in the Eternal State be portrayed?

Endnotes

1. Warren W. Wiersbe, *The Bible Exposition Commentary* (Wheaton, IL: Victor Books, 1996), Rev. 20:11.
2. John F. Walvoord, *The Revelation of Jesus Christ* (Chicago, IL: Moody, 1966), 313.

Conclusion

THE REVELATION OF God was given to mankind for clear and specific reasons. First, and foremost, God is calling out a people for Himself. However, it should be apparent that a significant part of the function of the Word of God is to reveal the events of the future. Otherwise, it is difficult to imagine why God would have given such great detail about His program for the end times. Rest assured that for believers in Christ, the future in store for us should not be feared. Rather, we should look forward to the coming Kingdom of God, knowing that our loving Creator has a glorious plan for His people.

The Apostle John was told about the revelation he had been given, "Do not seal the words of the prophecy of this book, for the time is at hand" (Rev. 22:10). We are certainly living in the last days. The Rapture of the Bride of Christ could take place at any moment, ushering in the fulfillment of God's prophetic Word and His end times program.

In some of the last recorded words of Jesus in Revelation, our Savior testified, "And behold, I am coming quickly, and My reward is with Me, to give to every one according to his work. I am the Alpha and the Omega, the Beginning and the End, the First and the Last" (Rev. 22:12-13). Jesus promised He would return. The assurance of rewards should be a powerful motivator for walking in obedience to Christ. The eternal and sovereign God will bring to completion what He has promised. Living in light of the eternal means that our focus should be on *what lies ahead*.

No better conclusion could be made than the final words written by John in the book of Revelation, "Even so, come, Lord Jesus! The grace of our Lord Jesus Christ be with you all. Amen" (Rev. 22:20-21).

Are you ready for His return? Have you ever trusted in Jesus Christ for eternal salvation? The reality is that every one of us is born a sinner. This is why the Bible teaches, "For all have sinned and fall short of the glory of God" (Rom. 3:23). Each of us has fallen short of God's standard of perfection. The bad news is that our sin has a penalty, which is eternal separation from God in a literal place of torment called hell. No amount of good works can take care of our sin problem. Entrance into heaven requires perfect righteousness.

The good news is that God has given us a gift, out of His love for us. The Bible teaches, "But God demonstrates His own love toward us, in that while we were still sinners, Christ died for us" (Rom. 5:8). God provided for our salvation when He sent His Son, Jesus, to die in our place on the Cross. Jesus' work on the Cross paid the penalty for our sin. This most certainly is good news.

The grace of God has provided mankind with hope. All who trust Jesus Christ, the Son of God, and Him alone, to forgive their sins and give them the free gift of eternal life will be saved. God wanted people to be rescued by the death and resurrection of His Son. This is why He wrote it down in His Word and told us, "But as many as received Him, to them He gave the right to become children of God, to those who believe in His name" (John 1:12). The message of the good news of Jesus Christ and His work on the cross saves those who believe it. When we believe the gospel message, Christ's perfect righteousness covers our sin and grants us entrance into heaven.

If you need encouragement or if you would like more information about how to have eternal life, please contact the authors at www. NotByWorks.org or www.LiteralTruth.org.

Appendix:
Sequential Order of End Times Events

By: J. B. Hixson, Ph.D.

www.NotByWorks.org

1. The Rapture of the Church (1 Thess. 4:13-18; 1 Cor. 15:51-58; 2 Thess. 2:1-12; John 14:1-3)
2. The Judgment Seat of Christ in heaven for all Church Age believers (1 Cor. 3:10-15; Rom. 14:10; 2 Cor. 5:10)
3. The Marriage of the Lamb (Rev. 19:7)
4. Formation of a Western Alliance, probably led by the future Antichrist, that invades Egypt (Dan. 11:40-43)
5. Battle of Gog & Magog (Ezek. 38-39)
    a. Formation of a Northern Alliance against Israel (Ezek. 38)
    b. Invasion of Israel by this Northern Alliance (Ezek. 38:16)
    c. The Western Alliance protests (Dan. 11:44).
    d. God supernaturally intervenes allowing the Western Alliance to defeat the Northern Alliance (Ezek. 38:21-39:7).
    e. This gives the Antichrist world notoriety and paves the way for his reign of terror (Dan. 9:27).
6. Unveiling of the Antichrist (2 Thess. 2:3)
7. The Antichrist signs a peace treaty with Israel (Dan. 9:27; 1 Thess. 5:3).
    • This constitutes the official commencement of Daniel's Seventieth Week (Matt. 24-25; Rev. 6-18). Daniel's Seventieth Week is also called the Great Day of the Lord's Wrath (Zeph. 1:15), the Time of Jacob's Trouble (Jer. 30:7), the Tribulation (Matt. 24), and the Day

of the Lord (many OT passages).

8. The Seal Judgments begin (Rev. 6)

9. The ministry of the 144,000 world-wide witnesses begins (Rev. 7, 14; cf. Matt. 24:14; 13:47-50).

10. The ministry of the two special witnesses begins (Rev. 11).

11. The Antichrist kills the two witnesses (Rev. 11).

12. The two witnesses are resurrected (Rev. 11).

13. The Antichrist's reign of terror intensifies. He sets himself up as God and demands worship (Dan. 9:27; Rev. 13; Matt. 24:15). This event is called the Abomination of Desolation.

14. The trumpet judgments begin (Rev. 8-9).

15. The False Prophet, second in command to the Antichrist, takes on an increased role (Rev. 13).

16. The False Prophet controls commerce (Rev. 13).

17. There is severe persecution of all Jews and all believers (Rev. 12-13).

18. The fall of geographic, political, and ecclesiastical Babylon (Rev. 18)

19. The bowl judgments begin (Rev. 15-16).

20. As the Antichrist proceeds with his program, nations from the East (the Orient) will unite and attempt to stop him. (Rev. 16:12-16).

21. The armies from the East and West will face off in a series of battles in an area around the mountains of Megiddo north of Palestine. This campaign is called Armageddon (Rev. 16:14; 19:17).

22. Climaxing the campaign of Armageddon, Christ will return to judge the nations and establish His Kingdom (Zech. 14:4; Matt. 25; Rev. 19:11-21).

23. The Antichrist and False Prophet are cast into the Lake of Fire (Rev. 19:17-21).

24. Christ will judge the world to see who may enter the Messianic Kingdom (Matt. 25:31-46).

25. The Marriage Supper of the Lamb takes place at the inauguration of the Messianic Kingdom (Rev. 19:9; Matt. 8:11).

26. The millennial reign of Christ over the earthly Kingdom (Rev. 20:1-6)

27. The binding of Satan during the millennial reign (Rev. 20:1-6)

28. The loosing of Satan at the end of the Millennium (Rev. 20:7-10)

29. One final battle between Satan and God called Gog and Magog (not the same as Ezek. 38-39) at the end of the Millennium (Rev. 20)

30. The Great White Throne judgment of all unbelievers (Rev. 20:11-15)

31. The final destruction of Satan, the Antichrist, the False Prophet and all unbelievers (Rev. 20:15)

32. The destruction of the old heaven and old earth and the recreation of heaven and earth in sinless perfection (Rev. 21)
33. The everlasting reign of Christ over the New Heaven and New Earth (Rev. 21)

Scripture Index

Bibliography

Books, Commentaries, and Reference Works

Anderson, Sir Robert. *The Coming Prince*, Galaxie Software, 2004.

Arndt, William, Frederick W. Danker, and Walter Bauer. *A Greek-English Lexicon of the New Testament and Other Early Christian Literature*. 3rd ed. Chicago, IL: University of Chicago Press, 2000.

Benware, Paul. *The Believer's Payday*. Chattanooga, TN: AMG Publishers, 2002.

——. *Understanding End Times Prophecy: A Comprehensive Approach*. Chicago, IL: Moody Publishers, 2006.

Cabal, Ted, Chad Owen Brand, E. Ray Clendenen et al. *The Apologetics Study Bible: Real Questions, Straight Answers, Stronger Faith*. Nashville, TN: Holman Bible Publishers, 2007.

Chafer, Lewis Sperry. *Dispensationalism*. Dallas, TX: Dallas Seminary Press, 1951.

——. *The Kingdom in History and Prophecy*. Chicago, IL: The Bible Institute Colportage Ass'n, 1936.

——. *Must We Dismiss the Millennium?* Florida: Biblical Testimony League, 1921.

——. *Systematic Theology*. Grand Rapids, MI: Kregel Publications, 1993.

Constable, Tom. *Tom Constable's Expository Notes on the Bible*, 2003.

Couch, Mal. et al. *Dictionary of Premillennial Theology*. Grand Rapids, MI: Kregel Publications, 1996.

Edwards, Randy H. *From the Rapture Until*. Mount Airy, NC: Ever-Read Publishing, 1993.

Elwell, Walter A. and Barry J. Beitzel. *Baker Encyclopedia of the Bible*. Grand Rapids, MI: Baker Book House, 1988.

Enns, Paul P. *The Moody Handbook of Theology*. Chicago, IL: Moody Press, 1997.

Feinberg Charles L. *Israel: At the Center of History and Revelation, 3d ed.* Portland, OR: Multnomah Press, 1980.

Gaebelein, Arno C. *The Annotated Bible, Volume 6: Matthew to The Acts.* Bellingham, WA: Logos Research Systems, Inc., 2009.

Galli, Mark and Ted Olsen. *131 Christians Everyone Should Know.* Nashville, TN: Broadman & Holman Publishers, 2000.

Gesenius, Wilhelm and Samuel Prideaux Tregelles. *Gesenius' Hebrew and Chaldee Lexicon to the Old Testament Scriptures.*

Hixson, J. B. *The Great Last Days Deception: Exposing Satan's New World Order Agenda.* Brenham, TX: Lucid Books, 2012.

Hixson, J. B. et al. *Freely By His Grace: Classical Free Grace Theology.* Duluth, MN: Grace Gospel Press, 2012.

Hoyt, Samuel L. *The Judgment Seat of Christ.* Milwaukee, WI: Grace Gospel Press, 2011.

———. "The Negative Aspects of the Christian's Judgment," *Bibliotheca Sacra* 137 (April–June 1980).

Ironside, H. A. *Not Wrath ... but Rapture: Or, Will the Church Participate in the Great Tribulation.* Neptune, NJ: Loizeaux Brothers, 1941.

———. *Setting the Stage for the Last Act of the Great World Drama.* Neptune, NJ: Loizeaux Brothers, 1937.

Josephus, Flavius and William Whiston. *The Works of Josephus: Complete and Unabridged.* Peabody, MA: Hendrickson Publishers, 1987.

Lightner, Robert P. *The Last Days Handbook.* Nashville, TN: Thomas Nelson Publishers, 1990.

MacArthur, John F., Jr. *The MacArthur Study Bible: New American Standard Bible.* Nashville, TN: Thomas Nelson Publishers, 2006.

New American Standard Bible: 1995 Update. LaHabra, CA: The Lockman Foundation, 1995.

Pentecost, J. Dwight. *Things To Come: A Study in Biblical Eschatology.* Grand Rapids, MI: Zondervan, 1964.

———. *Thy Kingdom Come: Tracing God's Kingdom Program and Covenant Promises Throughout History.* Grand Rapids, MI: Kregel Publications, 1995.

Radmacher, Earl D., Ronald Barclay Allen, and H. Wayne House. *Nelson's New Illustrated Bible Commentary.* Nashville, TN: Thomas Nelson Publishers, 1999.

Reid, Daniel G., Robert Dean Linder, Bruce L. Shelley, and Harry S. Stout. *Dictionary of Christianity in America.* Downers Grove, IL: InterVarsity Press, 1990.

Rice, John R. *The Coming Kingdom of Christ.* Wheaton, IL: Sword of the Lord Publishers, 1945.

Roberts, Alexander, James Donaldson, and A. Cleveland Coxe. *The Ante-Nicene Fathers Vol. I: Translations of the Writings of the Fathers Down to A.D. 325.*

Ryrie, Charles Caldwell. *Basic Theology: A Popular Systematic Guide to Understanding Biblical Truth.* Chicago, IL: Moody Press, 1999.

———. *The Basis of the Premillennial Faith.* Dubuque, IA: ECS Ministries, 2005.

———. *Dispensationalism*. Revised and expanded. Chicago, IL: Moody Publishers, 1995.

———. *The Final Countdown: God's Blueprint for Future Events*. Wheaton, IL: Victor Books, 1982.

———. *What You Should Know About the Rapture*. Current Christian Issues. Chicago, IL: Moody Press, 1981.

Showers, Renald E. *There Really Is a Difference! A Comparison of Covenant and Dispensational Theology*. Bellmawr, NJ: The Friends of Israel Gospel Ministry, Inc., 1990.

Strong, James. *Enhanced Strong's Lexicon*.

Tan, Paul Lee. *The Interpretation of Prophecy*. Rockville, MD: Assurance Publishers, 1974.

Thiessen, Henry C. *Lectures in Systematic Theology*. Grand Rapids, MI: William B. Eerdmans Publishing, 2001.

Thomas, Robert L. *Revelation 1-7: An Exegetical Commentary*. Chicago, IL: Moody Publishers, 1992.

———. *Revelation 8-22: An Exegetical Commentary*. Chicago, IL: Moody Publishers, 1995.

Vincent, Marvin Richardson. *Word Studies in the New Testament*. New York, NY: Charles Scribner's Sons, 1887.

Vine, W. E., Merrill F. Unger, and William White, Jr. *Vine's Complete Expository Dictionary of Old and New Testament Words*. Nashville, TN: Thomas Nelson Publishers, 1996.

Walvoord, John F. *Every Prophecy of the Bible*. Colorado Springs, CO: Chariot Victor Publishing, 1999.

———. *The Rapture Question*. Revised and Enlarged Edition. Grand Rapids, MI: Zondervan, 1979.

———. *The Revelation of Jesus Christ*, Chicago, IL: Moody, 1966.

Walvoord, John F., Roy B. Zuck, and Dallas Theological Seminary. *The Bible Knowledge Commentary: An Exposition of the Scriptures*. Wheaton, IL: Victor Books, 1985.

Wiersbe, Warren W. *The Bible Exposition Commentary*. Wheaton, IL: Victor Books, 1996.

Willis, Wesley R., and John R. Master, eds. *Issues in Dispensationalism*. Chicago, IL: Moody Press, 1994.

Wood, Leon J. *The Bible and Future Events*. Grand Rapids, MI: Zondervan Publishing House, 1973.

Internet Sources

"Black Death." http://www.middle-ages.org.uk/black-death.htm (accessed September 21, 2012).

Department of the Navy – Naval Historical Center. "USS S-4 (Submarine # 109, later SS-109), 1919-1936." http://www.history.navy.mil/photos/sh-usn/usnsh-s/ss109.htm (accessed May 31, 2012).

Fontaine, D.J. "Millennium Manor Castle." http://www.blountweb.com/millenniummanor/ (accessed December 25, 2012).

Lovell, John. "Death's Door." http://new.yankeemagazine.com/article/deaths-door (accessed April 8, 2012).

"The Mideast conflict: A look at the region's history." http://www.usatoday.com/graphics/news/gra/gisrael2/flash.htm (accessed July 5, 2012).

Thompson, Kalee." Alaska Ranger: Lessons from Coast Guard's most challenging rescue," http://coastguard.dodlive.mil/2011/01/alaska-ranger-lessons-from-coast-guards-most-challenging-rescue/ (accessed September 27, 2012).

———. "Inside the Coast Guard's Most Extreme Rescue," http://www.popular-mechanics.com/technology/aviation/crashes/4267469 (accessed September 27, 2012).

CPSIA information can be obtained at www.ICGtesting.com
Printed in the USA
LVOW10s1722110915

453800LV00001B/152/P